# UTAH & NEVADA CAMPING

by Gayen and Tom Wharton
Deke Castleman

Foghorn
Press

BOOKS BUILDING COMMUNITY™

ISBN 1-57354-012-9

51895

9 781573 540124

>Foghorn Press
>Rights Department
>555 DeHaro Street, Suite 220
>San Francisco, CA 94107
>foghorn@well.com

To order individual books, please call Foghorn Press: 1-800-FOGHORN (364-4676) or (415) 241-9550. Foghorn Press titles are distributed to the book trade by Publishers Group West, based in Emeryville, California. To contact your local sales representative, call 1-800-788-3123.

Although the author and publisher have made every effort to ensure that the information in this book was correct at press time, the author and publisher do not assume and hereby disclaim any liability to any party for any loss or damage caused by errors, omissions, or any potential travel disruption, whether such errors or omissions result from negligence, accident, or any other cause.

Library of Congress ISSN Data:
January 1997
*Utah & Nevada Camping*
*The Complete Guide to More Than 36,000 Campsites*
First Edition
ISSN: 1089-2702

**The Foghorn Press Commitment**

Foghorn Press is committed to the preservation of the environment. We promote Leave No Trace principles (see page 378) in all of our guidebooks. Additionally, our books are printed with soy-based inks on 100 percent recycled paper, which has a 50 percent post-consumer waste content.

Printed in the United States of America

# Contents

Utah Chapter Reference Map ..................................................... 6

Nevada Chapter Reference Map ................................................. 7

How to Use This Book ............................................................ 8

Camping Tips ....................................................................... 11

Getting Into Gear
*What to Pack for Your Camping Trip* ...................................... 12

Since We're Neighbors, Let's Be Friends
*A Guide to Campground Ethics* ............................................. 16

Helpful Hints for Hikers ....................................................... 19

Don't Let Scorpions Sleep in Your Boots
*And Other Safety/First-Aid Tips* ........................................... 22

Honey, I Packed the Kids
*Eight Great Tips for Camping with Children* ........................... 27

Utah Resource Guide ........................................................... 30

Nevada Resource Guide ........................................................ 40

Utah Campgrounds .............................................................. 45

Chapter A1 ........................................................................ 48
*Map on page 48.* Little Sahara Recreation Area, Onaqui Mountains, Pony Express Trail, Sawtooth National Forest, Snowville, Wasatch–Cache National Forest

Chapter A2 ........................................................................ 56
*Map on page 56.* American Fork, Antelope Island, Bear Lake, Big Cottonwood Canyon, Boulger Reservoir, Brigham City, Coalville, Currant Creek Reservoir, Daniels Canyon, Deer Creek Reservoir, Diamond Fork Canyon, Echo Reservoir, Farmington, Fishlake National Forest, Garden City, Great Salt Lake, Hobble Creek Canyon, Honeyville, Hyrum, Hyrum Reservoir, Jordanelle Reservoir, Jordanelle State Park, Kamas, Kaysville, Layton, Little Cottonwood Canyon, Logan, Lost Creek Reservoir, Manti–La Sal National Forest, Mantua Reservoir, Midway, Nephi, Ogden, East Canyon Reservoir, Park City, Payson, Plymouth, Price, Provo, Provo River, Richmond, Rockport State Park, Salt Lake City, Scofield Reservoir, Scofield State Park, Strawberry Reservoir, Uinta National Forest, Upper Birch Creek Reservoir, Utah Lake, Wasatch Mountain State Park, Wasatch National Forest, Wasatch–Cache National Forest, Willard Bay

Chapter A3 ..................................................................................... 124
*Map on page 124.* Ashley National Forest, Dinosaur National Monument, Flaming Gorge National Recreation Area, Flaming Gorge Reservoir, Manila, Moon Lake, Pelican Lake, Red Fleet Reservoir, Starvation Reservoir, Steinaker Reservoir, Vernal

Chapter B1 ..................................................................................... 150
*Map on page 150.* Beaver, Cedar Breaks National Monument, Cedar City, Clear Creek, Coral Pink Sand Dunes State Park, Delta, Dixie National Forest, Enterprise, Fillmore, Fishlake National Forest, Glendale, Gunlock Reservoir, Hatch, Hurricane, Kanab, Kanarraville, La Verkin, Leeds, Minersville Reservoir, Mount Carmel Junction, Quail Creek Reservoir, Orderville, Panguitch, Panguitch Lake, Parowan, Pine Valley, Snow Canyon State Park, Springdale, St. George, Zion National Park

Chapter B2 ..................................................................................... 188
*Map on page 188.* Bicknell, Boulder, Bryce Canyon National Park, Cannonville, Capitol Reef National Monument, Capitol Reef National Park, Circleville, Dixie National Forest, Escalante, Escalante Petrified Forest State Park, Ferron Reservoir, Fish Lake, Fishlake National Forest, Glen Canyon National Recreation Area, Gunnison, Henry Mountains, Huntington Reservoir, Huntington State Park, Joe's Valley Reservoir, Johnson Reservoir, Joseph, Kodachrome Basin State Park, Lake Powell, Lower Bown's Reservoir, Manti, Manti–La Sal National Forest, Marysville, Millsite Reservoir, Millsite State Park, Monroe, Otter Creek Reservoir, Palisade Reservoir, Palisade State Park, Panguitch, Paria River, Payson, Piute Reservoir, Richfield, Salina, Torrey, Tropic Reservoir, Wide Hollow Reservoir, Yearns Reservoir, Yuba Reservoir

Chapter B3 ..................................................................................... 224
*Map on page 224.* Arches National Park, Blanding, Bluff, Canyonlands National Park, Capitol Reef National Park, Colorado River, Dead Horse Point State Park, Glen Canyon National Recreation Area, Goblin Valley State Park, Goosenecks State Park, Green River, Green River State Park, Hanksville, Henry Mountains, Hovenweep National Monument, Lake Powell, Manti–La Sal National Forest, Mexican Hat, Moab, Monticello, Monument Valley, Natural Bridges National Monument, Oohwah Lake, San Juan River, San Rafael Swell, Warner Lake

**Nevada Campgrounds** ................................................................. 255

Chapter C1 ..................................................................................... 258
*Map on page 258.* Denio, Lovelock, Pyramid Lake, Pyramid Lake Paiute Reservation, Rye Patch Reservoir, Sheldon National Wildlife Refuge, Sutcliffe

Chapter C2 .......................................................................... 262
*Map on page 262.* Battle Mountain, Humboldt National Forest, Mountain City, Wilson Reservoir, Winnemucca

Chapter C3 .......................................................................... 268
*Map on page 268.* Angel Lake, Elko, Humboldt National Forest, Jackpot, Jarbridge Wilderness, Mountain City, Ruby Lake National Wildlife Refuge, Ruby Mountain Scenic Area, South Fork State Recreation Area, Wells, Wendover, Wildhorse Reservoir, Wildhorse State Recreation Area

Chapter D1 .......................................................................... 282
*Map on page 282.* Carson City, Carson River, Dayton, Dayton State Park, Fallon, Fort Churchill State Historic Park, Gardnerville, Genoa, Hawthorne, Lahontan State Recreation Area, Lake Lahontan, Lake Tahoe, Minden, Pyramid Lake Indian Reservation, Reno, Silver Springs, Sparks, Toiyabe National Forest, Topaz Lake, Truckee River, Virginia City, Wadsworth, Walker Lake, Walker River, Washoe Lake State Recreation Area, Yerington

Chapter D2 .......................................................................... 298
*Map on page 298.* Austin, Berlin–Ichthyosaur State Park, Gabbs, Mount Jefferson, Toiyabe National Forest, Tonopah

Chapter D3 .......................................................................... 304
*Map on page 304.* Baker, Beaver Dam State Park, Caliente, Cathedral Gorge State Park, Cave Lake State Recreation Area, Echo Canyon State Park, Ely, Great Basin National Park, Humboldt National Forest, Illipah Reservoir, Lehman Creek, Panaca, Pioche, Spring Valley State Park

Chapter E2 .......................................................................... 314
*Map on page 314.* Beatty, Death Valley National Park, Pahrump

Chapter E3 .......................................................................... 318
*Map on page 318.* Boulder City, Lake Mead National Recreation Area, Las Vegas, Laughlin, Mesquite, Overton, Overton Beach, Searchlight, Spring Mountains National Recreation Area, Toiyabe National Forest, Valley of Fire State Park

**Lake Tahoe Area Campgrounds** ........................................ 340
*Map on page 340.* D.L. Bliss State Park, Emerald Bay, Emerald Bay State Park, Fallen Leaf Lake, Homewood, Lake Tahoe, Meeks Bay, South Lake Tahoe, Stateline, Sugar Pine Point State Park, Tahoe City, Tahoe State Recreation Area, Tahoe Vista, Tahoma

**Index** ................................................................................ 350

# Utah Chapter Reference Map

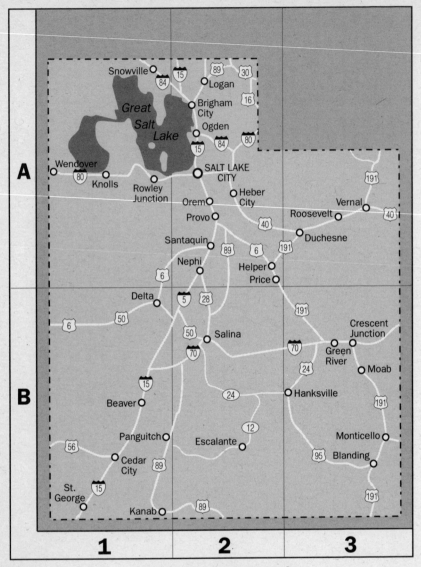

## Utah Campgrounds

Chapter A1 ............................ page 48

Chapter A2 ............................ page 56

Chapter A3 ............................ page 124

Chapter B1 ........................ page 150

Chapter B2 ........................ page 188

Chapter B3 ........................ page 224

# Nevada Chapter Reference Map

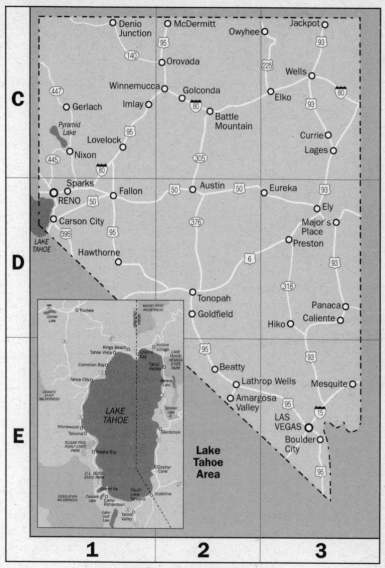

## Nevada Campgrounds

Chapter C1 .......................... page 258

Chapter C2 .......................... page 262

Chapter C3 .......................... page 268

Chapter D1 .......................... page 282

Chapter D2 .......................... page 298

Chapter D3 .......................... page 304

Chapter E2 .......................... page 314

Chapter E3 .......................... page 318

Lake Tahoe Area Campgrounds .................... page 340

# How to Use This Book

You can search for your ideal campsite in two ways:

1) If you know the name of the geographical area you'd like to visit, such as a town, national forest, or lake, look for it in the index beginning on page 350. If you'd like to find a particular campground, search for the campground's name in the index—the page number for each campground is listed in bold type.

2) To find a camp in a particular part of Utah or Nevada, turn to the state maps featured on pages 6 and 7. Find the grid you'd like to visit (such as A2 for the Salt Lake City, Utah, area or E3 for the Las Vegas, Nevada, area), then turn to the corresponding pages in the book.

At the bottom of every page, you'll find a reference for the chapter's corresponding map.

## What the Symbols Mean
Every camp listing has one or more symbols next to its name, which represent the recreational activities and sidetrip possibilities located at or near the campground. Other symbols identify whether the camps have RV hookups and wheelchair-accessible facilities (call ahead to make sure the camp's definition of wheelchair-accessible facilities suits your particular needs).

## Key to the Symbols

| Boating | Canoeing/Rafting | Fishing | Golf | Hiking | Historical Sites |

| Horseback Riding | Hot Springs | Swimming | Waterskiing | RV Sites | Wheelchair Access |

## What the Ratings Mean

Each campground in this book is designated with a scenic beauty rating of 1 through 10. The ratings are based solely on the campground's scenic beauty, and do not reflect quality issues such as the cleanliness of the camp or the temperament of the management, which can change from day to day.

## Scenic Rating

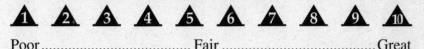

Poor..........................................Fair..........................................Great

## Note to RVers

*Utah & Nevada Camping* features this easy-to-spot RV symbol by every camp that has RV sites: **RV**. Occasionally a campground listing mentions RV sites but does not feature the RV symbol; these camps have access routes that may not be safe for RVs.

## Note to Tent Campers

If an RV symbol is pictured next to a campground listing, that does not necessarily mean that the camp is an exclusive RV resort or unsuitable for tent campers. Many camps offer quality sites for both tent and RV camping.

> *Every effort has been made to ensure that the campground information in* Utah & Nevada Camping *is as up-to-date as possible. However, details such as fees and telephone numbers are liable to change. Please contact the campgrounds you plan to visit for updated information.*

# Credits

| | |
|---|---|
| **Editor in Chief** | Rebecca Poole Forée |
| **Senior Editor** | Jean Linsteadt |
| **Production Manager** | Michele Thomas |
| **Contributing Editors** | Howard Rabinowitz, Cynthia Rubin |
| **Associate Editor** | Karin Mullen |
| **Assistant Editor** | Aimee Larsen |
| **Production Assistant** | Alexander Lyon |
| **Proofreader** | Annelise Zamula |
| **Acquisitions Editor** | Judith Pynn |
| **Indexer** | Leigh Anna Mendenhall |
| **Cover Photo** | Monument Valley, Utah, by Buddy Mays/FPG International |

# Camping
# Tips

# Getting Into Gear
## What to Pack for Your Camping Trip

Want to know how much gear to bring on your camping trip? Here's a tip: keep it simple. Campers often stuff lots of fancy gadgets into their packs and cars, but only a few items are essential: a sleeping bag, tent, stove, cooking utensils, cooler, light, and first-aid kit. The hard part is determining how much money to spend on those essentials. Your best bet is to play it safe and buy top-quality gear that will withstand whatever weather conditions you might encounter. Nothing is worse than a tent that leaks in a rainstorm or gets blown away by a strong gust of wind. And if a tent is too poorly made to weather a wicked storm, what good is it anyway? Camping is no fun when the main goal is survival.

Before you invest in some gear, consider how it's going to be transported. If you plan to car-camp with a van or a truck, you may have enough room for a large canvas tent, stoves and heaters fueled by propane tanks, and bulky sleeping bags, while folks in small cars will need more compact camping gear. If you're backpacking, purchase the lightest equipment you can find (and afford).

Here's what you should look for when buying the camping basics:

### Sleeping Bags and Pads

Selecting the appropriate sleeping bag for the varied terrain and temperatures of Utah and Nevada can be difficult. The desert's hot summer nights mandate a lightweight bag, whereas the cooler nights of alpine areas demand a heavy-duty model. Of course, the best plan of action is to buy two sleeping bags—one for cold weather and another for the hot desert temperatures. If funds are limited, however, invest in the cold-weather bag, which you can always sleep on top of during hot-weather spells, covering yourself with a blanket or sheet. Winter bags should be rated for freezing weather and still be light and small enough to strap onto a backpack. Mummy-style bags are ideal for cold nights because they're designed to cover your head. On nights when the temperature dips below 32-degrees Fahrenheit, sleep in a tent and wear a wool hat and at least one layer of clothing.

The best, most compact bags (and typically the costlier ones) are stuffed with goose down. But even down sleeping bags have their downfalls. They can be difficult to clean and, if they get wet on a camping trip, they're useless. Bags filled with artificial fibers are easier to clean and hold up better in wet weather. Couples should consider purchasing sleeping bags that can be zipped together—snuggling next to one another under the stars on a cool night is not only romantic, it generates heat.

Sleeping pads are recommended for extra comfort and warmth. Self-inflating pads cost more than traditional air mattresses or bulky foam, but they seldom spring a leak and take up little storage space. Cots are another option for those with circus-size tents.

## Tents

Backpackers and car campers tend to prefer small, lightweight nylon tents. But if you're taking the entire family car camping and you own a large vehicle, a roomier canvas tent might make the troops happier.

If you plan to buy a tent, find a store that specializes in camping equipment. Many of the best specialty stores have display tents set up for you to examine. Crawl inside several of them to check for roominess and compare other features. Inspect the tent's stitching; top-quality tents are double or triple stitched at all of the stress points. And be sure to find out if a tent is designed for four-season use or summer weather only. Summer-use tents tend to be lightweight, but not as weatherproof or as durable as their year-round counterparts. Finally, ask a salesperson to demonstrate the ABCs of assembling the tent you're seriously considering, and keep in mind that if a tent is too tricky to erect in the comfort of the store, it'll surely be too difficult to set up in the middle of a howling rainstorm in the dark.

## Stoves

The standard Coleman stove is a staple of most campers—it's virtually indestructible, works well in most weather conditions, and the fuel is typically less expensive than that of other brands. Several models of Coleman's basic two- and three-burner stove are available in different sizes. The only decision a camper may need to make is whether to purchase the model that operates on white gas or the newer version that burns either white or unleaded gas. The white-gas-only model requires pumping air into the stove before lighting it; if you want an instant flame (i.e., no pumping required), buy a stove that runs on propane. Propane stoves cost more, and although they don't work quite as well in cold weather or burn as hot as gas models, they light quickly and easily and are usually equipped with a barbecue grill. One disadvantage is that the fuel canisters are expensive; car campers with large vehicles may want to purchase a propane tank to save money. If you plan to backpack or car-camp with a small car, a tiny, lightweight, single-burner backpacking stove may be the best option. Most operate on white gas, unleaded gas, propane, or butane.

## Cooking Utensils

Picking out the right cooking equipment for a camping trip is primarily a matter of personal taste. Some prefer to keep it simple by packing an old frying pan, plastic utensils, paper plates and bowls, and disposable cups, although gourmands might be happiest toting their favorite wok, a grill, or even a Dutch oven that can be used over an open fire.

One of the simplest and handiest camping cookware sets consists of a "nesting" package—a medium-sized pot that contains a frying pan, one or two other pots, a coffeepot, handles for the pots and frying pan, and cups and plates. These cookware packages tend to last for years and won't set you back more than $50.

To save time when you're packing, keep the cooking basics—a can opener, ladle, large spoons, salt and pepper, spatula, and cleaning gear—together with the cookware in a large plastic storage box. Store standard supplies such as coffee, tea, hot chocolate, spices, a first-aid kit, and flashlights (with spare batteries) inside the box, and make sure you replace any used items after every trip.

## Coolers and Jugs

The size of the cooler and water jug you'll need often depends on the length of your trip, how much room you have in your vehicle, and how far from civilization you'll be. Since coolers are relatively inexpensive, consider buying a large one for extended trips in isolated places where you need to pack in a lot of food. Get a medium-sized cooler for weekend trips and a small one for day trips and overnighters.

Some campers prefer packaged "blue" ice, which can be reused, but it won't last longer than a couple of days. For extended trips, dry ice is preferable because it often lasts longer than cubed ice.

## Lights

A light for cooking, reading, or even finding your way to a campground rest room late at night is an essential part of any camping package. This light could be as simple as a miniature flashlight (the kind you might stash in your glove box) or as fancy as a propane-powered model.

Most campers tote along a Coleman gas lantern, which burns white gas or unleaded gas. They come in a variety of sizes: the large models emit more light, often burning two mantles at once, while the small lanterns fit better in compact cars. Some of these lanterns also use propane, which, although slightly more expensive, ignites more quickly than white or unleaded gas and doesn't require pumping air into a tank.

Some campers prefer a battery-operated fluorescent light. Although they're not quite as bright as the gas and propane models, they're easier to use—just flip the switch. They are also space savers because they can double as flashlights. Batteries can be expensive, however.

A reliable, no-frills flashlight will also do the job. A flashlight that snaps onto a headband or a headlamp, like those used by miners, works great as a reading lamp and as an all-purpose light source.

## Extra Gear

If you have room for more camping gear, consider packing a propane-powered heater. Your chances of finding wood for a campfire are scarce in many parts of Utah and Nevada, and in several desert regions wood-gathering is prohibited. Extra blankets might be handy, too.

In regions with a lot of biting insects, a mosquito-net tent that fits over a picnic table can make eating a meal in the outdoors much more pleasant. Such shelters also provide shade in the summer months (a godsend in the desert) and a windbreak on blustery days.

### Camping Gear Checklist

There's nothing like driving for hours to get to that prime campsite in the woods, only to discover that you forgot to pack your sleeping bag. Your best bet for avoiding such disasters is to make a list and check it twice. Create your own camping checklist and assign one of your camping buddies to check off each item as it is packed—it's one way to guarantee nothing gets left behind. Here's a list to get you started:

**Sleeping Gear**
- ☐ Ground cloth
- ☐ Tent
- ☐ Sleeping pad
- ☐ Sleeping bag
- ☐ Pillow
- ☐ Extra blankets

**Cooking Utensils**
- ☐ Stove
- ☐ Fuel
- ☐ Matches
- ☐ Cooking kit
- ☐ Grill
- ☐ Charcoal
- ☐ Cooler
- ☐ Water jugs
- ☐ Spatula
- ☐ Can opener
- ☐ Plates
- ☐ Cups
- ☐ Forks, knives, and spoons

- ☐ Aluminum foil
- ☐ Coffee
- ☐ Hot chocolate
- ☐ Salt and pepper
- ☐ Tablecloth

**Packing and Cleaning Supplies**
- ☐ Cloth towels
- ☐ Dish soap
- ☐ Paper towels
- ☐ Plastic bags (large and small)
- ☐ Sponge

**Recreational Gear**
- ☐ Binoculars
- ☐ Books and magazines
- ☐ Camera and film
- ☐ Car games for kids
- ☐ Deck of cards
- ☐ Field guides

- ☐ Fishing rod, reel, and tackle box
- ☐ Journal
- ☐ Portable stereo and tapes

**First-Aid Kit**
- ☐ See the checklist on page 26

**Miscellaneous Gear**
- ☐ Camp chairs
- ☐ Compass
- ☐ Daypack
- ☐ Firewood
- ☐ Flashlight and batteries
- ☐ Lantern
- ☐ Maps
- ☐ Mosquito-net tent
- ☐ Portable table
- ☐ Propane heater

# Since We're Neighbors, Let's Be Friends

## A Guide to Campground Ethics

As America's cities and towns become increasingly crowded, a growing number of people are turning to the outdoors for serenity, simplicity, and solitude. That's the good news. The bad news is that as urban centers become increasingly crowded, a growing number of people are bringing their bad habits—primarily thoughtlessness toward fellow campers and a disrespect for the land—into the backcountry. Even folks who have the best intentions sometimes unwittingly go awry, taking the "great" out of the Great Outdoors for others.

You may wonder what is meant by "campground ethics." It's simply another way of saying *use common sense and consideration while camping*. Common sense in a campground means keeping quiet; noise is the most common breach of campground ethics. It arrives in a variety of amplitudes, from the laughter of children sitting at a campfire roasting marshmallows at midnight to an all-out brawl between drinking buddies at the next campsite in the wee hours. A gas-powered electrical generator that can't be heard inside a well-insulated RV is torture for tent campers up to six sites away. A group that breaks up camp the moment the sun rises—rattling pots and pans, shouting orders, and running the car (or, worse, motorcycle) engine—can wake up everyone in the campground.

Other ways in which disrespect is manifested in the Great Outdoors are through carelessness with litter, spur-of-the-moment vandalism, and destruction of the natural environment. Litter—from trash left on a picnic table or strewn around a campsite to beer cans, aluminum foil, and glass tossed into a campfire pit—can be unsightly and annoying. It can also be a health hazard: have you ever been greeted by sewage left by an RVer who was too lazy to dispose of it at a dump station?

Vandalism and malicious destruction are increasing in the backcountry, too. Vandalism is immediately identifiable: marker and spray-paint graffiti; picnic tables and tree trunks carved with knives; and signs, garbage cans, and outhouses shot up for target practice. Considering recent and looming cuts in the budgets of the state and federal government agencies that oversee public lands, vandalized facilities may never be repaired or replaced. Worse, if picnic tables are smashed or cut up for firewood, toilets are removed from privies, and water pumps are knocked over by vehicles, the campground itself may be in danger of being closed permanently.

What can be done? Here are some suggestions:

• **Leave No Trace.** Public-land agencies and concerned environmentalists are mounting campaigns to publicize the principles of "minimum-impact" or "leave-no-trace" camping. For specific Leave No Trace guidelines, see page 378.

• **Take personal responsibility for backcountry ethics.** When entering a campground, even if only for a night, read the posted rules and observe them closely. Be sure to register and pay your camping fees promptly. This enables campground hosts and park rangers to spend their time maintaining the facilities, instead of informing you of campground rules and regulations or making sure you've paid your fees.

• **Observe quiet hours.** Most campgrounds have established quiet hours, usually between 10 P.M. and 7 A.M. During this time, campers should speak softly, use headphones for music, refrain from running generators, and keep children under complete control—in other words, be courteous to other campers. When setting up or breaking down camp, make as little noise as possible and, if it's dark, try to avoid shining bright flashlights or headlights everywhere.

• **Dispose of your litter.** Litter is pollution. Whenever you're tempted to leave garbage behind, think of how you feel when you find other people's plastic bags, tin cans, or aluminum foil in *your* yard. If you packed it in, pack it out. Properly dispose of your trash in frequently emptied public dumpsters. Even organic refuse, such as apple cores, orange peels, and eggshells (which take months to decompose), is trash. Always leave your campsite in better condition than when you found it, even if it means picking up the litter of those who came before you.

• **Keep rest-room facilities clean.** Tidy up messes you make when brushing your teeth, shaving, or using toiletries. Do not put any kind of garbage in vault toilets; trash, such as plastic bags, sanitary napkins, and diapers, cannot be pumped and have to be picked out, piece by piece, by some poor soul. If there is running water, use a biodegradable soap for washing dishes and cleaning up. If showers are available, bathe quickly so others can use the facilities.

• **Respect the land.** Leave the foliage and natural setting around the campground intact. Do not cut down limbs or branches or remove leaves from trees. If you want to build a fire, bring your own wood or buy some from a store or concessionaire. Before leaving a campsite, always make sure the fire is completely out.

• **Respect the animals that inhabit the area.** Don't feed or harass animals that visit your campground. Animals need to stick to their natural diets or else they might become ill. Keep your camp area clean, especially if you're in or near bear country, so you don't tempt any animals to visit your site.

• **Camp and hike in established areas.** Camp only in designated campsites, which are usually selected because they are resistant to constant use. Stay on the trails when walking to and from rest rooms, visitors centers, or stores, or when venturing into the backcountry. This is especially important in desert areas, where the cryptobiotic soil—a black crust that prevents erosion and takes years to form—is easily destroyed.

• **Avoid conflict and respect fellow campers.** If a situation arises with inconsiderate or uncooperative neighbors, try to avoid confrontations, which can easily escalate and turn ugly, especially when alcohol is involved. Talk to a campground host, park ranger, or someone with authority and let him or her address the problem. Meanwhile, make sure nobody has cause to complain about *you*. Show your camping neighbors the same respect that you expect from them and everyone will camp happily ever after.

# Helpful Hints for Hikers

Few spots on the planet have terrain as diverse as Utah and Nevada. In one weekend, hikers can trek up mountain peaks with elevations of more than 12,000 feet, then wander through a vast desert basin that's barely above sea level. Between these two extremes are a wide range of landscapes—from ponderosa pine forests and grassland prairies to slickrock canyons and lush river bottoms.

Not surprisingly, the climates in these distinct environments vary dramatically. The higher elevations of most mountain ranges are great for summer and fall hikes, but snow usually covers the trails and access roads from winter to early spring. The desert is an ideal setting in the winter, but it's potentially deadly in the summer. If you want to avoid places that are too hot or too cold, here's a good rule to live by: Hike in areas above 5,000 feet in the summer and fall, and seek out locations below 5,000 feet in the winter and spring.

## Drink Up!

Water is one of the most important supplies to take into the backcountry—especially in desert terrain. Day hikers and backpackers should carry at least one gallon of water per person per day. You'll probably need more than a gallon a day if you're visiting a desert area where the temperature is pushing 100 degrees Fahrenheit or if you'll be engaging in aerobic activity, such as climbing steep hills.

It's critical to carry all the water you'll need because, in most places in Utah and Nevada, finding groundwater is a rarity. And even if you encounter a flowing creek or stream, you shouldn't drink the water unless you treat or filter it. As with most backcountry locations in the lower 48 states, the bacteria *Giardia lamblia* abounds in the groundwater—even in seemingly pristine locations—due to animal waste.

## Hiking Gear Basics

Do you know how much a gallon of water weighs? Try eight pounds. Fortunately, in recent years equipment manufacturers have made it much easier for hikers to carry their own water. You may want to consider buying a Camelback insulated pouch, which straps on like a daypack and holds about two quarts. Various makers of fanny packs have also designed products with a liter-sized water holder that fits on either side of the hip bag.

In addition to water, other critical supplies include sunblock, sunglasses (with 100 percent UV protection), and a hat to guard against heat exhaustion. A light-colored, brimmed hat made of cotton or straw is ideal, or try one of those specially designed "desert rat" hats (which are white and have a duckbill brim and neck flap).

Traversing rugged terrain, whether you're in the mountains or the desert, requires a sturdy pair of hiking boots with lug soles. Heavy mountaineering-type boots aren't necessary, but you should at least have medium-weight, ankle-high boots. A rugged nylon and/or leather construction will stand up against sharp objects, such as cactus spines and rocks. If you hike through shallow snow or water during the cooler months, wear boots with a waterproof liner to keep your feet warm and dry. In hot weather, a fabric/leather boot offers the most ventilation—an important factor for minimizing sweaty feet and, ultimately, painful blisters. Be sure to begin breaking in a new pair of boots by wearing them around town for *at least* a week before setting off on an extended hike. All-leather boots require more break-in time than the fabric/leather variety; a general rule is to put 50 street miles on new boots before showing up at the trailhead.

A good pair of boots won't do much to prevent blisters or keep your feet warm if you aren't wearing quality hiking socks. Cheap cotton tube socks (the 10-in-a-pack specials) won't do the job. Wool socks work reasonably well, but socks made of a wool/synthetic blend are preferable. These materials wick away moisture, dry quickly, and provide extra padding.

A hiking staff can be a useful tool when traversing difficult desert or mountain terrain. It can help you hike down steep cliffs, climb up rocky hills, keep your footing steady when crossing streams, and, perhaps most importantly, divert angry rattlesnakes.

Before trekking into the backcountry, load a large fanny pack or daypack with the following essential items, which should help prepare you for an outdoor emergency:

| | |
|---|---|
| ☐ compass | ☐ map |
| ☐ extra clothing for cool conditions | ☐ matches |
| | ☐ moleskin |
| ☐ first-aid kit | ☐ sunblock |
| ☐ flashlight | ☐ Swiss Army knife |
| ☐ food | ☐ water |

## Keep on Track

Never go hiking in the backcountry without a map, and study your route prior to setting out. Most hiking trails in the region are charted on either U.S. Forest Service maps or National Park Service maps, which can be purchased at their respective ranger district and park offices. However, these maps provide little detail and often aren't sufficient for long hikes in remote areas.

Since there is so much public land in Utah and Nevada and the federal land-management agencies have limited recreational budgets, many excellent hiking trails are not maintained or marked. As long as you have the right U.S. Geological Survey (USGS) topographical map, this shouldn't be a huge problem; these maps show the landscape in great detail, including exact elevations and the location of springs, washes, and even abandoned roads and buildings. The 7.5-minute map series is preferable, because it shows the most detail; in many desert regions, however, only the less detailed 15-minute maps are available. USGS maps are sold for a few dollars at many outdoor stores or may be ordered by writing to: U.S. Geological Survey, Western Distribution Branch, Denver Federal Center, P.O. Box 25286, Denver, CO 80225.

If you're an avid hiker or plan to spend a lot of time exploring the backcountry, consider learning how to use a map and compass. Many books offer advice on orienteering skills. One particularly useful manual is *The Essential Wilderness Navigator: How to Find Your Way in the Great Outdoors,* by David Seidman (Ragged Mountain Press).

To ensure your hike is an enjoyable and safe adventure, contact the appropriate land-management office before heading out. A ranger or park official can usually tell you about the current trail conditions and offer other up-to-date information on the area.

# Don't Let Scorpions Sleep in Your Boots

## And Other Safety/First-Aid Tips

The Utah-Nevada region is a land of beautiful extremes, but one that requires visitors to be prepared for equally extreme conditions of hot and cold. The warm sunshine that so many people come to enjoy can cause serious sunburns and sunstroke, and getting caught in a summer thunderstorm at higher elevations can result in hypothermia, even if the temperature stays above 50 degrees Fahrenheit. Also bear in mind that there are few sources of water that don't require treatment before drinking, and when it comes to poisonous plants, animals, and insects, the region has its fair share. So before you set up camp, familiarize yourself with local hazards and take steps to ensure a safe and healthy trip.

### Sunburns

It's a commonly known fact that extended exposure to the sun's ultraviolet rays can cause skin cancer. For that reason, you'll see many savvy folks in the area wearing long-sleeved clothing and hats for protection. Sunscreen is also religiously applied to the skin throughout the day.

Sunscreen is assigned a numerical "sun protection factor" (SPF) rating. Use a sunscreen with an SPF of at least 15; anything lower won't provide enough protection. An SPF 15 rating means a user can stay in the sun without getting burned 15 times longer than without protection.

No matter what time of year you venture here, always apply sunscreen before heading out for an activity, and reapply it periodically throughout the day. Some of the worst sunburns are incurred during winter skiing and ice-fishing trips, because the bright sun is reflected off the snow and ice. If you forget to lather up with sunscreen or miss a hard-to-reach spot and get sunburned, treat the burned area by washing it with cold water; if available, add one teaspoon of boric acid per quart of water. Aloe vera gels will help restore moisture to the skin, but prevention, of course, is the best medicine.

### Heat Illnesses

Dehydration is a major cause of heat-related illnesses, such as heatstroke, which is a result of reduced blood flow to the brain. Symptoms range from hot, dry skin to light-headedness and fainting. To prevent a heat illness, force yourself to drink lots of water during hikes or any other activity in hot weather. Each person should carry at least one gallon of water per day. Replace electrolytes (salt, potassium, and bicarbonate) by drinking fruit juice or a soft drink occasionally. Although physicians once recommended that hikers take salt pills, they now believe that regular diets, including dehydrated foods that backpackers often bring on trips, provide enough salt without supplements.

If someone in your group becomes ill, stop exercising immediately and look for a place to sit in the shade. Cover the person's skin with wet towels or clothing to cool the body and give him or her some water to slowly replenish bodily fluids. A massage can help move blood to the extremities. If the person has lost consciousness, seek medical attention immediately. Even mild heat illness can become serious if not treated properly, so don't take any chances.

## Hypothermia

When your core body temperature falls dangerously low, you are suffering from hypothermia. Symptoms include impaired judgment, disorientation, and involuntary shaking, which is the body's way of trying to generate warmth. In advanced stages of hypothermia, a person might appear to have stopped breathing.

Treatment for mild hypothermia can be as simple as putting on warm, dry clothes and exercising to stimulate blood flow. Get out of the elements and seek any shelter that will reduce your exposure to wind and cold temperatures. Remove wet, cold clothing and drink warm liquids to help raise your body temperature. Curl up in a dry sleeping bag inside of a tent. If you are assisting someone in an advanced stage of hypothermia, soak towels or clothing in hot water and wrap them in plastic bags. Place the bags on the person's skin, especially around the lungs and heart, but be very careful not to scorch the skin. In extreme cases, CPR may be necessary.

## Water Treatment

No matter where campers venture in the outdoors, they face the challenge of making the water they find safe for drinking. Many campers use water filters to remove bacteria and parasitic cysts such as *Giardia lamblia* and *Cryptosporidium*. The popular Katadyn ceramic filters are dependable but expensive; the First Need filter is a less expensive option that also performs well. All filters are fairly easy to use, but they can be bulky. Filters can also become clogged if the water source is extremely dirty.

For increased safety, consider adding a chemical treatment to the filtered water. Chlorine or iodine products are readily available and capable of purifying water—even killing *Giardia*—if the correct amount is left in the water for a sufficient period of time. Most packaged iodine solutions come with instructions for the length of time the water must be treated (which varies depending on the water's temperature and its organic content). Follow instructions on the iodine treatment kit, and have a thermometer handy to measure water temperature. If you are allergic to iodine, boil the water for at least five minutes to eliminate bacteria and parasitic cysts (unfortunately, this may require using a fair amount of your cooking fuel supply).

## Cuts

When camping, your knife, hatchet, or ax can be your best friend—or one of your worst enemies. It only takes one bad swing with an ax or a careless slice with a knife to turn an enjoyable camping trip into a disaster, especially if you're 50 miles away from the nearest hospital. Always proceed cautiously before chopping wood or peeling the bark off a marshmallow stick.

If a cut occurs, apply direct pressure to the wound. This will collapse the blood vessel and allow clots to form. Use a sterile pad to stop the blood flow; anything from a gauze pad to a sanitary napkin will suffice. After the flow of blood has been slowed or stopped, carefully clean the wound. Physicians specializing in wilderness medicine encourage campers to carry a 10cc to 50cc syringe to flush out wounds with clean water.

Use butterfly bandages, wound-closure strips, or adhesive tape to close larger wounds instead of using sutures. (Sewing up a wound in the wilderness may only slow the healing process and trap infectious dirt or bacteria.) After closing the wound, cover it with a gauze dressing treated with an antibiotic ointment, then secure it with an elastic bandage or tape. If the cut is serious, consult a doctor as soon as possible.

## Blisters

The best way to prevent blisters is to spend a lot of time breaking in new boots or other footwear before you use them on a camping trip. Make sure your socks are clean and fit your feet, and avoid wrinkles in your socks, which can cause blisters. Wear a thin polypropylene sock inside a thick wool sock—some campers even wear three pairs of socks when backpacking. It's also wise to change your socks periodically and expose your feet to the air and give them time to dry off. Some campers apply antiseptic liquid bandages such as New Skin to their feet before hiking or backpacking.

To treat blisters and "hot spots" (areas on the foot where it feels like blisters are forming), cut a square of moleskin large enough to surround and protect the blister, then cut out a hole in the center of the square so the moleskin doesn't actually touch the blistered skin. After the moleskin is in place, tape it down snugly with adhesive tape. If necessary, drain the fluid from the blister with a sterile needle; however, the chance of getting an infection is reduced if the surface skin remains intact.

## Snakebites

Rattlesnakes are the most common venomous snakes in the region. Some are extremely poisonous, but your chances of getting bitten by a snake are very slim. Most people who die from snakebites are bitten while handling snakes. The rule of thumb here is quite clear: don't mess with them, and they won't mess with you.

On those rare occasions when a snake does strike, it usually does not inject venom into the victim. If venom is injected, you will probably experience immediate swelling and pain. For most bites, if you are within an hour or two of a hospital, you only need to remove rings, watches, bracelets, and other constrictions near the bite and get medical help as soon as possible. Keep the injured limb on the same level as the heart; this helps keep the venom from pooling if the wound is below the heart, or spreading if it is above the heart.

If you're more than a two-hour trip from a hospital, suction is recommended. Do not cut the fang marks, even with a sterilized blade. Use a venom extractor (available at mountaineering shops) to remove the venom; follow the explicit directions included in the kit. Extraction should be attempted within 30 minutes of being bitten. Always seek professional medical attention promptly.

## Scorpions
The sting of these arachnids can be deadly. To avoid scorpions, check your clothing carefully before dressing in the morning (especially your shoes or boots, which are favorite hiding spots) and use caution when moving sticks and rocks, which they may be hiding under. Scorpion stings can cause convulsions, especially in children. Applying ice to the wound can ease the pain, but administering the antivenin—available at most hospitals in Arizona—is essential.

## Ticks and Other Insects
While tick bites are not a major problem in Utah or Nevada, they occur occasionally and can cause Lyme disease. Sometimes a pair of tweezers can be used to successfully extract a tick from your body, but it depends on how deeply the tick is imbedded into your skin. To avoid the risk of breaking the tick in half (leaving a portion of the critter burrowed inside you), get medical help. Always save the tick in a plastic bag—your doctor might be able to identify the species if the bite becomes infected. Mosquitoes are a more prevalent problem, particularly near ponds and rivers. Your best defense is to carry insect repellent. If you get a nasty bite that's itching like crazy, you might want to use an extractor—the same kind used to remove snake venom—to treat the bite. Extractor kits are available at sporting-goods and mountaineering stores such as REI.

## Plague
Parts of southern Utah have several types of plague, which are transmitted through flea bites or contact with a sick animal. The disease is predominantly carried by prairie dogs, rock squirrels, field rats, and

---

chipmunks. Campers should not handle any animal—especially an animal that appears to be ill. The symptoms of plague include acute fever, malaise, and swelling of the lymph nodes, usually in the neck or groin. Typically, plague victims contract the disease from their own pets, often dogs or cats. Once symptoms appear, seek immediate medical attention; antibiotics must be administered as soon as possible.

## Hantavirus Pulmonary Syndrome

In 1993, a mysterious illness killed several people who lived in or visited rural areas of New Mexico and southern Utah. Eventually the culprit was identified and named Hantavirus Pulmonary Syndrome, a disease that's spread through the bodily waste of deer mice and causes fever, muscle aches, and coughing, followed by rapidly developing lung disease. Any home, building, or woodpile infested with rodents could be a source of the disease, but campers have a very small chance of contracting Hantavirus. For more information, call the Centers for Disease Control and Prevention's Hantavirus Hot Line: (800) 532-9929.

## First-Aid Kits

If you ask some campers about the contents of their first-aid kits, many will tell you they carry the usual things needed for headaches, blisters, and minor cuts, such as aspirin, Band-Aids, and moleskin. But that's not enough. Don't wait for a major accident to happen in the outdoors to convince you that you need a fully equipped kit. Here's what every camper should bring along:

- ☐ Acetaminophen, ibuprofen, or aspirin, for pain relief
- ☐ Adhesive tape
- ☐ Aloe vera–based burn ointment
- ☐ Antibiotic ointment, for minor cuts and scrapes
- ☐ Band-Aids, for minor cuts and scrapes
- ☐ Betadine solution, for disinfection
- ☐ Elastic bandages, to wrap sprains
- ☐ Extractor, for snake venom
- ☐ Gauze pads (extra thick and four inches square) or sanitary napkins, to reduce the flow of blood from major wounds
- ☐ Insect repellent
- ☐ Moleskin, to treat blisters
- ☐ Notebook and pencil, to record the details of any accident or injury that might be needed by a physician
- ☐ Sunscreen (at least SPF 15), to prevent sunburn
- ☐ Syringe (10cc to 50cc), to flush wounds
- ☐ Thermometer
- ☐ Tweezers
- ☐ Water filter, plus chlorine or iodine treatment

# Honey, I Packed the Kids
## Eight Great Tips for Camping with Children

Camping is a terrific way to introduce a child to the world of nature. Everything—playing, eating, sleeping, learning—is done under the sun and the clouds and the moon and the stars. More than a fun vacation (although it should be that, too), it's a chance to learn lifelong skills and experience nature outside of the everyday routine.

In addition, camping is one of the more affordable trips families can take. Sleeping in campgrounds is much less expensive than staying at a motel or hotel, and activities such as hiking, fishing, and exploring nature are not as pricey as amusement-park admission fees. And since you're cooking your meals at the campsite, the high cost of eating in a restaurant is avoided.

When planning a camping trip with the kids, remember a few simple rules: Tailor the trip to their capabilities; focus on their interests; and adjust to their limitations, which are generally defined by their age and development level.

Babies can be great campers, as long as you're prepared to limit your outdoor activities and can address their special requirements (crib, stroller, formula, diapers, etc.). Toddlers especially appreciate exploring a new environment. They love to get dirty and wet, collect leaves and rocks, and watch wildlife and insects.

Elementary school–age children are typically enthusiastic campers, anxious to learn about the outdoors, help with the chores, and participate in all the camping activities. They like to swim, hike, build fires, and roast hot dogs. And they can't resist hearing a good ghost story or tall tale about falling stars or wild animals.

Teenagers? Well, you're on your own there. Some teens like to camp, especially if it's an annual family vacation routine. Others consider it a drag and will take every opportunity to remind you of it. Try to involve teens in every aspect of the trip: deciding where to go, what to take, what to eat, what to do. Let them bring a friend and give them a little more freedom than they get at home. They'll be much better company during group activities and meals if they know they'll be able to go off and hike, fish, or swim on their own later.

Here are some tips on how to ensure that a fun, rewarding vacation is had by all:

• **Expect short attention spans.** By staying a step or two ahead of the kids in the planned activities department, you can keep them from getting bored or into trouble. Unlike adults, the kids need action on a vacation. Plan activities and games to keep them occupied. That means staying prepared by knowing what the next fun event will be—an activity that will inspire or distract a restless child.

• **Bring the right gear and games.** What you pack partly depends on where you'll be camping and what your children like to do. Are you camping at a sandy lake with toddlers? Then buckets, shovels, sieves, toy trucks, and plastic molds are in order. Will you be sleeping on top of old Smoky? Then binoculars, a telescope and star chart, a magnifying glass, and an altimeter are ideal. Will there be a river nearby? Then bring along a fishing rod. No matter where you go, pack along a ball, a Frisbee, a pack of cards, pens and paper, or crayons and coloring pads for younger kids.

• **Have a camera ready to capture the moment.** A still or video camera is a great thing to tote along. Photographs or videos of your family in the outdoors—hiking up a mountain, catching a fish, taking down the tent—will go a long way toward helping your kids hang on to memories of the last trip and build up a head of steam for the next.

• **Let your kids help with the practical stuff.** When you're camping, there are essential campground tasks that must be done—such as setting up camp, building a fire, cooking dinner—and kids would rather be involved than just watch you do everything. Show them how to help put up the tent, collect sticks for the campfire, add water and stir the pancake mix, read a compass.

• **Help your children learn, but also let them play.** Spending time outdoors provides the opportunity to teach them outdoor skills and safety, campground ethics, even some lessons about life. While teaching them to pick up after themselves (and others) and to respect the outdoors is very important, remember that taking your children to the woods, mountains, or desert doesn't have to be strictly an educational experience. This is first and foremost a vacation—and kids need to relax, too.

• **Let them have a say in the agenda.** It's everybody's trip. Listen to what the kids want to do and don't want to do. If a hike is planned and they want to spend the day swimming or tossing a Frisbee instead, let the majority rule. Follow their lead sometimes, go with their flow, let the adventure happen.

• **Set rules for acceptable behavior.** Giving the youngsters a say in the agenda doesn't mean letting them run wild. Rules and limits are essential to ensure kids' safety and their consideration for other campers. Let them know what behavior is acceptable around a campfire, how close they can come to a cliff or wildlife, and why it's important to stay within sight.

• **Prepare kids for the ups and the downs.** Enthusiasm is a key ingredient for a successful camping trip, but letting children become excessively excited can backfire when things don't go their way. If it rains or is unseasonably cold, if the fish aren't biting, or if one of them twists an ankle or catches a cold, it could ruin the whole experience for them. Tell them about the possible negative as well as the positive aspects of the trip—that way they'll be better prepared for whatever little disasters or disappointments come their way.

# Utah Resource Guide

## National Forests

Utah's six national forests cover 8.2 million acres, most of which are located in high alpine regions. They provide thousands of campsites, prime fishing spots, the bulk of the state's designated wilderness, and land for the majority of Utah's downhill ski resorts.

Some, such as Wasatch–Cache and Uinta, are situated near heavily populated areas, offering thousands of urbanites a quiet retreat. Others, including the more remote Ashley, Dixie, Fishlake, and Manti–La Sal, are in primarily rural settings where campers and outdoor recreation enthusiasts share the land with ranchers and other agricultural interests.

The Wasatch–Cache National Forest, which encompasses most of the mountainous areas from Salt Lake County north to the Utah-Idaho border along the Wasatch Front, manages 1.2 million acres. Some of the state's most popular ski areas, including Alta, Snowbird, Brighton, Solitude, Snowbasin, and Beaver Mountain, are on these lands. Canyons to the east and north of urban population centers such as Salt Lake City, Ogden, and Logan provide city dwellers with a welcome break from urban life. Also within the forest boundaries are the Mount Olympus, Twin Peaks, Mount Naomi, and Wellsville Mountain Wilderness Areas, plus most of Lone Peak and half of the High Uintas. Campers and anglers especially enjoy the dozens of camping spots and fishing areas along Utah Highway 150 between Kamas and Evanston, Wyoming, known by locals as the Mirror Lake Highway.

The 947,000-acre Uinta National Forest also serves as a major urban recreation area for campers, anglers, and hikers. Located east of Utah County in Wasatch County, this forest contains two wilderness areas: Mount Nebo and Mount Timpanogos, as well as dozens of developed sites, many of which have been refurbished in recent years. The huge Strawberry Reservoir recreation complex, which includes a visitors center, several large campgrounds, boat-launching ramps, and day-use areas, is one of Utah's most important Forest Service recreation sites thanks to the reservoir's reputation as one of the nation's top trout fisheries. There are excellent horse-camping areas in Payson Canyon's Blackhawk facility and at Currant Creek Reservoir. The Alpine Loop Drive, which connects Provo and American Fork Canyons, and the Nebo Loop Drive, which connects the towns of Payson and Nephi, are among Utah's most popular fall destinations.

Covering 1.4 million acres, Ashley National Forest in northeastern Utah offers contrasting styles of recreation. The huge Flaming Gorge National Recreation Area provides every type of facility a camper could need, including marinas, boat-in campsites, highly developed camp-grounds, beaches, geology tours and tours of the Flaming Gorge Dam, a national recreation trail, and two large visitors centers. By contrast, less developed and more primitive areas are located on the edge of Ashley's half of the High Uintas Wilderness Area, slow-paced spots like Spirit Lake, Moon Lake, White Rocks Canyon, Rock Creek Canyon, and Upper Stillwater Reservoir.

Utah's largest forest at nearly two million acres, Dixie National Forest in southern Utah provides an alpine alternative near Zion and Bryce Canyon National Parks, as well as some of the more remote country in the state. Elevations vary greatly, from as low as 2,800 feet near St. George to 11,322-foot Blue Bell Knoll on the remote Boulder Mountain north of Escalante. The Pine Valley Mountains, Ashdown Gorge, and Box Death Hollow Wilderness Areas are also found within the forest boundaries. Some of the best developed campgrounds include those in the Pine Valley area surrounding a small fishing lake; near Panguitch Lake, a popular fishing resort; in the Boulder Mountain area near some popular fishing lakes; and in the spectacular Red Canyon near the entrance to Bryce Canyon National Park. The forest also leases land to the Brian Head Ski Resort, the largest downhill resort in southern Utah. Forest lands in the area also offer excellent cross-country skiing and mountain-biking trails.

Fishlake National Forest, covering 1.5 million acres, is located in a more rural part of central Utah and features 19 campgrounds. The most developed are around Fish Lake, a popular fishing and resort area south of Salina. Anglers often fill beautiful campgrounds situated in pines and quaking aspens on busy summer weekends, enjoying both the scenery and the famous catches of trout and yellow perch. The popular Paiute ATV Trail, one of the longest developed motorized trails of its kind in the country, stretches across the Pahvant Range. The Great Western Trail near Fish Lake also offers good snowmobiling, all-terrain vehicle riding, and horseback riding.

Portions of 1.3-million-acre Manti–La Sal National Forest can be found in southeastern Utah. The La Sal Mountains, near Arches National Park, and the Blue or Abajo Mountains, near Canyonlands National Park, offer alpine camping and hiking alternatives to the blazing deserts of the slickrock parks. Dark Canyon Wilderness, west of Monticello, contains many Anasazi cliff-dwelling sites. The other major portion of this forest is on the Wasatch Plateau, which separates the towns of Manti and Ephraim on the west and Castle Dale, Ferron, and Huntington on the east. Skyline Drive, which stretches from Salina to Spanish Fork Canyon, offers one of the state's most popular four-wheel-drive adventures, especially in the fall when the leaves are changing color.

Campers wishing to use undeveloped campsites should first check with the forest supervisor's office or one of the district offices listed below to obtain a travel plan. Due to damage from overuse, Utah's national forest managers are increasingly restricting camping on undeveloped sites, and encouraging use of more developed areas. Many, but not all, developed campgrounds can be reserved for a nonrefundable $7.50 reservation fee by calling the U.S. Forest Service National Reservation System at (800) 280-CAMP (2267).

You are permitted to bring your dog into most national forests without paying an extra charge. The exception is Big and Little Cottonwood Canyons in Salt Lake County, where dogs are banned in order to protect Salt Lake City's water supply.

Maps of national forests are available from forest supervisor offices and district ranger offices. They can also be obtained by contacting the Wasatch National Forest Supervisor's Office in Salt Lake City at 125 South State Street, Salt Lake City, UT 84138; (801) 524-5030. There is a small charge for the maps, between $3 and $5. For more detailed maps, contact the U.S. Geological Survey or one of the private map companies listed on page 38.

Stopping by a ranger district office before visiting a forest is a good idea. When addresses aren't given in the following list, it means that the town is very small and the Forest Service district office is clearly marked and easy to find.

## Ashley National Forest
**Headquarters:** Ashton Energy Center, 355 North Vernal Avenue, Vernal, UT 84078; (801) 789-1181.

**Ranger Districts:**
  **Duchesne Ranger District,** 85 West Main Street (P.O. Box 981), Duchesne, UT 84021; (801) 738-2482.

  **Flaming Gorge Headquarters,** P.O. Box 279, Manila, UT 84046; (801) 784-3445.

  **Flaming Gorge Dutch John Office,** P.O. Box 157, Dutch John, UT 84023; (801) 781-5240.

  **Roosevelt Ranger District,** 244 West Highway 40 (P.O. Box 333-6), Roosevelt, UT 84066; (801) 722-5018.

  **Vernal Ranger District,** Ashton Energy Center, 355 North Vernal Avenue, Vernal, UT 84078; (801) 789-0323.

## Dixie National Forest
**Headquarters:** 82 North 100 East, Cedar City, UT 84720; (801) 865-3700.

**Ranger Districts:**

**Cedar City Ranger District,** 82 North 100 East (P.O. Box 627), Cedar City, UT 84720; (801) 865-3700.

**Escalante Ranger District,** 755 West Main Street (P.O. Box 246), Escalante, UT 84726; (801) 826-5400.

**Pine Valley Ranger District,** 196 East Tabernacle Street, St. George, UT 84770; (801) 652-3100.

**Powell Ranger District,** 225 East Center (P.O. Box 80), Panguitch, UT 84759; (801) 676-8815.

**Teasdale Ranger District,** P.O. Box 99, Teasdale, UT 84773; (801) 425-3435.

## Fishlake National Forest
**Headquarters:** 670 North Main Street, Richfield, UT 84701; (801) 896-4491.

**Ranger Districts:**

**Beaver Ranger District,** 575 South Main Street (P.O. Box E), Beaver, UT 84713; (801) 836-2436.

**Fillmore Ranger District,** 390 South Main Street, Fillmore, UT 84631; (801) 743-5721.

**Loa Ranger District,** 138 South Main Street (P.O. Box 129), Loa, UT 84747; (801) 836-2811.

**Richfield Ranger District,** 670 North Main Street, Richfield, UT 84701; (801) 896-4491.

## Manti–La Sal National Forest
**Headquarters:** 599 West Price River Drive, Price, UT 84501; (801) 637-2817.

**Ranger Districts:**

**Ferron Ranger District,** 115 West Canyon Road (P.O. Box 310), Ferron, UT 84523; (801) 384-2372.

**Moab Ranger District,** 2290 South West Resource Boulevard (P.O. Box 386), Moab, UT 84532; (801) 259-7155.

**Monticello Ranger District,** 496 East Central Street (P.O. Box 820), Monticello, UT 84535; (801) 587-2114.

**Price Ranger District,** 599 West Price Drive, Price, UT 84501; (801) 637-2816.

**Sanpete Ranger District,** 540 North Main Street (P.O. Box 32-14), Ephraim, UT 84627; (801) 283-4151.

## Uinta National Forest
**Uinta Supervisor's Office:** 88 West 100 North (P.O. Box 1428), Provo, UT 84603; (801) 342-5100.

**Ranger Districts:**
**Heber Ranger District,** 2460 South Highway 40 (P.O. Box 190), Heber City, UT 84032; (801) 654-0470.

**Pleasant Grove Ranger District,** 390 North 100 East (P.O. Box 228), Pleasant Grove, UT 84062; (801) 342-5250.

**Spanish Fork Ranger District,** 44 West 400 North, Spanish Fork, UT 84660; (801) 342-5260.

## Wasatch–Cache National Forest
**Wasatch–Cache Supervisor's Office:** 8226 Federal Building, 125 South State Street, Salt Lake City, UT 84138; (801) 524-5030.

**Ranger Districts:**
**Evanston Ranger District,** 1565 Highway 150, Suite A (P.O. Box 1880), Evanston, WY 82930; (307) 789-3194 (year-round), (801) 642-6662 (in the summer).

**Kamas Ranger District,** 50 East Center Street (P.O. Box 68), Kamas, UT 84036; (801) 783-4338.

**Logan Ranger District,** 1500 East Highway 89, Logan, UT 84321; (801) 755-3620.

**Mountain View Ranger District,** Lone Tree Road, 321 Highway 414 East (P.O. Box 129), Mountain View, WY 82939; (307) 782-6555.

**Salt Lake Ranger District,** 6944 South 3000 East, Salt Lake City, UT 84121; (801) 943-1794.

## National Parks
With five national parks, two national recreation areas, six national monuments, and one national historic area, the state offers visitors incredible scenic and cultural diversity. From the high alpine red-rock country of Bryce Canyon National Park to the water-oriented Flaming Gorge and Glen Canyon National Recreation Areas to the cultural resources of Hovenweep National Monument and Golden Spike National Historic Site, Utah's parks rank among the world's best.

Camping spots at the state's national parks fill quickly. This is especially true at Arches, Canyonlands, and Capitol Reef, where facilities are small. Though much larger, campgrounds do fill at Zion and Bryce as well. Since no reservations are taken for individual camping sites, those wishing to secure a spot should arrive as early in the day as possible. At Arches and Canyonlands, 9 A.M. is often not early enough.

Only Timpanogos Cave and Cedar Breaks National Monuments close in the winter, and even those offer limited access. The visitors center at Timpanogos Cave is open year-round, and cross-country skiers and snowmobilers can enjoy Cedar Breaks in the winter months. The best time to see southern Utah's national parks is often the off-season, when trails are less crowded and the scorching desert heat isn't a problem.

Pick up maps at park entrance stations or locally operated visitors centers. Or, contact the Utah Travel Council, Council Hall/Capitol Hill, Salt Lake City, UT 84114; (801) 538-1030.

## National Parks, Monuments, Recreation Areas, and Historic Areas:

**Arches National Park,** P.O. Box 907, Moab, UT 84532; (801) 259-8161.

**Bryce Canyon National Park,** P.O. Box 170001, Bryce Canyon, UT 84717; (801) 834-5322.

**Canyonlands National Park,** 2282 Southwest Resource Boulevard, Moab, UT 84532; (801) 259-7164.

**Capitol Reef National Park,** HC 70, Box 15, Torrey, UT 84775; (801) 425-3791.

**Cedar Breaks National Monument,** 2390 West Highway 56, Suite 11, Cedar City, UT 84720; (801) 586-9451.

**Dinosaur National Monument,** Dinosaur, CO 81610; (970) 374-3000 or (801) 789-2115 (Dinosaur Quarry Visitors Center).

**Escalante–Grand Staircase National Monument,** 318 North First East, Kanab, UT 84741; (801) 644-2672.

**Flaming Gorge National Recreation Area,** P.O. Box 279, Manila, UT 84046; (801) 784-3445.

**Glen Canyon National Recreation Area,** Box 1507, Page, AZ 86040; (520) 608-6404.

**Golden Spike National Historic Site,** P.O. Box 897, Brigham City, UT 84302; (801) 471-2209.

**Natural Bridges National Monument,** Box 1, Lake Powell, UT 84533; (801) 692-1234.

**Rainbow Bridge National Monument,** Glen Canyon National Recreation Area, P.O. Box 1507, Page, AZ 86040; (520) 608-6404.

**Timpanogos Cave National Monument,** Route 3, Box 200, American Fork, UT 84003; (802) 756-5239 (winter), (801) 756-5238 (summer).

**Zion National Park,** P.O. Box 1099, Springdale, UT 84767; (801) 772-3256.

## State Parks

Some of Utah's best camping opportunities are found in its 45 state parks, many of which are in close proximity to national parks. Facilities at some state parks include full hookups, showers, and playgrounds. Depending on the facilities, fees for overnight camping range from about $5 to $13.

Campgrounds at parks in southern Utah such as Snow Canyon, Dead Horse Point, Goblin Valley, Kodachrome Basin, Escalante, and Quail Creek tend to fill in the spring and fall and on holiday weekends. During the summer months, northern Utah's water-oriented parks, including Rockport, East Canyon, Willard Bay, Jordanelle, and Wasatch Mountain, host hordes of visitors.

The state park camping reservation system makes planning a trip to one of these Utah parks quite simple. Reservations for individual campsites may be made from three to 120 days in advance of your trip by calling (801) 322-3770 or (800) 322-3770, Monday through Friday from 8 A.M. to 5 P.M. (Mountain Standard Time).

### Park Offices:

**Utah Division of Parks and Recreation State Office,** 1594 West North Temple, Suite 116, Salt Lake City, UT 84116-3156; (801) 538-7220.

**Northeast Region Office**, P.O. Box 309, Heber City, UT 84032-0309; (801) 645-8036.

**Northwest Region Office,** 1084 North Redwood Road, Salt Lake City, UT 84116-1555; (801) 533-5127.

**Southeast Region Office,** 1165 South Highway 191, Suite 7, Moab, UT 84532-3062; (801) 259-3750.

**Southwest Region Office,** 585 North Main Street (P.O. Box 1079), Cedar City, UT 84720-1079; (801) 586-4497.

## Bureau of Land Management

Though not as well known as the national parks and forests and the state parks, some of the more popular developed campgrounds run by the Bureau of Land Management (BLM) rank among the best in the state of Utah. This is especially true of the Little Sahara sand dunes near Nephi, the Calf Creek Falls Recreation Area near Escalante, the Dixie Red Cliffs facility near Saint George, and the Slickrock Bicycle Trail and Colorado River camping complex near Moab. With such remote gems as the Starr Springs and McMillan Springs sites on the Henry Mountains or Simpson Springs along the Pony Express Trail in Utah's West Desert region, campers should not pass up a stay at a BLM site.

Many spectacularly beautiful BLM lands in Utah are also open to dispersed camping. After all, the agency manages about 22 million acres—approximately 42 percent of the state of Utah. Check with the local district or resource offices listed below for rules governing the use of such lands.

**BLM Utah State Office:**
  **Information Access Center**, 324 South State Street, Suite 400, Salt Lake City, UT 84111; (801) 539-4001.

**Field Offices:**
  **Cedar City Field Office,** 176 East D. L. Sargent Drive, Cedar City, UT 84720; (801) 865-3053.

  **Dixie Field Office,** 225 North Bluff Street, St. George, UT 84770; (801) 628-4491.

  **Escalante Field Office,** P.O. Box 225, Escalante, UT 84726; (801) 826-4291.

  **Fillmore Field Office,** P.O. Box 778, Fillmore, UT 84631; (801) 743-6811.

  **Kanab Field Office,** 318 North First East, Kanab, UT 84741; (801) 644-2672.

  **Moab Field Office,** 82 East Dogwood, Suite M, Moab, UT 84532; (801) 259-6111.

  **Price Field Office,** 125 South 600 West (P.O. Box 7004), Price, UT 84501; (801) 636-3600.

  **Richfield Field Office,** 150 East 900 North, Richfield, UT 84701; (801) 896-8221.

  **Salt Lake Field Office,** 2370 South 2300 West, Salt Lake City, UT 84119; (801) 977-4300.

  **San Juan Field Office,** 435 North Main Street (P.O. Box 7), Monticello, UT 84535; (801) 587-2141.

  **Vernal Field Office,** 170 South 500 East, Vernal, UT 84078; (801) 781-4400.

# National Wildlife Refuges
There are three national wildlife refuges in Utah: the Bear River Migratory Bird Refuge west of Brigham City on the edge of the Great Salt Lake; the Fish Springs National Wildlife Refuge on the Pony Express Trail in a remote part of Utah's West Desert region southwest of Tooele; and the Ouray National Wildlife Refuge southeast of Roosevelt in eastern Utah. For more information, contact the state office of the U.S. Fish and Wildlife Service at 145 East 1300 South, Suite 404, Salt Lake City, UT 84115.

## RV Parks

Utah offers dozens of RV parks, which are particularly attractive to budget travelers because they provide an alternative to staying in costly hotels and motels. The RV parks range from simple gravel parking lots equipped with electricity and water hookups to elaborate facilities that include golf courses, swimming pools, hot tubs, water slides, and access to nearby theme parks. Some, like the huge campgrounds in the St. George area in southwestern Utah, provide a place for retired citizens to spend the winter months in a warm climate. There are several big parks near Salt Lake City, Ogden, and Provo that give travelers on a budget a place to spend the night near a big city, where they can enjoy sights such as Salt Lake City's Temple Square, the Great Salt Lake, or downtown shopping and tourist attractions. Some facilities, such as those in the Moab area in southeastern Utah, fill a need for camping space. Federal and state agencies in that part of the state haven't been able to keep up with the high demand for campgrounds, whereas private operators have been more than willing to make up for it by constructing some of the state's newest all-purpose RV campgrounds.

## Native American Land

Native American lands are scattered throughout rural Utah, but they provide little in the way of recreation. One exception is the Navajo Reservation in southeastern Utah, which offers a campground, tours of Monument Valley, and the Tribal Park Visitor Center. The other is Four Corners, the monument where Utah, New Mexico, Arizona, and Colorado meet; it is the only site in the United States where a person can stand in four states at once. For information, write to Navajo Tribal Park, P.O. Box 360289, Monument Valley, UT 84536, or call the Parks and Recreation Department in Window Rock, AZ, at (520) 871-6647. The Utah Travel Council (see their number in "Other Useful Organizations" below) produces an annual listing of Native American celebrations held throughout the year.

## Map Companies

Maps of individual national forests are available at U.S. Forest Service headquarters and district ranger offices. Some maps can also be obtained from the Bureau of Land Management. The Utah Travel Council (see "Other Useful Information") offers a series of five sectional maps designed for tourists. Other sources of detailed Utah maps are:

**DeLorme Mapping Company,** P.O. Box 298, Freeport, ME 04032; (800) 642-0970.

**Trails Illustrated,** P.O. Box 4357, Evergreen, CO 80437-4357; (800) 962-1643.

**U.S. Geological Survey,** 2222 West 2300 South, West Valley City, UT 84119; (801) 975-3742.

**Utah Geological Survey,** 1594 West North Temple, Salt Lake City, UT 84116; (801) 537-3300.

## Other Useful Organizations

**Bed and Breakfast Inns of Utah,** P.O. Box 3066, Park City, UT 84060; (801) 645-8068.

**Bicycle Vacation Guide,** P.O. Box 738, Park City, UT 84060; (801) 649-5806.

**Office of Museum Services,** 324 South State Street, Suite 500, Salt Lake City, UT 84114-7910; (801) 533-4235.

**Ski Utah,** 150 West 500 South, Salt Lake City, UT 84101; (801) 534-1779.

**Utah Campground Owners Association,** 1320 West North Temple, Salt Lake City, UT 84116; no phone.

**Utah Department of Natural Resources Book Store,** 1596 West North Temple, Salt Lake City, UT 84116; (801) 527-3320.

**Utah Department of Transportation,** 4501 South 2700 West, Salt Lake City, UT 84119; (800) 964-6000 (within Salt Lake City only), (800) 492-2400 (nationwide; road condition report).

**Utah Division of Wildlife Resources,** 1596 West North Temple, Salt Lake City, UT 84116; (801) 538-4700.

**Utah Guides and Outfitters,** 153 East 7200 South, Midvale, UT 84047; (801) 566-2662.

**Utah Hotel-Motel Association,** 9 Exchange Place, Suite 812, Salt Lake City, UT 84116; (801) 359-0104.

**Utah Travel Council,** Council Hall/Capitol Hill, Salt Lake City, UT 84114; (801) 538-1030 or (800) 200-1160.

# Nevada Resource Guide

## National Forests

The U.S. Forest Service manages millions of acres of Nevada land, though you won't find trees on all of them. Tree line in Nevada begins at around 4,000 feet; forests as they're typically thought of are in the 7,000- to 11,000-foot range. Between these elevations lie the majority of the Forest Service campgrounds. Most provide running water, flush or vault toilets, picnic tables, grills, and fire rings. Some are right on the beaten track, while others are at the end of mountainous dirt roads miles from civilization.

Of the two dozen or so developed Forest Service campgrounds in the state, approximately half a dozen accept reservations. The more popular and less remote sites, such as those at Lake Tahoe, recommend making reservations as far in advance as possible and charge upwards of $16; other popular campgrounds, including those on Mount Charleston near Las Vegas, accept reservations for group sites only and charge around $10. To reserve one of these campsites, call the U.S. Forest Service National Reservation System at (800) 280-CAMP (2267). Most campgrounds on this system take reservations up to 180 days, but no less than three to seven days, in advance.

Ranger district offices handle reservations for the other Forest Service campgrounds that accept them, such as Lye Creek, Angel Lake, and Thomas Canyon. Fees for these sites generally run between $4 and $6. Dogs are permitted in national forests at no extra charge.

The U.S. Forest Service is a good source of detailed national forest maps; for information, contact: U.S. Forest Service, Office of Information, Pacific Southwest Region, 630 Sansome Street, San Francisco, CA 94111; (415) 705-2874. Regional maps for Nevada's two national forests can be obtained from ranger district offices; they cost $4 each.

For specific, up-to-date information on a national forest in Nevada, contact the forest superintendent or one of the following ranger district offices:

## Humboldt National Forest

**Superintendent:** 2035 Last Chance Road, Elko, NV 89801; (702) 738-5171.

**Ranger Districts:**

**Ely Ranger District,** 350 Eighth Street (P.O. Box 539), Ely, NV 89301; (702) 289-3031.

**Mountain City Ranger District,** P.O. Box 276, Mountain City, NV 89831; (702) 763-6691.

**Ruby Mountain Ranger District,** 428 Humboldt Avenue (P.O. Box 246), Wells, NV 89835; (702) 752-3357.

**Santa Rosa Ranger District,** 1200 East Winnemucca Boulevard, Winnemucca, NV 89445; (702) 623-5025.

# Toiyabe National Forest
**Superintendent:** 1200 Franklin Way, Sparks, NV 89431; (702) 331-6444.

**Ranger Districts:**
   **Austin Ranger District,** 100 Midas Canyon Road (P.O. Box 130), Austin, NV 89310; (702) 964-2671.

   **Carson Ranger District,** 1536 South Carson Street, Carson City, NV 89701; (702) 882-2766.

   **Las Vegas Ranger District,** 2881 South Valley View Boulevard, Suite 16, Las Vegas, NV 89102; (702) 222-1597.

   **Tonopah Ranger District,** 1400 South Erie Main Street, Tonopah, NV 89049; (702) 482-6286.

# National Parks
Nevada's sole national park is Great Basin. Established in 1986, it's one of the newest and smallest members of the national park system. Features include Lehman Caves, Wheeler Peak (13,063 feet), and 77,000 acres of fairly remote, rugged backcountry. Reservations are not accepted for the four campgrounds within park boundaries, which are strictly first come, first served. You can obtain maps at the visitors center or by contacting the park at: Superintendent, Great Basin National Park, Baker, NV 89311; (702) 234-7331.

The state is also home to one national recreation area, Lake Mead, the largest in the lower 48 states at 1.5 million acres. All campgrounds in the Lake Mead National Recreation Area are available on a first come, first served basis. For information and maps, contact: Lake Mead, 601 Nevada Highway, Boulder City, NV 89005; (702) 293-8906.

# State Parks
There are 22 state parks, recreation areas, and historic sites in Nevada. Fifteen of these offer camping opportunities. Contrary to the popular misconception that Nevada is an arid wasteland, most of the campsites are within walking distance of a lake, reservoir, or river. None of the state park campgrounds accept reservations; sites are available only on a first come, first served basis.

The most popular state parks for camping are Lake Tahoe–Nevada, Lahontan, Cave Lake, Valley of Fire, Berlin-Ichthyosaur, and Cathedral

Gorge. Sites are almost always available during the week, but campers are advised to arrive early on weekends to secure a place.

For general information on the state park system, contact: Nevada Department of Conservation and National Resources, Division of State Parks, 1300 South Curry Street, Capitol Complex, Carson City, NV 89710; (702) 687-4370.

## Bureau of Land Management

The federal government owns more of Nevada than any other state in the country: 60 million acres, or 85.3 percent of the total land area. The Bureau of Land Management oversees 50 million of those acres, and true to form, the agency manages a handful of remote and primitive campgrounds, most of which are far from pavement. Three charge camping fees, and one accepts reservations. For information on individual campgrounds, contact the BLM district offices listed below.

**BLM Nevada State Office**
  **Headquarters:** 850 Harvard Way, Reno, NV 89520, or P.O. Box 12000, Reno, NV 89502; (702) 785-6586.

**District Offices:**
  **Battle Mountain District Office,** 50 Bastion Road (P.O. Box 1420), Battle Mountain, NV 89820; (702) 635-4000.

  **Carson City District Office,** 1535 Hot Springs Road, Suite 300, Carson City, NV 89706; (702) 885-6000.

  **Elko District Office,** 3900 East Idaho Street (P.O. Box 831), Elko, NV 89801; (702) 753-0200.

  **Ely District Office,** 702 North Industrial Way (P.O. Box 33500), Ely, NV 89301; (702) 289-4865.

  **Las Vegas District Office,** 4765 West Vegas Drive, Las Vegas, NV 89108; (702) 647-5000.

  **Winnemucca District Office,** 5100 East Winnemucca Boulevard, Winnemucca, NV 89445; (702) 623-1500.

## National Wildlife Refuges

Nevada has seven national wildlife refuges, from the 248-acre Anaho Island National Wildlife Refuge, which protects the nesting grounds of American white pelicans in the middle of Pyramid Lake, to the 1.6-million-acre Desert National Wildlife Refuge, a vast and secure habitat for bighorn sheep. The others include the 5,300-acre Pahranagat National Wildlife Refuge, 90 miles north of Las Vegas; 12,700-acre Ash Meadows National Wildlife Refuge, home of the indigenous pupfish; 37,600-acre Ruby Lake National Wildlife Refuge, 60 miles south of

Elko; 140,000-acre Stillwater National Wildlife Refuge, 20 miles north-west of Fallon; and the 575,000-acre Sheldon National Wildlife Refuge, home to thousands of pronghorn sheep and the best place in the state to view wildlife en masse. For more information, contact the U.S. Fish and Wildlife Service Office in Las Vegas at 500 North Decatur Boulevard, Las Vegas, NV 89107, (702) 646-3401, or in Reno at 4600 Kietzke Lane, Building C, Room 125, Reno, NV 89502, (702) 784-5227.

## RV Parks

Some RV parks in Nevada date back to 1927, while others have been around for less than a year. You'll find them practically everywhere: in the heart of big cities, on the edge of small rural towns, along interstates and national highways, on Indian reservations, and in parking lots at casinos and even churches. Hookup fees average $15 a night, but RV parks at casinos are often less expensive, since they're among the amenities subsidized by gambling profits. It's wise to reserve a spot in a big-city RV park as soon as possible; space is limited in Reno and Las Vegas, and parks there fill up fast, especially during the high season. There's no central reservation service for RV parks in Nevada. To reserve, you must call the individual park and leave a credit card number; be sure to ask about their cancellation policy.

## Native American Land

Several Indian tribes in Nevada allow camping on their reservations. For information, contact any of the following:

**Duck Valley Indian Reservation,** Shoshone-Paiute Business Council, P.O. Box 219, Owyhee, NV 89832; (702) 757-3211.

**Pyramid Lake Paiute Reservation,** Pyramid Lake Paiute Tribal Council, P.O. Box 256, Nixon, NV 89424; (702) 574-1000.

**Walker River Indian Reservation,** Walker River Paiute Tribal Council, P.O. Box 220, Schurz, NV 89427; (702) 773-2306.

## Map Companies

The Nevada Department of Transportation is the most complete source of state maps; contact them at 1263 South Stewart Street, Carson City, NV 89712, (702) 888-7000. Raven Maps produces the largest, most informative, and most artistic map of Nevada; contact them at P.O. Box 850, Medford, OR 97501-0253, (800) 237-0798. Maps are also available from the U.S. Forest Service (see page 40) and the U.S. Geological Survey (see page 44).

In the Reno area, a good place to buy maps is at Oakman's, 634 Ryland Street, Reno, NV 89502, (702) 786-4466, and the local AAA office, 199 East Moana Lane, Reno, NV 89510, (702) 826-8800.

In Las Vegas, you can purchase maps at Front Boy, 1149 Maryland Parkway South, Las Vegas, NV 89106, (702) 384-7220, and at the local AAA office, 3312 West Charleston Boulevard, Las Vegas, NV 89102, or P.O. Box 26719, Las Vegas, NV 89126, (702) 870-9171.

## Other Useful Organizations

**Nevada Bureau of Mines and Geology,** Publications Sales, Mail Stop #178, University of Nevada, Reno, NV 89557-0088; (702) 784-6691. (Their rockhounders map costs $5.)

**Nevada Commission on Tourism,** 5151 South Carson Street, Carson City, NV 89701; (702) 687-4322 or (800) 638-2328. (Stop by for maps, a coupon book, and brochures on ghost towns, outfitters and guides, and special events.)

**Nevada Department of Wildlife,** 1100 Valley Road, Reno, NV 89512; (702) 688-1500. (Licenses and brochures on boating, fishing, and hunting are available here.)

**U.S. Geological Survey,** Western Distribution Branch, Denver Federal Center, P.O. Box 25286, Denver, CO 80225; (303) 202-4700.

# Utah Campgrounds

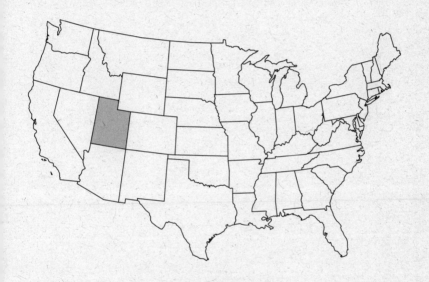

## Scenic Rating

Poor ........................................ Fair ........................................ Great

## Key to the Symbols

 Boating

Canoeing/ Rafting

Fishing

Golf

Hiking

 Historical Sites

 Horseback Riding

Hot Springs

Swimming

Waterskiing

RV Sites

Wheelchair Access

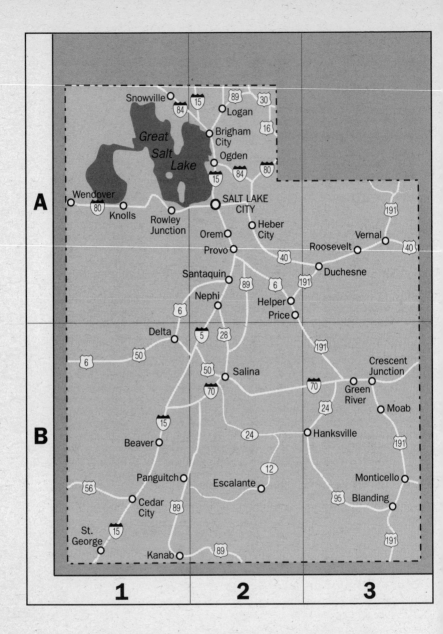

# Utah Campgrounds—Pages 48-253

**Chapter A1** ................................. **48**
*Map on page 48.* Little Sahara Recreation Area, Onaqui Mountains, Pony Express Trail, Sawtooth National Forest, Snowville, Wasatch–Cache National Forest

**Chapter A2** .................................. **56**
*Map on page 56.* American Fork, Antelope Island, Bear Lake, Big Cottonwood Canyon, Boulger Reservoir, Brigham City, Coalville, Currant Creek Reservoir, Deer Creek Reservoir, Diamond Fork Canyon, Echo Reservoir, Farmington, Fishlake National Forest, Garden City, Great Salt Lake, Hobble Creek Canyon, Honeyville, Hyrum, Hyrum Reservoir, Jordanelle Reservoir, Jordanelle State Park, Kamas, Kaysville, Layton, Little Cottonwood Canyon, Logan, Lost Creek Reservoir, Manti–La Sal National Forest, Mantua Reservoir, Midway, Nephi, Ogden, East Canyon Reservoir, Park City, Payson, Plymouth, Price, Provo, Provo River, Richmond, Rockport State Park, Salt Lake City, Scofield Reservoir, Scofield State Park, Strawberry Reservoir, Uinta National Forest, Upper Birch Creek Reservoir, Utah Lake, Wasatch Mountain State Park, Wasatch–Cache National Forest, Willard Bay

**Chapter A3** .................................. **124**
*Map on page 124.* Ashley National Forest, Dinosaur National Monument, Flaming Gorge National Recreation Area, Flaming Gorge Reservoir, Manila, Moon Lake, Pelican Lake, Red Fleet Reservoir, Starvation Reservoir, Steinaker Reservoir, Vernal

**Chapter B1** .................................. **150**
*Map on page 150.* Beaver, Cedar Breaks National Monument, Cedar City, Clear Creek, Coral Pink Sand Dunes State Park, Delta, Dixie National Forest, Enterprise, Fillmore, Fishlake National Forest, Glendale, Gunlock Reservoir, Hatch, Hurricane, Kanab, Kanarraville, La Verkin, Leeds, Minersville Reservoir, Mount Carmel Junction, Quail Creek Reservoir,

Orderville, Panguitch, Panguitch Lake, Parowan, Pine Valley, Snow Canyon State Park, Springdale, St. George, Zion National Park

**Chapter B2** .................................. **188**
*Map on page 188.* Bicknell, Boulder, Bryce Canyon National Park, Cannonville, Capitol Reef National Monument, Capitol Reef National Park, Circleville, Dixie National Forest, Escalante, Escalante Petrified Forest State Park, Ferron Reservoir, Fish Lake, Fishlake National Forest, Glen Canyon National Recreation Area, Gunnison, Henry Mountains, Huntington Reservoir, Huntington State Park, Joe's Valley Reservoir, Johnson Reservoir, Joseph, Kodachrome Basin State Park, Lake Powell, Lower Bown's Reservoir, Manti, Manti–La Sal National Forest, Marysville, Millsite Reservoir, Millsite State Park, Monroe, Otter Creek Reservoir, Palisade Reservoir, Palisade State Park, Panguitch, Paria River, Payson, Piute Reservoir, Richfield, Salina, Torrey, Tropic Reservoir, Wide Hollow Reservoir, Yearns Reservoir, Yuba Reservoir

**Chapter B3** .................................. **224**
*Map on page 224.* Arches National Park, Blanding, Bluff, Canyonlands National Park, Capitol Reef National Park, Colorado River, Dead Horse Point State Park, Glen Canyon National Recreation Area, Goblin Valley State Park, Goosenecks State Park, Green River, Green River State Park, Hanksville, Henry Mountains, Hovenweep National Monument, Lake Powell, Manti–La Sal National Forest, Mexican Hat, Moab, Monticello, Monument Valley, Natural Bridges National Monument, Oohwah Lake, San Juan River, San Rafael Swell, Warner Lake

# MAP A1

Map of Utah ........................ see page 46

**Beyond This Region:**

North ............................................. Idaho
East (Map A2) .................. see page 56
South (Map B1) .............. see page 150
West .......................................... Nevada

15 Campgrounds
Pages 48–55

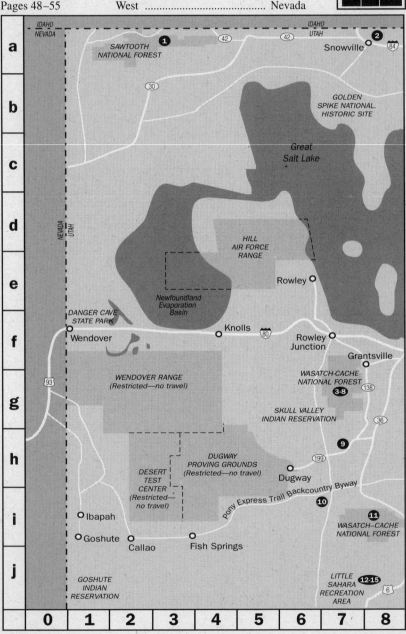

**Chapter A1 features:**

1. Clear Creek
2. Lottie Dell Campground
3. Cottonwood
4. Intake
5. Boy Scout
6. Lower Narrows
7. Upper Narrows
8. Loop
9. Clover Springs
10. Simpson Springs
11. Uinta Little Valley
12. White Sands
13. Oasis
14. Jericho
15. Sand Mountain

## 1. CLEAR CREEK

*Reference:* **In Sawtooth National Forest; map A1, grid a3.**

*Campsites, facilities:* There are 10 sites with picnic tables and fire grills. Vault toilets and drinking water are available.

*Reservations, fee:* Sites are free and are first come, first served.

*Contact:* Call the Burley Ranger District of Sawtooth National Forest in Idaho at (208) 678-0430.

*Location:* From Snowville, head west on State Route 30. In about 18 miles, look for the junction with State Route 42. Take State Route 42 about 8.5 miles, keeping an eye out for the Strevell Road 3600 South sign. (Note: It's a small street sign that can be difficult to see at night.) Turn left onto Strevell Road, go about 3.2 miles to Clear Creek Campground Road, turn left, and continue for another six miles.

*Trip notes:* Despite its remote location, this campground set in somewhat open country can fill up quickly on weekends. A small, fishable stream is nearby, and hikers and bicyclists will discover plenty of pines and wildflower-covered fields. Also close by is the Bull Flat Trailhead, accessible to hikers, horses, mountain bikes, and all-terrain vehicles. On the Bull Flat Trail, hikers can either take the turnoff to Bull Flat or continue on the main path to the Lake Fork Trail; this leads to Bull Lake, located beneath sheer, glacier-formed quartzite cliffs.

*Season:* June through September.

## 2. LOTTIE DELL CAMPGROUND

*Reference:* **In Snowville; map A1, grid a8.**

*Campsites, facilities:* There are 34 sites with hookups, 14 camping cabins, and a large, grassy area for tents. Laundry facilities, rest rooms, showers, picnic tables, and a public phone are available. Pets are allowed.

*Reservations, fee:* Reservations are accepted. Sites with hookups are $15, tent sites are $11, and cabins are $20.

*Contact:* Call the campground at (801) 872-8273.

*Location:* Follow Interstate 84 to Snowville, then take either exit 5 or 7 and drive into town, where the campground is located.

*Trip notes:* This campground is located within the boundaries of Snowville, a quiet small town. Not far away is the Golden Spike National Historic Site, where the tracks of the Transcontinental Railroad were joined in 1869. Here, during the summer, one of two steam engines periodically chugs out of the train-house, providing a touch of living history; exhibits also tell the story of the momentous event.

*Season:* Open year-round.

---

## 3. COTTONWOOD

*Reference:* **In Wasatch–Cache National Forest; map A1, grid g7.**

*Campsites, facilities:* There are three sites with picnic tables and vault toilets, but there is *no drinking water.*

*Reservations, fee:* Sites are $5 and are first come, first served.

*Contact:* Call the Salt Lake Ranger District at (801) 943-1794.

*Location:* From Salt Lake City, drive west on Interstate 80. Take exit 99 and go left on State Route 36, following the signs to Grantsville and Tooele. After about 10 miles, turn right on State Route 138 to Grantsville. Drive most of the way through town, and look for the brown sign with directions to the Wasatch National Forest Recreation Areas of South Willow and North Willow. Turn left on 400 West and, after about five miles, take the right turnoff to South Willow. Follow the paved road to the Forest Service boundary, then continue on the gravel (passable by two-wheel-drive vehicles) for another 9.2 miles to the campground.

*Trip notes:* Named for its tall and sheltering cottonwood trees, this campground basically consists of a small parking area to the left of the road; like most of the campgrounds nearby, it's sandwiched between the road and the steep walls of South Willow Canyon. Hikers come here to tackle 11,031-foot Deseret Peak, set in the heart of a beautiful designated wilderness area not far away. Those who make the summit enjoy spectacular views of the Wasatch Mountains, the Great Salt Lake, Great Basin, and the Bonneville Salt Flats. A small stream flows through the campground and is occasionally stocked with catchable rainbow trout. Campers must haul their gear down to the sites closest to the stream. The alpine canyon provides a cool and shady counterpoint to the stark, arid surroundings.

*Season:* May through October.

---

## 4. INTAKE

*Reference:* **In Wasatch–Cache National Forest; map A1, grid g7.**

*Campsites, facilities:* There are four sites with picnic tables and fire grills. Vault toilets are available, but there is *no water.*

*Reservations, fee:* Sites are $5 and are first come, first served.

*Contact:* Call the Salt Lake Ranger District of Wasatch National Forest at (801) 943-1794.

*Location:* From Salt Lake City, take Interstate 80 west to exit 99, then turn left on State Route 36 and follow the directions to Grantsville (see Cottonwood campground above). Continue past Cottonwood a short distance up the canyon. The campground is 9.9 miles from Grantsville.

*Trip notes:* The road to Intake campground is a sharp jag to the left down a dirt road; as with most campgrounds in South Willow Canyon, there's some-

---

times a fine cover of road dust. Still, the campsites here, set along a small stream, are a little more secluded from the road and spaced farther apart than at other campgrounds nearby, and they're shaded by box elder and Rocky Mountain big-tooth maple trees. There's good fishing at nearby Grantsville Reservoir for planted rainbow trout, especially in the spring. Hikers can explore the designated wilderness area of nearby 11,031-foot Deseret Peak or attempt the summit itself.

*Season:* May through October.

## 5. BOY SCOUT

*Reference:* **In Wasatch–Cache National Forest; map A1, grid g7.**

*Campsites, facilities:* There are five sites with picnic tables and fire grills. Vault toilets are available, but there is *no water.*

*Reservations, fee:* Sites are $5 and are first come, first served.

*Contact:* Call the Salt Lake Ranger District of Wasatch National Forest at (801) 943-1794.

*Location:* From Salt Lake City, follow the directions to Cottonwood campground in South Willow Canyon (see page 50), continuing on past Cottonwood for about another quarter of a mile. Boy Scout campground is 10.2 miles southwest of Grantsville.

*Trip notes:* Boy Scout is an excellent little spot in which to beat the heat and avoid all the crowds in the campgrounds located closer to the Wasatch Front. Since it is equipped with long tables, it's also well suited to larger groups, as the name "Boy Scout" suggests. The campground is separated from the road by a stream and shaded by cottonwood trees. Hikers who are not up for climbing nearby Deseret Peak can opt for shorter walks from the trailhead instead.

*Season:* May through October.

## 6. LOWER NARROWS

*Reference:* **In Wasatch–Cache National Forest; map A1, grid g7.**

*Campsites, facilities:* There are five sites with picnic tables and fire grills. Vault toilets are available, but there is *no water.*

*Reservations, fee:* Sites are $5 and are first come, first served.

*Contact:* Call the Salt Lake Ranger District of Wasatch National Forest at (801) 943-1794.

*Location:* From Salt Lake City, follow the directions for Cottonwood campground in South Willow Canyon (see page 50) and continue on to Lower Narrows. The campground is half a mile up the canyon, 10.7 miles southwest of Grantsville.

*Trip notes:* Campers must haul their gear across a bridge to this campground, since parking is only along the road and the sites are across the stream. Many campers come to Lower Narrows to explore the nearby Deseret Peak Wilderness Area or to fish for rainbow trout in the small creek that runs through South Willow Canyon.

*Season:* May through October.

# 7. UPPER NARROWS

*Reference:* **In Wasatch–Cache National Forest; map A1, grid g7.**

*Campsites, facilities:* There are eight sites with picnic tables and fire grills. Vault toilets are available, but there is *no water.*

*Reservations, fee:* Sites are $5 and are first come, first served.

*Contact:* Call the Salt Lake Ranger District of Wasatch National Forest at (801) 943-1794.

*Location:* From Salt Lake City, follow the directions for Cottonwood campground in South Willow Canyon (see page 50). This campground is .8 miles farther up the canyon, 11.5 miles southwest of Grantsville.

*Trip notes:* Tooele County residents know this small campground is a great place to escape the pounding summer heat. Campers can spend a day at the Great Salt Lake State Park beaches northwest of Grantsville, then head back into the forest. Anglers can fish for rainbow trout in the nearby small stream or down the road at Grantsville Reservoir. All parking is along the road; campers must walk to their sites along the stream, just before the narrowest part of the canyon.

*Season:* May through October.

# 8. LOOP

*Reference:* **In Wasatch–Cache National Forest; map A1, grid g7.**

*Campsites, facilities:* There are nine sites with picnic tables and fire grills. Vault toilets are available, but there is *no water.*

*Reservations, fee:* Sites are $5 and are first come, first served.

*Contact:* Call the Salt Lake Ranger District of Wasatch National Forest at (801) 943-1794.

*Location:* From Salt Lake City, follow the directions to Cottonwood campground in South Willow Canyon (see page 50) and continue for almost four miles. Loop campground is at the end of the canyon, 13 miles southwest of Grantsville.

*Trip notes:* This campground serves as the trailhead for 11,031-foot Deseret Peak, a popular place for hikers who love a breathtaking view (see Cottonwood campground on page 50). It's also a great base for anglers looking to find rainbow trout at Grantsville Reservoir or the nearby small stream. The well-spaced campsites are located along the road under a grove of tall aspens, which in mid-September are brilliantly ablaze with the colors of fall.

*Season:* May through October.

# 9. CLOVER SPRINGS

*Reference:* **In the Onaqui Mountains; map A1, grid h7.**

*Campsites, facilities:* There are 11 camping spaces with no hookups, plus group facilities and vault toilets. Equestrian facilities include horse tie-ups, unloading docks, and feeding troughs.

*Reservations, fee:* Camping is free and sites are first come, first served.

*Contact:* Call the Bureau of Land Management at (801) 977-4300.

*Location:* Driving south from Tooele, take State Route 36 south to Highway 199; head west eight miles to the campground.

*Trip notes:* This campground is in a popular horseback-riding area in one of the more remote parts of Utah. Across the road are some developed horse and hiking trails, but the wide-open country beckons adventurers to ramble off the beaten path. The camping itself is in a riparian canyon at an elevation of 6,000 feet, so temperatures can be on the cool side. Campers looking for a quiet spot should enjoy this one.

*Season:* April through November.

---

## 10. SIMPSON SPRINGS

*Reference:* **On the Pony Express Trail; map A1, grid i6.**

*Campsites, facilities:* There are 14 sites (plus a large overflow area) with no hookups. Picnic tables, fire grills, and vault toilets are available, but there is *no water.*

*Reservations, fee:* Campsites are $2 and are first come, first served.

*Contact:* Call the Bureau of Land Management at (801) 977-4300.

*Location:* This extremely remote campground is about 120 miles from the cities of Provo (via Lehi) and Salt Lake City (via Tooele), off State Route 36. Turn off State Route 36 at Vernon, and head west for 31 miles on the graveled Pony Express Trail Backcountry Byway. Look for the signs directing visitors to the Pony Express Trail and Fish Springs National Wildlife Refuge.

*Trip notes:* The stark desert scenery of the Great Basin takes some getting used to if you're accustomed to greener terrain, but the desolate beauty has an appeal all its own. History buffs will enjoy touring the remains of the Pony Express Trail Station on the dirt road near the entrance, where interpretive signs tell the story of the historic route. This is literally wide-open territory for horseback riders and hikers, with few developed trails; mountain bikers often use the dirt road. Bird-watchers can spot many different types of migrating shorebirds, waterfowl, and raptors at the nearby Fish Springs National Wildlife Refuge. Note: Simpson Springs campground is quite popular with off-road-vehicle enthusiasts and can be crowded in spring and fall.

*Season:* Open year-round.

---

## 11. UINTA LITTLE VALLEY

*Reference:* **In Wasatch–Cache National Forest; map A1, grid i8.**

*Campsites, facilities:* There are six sites with picnic tables and fire grills. Vault toilets are available, but there is *no water.*

*Reservations, fee:* All sites are free and first come, first served.

*Contact:* Call the Spanish Fork Ranger District at (801) 798-3571.

*Location:* This remote campground, off State Route 36 and south of Vernon, is 120 miles from both Provo (via Lehi) and Salt Lake City (via Tooele). Take State Route 36 to Vernon, turn onto Forest Road 005, and head south for 11 miles to the campground.

*Trip notes:* Here's a truly out-of-the-way spot that's perfect if you're trying to avoid the crowds. Fishing for stocked trout at nearby Vernon Reservoir can

---

be good, especially in the spring. Though the launching facilities are somewhat primitive, small boats, canoes, and rafts are allowed on the reservoir. The campground is in Wasatch-Cache National Forest, but it is managed by Uinta National Forest.

*Season:* April through November.

## 12. WHITE SANDS

*Reference:* **In Little Sahara Recreation Area; map A1, grid j7.**

*Campsites, facilities:* There are 50 sites with picnic tables, fire grills, rest rooms with flush toilets, drinking water, and a fenced recreation area in the dunes.

*Reservations, fee:* Sites are $5 and are first come, first served.

*Contact:* Call the Bureau of Land Management in Fillmore at (801) 743-6811.

*Location:* Drive 24 miles north of Delta or 18 miles south of Eureka on U.S. Highway 6 to Jericho Junction. Just past the visitors center, take the first road north and drive 4.5 miles to the campground.

*Trip notes:* The surrounding Little Sahara Recreation Area is a huge complex of dunes, so this campground is popular with off-road vehicle owners. The fenced-in play area protects kids and adults from the dune buggies and dirt bikes. Hiking the shifting dunes is more like a freewheeling romp in the sand. The campsites are set against the sandy hills near juniper trees.

*Season:* Open year-round, though the water may be turned off in the winter.

## 13. OASIS

*Reference:* **In Little Sahara Recreation Area; map A1, grid j7.**

*Campsites, facilities:* There are 84 sites with no hookups (this is a popular place to bring self-contained RVs). Picnic tables, fire grills, flush toilets, and drinking water are available.

*Reservations, fee:* Sites are $5 and are first come, first served.

*Contact:* Call the Bureau of Land Management in Fillmore at (801) 743-6811.

*Location:* Take U.S. Highway 6 to Jericho Junction, located 24 miles north of Delta and 18 miles south of Eureka. Then follow the signs to the campground, heading south and west for about seven miles.

*Trip notes:* This campground is the number-one favorite with folks who like to take their dune buggies, dirt bikes, or other all-terrain vehicles onto the extensive dune system at Little Sahara. That means hikers need to be careful on the dunes. Like other campgrounds nearby, this one is in a hilly, sandy area in the midst of some juniper trees.

*Season:* Open year-round, though the water may be turned off in the winter.

## 14. JERICHO

*Reference:* **In Little Sahara Recreation Area; map A1, grid j7.**

*Campsites, facilities:* There are 41 sites with no hookups. Picnic tables, fire grills, flush toilets, and drinking water are available, along with a fenced sandy play area that's off-limits to all-terrain vehicles.

*Reservations, fee:* Sites are $5 and are first come, first served.

*Contact:* Call the Bureau of Land Management in Fillmore at (801) 743-6811.

*Location:* On U.S. Highway 6, travel 24 miles north of Delta or 18 miles south of Eureka to Jericho Junction. Then follow the signs to the campground, heading southwest for just over seven miles.

*Trip notes:* Set in the dunes, this might be the best camping spot in the area for families with young children. Here, in the big fenced play area, kids and adults can build sand castles, roll down the sandy slopes, or gaze at the dramatic scenery without worrying about collisions with all-terrain vehicles. The campground terrain is largely open; covered picnic tables provide the only shade.

*Season:* Open year-round, though the water may be turned off in the winter.

## 15. SAND MOUNTAIN

*Reference:* **In Little Sahara Recreation Area; map A1, grid j7.**

*Campsites, facilities:* There are no designated campsites; this is a popular spot for self-contained RVs. Vault toilets are available, but there is *no water.*

*Reservations, fee:* Campsites are $5 and are first come, first served.

*Contact:* Call the Bureau of Land Management in Fillmore at (801) 743-6811.

*Location:* On U.S. Highway 6, drive 24 miles north from Delta or 18 miles south from Eureka to Jericho Junction. Then follow the signs, heading southwest for just over 12 miles to the end of the road near Sand Mountain.

*Trip notes:* Off-highway vehicle owners love the wide-open spaces of Sand Mountain. All hiking is on the dunes, with no marked trails. Though facilities are limited, the area can accommodate large numbers overnight. Campers park their RVs at the base of Sand Mountain, one of the largest dunes in the 60,000-acre area.

*Season:* Open year-round.

# MAP A2

Map of Utah ...................... see page 46
Beyond This Region:
North ............................................ Idaho
East (Map A3) ................. see page 124
South (Map B2) ............... see page 188
West (Map A1) ................... see page 48

154 Campgrounds
Pages 56–123

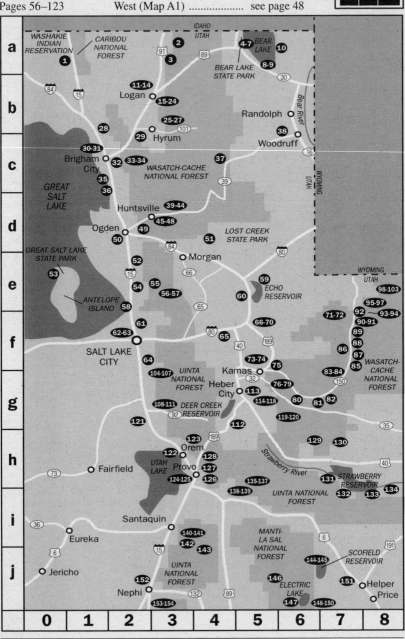

**Chapter A2 features**:

1. Belmont Hot Springs
2. High Creek
3. Smithfield Canyon
4. Bear Lake State Recreation Area
5. Bear Lake KOA
6. Sunrise
7. Bluewater Beach Campground
8. Sweetwater RV Park and Marina
9. Bear Lake Rendezvous Beach State Park
10. Bear Lake South Eden
11. Western Park Campground
12. Bandits Cove
13. River Side RV Park and Campground
14. Country Cuzzins RV Park
15. Wood Camp
16. Lodge
17. Lewis M. Turner
18. Red Banks
19. Tony Grove
20. Bridger
21. Spring Hollow
22. Guinavah-Malibu
23. Sunrise
24. Preston Valley
25. Friendship
26. Spring
27. Pioneer
28. Crystal Springs Resort
29. Hyrum State Park
30. Golden Spike RV Park
31. Brigham City KOA
32. Mountain Haven Campground
33. Box Elder
34. Willard Basin
35. Willard Bay North
36. Willard Bay South
37. Monte Cristo
38. Birch Creek
39. Botts
40. South Fork
41. Perception Park
42. Lower Meadows
43. Upper Meadows
44. Willows
45. Anderson Cove
46. Jefferson Hunt
47. Magpie
48. Hobble
49. The Maples
50. Century RV Park
51. Lost Creek State Park
52. Circle L. Mobile Home Park
53. Antelope Island State Park
54. Cherry Hill Campground
55. Sunset
56. Bountiful Peak
57. East Canyon State Park
58. Great Salt Lake State Park
59. Echo Resort on Echo Reservoir
60. Holiday Hills Campground
61. Lagoon Pioneer Village Campground
62. Salt Lake City VIP
63. Mountain Shadows RV Park
64. Shady Haven RV Park
65. Hidden Haven Campground
66. Juniper and Cedar Point
67. Cottonwood
68. Twin Coves
69. Pinery
70. Crandall's
71. Smith and Morehouse
72. Ledgefork
73. Hailstone Campground
74. Rock Cliff Campground
75. Yellow Pine RV
76. Beaver Creek
77. Taylor Fork
78. Shingle Creek
79. Lower Provo
80. Soapstone
81. Shady Dell
82. Cobblerest
83. Trial Lake
84. Lilly Lake
85. Lost Creek
86. Moosehorn
87. Mirror Lake
88. Butterfly

*(continued on page 58)*

| | |
|---|---|
| 89. Sulphur | 122. Utah Lake State Park |
| 90. Beaver View | 123. Hope |
| 91. Hayden Fork | 124. Lakeside Campground |
| 92. Wolverine ATV Trailhead | 125. Provo KOA |
| 93. Christmas Meadows | 126. Frazier Trailer Park |
| 94. Stillwater | 127. Deer Creek Park |
| 95. Bear River | 128. River Bend Trailer Park |
| 96. East Fork | 129. Lodgepole |
| 97. Little Lyman Lake | 130. Currant Creek |
| 98. China Meadows | 131. Strawberry Bay |
| 99. China Meadows Trailhead | 132. Renegade Point |
| 100. Marsh Lake | 133. Soldier Creek |
| 101. Bridger Lake | 134. Aspen Grove |
| 102. State Line | 135. Whiting |
| 103. Hoop Lake | 136. Cherry |
| 104. Spruces | 137. Balsam |
| 105. Redman | 138. Palmyra |
| 106. Tanners Flat | 139. Diamond |
| 107. Albion | 140. Maple Bench |
| 108. Little Mill | 141. Payson Lakes |
| 109. Granite Flat | 142. Tinney Flat |
| 110. Mount Timpanogos | 143. Blackhawk |
| 111. Timpanoke | 144. Mountain View |
| 112. Deer Creek State Park | 145. Madsen Bay |
| 113. Mountain Spa | 146. Gooseberry |
| 114. Oak Hollow | 147. Flat Canyon |
| 115. Mahagony | 148. Old Folks Flat |
| 116. Cottonwood | 149. Forks of the Huntington |
| 117. Deer Creek | 150. Indian Creek |
| 118. Heber Valley RV Park | 151. Price Canyon Recreation Area |
| 119. Wolf Creek | 152. Nephi KOA |
| 120. Mill Hollow | 153. Chicken Creek |
| 121. American Campground | 154. Maple Canyon |

## 1. BELMONT HOT SPRINGS

*Reference:* **In Plymouth; map A2, grid a1.**

*Campsites, facilities:* There are 70 sites with full hookups and a grassy area for tents. Rest rooms, showers, picnic tables, a video game room, a snack shop, a nine-hole golf course, and a mineral hot pool are available.

*Reservations, fee:* Reservations are recommended. Sites are $15 for full hookups, $8 for RV parking without hookups, and $2 per person for tent camping.

*Contact:* Belmont Hot Springs, P.O. Box 36, Fielding, UT 84311; (801) 458-3200.

*Location:* From Brigham City, drive north on Interstate 15 about 30 miles. Take exit 394, turn right after the exit, and drive past the truck stop. At the stop sign, turn right on State Route 13, go three miles, turn right at the sign for Belmont Hot Springs, and proceed another half of a mile to the resort.

*Trip notes:* Overnight amenities are somewhat limited at this resort, so it's really better for daytime visits, unless you have a self-contained RV. Tent sites are exposed, picnic tables are scarce, and the showers and rest rooms are confined to the swimming pool area, so it's port-a-potties only at night. The RV sites, more pleasantly situated on a hill above the resort, are cooler and command a tranquil valley view.

*Season:* April through mid-October.

---

## 2. HIGH CREEK

*Reference:* **Northeast of Richmond; map A2, grid a3.**

*Campsites, facilities:* There are six sites for tents or RVs (but no hookups) with picnic tables, fire grills, and vault toilets, but *no water.*

*Reservations, fee:* Sites are free and are first come, first served.

*Contact:* Call the Logan Ranger District at (801) 755-3620.

*Location:* From Logan, drive 14 miles north on U.S. 91, past Richmond. Then head east on High Creek Road approximately four miles (the road eventually becomes Forest Road 48) to the campground, which is about 2.5 miles east of the forest boundary.

*Trip notes:* High Creek (elevation 5,000) is a favorite with hikers, who like to take the trail that leads from here to another local campground called Tony Grove. It's also small enough to offer an escape from the weekend crowds—if you come early enough to get a site.

*Season:* June through September.

---

## 3. SMITHFIELD CANYON

*Reference:* **In Smithfield Canyon; map A2, grid a3.**

*Campsites, facilities:* There are six sites with picnic tables and fire pits. Vault toilets and drinking water are available.

*Reservations, fee:* Sites are $8 and are first come, first served.

*Contact:* Call the Logan Ranger District at (801) 755-3620.

*Location:* From Logan, drive north on U.S. 91 to Smithfield, head northeast five miles on Smithfield Canyon Road, and take Forest Road 49 to the campground.

*Trip notes:* Located in a shaded area by the river, this campground is largely paved, and the road is also paved all the way to the National Forest Service boundary. There's a communal area for group activities.

*Season:* May 15 through September 15.

---

## 4. BEAR LAKE STATE RECREATION AREA

*Reference:* **On Bear Lake; map A2, grid a5.**

*Campsites, facilities:* There are 15 lakeside campsites adjacent to a marina located in a sheltered harbor, with 176 boat slips and an 80-foot-wide concrete launching ramp. Handicapped-accessible rest rooms and hot showers are also available. A park visitors center and marina sanitary disposal station are nearby.

---

*Reservations, fee:* Reservations are available 20 days in advance for a nonrefundable $5 fee per site; call (800) 322-3770 Monday through Friday from 8 A.M. to 5 P.M. Sites are $13. Utah residents age 62 or older with a Special Fun Tag get a $2 discount Sunday through Thursday, excluding holidays.

*Contact:* Call park headquarters (open year-round) at (801) 946-3343.

*Location:* From Garden City on U.S. 89, drive two miles north and look for the turnoff to Bear Lake. The marina and campground are next to the lake.

*Trip notes:* This marina campground is right at the edge of turquoise-blue, 71,000-acre Bear Lake. Though the water can be on the chilly side, it's a popular place for boating, fishing, sailing, and waterskiing, and two privately operated golf courses are not far away. Nearby Logan Canyon has hiking trails for short nature walks as well as all-day treks. In summer when the raspberries are ripe, visitors pick their own or enjoy berry shakes and sundaes at one of the drive-in snack bars. All campsites are in the marina area, with a corresponding row of parking spaces in a lot by the beach. A grassy area separates the parking lot from the beach, where campers can also pitch their tents.

*Season:* May 1 through October 1.

## 5. BEAR LAKE KOA

*Reference:* In Garden City; map A2, grid a5.

*Campsites, facilities:* There are 100 RV sites and 50 tent sites. Amenities include rest rooms, showers, a video game room, and a swimming pool.

*Reservations, fee:* Reservations, available year-round, are highly recommended in July and August. Sites with full RV hookups are $20.50 (subject to increase); smaller sites with water are $15.50.

*Contact:* Bear Lake KOA, U.S. Highway 89, Garden City, UT 84028; (801) 946-3454.

*Location:* From Salt Lake City, take Interstate 15 to Brigham City; then follow U.S. 89 to Logan and continue on to Garden City and Bear Lake. Take U.S. 89 north for one mile, toward the Bear Lake Marina. The KOA is on the north side of the road.

*Trip notes:* Located across the highway from Bear Lake, this grassy campground is in mostly open terrain, affording a good view of the sagebrush-covered mountains and the lake. The sites are rather close together, but amenities abound, including a gas station and a car wash, tennis and horseshoe facilities, and even miniature golf (for an extra charge).

*Season:* Open year-round.

## 6. SUNRISE

*Reference:* In Garden City near Bear Lake; map A2, grid a5.

*Campsites, facilities:* There are 40 sites with water and electricity, picnic tables, and fire grills; rest rooms and showers are available.

*Reservations, fee:* Reservations are accepted. Fees are $15 to $20, depending on the size of the site.

*Contact:* Call the campground at (801) 946-8620.

*Location:* From Salt Lake City, take Interstate 15 to Brigham City; then take U.S. 89 to Logan and continue on to Garden City and Bear Lake. Follow the highway north to the Bear Lake Marina. The campground is located just north of the marina on the west side of the road.

*Trip notes:* The sites here are mostly out in the open on a hill overlooking Bear Lake, one of the state's most popular water recreation areas, where anglers can fish for lake and cutthroat trout. Golf enthusiasts will find several golf courses nearby.

*Season:* Memorial Day through Labor Day.

## 7. BLUEWATER BEACH CAMPGROUND

*Reference:* **In Garden City; map A2, grid a5.**

*Campsites, facilities:* There are 120 sites; 50 have full RV hookups, and 70 have water and electricity (for tents or RVs). Also available are rest rooms, showers, laundry facilities, an RV disposal site, picnic tables, a lounge, barbecue grills, a swimming pool, a public phone, and volleyball and basketball courts. Some facilities are handicapped accessible.

*Reservations, fee:* Reservations are recommended in the summer. Sites with full hookups are $29; all others are $25.

*Contact:* Bluewater Beach Campground, 2126 South Bear Lake Boulevard, Garden City, UT 84028; (801) 946-3333.

*Location:* From Salt Lake City, take Interstate 15 north to Brigham City; then take U.S. 89 to Logan and continue on to Garden City and Bear Lake. From there, take State Route 30 south for four miles to the campground.

*Trip notes:* Like the other campgrounds on Bear Lake, this one isn't really much to look at: it's basically a gravel and grass parking lot surrounded by trees, with the sites themselves clumped very close together. The big draw here is the lake, with its scenic appeal and various water sports. The beach, where Jet Ski and boat rentals are available, is a short walk away, depending on the water level. There's also a basketball and a volleyball court on the premises, with a golf course across the street.

*Season:* May 29 through September 30.

## 8. SWEETWATER RV PARK AND MARINA

*Reference:* **In Garden City on Bear Lake; map A2, grid a5.**

*Campsites, facilities:* There are 24 sites for self-contained RVs only. *No water* or rest rooms are available.

*Reservations, fee:* Reservations are recommended. Sites are $12.

*Contact:* Call the Ideal Beach Resort at (801) 946-2711.

*Location:* From Salt Lake City, drive north on Interstate 15 to Brigham City; then take U.S. 89 to Logan and continue another 40 miles to Garden City, located on Bear Lake. Take the turnoff for State Route 30 south, drive past the Bluewater Beach Campground, and look on the left (east) side of the road for a large campground sign just around a bend in the road.

*Trip notes:* During summer, especially holiday weekends, this place is packed, notably with water buffs lured by the Jet Ski and boat rentals at the Ideal Beach Resort a quarter of a mile away. The campsites, too, are packed close together on what's basically a big patch of gravel and grass, and there's no beach.

*Season:* May through September.

## 9. BEAR LAKE RENDEZVOUS BEACH STATE PARK

*Reference:* On Bear Lake; map A2, grid a5.

*Campsites, facilities:* There are 138 sites, spread out among three different areas—Big Creek, Cottonwood, and Willow—with handicapped-accessible rest rooms, hot showers, and sewer and electrical hookups. Camping is adjacent to a 1.25-mile sandy beach, one of the longest stretches of public shorefront on Bear Lake. A concessionaire rents small boats.

*Reservations, fee:* Reservations are available 120 days in advance for a nonrefundable $5 per site; call (800) 322-3770. The 46 full-hookup sites in the Big Creek campground are $15; at Cottonwood (60 sites) and Willow (32 sites), fees are $11. Utah residents 62 years and older with a Special Fun Tag get a $2 discount Sunday through Thursday, excluding holidays.

*Contact:* Call the state park at (801) 946-3343.

*Location:* From Salt Lake City, follow the directions to the Bear Lake area (see Bear Lake State Recreation Area on page 59). Then, on State Route 30, drive just west of Laketown to the park entrance.

*Trip notes:* Set in the midst of towering cottonwoods, this campground is the nicest on Bear Lake and tends to fill up fast, especially on summer weekends. Beach lovers come here to swim, build sand castles, and play sand volleyball or Frisbee. The Cottonwood section is set along a car-and-RV parking strip, with a grassy area separating the asphalt from the beach. Big Creek is bordered by a stream to the south and by Bear Lake to the north, and the vehicle back-ins and pull-throughs are on a paved loop that runs partly by the lake and partly under the trees.

*Season:* May 1 through October 1, except Big Creek, which is open all year.

## 10. BEAR LAKE SOUTH EDEN

*Reference:* On Bear Lake; map A2, grid a5.

*Campsites, facilities:* There are 20 primitive campsites with handicapped-accessible vault toilets. There is *no water.*

*Reservations, fee:* Reservations are available 120 days in advance for a nonrefundable $5 fee per site; call (800) 322-3770 Monday through Friday from 8 A.M. to 5 P.M. Sites are $6. Utah residents 62 years and older with a Special Fun Tag get a $2 discount Sunday through Thursday, excluding holidays.

*Contact:* Call the state park at (801) 946-3343.

*Location:* From Salt Lake City, follow the directions to the Bear Lake area (see Bear Lake State Recreation Area on page 59). Then, from State Highway

30, drive 10 miles north of Laketown on the narrow, unlabeled road that heads west along the east side of the lake.

*Trip notes:* Located on Bear Lake's eastern, more primitive side, this place is a favorite with scuba divers as well as anglers looking for cutthroat, white-fish, and lake trout. In January, fishing buffs also come with dip nets to catch the six-inch-long cisco, a sardinelike fish found only in Bear Lake (prompting locals to nickname these parts Cisco Beach). There's a 28-foot-wide concrete launch ramp for small fishing boats.

*Season:* Open year-round.

## 11. WESTERN PARK CAMPGROUND

*Reference:* **In Logan; map A2, grid b2.**

*Campsites, facilities:* There are 13 RV sites with water and electricity, and a grassy area for tents.

*Reservations, fee:* Reservations are available. Sites with water and electricity are $15 and tent sites are $12.

*Contact:* Call the campground at (801)752-6424.

*Location:* In Logan, turn west off Main Street at 800 South. Go three blocks west, turn left at 300 West, and continue to 350 West, where the campground is located.

*Trip notes:* This campground, part of a suburban mobile home park, consists of a few open spaces for overnighters on the gravel. In other words, it's basically an option if you are desperate for a place to spend the night.

*Season:* Open year-round.

## 12. BANDITS COVE

*Reference:* **In Logan; map A2, grid b2.**

*Campsites, facilities:* There are 12 sites with full hookups, rest rooms, showers, laundry facilities, an RV disposal site, picnic tables, and cable TV.

*Reservations, fee:* Sites are $17 and are first come, first served, with a self-serve check-in system.

*Contact:* Bandits Cove, 590 South Main Street, Logan, UT 84321; call (801) 752-4539.

*Location:* The park is in downtown Logan on South Main Street, next to the Riverside Angler Full Service Fly Shop.

*Trip notes:* This oddly located RV park with pull-throughs—in a downtown parking lot—is fine if you prefer camping in town to the abundant national forest lands nearby.

*Season:* Open year-round.

## 13. RIVER SIDE RV PARK AND CAMPGROUND

*Reference:* **In Logan; map A2, grid b2.**

*Campsites, facilities:* There are 10 sites with full hookups, four sites with water and electricity only, and a grassy area for tents. The campground has handicapped-accessible rest rooms, showers, laundry facilities, a couple of picnic tables, and a few barbecue grills in the tent area. No dogs weighing over 20 pounds are allowed.

*Reservations, fee:* Reservations are recommended on holidays. RV sites are $16.34 for full hookups or water and electricity; tent sites are $9.81.

*Contact:* Call the campground at (801) 245-4469.

*Location:* Take U.S. 89 into Logan, then follow Main Street to the south side of town. Just north of a warehouse on 1700 South, look for the sign and turn right. The campground is just past the railroad tracks on the left.

*Trip notes:* This is yet another strangely located Logan RV park—basically a parking lot in an industrial part of the city. Small and out in the open, the sites consist of cement pads with grass in between. Again, it's only a good choice if you can't find a camping spot in the nearby National Forest or need to stay in town.

*Season:* Open year-round.

---

## 14. COUNTRY CUZZINS RV PARK

*Reference:* **In Logan, map A2, grid b2.**

*Campsites, facilities:* There are 26 sites with full hookups. Tent sites are on a grassy area. The park has a rest room, showers, laundry facilities, an RV disposal site, picnic tables, public phones, and a convenience/gift store.

*Reservations, fee:* Reservations are accepted. Campsites are $14.

*Contact:* Country Cuzzins RV Park, 1936 North Main Street, Logan, UT 84341; (801) 753-1025.

*Location:* In Logan, take Main Street to the north part of town. The park is at the junction of U.S. 89 and U.S. 91, behind the Phillips 66 gas station.

*Trip notes:* Although stuck way at the back of a gas station, this RV park is also at the edge of town, so at least it's somewhat in the open with views of the mountains. The sites are strips of gravel surrounded by grass. The showers and rest room are next to the gas station's car wash. Again, it's an okay choice if you need to be in town.

*Season:* Open year-round.

---

## 15. WOOD CAMP

*Reference:* **In Wasatch–Cache National Forest; map A2, grid b3.**

*Campsites, facilities:* There are seven sites with picnic tables and fire pits. Vault toilets are available, but there's *no water.*

*Reservations, fee:* Sites are $6 and are first come, first served.

*Contact:* Call the Logan Ranger District at (801) 755-3620.

*Location:* From Logan, drive 10.3 miles up Logan Canyon on U.S. 89. The campground is on the left side of the road.

*Trip notes:* As with all campgrounds in narrow Logan Canyon, this one is close to the highway. Still, the place is situated amid tall deciduous trees, with a view of the river and the mountains. Sites are set along a row of pull-throughs, one right after the other, and there's a horse-unloading ramp for riding fans. This is basically an RV campground; site six, however, would be nice for a tent. Anglers can fish for brown trout and planted rainbow trout nearby in

---

the Logan River. West of the property, the Jardine Juniper Trailhead offers a short nature walk for hikers.

*Season:* April through October.

---

## 16. LODGE

*Reference:* **In Wasatch–Cache National Forest; map A2, grid b3.**

*Campsites, facilities:* There are 10 sites, plus drinking water, vault toilets, picnic tables, and fire grills.

*Reservations, fee:* All sites are $7 and are first come, first served.

*Contact:* Call the Logan Ranger District at (801) 755-3620.

*Location:* From Logan, drive 12.7 miles east on U.S. 89 in Logan Canyon to the campground.

*Trip notes:* Located near the Logan River, this campground is a good place for anglers hoping to find trout in either the river or the impoundments adjacent to the property. It's also one of the smaller campgrounds in this scenic alpine setting (elevation 5,600).

*Season:* Late May through mid-September.

---

## 17. LEWIS M. TURNER

*Reference:* **In Wasatch–Cache National Forest; map A2, grid b3.**

*Campsites, facilities:* There are 10 sites, plus picnic tables and fire pits. Flush toilets and water are available.

*Reservations, fee:* All sites are $9 and are first come, first served.

*Contact:* Call the Logan Ranger District at (801) 755-3620.

*Location:* From Logan, follow U.S. 89 about 19 miles up Logan Canyon. Take the turnoff to the Tony Grove Lake area.

*Trip notes:* This forested campground is located near prime hiking country: the Mount Naomi Wilderness Area. There's also good canoeing on nearby Tony Grove Lake, and fishing fans can choose from either the lake or the nearby Logan River.

*Season:* July through October.

---

## 18. RED BANKS

*Reference:* **In Wasatch–Cache National Forest; map A2, grid b3.**

*Campsites, facilities:* There are 12 sites with picnic tables and fire pits. Water and vault toilets are available.

*Reservations, fee:* Sites are $8 and are first come, first served.

*Contact:* Call the Logan Ranger District at (801) 755-3620.

*Location:* From Logan, take U.S. 89 and go 20.2 miles up Logan Canyon. Look for the campground on the left side of the highway.

*Trip notes:* Named for the deep red-orange exposed earth of the mountain behind it, this campground is situated in an open area amid the aspen trees. To the south, a rail fence affords views of a meadow and the mountains. The Logan River is a favorite with fly-fishing buffs. The pull-through sites are located near the river.

*Season:* May through October.

---

## 19. TONY GROVE

*Reference:* **In Wasatch–Cache National Forest; map A2, grid b3.**

*Campsites, facilities:* There are 39 sites with picnic tables and fire pits. Drinking water and both flush and vault toilets are available.

*Reservations, fee:* Reservations are strongly recommended during summer; call the U.S. Forest Service National Reservation System at (800) 280-2267. Sites are $11.

*Contact:* Call the Logan Ranger District at (801) 755-3620.

*Location:* From Logan, take U.S. 89 and go 19.2 miles up Logan Canyon. Take the turnoff to the Tony Grove Lake Area and continue for another seven miles to the campground.

*Trip notes:* Reached by a seven-mile paved, winding, uphill road, Tony Grove campground is surrounded by the high cliffs of a glacial cirque, near a picturesque forest and lake. There's a horse ramp on the premises for riders; for hikers, a parking lot serves as a trailhead for paths leading several directions. A nature trail goes around the lake, which is popular for rafting and canoeing.

*Season:* July through October.

## 20. BRIDGER

*Reference:* **In Wasatch–Cache National Forest; map A2, grid b3.**

*Campsites, facilities:* There are 10 sites with picnic tables and fire pits. Water and flush toilets are available.

*Reservations, fee:* All sites are $9 and are first come, first served.

*Contact:* Call the Logan Ranger District at (801) 755-3620.

*Location:* From Logan, take U.S. 89 and go 3.3 miles up Logan Canyon. The campground is on the right side of the highway.

*Trip notes:* Nicely located across the river and away from the highway, sites at this campground are also set farther apart than most others in the Logan Canyon area. And they're well sheltered by the streamside vegetation and tall deciduous trees. Fishing in the Logan River is a favorite activity here. The road is paved, and sites are gravel.

*Season:* May through October.

## 21. SPRING HOLLOW

*Reference:* **In Wasatch–Cache National Forest; map A2, grid b3.**

*Campsites, facilities:* There are 12 sites with picnic tables and fire pits. Drinking water and both flush and vault toilets are available.

*Reservations, fee:* For reservations, call the U.S. Forest Service National Reservation System at (800) 280-2267. Sites are $9.

*Contact:* Call the Logan Ranger District at (801) 755-3620.

*Location:* From Logan, take U.S. 89 and go 4.3 miles up Logan Canyon. The campground is on the right side of the highway, just up the canyon from a broad, flat spot in the Logan River.

*Trip notes:* Spring Hollow is right on the highly fishable Logan River. Set at a lower elevation than other campgrounds along the river, this one sometimes

gets a little wetter in rainy years, but its sites are also a bit farther apart. Some sites are better suited to RVs; others can accommodate tents.
*Season:* May through October.

---

## 22. GUINAVAH-MALIBU

*Reference:* **In Wasatch–Cache National Forest; map A2, grid b3.**

*Campsites, facilities:* There are 40 sites with picnic tables and fire pits. Water and flush toilets are available.

*Reservations, fee:* Reservations are strongly recommended for weekends during the summer; call the U.S. Forest Service National Reservation System at (800) 280-2267. Sites are $10.

*Contact:* Call the Logan Ranger District at (801) 755-3620.

*Location:* From Logan, take U.S. 89 and go 5.3 miles up Logan Canyon. The campground is on the right side of the highway.

*Trip notes:* This place is really two campgrounds: Guinavah is to the right as you turn off the highway, Malibu is to the left. Both have paved roads and gravel sites that are well spaced. In Guinavah, the sites are under tall cottonwood trees, and there's a bridge over the river; Malibu is in a more open, grassy area with broad, flat sites. In each facility, one loop is designated for tents and one for RVs, though some sites can accommodate either.

*Season:* May 15 through September.

---

## 23. SUNRISE

*Reference:* **In Wasatch–Cache National Forest; map A2, grid b3.**

*Campsites, facilities:* There are 27 sites with picnic tables and fire pits. Water and vault toilets are available.

*Reservations, fee:* Reservations are strongly recommended during the summer; call the U.S. Forest Service National Reservation System at (800) 280-2267. Sites are $11.

*Contact:* Call the Logan Ranger District at (801) 755-3620.

*Location:* From Logan, take U.S. 89 and go 31 miles up Logan Canyon. The campground is on the right side of the highway.

*Trip notes:* Nestled in a stand of aspen and pine trees, this is the last campground at the end of Logan Canyon, and the last U.S. Forest Service campground before you come to Bear Lake. Some Bear Lake fans stay here to enjoy the trees and high terrain, commuting to the lake for the fishing and water sports. Other campers like the proximity to the Limber Pine Trailhead, a popular hiking spot. The campground road and sites are paved, with relatively level pull-throughs and back-ins; the best tent sites are well spaced and set back from the road among the trees.

*Season:* June through October.

---

## 24. PRESTON VALLEY

*Reference:* **In Wasatch–Cache National Forest; map A2, grid b3.**

*Campsites, facilities:* There are nine sites with picnic tables and fire pits. Water and flush toilets are available.

---

*Reservations, fee:* Sites are $9 and are first come, first served.

*Contact:* Call the Logan Ranger District at (801) 755-3620.

*Location:* From Logan, drive 7.8 miles up Logan Canyon on U.S. 89. The campground is on the right side of the highway.

*Trip notes:* Though the sites here are gravel and close together, they're nicely separated from each other by a screen of vegetation and conveniently located near the river and the paved road. The river fishing is excellent. Hikers can pick up information about local trails in the Logan Ranger District office at the mouth of the canyon.

*Season:* May 15 through September.

## 25. FRIENDSHIP

*Reference:* **In Wasatch–Cache National Forest; map A2, grid b3.**

*Campsites, facilities:* There are six sites with picnic tables, fire pits, and pit toilets, but *no drinking water.*

*Reservations, fee:* Sites are free and are first come, first served.

*Contact:* Call the Logan Ranger District at (801) 755-3620.

*Location:* From Hyrum, drive east on State Highway 101. Look for Forest Road 245, a gravel road heading north and east, and take it three miles to the campground.

*Trip notes:* Friendship campground is set on a gravel road in a canopy of maple trees, near the excellent fishing on the Left Fork of the Blacksmith Fork River. The gravel road is primitive but is usually passable for two-wheel-drive vehicles.

*Season:* May 15 through September 15.

## 26. SPRING

*Reference:* **In Wasatch–Cache National Forest; map A2, grid b3.**

*Campsites, facilities:* There are three sites with picnic tables, fire pits, and pit toilets, but *no drinking water.*

*Reservations, fee:* All sites are free and are first come, first served.

*Contact:* Call the Logan Ranger District at (801) 755-3620.

*Location:* From Hyrum, drive east on State Highway 101. Look for Forest Road 245, a gravel road heading north and east, and take it three miles to the campground.

*Trip notes:* This out-of-the-way campground is surrounded by maple trees, in a beautiful canyon near the Left Fork of the Blacksmith Fork River. Drive up the canyon to see the creatures and interpretive displays at the Utah Division of Wildlife's Hardware Ranch, where as many as 800 elk spend the winter.

*Season:* May 15 through October 31.

## 27. PIONEER

*Reference:* **In Wasatch–Cache National Forest; map A2, grid b3.**

*Campsites, facilities:* There are 18 sites with picnic tables and fire pits. Water and vault toilets are available.

*Reservations, fee:* Sites are $9 and are first come, first served.

*Contact:* Call the Logan Ranger District at (801) 755-3620.

*Location:* In Hyrum, take State Route 101 right to Hyrum State Park. Follow the signs to Hardware Ranch and turn off the highway at the sign to Pioneer campground. The campground is nine miles from Hyrum.

*Trip notes:* This campground has large, secluded sites under tall trees, on the eminently fishable Blacksmith Fork River. The road through the campground is unpaved, and not always RV-friendly. Sites 16 through 18 are not on a loop, and the road is too narrow to turn around a large vehicle; the very private sites 3 through 5, set on spurs, don't have much turnaround room either. Best bets for RVs are sites 6 through 15, set along a loop road.

*Season:* May through October.

---

## 28. CRYSTAL SPRINGS RESORT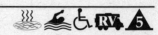

*Reference:* **In Honeyville; map A2, grid b1.**

*Campsites, facilities:* The resort has 83 full hookups and a grassy area for tents, plus handicapped-accessible rest rooms, showers, laundry facilities, picnic tables, a game room, a playground, and several mineral pools.

*Reservations, fee:* Reservations are recommended in the summer. Sites are $16 to $18 for RVs and $9 for tents.

*Contact:* Crystal Springs Resort, 8215 North Highway 38, Honeyville, UT 84314; (801) 279-8104.

*Location:* From Brigham City, drive north on Interstate 15 about 10 miles, and take exit 375 to Honeyville. Go east one mile to Highway 69 North. Take it north one mile to Crystal Hot Springs, and continue for about three miles to the campground.

*Trip notes:* Honeyville is a rural community, so campers here have a full view of the valley and the mountains to the east. The sites are in the open, with the camping area bordered by tall cottonwood trees; tents are in an area separate from the RVs. Rest rooms are a short walk from the campground, and showers are part of the swimming complex. This resort's big attraction, the mineral pools, vary in temperature from cool to warm.

*Season:* Open year-round.

---

## 29. HYRUM STATE PARK

*Reference:* **On Hyrum Reservoir; map A2, grid c2.**

*Campsites, facilities:* There are 40 sites (most of them near the reservoir) and a group camping area, plus a swimming beach, a boat-launching ramp, and modern rest rooms, but no showers.

*Reservations, fee:* Reservations are available 120 days in advance for a nonrefundable $5 fee; call (800) 322-3770 Monday through Friday from 8 A.M. to 5 P.M. Sites are $10. Utah residents age 62 and older with a Special Fun Tag get a $2 discount Sunday through Thursday, excluding holidays.

*Contact:* Call the park at (801) 245-6866.

*Location:* Take U.S. 89/91 between Logan and Brigham City. Turn east on State Route 101, and go about 19 miles toward the town of Hyrum. Follow the signs to the park, which is on the southern city limits.

---

*Trip notes:* This campground is set partly in the open. In one section, sites overlook Hyrum Reservoir in a broad, high mountain valley, and flush toilets are available. Another section has sites along a parking area near a grassy picnic spot, with vault toilets and stairs leading to the water. No matter where you sleep, the fishing for yellow perch and rainbow trout can be good here (even through the ice in the winter). The 470-acre reservoir is also a good spot for power boating, and parents will appreciate the roped-off swimming beach near the day-use area. As a side trip, try driving 16 miles up Blacksmith Fork Canyon for more fishing and a look at the wildlife at Hardware Ranch. Kids should also enjoy the nearby Ronald Jensen Historical Farm on U.S. 89/91.

*Season:* April through October.

## 30. GOLDEN SPIKE RV PARK

*Reference:* **In Brigham City; map A2, grid c1.**

*Campsites, facilities:* There are 60 sites, 38 with full hookups, plus 20 for tents and two cabins. Also available are rest rooms, showers, laundry facilities, an RV disposal site, picnic tables, a hot tub, cable TV, a small convenience store, a putting green, and a swing set.

*Reservations, fee:* Reservations are accepted but not usually necessary. RV sites are $18 to $19, tent sites are $13 to $14, and cabins are $14 to $15.

*Contact:* Golden Spike RV Park, 905 West 1075 South, Brigham City, UT 84302; (801) 723-8858.

*Location:* From Ogden, take Interstate 15 to the Brigham City turnoff, exit 364, and go east over the viaduct. Drive one mile east on U.S. 89 to the campground, which is on the north side of the road.

*Trip notes:* This campground has a grassy farmland setting, with open views and a few young, tall trees. Though right off the highway, it's protected by a barrier of vegetation. The rest room building is newer than most.

*Season:* Open year-round.

## 31. BRIGHAM CITY KOA

*Reference:* **In Brigham City; map A2, grid c1.**

*Campsites, facilities:* There are 55 sites, including 25 with full hookups and 25 with water and electricity only, plus a grassy area on the perimeter for tents. Most sites have barbecue grills. Also available are rest rooms, showers, laundry facilities, an RV disposal site, picnic tables, a game room, a convenience and gift store, and a playground. Wheelchair access is limited.

*Reservations, fee:* Reservations are recommended from June through August. Sites with full hookups are $21.25, sites with water and electricity are $19.25, and tent sites are $16.25.

*Contact:* Brigham City KOA, P.O. Box 579, Brigham City, UT 84302; (801) 723-5503.

*Location:* From Salt Lake City, take Interstate 15 north to Brigham City and get off at exit 364. Go east over the viaduct and east on U.S. 89 to the light. Turn right and drive south for four miles. A KOA sign marks the turnoff to the campground, a little farther down the road past the cherry orchards.

*Trip notes:* This campground is in an orchard and farmland setting, with some tall, venerable trees. There's a nice grassy area for tents, plus some pull-through sites in the middle. All sites are fairly close together.

*Season:* Open year-round.

---

## 32. MOUNTAIN HAVEN CAMPGROUND

*Reference:* **On Mantua Reservoir; map A2, grid c2.**

*Campsites, facilities:* There are 52 sites with full hookups, and a grassy area for tents. The campground has rest rooms, showers, an RV disposal site, picnic tables, a game room, barbecue grills, a public phone, a convenience and gift store, cable TV hookups, and a playground. Pets are allowed on a leash.

*Reservations, fee:* Reservations are recommended, especially on summer weekends. All sites are $14.

*Contact:* Mountain Haven Campground, 830 North Main Street, Mantua, UT 84324; (801) 723-7615.

*Location:* From Salt Lake City, take Interstate 15 north and get off at the Brigham City exit; then take U.S. 89 (which turns into U.S. 91) and go four miles to Mantua Reservoir. The campground is on the west side of the reservoir.

*Trip notes:* True to its name, this reservoir campground is in a high mountain valley, in mostly unforested sagebrush country. Yet the property itself, surrounded by farmland, is grassy and shady. A trail leads from the campground up the hill to the water. To the north is a boat ramp for campers' use. Kids will especially like the selection of penny and nickel candy in the small store.

*Season:* April through October.

---

## 33. BOX ELDER

*Reference:* **In Wasatch National Forest; map A2, grid c3.**

*Campsites, facilities:* There are 26 sites with picnic tables and fire pits. Vault toilets and water are available.

*Reservations, fee:* For reservations, call the U.S. Forest Service National Reservation System at (800) 280-2267. Sites are $9.

*Contact:* Call the Ogden Ranger District at (801) 625-5112.

*Location:* From Brigham City, take U.S. 89 northeast to Mantua, get off at the Mantua exit, and turn right. Where the road comes to a T before entering the town, go left at the signs to the campground.

*Trip notes:* This is a little out-of-the-way campground on a stream, smack in the middle of tall cottonwoods and other stream-loving trees. Boating is popular on nearby Mantua Reservoir, and a side trip to the Mantua fish hatchery is a good bet with kids.

*Season:* May 15 through September 30.

---

## 34. WILLARD BASIN

*Reference:* **In Wasatch National Forest; map A2, grid c2.**

*Campsites, facilities:* There are four tent sites with pit toilets, picnic tables, and fire grills, but *no water.*

---

*Reservations, fee:* Sites are free and are first come, first served.

*Contact:* Call the Ogden Ranger District at (801) 625-5112.

*Location:* From the town of Mantua, drive eight miles south on Forest Road 084 to the campground.

*Trip notes:* This small, remote campground (elevation 9,000) is a favorite overnight stop for hikers planning to tackle the summit of 9,764-foot-high Willard Peak, with its fantastic views of the Great Salt Lake.

*Season:* June through October.

---

## 35. WILLARD BAY NORTH

*Reference:* **On Willard Bay of the Great Salt Lake; map A2, grid c2.**

*Campsites, facilities:* There are 62 sites with no hookups. Facilities include picnic tables, fire grills, handicapped-accessible rest rooms, hot showers, some covered areas, a dump station, fish-cleaning stations, beaches, a boat ramp, and boat-slip rentals during the season.

*Reservations, fee:* Reservations are available for a nonrefundable $5 fee per site; call (800) 322-3770 Monday through Friday from 8 A.M. to 5 P.M. Sites are $10. Utah residents 62 years and older with a Special Fun Tag get a $2 discount Sunday through Thursday, excluding holidays.

*Contact:* Call Willard Bay State Park at (801) 734-9494.

*Location:* From Ogden, drive 15 miles north on Interstate 15, looking for the Willard exit. Signs on the interstate direct you to the campground, which is visible to the west.

*Trip notes:* Boating is the number-one draw at this 9,900-acre freshwater reservoir, but the relatively low elevation (4,200) and proximity to Wasatch Front also make it a summer favorite with water-skiers and watercraft owners. And don't forget the fishing rods: anglers can catch crappie and walleye, and ice-fishing fans will find the state park and some of its facilities open in winter. The campground itself is pleasantly shaded by trees, with paved road loops, covered picnic areas, and sandy beaches within walking distance.

*Season:* Early May through early October.

---

## 36. WILLARD BAY SOUTH

*Reference:* **On Willard Bay of the Great Salt Lake; map A2, grid c2.**

*Campsites, facilities:* There are 30 sites with no hookups. Facilities include picnic tables and fire pits, handicapped-accessible rest rooms with flush toilets (but no showers), a boat ramp, and a small commercial marina.

*Reservations, fee:* Campsites are $10 and are first come, first served.

*Contact:* Call Willard Bay State Park at (801) 734-9494.

*Location:* From Ogden, drive eight miles north on Interstate 15, then follow the signs to Willard Bay South, heading north and west on a paved road to the marina.

*Trip notes:* This campground is located east of the tall dike that created 9,900-acre Willard Bay as a freshwater arm of the Great Salt Lake. Though there

---

are some shade trees, Willard Bay South is more in the open than its neighbor to the north (see Willard Bay North on page 72). The marina offers excellent boating close to the Wasatch Front. Those who enjoy picking through army surplus might want to stop at the nearby Smith & Edwards store.
*Season:* April through October.

## 37. MONTE CRISTO

*Reference:* **In Wasatch National Forest near Ogden; map A2, grid c4.**
*Campsites, facilities:* There are 47 sites with picnic tables and fire pits. Flush and vault toilets and water are available.
*Reservations, fee:* Sites are $9 and are first come, first served.
*Contact:* Call the Ogden Ranger District at (801) 625-5112.
*Location:* From Woodruff, drive 22 miles southwest on State Route 39.
*Trip notes:* This is a magnificent setting high in the mountains—a haven of lush grass, wildflowers, and tall trees. The paved road has pull-throughs and back-ins; the sites (also paved) include some great places for tents and are spaced far apart. The privacy, together with the distance from the highway, makes this a quiet, reflective place to spend the night.
*Season:* July through September.

## 38. BIRCH CREEK

*Reference:* **On Bureau of Land Management property near Upper Birch Creek Reservoir; map A2, grid c5.**
*Campsites, facilities:* There are four sites plus overflow space for self-contained RVs. Pit toilets and seven picnic tables are available, but there is *no water.*
*Reservations, fee:* Sites are free and are first come, first served.
*Contact:* Call the Salt Lake City office of the Bureau of Land Management at (801) 977-4300.
*Location:* From Woodruff, take State Route 16 to State Route 39 and drive nine miles west. Look for the sign for the reservoirs on the north side of the highway.
*Trip notes:* The main attraction here is the fishing at Upper Birch Creek Reservoir, stocked with catchable rainbows on a regular basis by the Utah Division of Wildlife Resources. The campsites themselves are primitive and in an open, arid, sparsely vegetated setting.
*Season:* Open year-round.

## 39. BOTTS

*Reference:* **In Wasatch National Forest near Ogden; map A2, grid d3.**
*Campsites, facilities:* There are eight individual sites with no hookups. Picnic tables, fire grills, drinking water, and vault toilets are available.
*Reservations, fee:* Sites are $8 and are first come, first served.
*Contact:* Call the Ogden Ranger District at (801) 625-5112.
*Location:* From Ogden, drive east on State Highway 39 past Pineview Reservoir. The campground is on the south side of the road, 6.5 miles east of Huntsville.

*Trip notes:* Botts is your basic Forest Service campground, set along the banks of the South Fork of the Ogden River, but it makes a nice, quiet alternative to the more hectic campgrounds on nearby Pineview Reservoir. The graveled sites are shaded by cottonwood and box elder trees, and there's decent fishing in the river and at the reservoir.
*Season:* May 15 through October 31.

## 40. SOUTH FORK

*Reference:* **In Wasatch National Forest near Ogden; map A2, grid c3.**
*Campsites, facilities:* There are 37 sites with picnic tables and fire pits. Vault toilets and drinking water are available.
*Reservations, fee:* Sites are $8 and are first come, first served.
*Contact:* Call the Ogden Ranger District at (801) 625-5112.
*Location:* From Ogden, drive east on State Route 39 past Pineview Reservoir. The campground is on the south side of the road, seven miles east of Huntsville.
*Trip notes:* This is the largest of the campgrounds on the South Fork of the Ogden River, making it a popular summer spot for anglers and kids who like riding their inner tubes downstream. At an elevation of 5,200 feet, this is also a good place to see the changing fall colors of the oaks, maples, and aspens of the nearby canyon.
*Season:* May 15 through October 31.

## 41. PERCEPTION PARK

*Reference:* **In Wasatch National Forest near Ogden; map A2, grid c3.**
*Campsites, facilities:* There are 24 individual sites and three group sites with picnic tables, fire grills, vault toilets, and a paved, wheelchair-accessible interpretive trail along the river. There is *no water.*
*Reservations, fee:* Reservations are available for some sites; call the U.S. Forest Service National Reservation System at (800) 280-2267. Individual sites are $11. Group sites vary.
*Contact:* Call the Ogden Ranger District at (801) 625-5112.
*Location:* From Ogden, drive east on State Highway 39. The campground is on the south side of the road, 7.5 miles east of Huntsville.
*Trip notes:* This might be Utah's best Forest Service campground for people with disabilities. The paved, wheelchair-accessible nature trail has signs in braille; several fishing piers are wheelchair accessible as well. With its shady setting, high elevation (5,200 feet), and proximity to the fishable South Fork of the Ogden River, this campground also has much to recommend it to families.
*Season:* May 15 through September 20.

## 42. LOWER MEADOWS

*Reference:* **In Wasatch National Forest near Ogden; map A2, grid c3.**
*Campsites, facilities:* There are 17 individual sites with picnic tables and fire grills. Drinking water and vault toilets are available.

*Reservations, fee:* Campsites are $8 and are first come, first served.

*Contact:* Call the Ogden Ranger District at (801) 625-5112.

*Location:* From Ogden, drive east for about 16 miles on State Highway 39. The campground is eight miles east of Huntsville.

*Trip notes:* This small retreat is located by the highway next to the fishable South Fork of the Ogden River, under some towering cottonwood trees. At an elevation of 5,300 feet, Lower Meadows is popular with valley people hoping to escape the summer heat. It's also a fine place to spot elk, mule deer, and the occasional moose.

*Season:* May 15 through September 30.

## 43. UPPER MEADOWS

*Reference:* **In Wasatch National Forest near Ogden; map A2, grid c3.**

*Campsites, facilities:* There are nine sites with picnic tables and fire grills. Vault toilets and drinking water are available.

*Reservations, fee:* Sites are $8 and are first come, first served.

*Contact:* Call the Ogden Ranger District at (801) 625-5112.

*Location:* From Ogden, drive east for about 16 miles on State Highway 39. The campground is eight miles east of Huntsville.

*Trip notes:* In the fall, this can be a spectacular place to camp; the maple, aspen, and oak trees typically begin to turn in mid-September. The 5,300-foot elevation also keeps things comfortable in summer yet relatively warm in spring and fall as well. Anglers can find whitefish and rainbow trout in the South Fork of the Ogden River.

*Season:* May 15 through September 30.

## 44. WILLOWS

*Reference:* **In Wasatch National Forest near Ogden; map A2, grid c3.**

*Campsites, facilities:* There are 13 sites with picnic tables and fire pits. Drinking water and vault toilets are available.

*Reservations, fee:* Sites are $8 and are first come, first served.

*Contact:* Call the Ogden Ranger District at (801) 625-5112.

*Location:* From Ogden, drive east for about 16 miles on State Highway 39. The campground is eight miles east of Huntsville.

*Trip notes:* Of the cluster of Forest Service campgrounds in the area, this one, on the banks of the South Fork of the Ogden River, is the farthest from the city. That means it's slightly more remote than the others, though still popular on weekends. Wildlife watchers should keep an eye out for deer, elk, and even an occasional moose.

*Season:* May 15 through September 30.

## 45. ANDERSON COVE

*Reference:* **In Wasatch National Forest near Ogden; map A2, grid d3.**

*Campsites, facilities:* There are 68 individual sites and two group sites with picnic tables and fire grills. Drinking water, vault toilets, and a dump station are available.

*Reservations, fee:* Reservations are recommended for summer weekends; call the U.S. Forest Service National Reservation System at (800) 280-2267. Sites are $11.

*Contact:* Call the Ogden Ranger District at (801) 625-5306.

*Location:* The campground is just off State Highway 39 on Pineview Reservoir, 2.5 miles southwest of Huntsville and about eight miles east of Ogden.

*Trip notes:* This campground, located close to the reservoir near the Wasatch Front, fills quickly on summer weekends, so be sure to make reservations. The main appeal is the warm water of 110,000-acre Pineview Reservoir, one of Utah's most popular boating and water-skiing lakes. And anglers will find that the crappie, bluegill, bullhead catfish, and yellow perch often bite fast, making this an ideal place to teach children to fish. The reservoir has two boat ramps, two swimming areas, and nature hiking trails, with golf nearby. Shade trees shelter many of the campsites.

*Season:* May 15 through September 30.

## 46. JEFFERSON HUNT

*Reference:* **In Wasatch National Forest near Ogden; map A2, grid d3.**

*Campsites, facilities:* There are 29 individual sites that are also suitable for families, with picnic tables and fire grills. Wheelchair-accessible vault toilets and drinking water are available.

*Reservations, fee:* Sites are $9 and are first come, first served.

*Contact:* Call the Ogden Ranger District at (801) 625-5306.

*Location:* The campground is north of State Highway 39, approximately nine miles east of Ogden and two miles southwest of Huntsville.

*Trip notes:* Located on the southeast corner of popular Pineview Reservoir, Jefferson Hunt fills fast, especially on weekends, so plan to arrive early. In addition to all the boating and fishing, campers can visit the nearby Trappist Monastery in Huntsville, where vespers and some other services are open to the public. The monks also sell flavored honey and fresh whole-wheat bread at a small visitors center.

*Season:* June through September.

## 47. MAGPIE

*Reference:* **In Wasatch National Forest near Ogden; map A2, grid d3.**

*Campsites, facilities:* There are 27 individual sites with picnic tables and fire grills. Vault toilets and drinking water are available.

*Reservations, fee:* Sites are $8 and are first come, first served.

*Contact:* Call the Ogden Ranger District at (801) 625-5112.

*Location:* From Ogden, drive east for about 16 miles through Ogden Canyon on State Route 39. The campground is six miles east of Huntsville on the south side of the road.

*Trip notes:* Contrary to its name, this is a truly soothing place to camp—set in a riparian area along the South Fork of the Ogden River, amid the sound of flowing water and the shade of tall trees. The river is great for summer inner-tube trips and for fishing (especially in spring and fall, when the tubing traffic abates).

*Season:* May 15 through October 31.

---

## 48. HOBBLE

*Reference:* **In Wasatch National Forest near Ogden; map A2, grid d3.**

*Campsites, facilities:* There are eight sites with picnic tables, fire grills, and one vault toilet, but *no drinking water.*

*Reservations, fee:* Sites are $5 and are first come, first served.

*Contact:* Call the Ogden Ranger District at (801) 625-5112.

*Location:* From Ogden, drive east from Ogden on State Highway 39, through Ogden Canyon and past Pineview Reservoir. The campground is on the north side of the highway, six miles east of Huntsville.

*Trip notes:* Campers will find only the basics at this small spot on the South Fork of the Ogden River (elevation 5,200), but it's just the ticket for anyone on a budget. Box elder and cottonwood trees shade the rather primitive sites, and drinking water can be obtained at nearby Forest Service campgrounds. Look for deer and elk on the sides of the nearby canyons.

*Season:* May 15 through October 31.

---

## 49. THE MAPLES

*Reference:* **In Wasatch National Forest near Ogden; map A2, grid d3.**

*Campsites, facilities:* There are 15 sites with picnic tables and fire grills. Vault toilets are available, but there's *no drinking water.*

*Reservations, fee:* Sites are free and are first come, first served.

*Contact:* Call the Ogden Ranger District at (801) 625-5112.

*Location:* From Ogden, drive east on State Route 39 through Ogden Canyon. Look for the turnoff to the Snowbasin Ski Area, and travel on the paved road approximately three miles to the campground.

*Trip notes:* This campground is unpaved, on a loop just off the highway, with sites set close together under cottonwood trees. Some sites are pull-throughs, some are back-ins. Nearby is a fishable river. Water sports are available at Pineview Reservoir, about eight miles away.

*Season:* June through October.

---

## 50. CENTURY RV PARK

*Reference:* **In Ogden; map A2, grid d2.**

*Campsites, facilities:* There are 180 RV spaces, with a grassy area for tents, plus rest rooms, showers, laundry facilities, an RV disposal site, picnic tables, a game room, a swimming pool, two public phones, cable TV, a store with light groceries, and a playground.

*Reservations, fee:* Reservations are recommended in the summer. Sites are $20.50 with full hookups, and $19.75 with water and electricity. Tent sites are $15.25.

*Contact:* Century RV Park, 1399 West 2100 South, Ogden, UT 84401; (801) 731-3800.

---

*Location:* In Ogden, take exit 346 off Interstate 15, and go east on 2100 South. The campground is on the left side of the road at 1399 West 2100 South.

*Trip notes:* This campground is in a residential mobile home park, with the permanent structures located near the back. But its outside-of-town location makes for a fairly rural setting.

*Season:* Open year-round.

## 51. LOST CREEK STATE PARK

*Reference:* **On Lost Creek Reservoir; map A2, grid d4.**

*Campsites, facilities:* This is an undeveloped campground with a few scattered picnic tables, pit toilets, and a boat-launching ramp.

*Reservations, fee:* Campsites are free and are first-come, first served.

*Contact:* Call East Canyon State Park headquarters at (801) 829-6866.

*Location:* From Morgan, travel north on Interstate 84 and take the Croyden exit. Follow the signs for about 10 miles to Lost Creek Reservoir, heading northeast on a county road that turns from pavement to dirt. The campground and boat ramp are located on the southeast part of the reservoir.

*Trip notes:* There's not much to this state park, located near the banks of the Lost Creek Reservoir in open terrain, other than the most basic facilities. But there *is* much to recommend if you like trout fishing: because of the 6,000-foot elevation, the water stays cool well into the summer, keeping the fish active and hungry.

*Season:* Open year-round.

## 52. CIRCLE L. MOBILE HOME PARK

*Reference:* **In Layton; map A2, grid e2.**

*Campsites, facilities:* There are 13 sites with full hookups and a grassy area for tents. The park has a rest room, showers, laundry facilities, an RV disposal site, picnic tables, barbecue grills, and a playground.

*Reservations, fee:* Reservations are accepted. Campsites are $10 to $12.

*Contact:* Circle L. Mobile Home Park, 78 Layton Circle, Layton, UT 84041; (801) 544-8945.

*Location:* Traveling south from Ogden or north from Salt Lake City on Interstate 15, get off at exit 332 in Layton. Turn north on Main Street; go over the viaduct and through the first light. The park is on the left at 229 Main Street.

*Trip notes:* This place definitely has the feel of a mobile home park stuck in the middle of Main Street—and indeed, most of the RVs, parked on the black-top at the end of the park, are permanent. The setting is well shaded. Still, campers can do better in the mountains nearby.

*Season:* Open year-round.

## 53. ANTELOPE ISLAND STATE PARK

*Reference:* **On Antelope Island in the Great Salt Lake; map A2, grid e0.**

*Campsites, facilities:* There are 12 individual sites and five large group camping areas, all with picnic tables, fire grills, and vault toilets, near a white-sand beach. There's also beach parking for self-contained trailers and RVs, located next to some covered picnic pavilions, plus a visitors center and rest rooms with running water and showers.

**Reservations, fee:** This is the only state park not on the automated reservation system. For reservations, call the park directly at (801) 773-2941. Sites are $9 per vehicle per night, including a $5 park entrance fee.

**Contact:** Call Great Salt Lake State Park at (801) 773-2941.

**Location:** Traveling south from Ogden or north from Salt Lake City on Interstate 15, take the Syracuse exit, then turn onto Gentile Drive. Drive west for nine miles, and cross to the island on a paved 7.5-mile causeway.

**Trip notes:** This is *the* place for a wonderful experience on the Great Salt Lake. Swimmers off the white-sand beaches can float like a cork in the salty water. On the hiking, mountain-biking, and horseback-riding trails, campers can try to spot birds, or perhaps one of the herd of 800 buffalo who call the park home. (For close-ups, check out the park's buffalo roundup in early November.) Another attraction is the Fielding Garr ranch house on the southwest corner of the island; open weekends during spring, summer, and fall, it's the oldest home still standing on its original foundation in the entire state. The park itself is an interesting place to visit in any season.

**Season:** Open year-round.

## 54. CHERRY HILL CAMPGROUND

**Reference:** In Kaysville; map A2, grid e2.

**Campsites, facilities:** There are 240 sites, including 119 with full hookups, 40 with water and electricity, 22 with electricity only, and 59 without hookups. Also available are rest rooms, showers, laundry facilities, an RV disposal site, picnic tables, two game rooms, a public phone, a pool, a convenience and gift store, a playground, a group picnic pavilion, and rentable barbecue grills. The rest rooms are wheelchair accessible; the showers are not.

**Reservations, fee:** Reservations are recommended, especially on weekends and holidays. Sites with full hookups are $21.85, sites with water and electricity are $20.76, and tent sites are $17.48. Groups of more than two pay an additional $1.50 per person.

**Contact:** Cherry Hill Campground, 1325 South Main Street, Kaysville, UT 84037; (801) 451-5379.

**Location:** From Salt Lake City, drive north on Interstate 15 to Kaysville. Get off at exit 326 and take U.S. 89 two miles north. The campground is on the left side of the highway.

**Trip notes:** Cherry Hill Campground is more like a bona fide resort: though the grassy sites are close together, there's a full-scale water park, facilities for miniature golf and arrowball (a trampoline game with elements of volleyball and basketball), batting cages, a children's play area called Hamster Haven, two snack bars, a restaurant, and a group pavilion. And if that's not enough, it's all located just north of Lagoon, Utah's largest amusement park, with myriad roller coasters, midway, assorted rides, huge water park, and historical Pioneer Village.

**Season:** April through October.

## 55. SUNSET

*Reference:* **In Wasatch National Forest near Farmington; map A2, grid e3.**

*Campsites, facilities:* There are 10 sites with picnic tables, fire grills, and vault toilets, but *no water.*

*Reservations, fee:* Sites are free and are first come, first served.

*Contact:* Call the Wasatch–Cache National Forest supervisor's office at (801) 524-5030.

*Location:* Take the Farmington exit off Interstate 15 between Ogden and Salt Lake City. Drive through Farmington and head four miles northeast of town on Forest Road 007 to the campground.

*Trip notes:* Set in a narrow, forested canyon along a popular scenic drive, this campground (elevation 6,400) is a pretty place to watch the changing fall colors and escape the hype and the hordes at the huge Lagoon amusement park west of Farmington.

*Season:* June through September.

## 56. BOUNTIFUL PEAK

*Reference:* **In Wasatch National Forest near Farmington; map A2, grid e3.**

*Campsites, facilities:* There are 26 individual sites and one group site with picnic tables and fire grills, a trailhead for motorized recreation, vault toilets, and drinking water.

*Reservations, fee:* Individual sites are free and are first come, first served; for group site information, call (801) 524-5030.

*Contact:* Call the Wasatch–Cache National Forest supervisor's office at (801) 524-5030.

*Location:* From Bountiful, go east on Forest Road 279 to Forest Road 008 (or, from Farmington, go northeast on Forest Road 007 until it becomes Forest Road 008) and continue to the campground. The campground is located about 9.3 miles northeast of Farmington.

*Trip notes:* This campground is located at an elevation of 7,500 feet in a beautiful, wooded area near the top of Bountiful Peak, which overlooks Davis County north of Salt Lake City. The chief draw here is the spectacular drive, which takes travelers from the valley bottom to the top of the mountains, offering fantastic views of the Great Salt Lake to the west. This is an especially scenic place to view the changing foliage of fall.

*Season:* June 15 through September 7.

## 57. EAST CANYON STATE PARK

*Reference:* **On East Canyon Reservoir; map A2, grid e3.**

*Campsites, facilities:* There are 31 sites with no hookups near a 680-acre reservoir. Picnic tables, fire grills, and modern rest rooms with running water and showers are available, along with covered group picnic areas, a fish-cleaning station, a concrete boat-launching ramp, a concessionaire, boat and Jet Ski rentals, groceries, and a small snack bar.

*Reservations, fee:* Reservations are available 120 days in advance for a nonrefundable $5 fee; call (800) 322-3770 Monday through Friday from 8 A.M. to 5 P.M. Sites are $10. Utah residents 62 years and older with a Special Fun Tag get a $2 discount Sunday through Thursday, excluding holidays.

*Contact:* Call East Canyon State Park at (801) 829-6866.

*Location:* From Salt Lake City, take Interstate 80 east to State Route 65 and follow it to the campground. From Morgan, travel 12 miles south on State Route 65.

*Trip notes:* This is a popular summer destination for Salt Lake City folks wanting to get out on the reservoir with their water skis, power boats, or personal watercraft. Fishing can also be good, especially in spring or fall when there aren't as many boats. Though camping shuts down in the fall, the park itself is open year-round and is popular with ice fishers.

*Season:* Open year-round, with camping available April 1 through October 15.

---

## 58. GREAT SALT LAKE STATE PARK

*Reference:* **On the Great Salt Lake; map A2, grid f2.**

*Campsites, facilities:* There are 25 sites near a sandy beach of the lake, with outdoor showers, modern rest rooms, and picnic tables, and a 240-slip marina and boat ramp nearby. Nearby Saltair Resort features a county-operated visitors center, souvenir shops, and camel rides.

*Reservations, fee:* Sites are $10 and are first come, first served. Utah residents 62 and older with a Special Fun Tag get a $2 discount Sunday through Thursday, excluding holidays.

*Contact:* Call Great Salt Lake State Park at (801) 250-1898.

*Location:* Drive 16 miles west of Salt Lake City on Interstate 80 and take the exit to the park.

*Trip notes:* This campground has the closest access to the Great Salt Lake from Salt Lake City, so it's heavily used. The large beach leads to a shallow portion of the lake, where the gradual drop-off forces swimmers to walk several hundred yards before reaching waist-deep water. Sailboating is popular, as are concerts and dances at Saltair. Traffic noise from Interstate 80 can be a distraction to campers.

*Season:* April through October.

---

## 59. ECHO RESORT ON ECHO RESERVOIR

*Reference:* **On Echo Reservoir; map A2, grid e5.**

*Campsites, facilities:* This is essentially a trailer park with some dispersed camping. Facilities include full hookups, rest rooms with showers, a grassy picnic area, a snack bar, and a boat-launching ramp.

*Reservations, fee:* Reservations are accepted. Sites are $7.50 per person.

*Contact:* Call the resort at (801) 336-9894.

*Location:* From Salt Lake City, take Interstate 80 east and look for the turnoff to Echo Reservoir, before the junction with Interstate 84. Then take the small road east to the east side of the reservoir.

---

*Trip notes:* Fishing and waterskiing are the prime attractions here. The camping quarters are rather close. Trailers are packed together as tightly as possible, though in late summer campers can pitch tents on the beach whenever the water retreats. The picnic area is pleasantly shaded. The South Beach, located south of the main area, has pit toilets, no tables, and generally limited facilities; it's basically a place to park an RV or pitch a tent. This spot is the end of the historic Union Pacific Rail Trail, a 27-mile-long former railbed originating in Park City that's now popular with mountain bikers, hikers, and horseback riders.

*Season:* Memorial Day through Labor Day.

## 60. HOLIDAY HILLS CAMPGROUND

*Reference:* In Coalville; map A2, grid e5.

*Campsites, facilities:* There are about 40 sites for RVs and tents, with full hookups, rest rooms, showers, laundry facilities, a swimming pool, a public phone, a communal covered picnic area, and a gas station/grocery store.

*Reservations, fee:* Reservations are recommended. Sites with full hookups are $17, and tent sites are $10.

*Contact:* Holiday Hills Campground, 500 West 100 South, Coalville, UT 84017; (801) 336-4421.

*Location:* From Salt Lake City on Interstate 80, take the Coalville turnoff (exit 164). The campground is just west of the interstate.

*Trip notes:* Except for the one at Echo Reservoir (see page 81), this is the only private campground in the area that isn't for members only. As with many private campgrounds, the sites are close together. On the plus side, the setting is a broad, high mountain valley that's pleasantly scenic and usually cool. While the property is not especially woodsy, shade is provided by some tall cottonwood and birch trees. And for anglers, there's ready access to the Weber River.

*Season:* Open year-round.

## 61. LAGOON PIONEER VILLAGE CAMPGROUND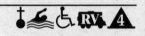

*Reference:* In Farmington; map A2, grid f2.

*Campsites, facilities:* There are 209 sites; 44 have full hookups, 49 have water and electricity, and 69 are for tents; 46 others are pull-throughs with full hookups. The campground has rest rooms, showers, laundry facilities, an RV disposal site, picnic tables, a public phone, and a convenience and grocery store.

*Reservations, fee:* Reservations are recommended from June through September. Sites with full hookups are $19, sites with pull-throughs are $19, sites with water and electricity are $15.50, and tent sites are $14. Groups of more than two pay an additional $1 for each extra person over age four, and another $1 for each additional vehicle per site.

*Contact:* Lagoon Pioneer Village Campground, P.O. Box 269, Farmington, UT 84025; (801) 451-8100.

*Location:* From Salt Lake City, go north on Interstate 15 and take exit 325. Follow the signs to Lagoon and camping areas. Turn right through the stone pillars to the campground.

*Trip notes:* The main attraction here is Lagoon—the second-oldest family owned amusement park in the United States. It has kept up with the times and adds something new almost every year. Along with its several roller coasters, midway, assorted rides, and special ride area for kids, the place offers musical entertainment, a large water-slide park, and historical Pioneer Village, a collection of pioneer-era buildings and artifacts from around the state. The campground itself, grassy and well shaded with closely spaced sites, is smack-dab between a horse corral and an old and rather noisy wooden roller coaster.

*Season:* April through October.

---

## 62. SALT LAKE CITY VIP

*Reference:* **In Salt Lake City; map A2, grid f2.**

*Campsites, facilities:* There are 530 sites, including 350 with full hookups, 130 with water and electricity, 45 for individual tents, and several group areas for tents; two camping cabins are also available. Amenities include water and toilets.

*Reservations, fee:* Reservations are recommended in the summer. Sites with full hookups are $24.95, sites with water and electricity are $21.95, RV sites with no hookups are $18.95, tent sites are $18.95, and cabins are $30.95. Groups of more than two pay an additional $2 for each extra person; there's also a $2 charge for 50-amp hookups or air conditioning.

*Contact:* Salt Lake City VIP, 1400 West North Temple, Salt Lake City, UT 84116; (801) 355-1214.

*Location:* In Salt Lake City, take the Redwood Road exit off Interstate 80. Drive north on Redwood Road to North Temple, then east on North Temple to 1400 West North Temple. The campground is on the north side of the road.

*Trip notes:* Located in an industrial area close to the Salt Lake Tabernacle and Mormon Temple, not far from the Utah State Fairpark and Salt Lake International Airport, this is largely a place for folks looking to camp in the city near some major amenities and attractions. While geared toward RVs, it does offer shade and grass for tent campers.

*Season:* Open year-round.

---

## 63. MOUNTAIN SHADOWS RV PARK

*Reference:* **In Salt Lake City; map A2, grid f2.**

*Campsites, facilities:* There are 96 sites with full hookups, 34 sites with water and electricity, and 10 tent sites. Facilities include rest rooms, showers, an indoor and outdoor hot tub, a Laundromat and store, and a recreation room.

*Reservations, fee:* Sites are $20.50 with full hookups, $16.20 with partial hookups, and $14.85 for tents.

*Contact:* Mountain Shadows RV Park, 13275 South Minuteman Drive, Draper, UT 84020; (801) 571-4024.

---

*Location:* On Interstate 15 in Salt Lake City, take exit 294, the Draper Riverton exit. Turn east toward Draper on 12300 South. Turn south on the frontage road at the light. Drive 1.1 miles south to the campground at 13275 Minuteman Drive.

*Trip notes:* Someone is clearly concerned about the aesthetics around here: the property includes a flower garden with a pond, a fenced-in tent area, and well-landscaped sites, plus a basketball court and modernized central office. Not surprisingly, some campers are year-round residents. The sites are close together but shaded by tall trees. Mountain Shadows is just north of Magic Waters, Salt Lake's least-expensive water slide park.

*Season:* Open year-round.

## 64. SHADY HAVEN RV PARK

*Reference:* **In Salt Lake City; map A2, grid f2.**

*Campsites, facilities:* There are 40 sites, all with full hookups, plus laundry facilities, an RV disposal site, a small playground, and a few picnic tables. Small pets are allowed.

*Reservations, fee:* Reservations are recommended. Campsites are $14.

*Contact:* Shady Haven RV Park, 8875 South 255 West, Sandy UT 84070; (801) 561-1744.

*Location:* In Salt Lake City on Interstate 15, take the 90th South/Sandy exit. Turn east and drive under the freeway on State Route 209. Go to the second light, turn left, and take the frontage road for a quarter of a mile. An old sign on the east side of the road directs you to Shady Haven RV Park.

*Trip notes:* This campground, in a business and industrial part of Salt Lake City, consists of some closely spaced sites under elm and Russian olive trees. Its chief redeeming feature: the view of Lone Peak to the east.

*Season:* May through September.

## 65. HIDDEN HAVEN CAMPGROUND

*Reference:* **Near Park City; map A2, grid f4.**

*Campsites, facilities:* There are 75 sites, including 20 with full hookups, 35 with water and electricity, and 20 for tents. The campground has rest rooms, showers, laundry facilities, an RV disposal site, picnic tables, a game room, barbecue grills, a public phone, limited groceries, and a swing set.

*Reservations, fee:* Reservations are recommended. Sites with full hookups are $17, sites with water and electricity are $16, and tent sites are $13.

*Contact:* Hidden Haven Campground, 2200 Rasmussen Road, Park City, UT 84098; (801) 649-8935.

*Location:* From Salt Lake City, take Interstate 80 toward Park City. Get off at exit 145 and go east on the frontage road for one mile. The campground is on the east side of the road.

*Trip notes:* Hidden Haven is within five miles of the golf courses of Jeremy Ranch and the ski runs of the Park City resort. Park City also offers shopping, a summertime alpine slide, and a 28-mile bike trail to Coalville. Though many of the campsites are in view of the freeway and close together, there are some nicer ones down by the river. Since it's open year-round, skiers come here to park their RVs.

*Season:* Open year-round.

---

# 66. JUNIPER AND CEDAR POINT

*Reference:* **In Rockport State Park; map A2, grid f5.**

*Campsites, facilities:* There are 30 sites at Juniper and four tent sites at the adjacent Cedar Point. Juniper facilities include showers, partial hookups, modern rest rooms, fire pits, grills, picnic tables, and a dump station. Cedar Point offers one vault toilet, but tent campers can walk to Juniper's modern rest rooms. There's a boat ramp nearby.

*Reservations, fee:* Reservations are available 120 days in advance for a $5 nonrefundable fee per site; call (800) 322-3770 Monday through Friday from 8 A.M. to 5 P.M. Sites are $13. Utah residents 62 and older with a Special Fun Tag get a $2 discount Sunday through Thursday, excluding holidays.

*Contact:* Call Rockport State Park at (801) 336-2241.

*Location:* From Salt Lake City, drive 45 miles east on Interstate 80, past the Park City and Heber City exits. Take the Wanship exit and drive four miles south on State Highway 189. Enter the state park on the south end of Rockport Reservoir, crossing the Weber River. The campground is located on the northeast part of the reservoir, on a paved road.

*Trip notes:* These campgrounds are located in the midst of juniper trees, at a cool and comfy elevation of 6,000 feet. Sites are within walking distance of the reservoir, which is popular for boating, swimming, and waterskiing. Anglers can find rainbow trout, both here and on the Weber River at the reservoir's upper end.

*Season:* May 10 through September 15.

---

# 67. COTTONWOOD

*Reference:* **In Rockport State Park; map A2, grid f5.**

*Campsites, facilities:* There are 20 campsites. Amenities include picnic tables, fire grills, drinking water, and pit toilets. A dump station and boat ramp are located nearby.

*Reservations, fee:* Reservations are available 120 days in advance for a nonrefundable $5 fee per site; call (800) 322-3770 Monday through Friday from 8 A.M. to 5 P.M. Sites are $6.

*Contact:* Call Rockport State Park at (801) 336-2241.

*Location:* From Salt Lake City, drive 45 miles east on Interstate 80, past the Park City and Heber City exits. Take the Wanship exit and drive four miles south on State Route 189. Enter the state park on the south end of Rockport Reservoir, crossing the Weber River. The campground is located on the northeast part of the reservoir, on a paved road.

*Trip notes:* The terrain here is somewhat open, though large shade trees grow along the Weber River nearby. Fishing is decent on the Weber, which is stocked regularly with catchable rainbow trout and occasionally offers up a

---

large brown trout as well. This campground is also a short distance from Rockport Reservoir.

*Season:* May 1 through October 15.

---

## 68. TWIN COVES

*Reference:* **In Rockport State Park; map A2, grid f5.**

*Campsites, facilities:* There are 22 sites with picnic tables, fire pits, drinking water, and vault toilets. A boat ramp and dump station are nearby.

*Reservations, fee:* Reservations are available 120 days in advance for a nonrefundable $5 per site; call (800) 322-3770 Monday through Friday from 8 A.M. to 5 P.M. Sites are $6.

*Contact:* Call Rockport State Park at (801) 336-2241.

*Location:* From Salt Lake City, drive 45 miles east on Interstate 80, past the Park City and Heber City exits. Take the Wanship exit and drive four miles south on State Route 189. Enter the state park on the south end of Rockport Reservoir, crossing the Weber River. The campground is located on the northeast part of the reservoir, on a paved road.

*Trip notes:* This campground sits on a hill overlooking Wanship Reservoir. Junipers provide some shade, but it's largely open terrain. Fishing and boating on the lake are the most popular activities.

*Season:* May 10 through September 15.

---

## 69. PINERY

*Reference:* **In Rockport State Park; map A2, grid f5.**

*Campsites, facilities:* This campground consists of an open field with no designated sites. Vault toilets, fire pits, and a few scattered picnic tables are available.

*Reservations, fee:* Campsites are $5 and are first come, first served.

*Contact:* Call Rockport State Park at (801) 336-2241.

*Location:* From Salt Lake City, drive 45 miles east on Interstate 80, past the Park City and Heber City exits. Take the Wanship exit and drive four miles south on State Route 189. Enter the state park on the south end of Rockport Reservoir, crossing the Weber River. The campground is located on the northeast part of the reservoir, on a paved road.

*Trip notes:* The wide-open spaces at this campground near Wanship Reservoir should appeal to folks who don't like regimented, commercialized camping. When it's uncrowded, the grassy turf is an ideal place to toss Frisbees; when other campgrounds are crowded, this one makes a good overflow spot.

*Season:* May 10 through September 15.

---

## 70. CRANDALL'S

*Reference:* **In Rockport State Park, map A2, grid f5.**

*Campsites, facilities:* There are five sites with picnic tables, fire pits, and a pit toilet. There is *no water.*

*Reservations, fee:* Sites are $5 and are first come, first served.

*Contact:* Call Rockport State Park at (801) 336-2241.

---

*Location:* From Salt Lake City, drive 45 miles east on Interstate 80, past the Park City and Heber City exits. Take the Wanship exit and drive four miles south on State Route 189. Enter the state park on the south end of Rockport Reservoir, crossing the Weber River. The campground is located on the northeast part of the reservoir, on a paved road.

*Trip notes:* Most state park campgrounds next to reservoirs are large, but this one in Rockport State Park is a nice small-scale alternative. Still, the size and first-come, first-served policy means it fills up with campers early in the day, especially on weekends. There's excellent boating and fishing at the reservoir nearby, as well as on the Weber River, which is stocked regularly with rainbow trout.

*Season:* May 10 through September 15.

## 71. SMITH AND MOREHOUSE

*Reference:* **In Wasatch–Cache National Forest; map A2, grid g5.**

*Campsites, facilities:* There are 34 sites with picnic tables and fire rings. Handicapped-accessible vault toilets and water are available.

*Reservations, fee:* For reservations, call the U.S. Forest Service National Reservation System at (800) 280-2267. Sites are $13.

*Contact:* Call the Kamas Ranger District at (801) 783-4338.

*Location:* Driving east from Salt Lake City on Interstate 80, take the Wanship exit. Travel southeast on State Route 32 to Oakley. Turn east and take Weber Canyon Road for 11 miles to the campground.

*Trip notes:* Get to a campsite early, especially on weekends; better yet, get a reservation. The combination of good fishing on nearby Smith and Morehouse Reservoir, remodeled facilities, and campsites tucked away in an alpine forest setting (elevation 7,700) make this one of the area's most-frequented campgrounds.

*Season:* June through October.

## 72. LEDGEFORK

*Reference:* **In Wasatch–Cache National Forest; map A2, grid g5.**

*Campsites, facilities:* There are 73 sites with picnic tables and fire rings. Vault toilets and water are available.

*Reservations, fee:* For reservations, call the U.S. Forest Service National Reservation System at (800) 280-2267. Sites are $11.

*Contact:* Call the Kamas Ranger District at (801) 783-4338.

*Location:* Driving east from Salt Lake City on Interstate 80, take the Wanship exit. Travel southeast on State Route 30 to Oakley. Drive east, to the end of Weber Canyon Road, for 12 miles to the campground.

*Trip notes:* Many campers come to this spot to hike the trail leading from the campground into the High Uintas Wilderness Area, or to fish for the planted trout in nearby Smith and Morehouse Reservoir. Located in a pretty pine forest (elevation 8,000), this popular place does fill fast, so reservations are advised.

*Season:* June through October.

## 73. HAILSTONE CAMPGROUND

*Reference:* **On Jordanelle Reservoir; map A2, grid f5.**

*Campsites, facilities:* There are 230 sites with water and electricity, plus modern rest rooms, showers, laundry facilities, a dump station, a park visitors center, sandy beaches, group-use picnic areas, sun shelters, an 80-slip boat marina with utility hookups, a boat fuel dock, a general store, a restaurant, and three play areas for children.

*Reservations, fee:* Reservations are available 120 days in advance for a nonrefundable $5 per site; call (800) 322-3770 Monday through Friday from 8 A.M. to 5 P.M. Sites are $13. Utah residents 62 and older with a Special Fun Tag get a $2 discount Sunday through Thursday, excluding holidays.

*Contact:* Call Jordanelle State Park at (801) 645-8036.

*Location:* From Heber City, drive six miles north on U.S. 40. The campground is just east of the highway on the west shore of Jordanelle Reservoir.

*Trip notes:* This might be the best campground of its kind in the state park system, and it's also one of the largest. It offers walk-in sites for tent campers, hookups for large RVs, and everything in between. The sites are in somewhat open terrain with good views of the reservoir. Because Hailstone is so close to Park City and Salt Lake City, however, it can get pretty crowded. Rangers limit the boats on the water to 300 at a time. There's an excellent day-use area and beach, and rainbow trout fishing is one of the most popular activities. The park isn't far from the historic Union Pacific Rail Trail State Park, a 28-mile mountain-biking, horseback-riding, and walking trail.

*Season:* April through October.

## 74. ROCK CLIFF CAMPGROUND

*Reference:* **On the Provo River in Jordanelle State Park; map A2, grid f5.**

*Campsites, facilities:* This is primarily a tent-camping area with 50 walk-in sites. Other facilities include modern rest rooms with showers, a nature center, boardwalk nature trails, and a small boat access ramp.

*Reservations, fee:* Reservations are available 120 days in advance for a nonrefundable $5 per site; call (800) 322-3770 Monday through Friday from 8 A.M. to 5 P.M. Sites are $11. Utah residents 62 and older with a Special Fun Tag get a $2 discount Sunday through Thursday, excluding holidays.

*Contact:* Call Jordanelle State Park at (801) 645-8036.

*Location:* From Francis, drive two miles west on State Route 32. A sign points the way to the campground, which is located in a clump of trees down the hill next to the Provo River.

*Trip notes:* This is a nice, quiet, shady spot for tent campers hoping to get away from RVs. Fishing is big on the Provo River or on nearby Jordanelle Reservoir, and hikers like the 17-mile trail around the reservoir. Check with park headquarters for special events associated with the nature center, one of the newest in Utah. All campsites are walk-in; many have covered picnic tables.

*Season:* May 15 to October 15.

## 75. YELLOW PINE RV

*Reference:* **In Wasatch National Forest near Kamas; map A2, grid f5.**

*Campsites, facilities:* There are 33 sites; 10 of these are pull-throughs. Vault toilets, picnic tables, and fire pits are available. There is *no water.*

*Reservations, fee:* Sites are $5, with $3 for each additional vehicle, and are first come, first served.

*Contact:* Call the Kamas Ranger District at (801) 783-4338 .

*Location:* From Kamas, take State Route 150 east for 6.8 miles. The campground is on the north side of the highway.

*Trip notes:* Yellow Pine is the first and lowest-elevation campground (7,200 feet) on what is called the Mirror Lake Scenic Byway. That means it's less crowded than other campgrounds in this area and has a longer season, particularly since higher elevations can have snow on the ground until July. A dirt road services the facility. Tall conifers grace the upper part of the campground. Beaver Creek, which is located across the highway, is a decent stream-fishing spot. Horseback riders and all-terrain vehicle enthusiasts will find a trailhead less than a mile to the west.

*Season:* June through October.

## 76. BEAVER CREEK

*Reference:* **In Wasatch National Forest near Kamas; map A2, grid g5.**

*Campsites, facilities:* There are 14 sites; five of these are pull-throughs. There is *no water,* but vault toilets, picnic tables, and fire pits are available.

*Reservations, fee:* Sites are $5, plus $3 for each additional vehicle, and are first come, first served.

*Contact:* Call the Kamas Ranger District at (801) 783-4338.

*Location:* From Kamas, take State Route 150 east of Kamas. Beaver Creek is 8.4 miles from town on the south side of the highway.

*Trip notes:* At this campground on the Mirror Lake Scenic Byway, sites are set along Beaver Creek, in an open meadow with tall grass, wildflowers, willows, and a few trees. The creek, traversed by a small bridge, offers plenty of good fishing. Hikers can stroll by the creek or in the mountains nearby. The road and sites are unpaved.

*Season:* June through October.

## 77. TAYLOR FORK

*Reference:* **In Wasatch National Forest near Kamas; map A2, grid f6.**

*Campsites, facilities:* There are 11 sites with picnic tables and fire pits. Water and vault toilets are available.

*Reservations, fee:* Sites are $9, plus $4.50 for each additional vehicle, and are first come, first served.

*Contact:* Call the Kamas Ranger District at (801) 783-4338.

*Location:* From Kamas, drive 9.1 miles east on State Route 150. The campground is on the south side of the highway.

*Trip notes:* This campground off the Mirror Lake Scenic Byway is a staging area for all-terrain vehicles: The ATV trail here is the best in northern Utah, and the west end is a parking lot with special ramps for loading and unloading ATVs from trailers or trucks. The roads are dirt. The unpaved, well-shaded, generously spaced campsites are dispersed along Beaver Creek, and have views of the meadow and creek. Fishing is excellent on the creek and in the old beaver pond at the campground's eastern end.

*Season:* June through October.

## 78. SHINGLE CREEK

*Reference:* **In Wasatch National Forest near Kamas; map A2, grid f6.**

*Campsites, facilities:* There are 21 sites, nine of them pull-throughs, plus picnic tables and fire pits. Water and vault toilets are available.

*Reservations, fee:* Sites are $10, plus $5 for each additional vehicle, and are first come, first served.

*Contact:* Call the Kamas Ranger District at (801) 783-4338.

*Location:* From Kamas, drive 9.5 miles east on State Route 150. The campground is on the south side of the highway.

*Trip notes:* This campground contains the trailhead to Shingle Creek Lake, which, along with nearby Shingle Creek to the north, is a popular fishing spot. An ATV trail takes off from the western end of the campground. The main road and sites are dirt, and half of the loop faces Beaver Creek. The sites themselves are not very level, but in the plus department, the vault toilets are newer than most in the area, and the picnic tables in the upper loop are set back from the road. As with most campgrounds on the Mirror Lake Scenic Byway, this one fills almost every summer weekend.

*Season:* June through October.

## 79. LOWER PROVO

*Reference:* **In Wasatch National Forest near Kamas; map A2, grid g6.**

*Campsites, facilities:* There are 10 sites with picnic tables and fire pits. Water and vault toilets are available.

*Reservations, fee:* For reservations, call the U.S. Forest Service National Reservation System at (800) 280-2267. Sites are $9, plus $4.50 for each additional vehicle.

*Contact:* Call the Kamas Ranger District at (801) 783-4338.

*Location:* From Kamas, drive 10.7 miles east on State Route 150, and look for the sign on the right side of the highway. The campground is three-quarters of a mile down a dirt road south of the highway.

*Trip notes:* The best thing about this campground is that it's off the well-traveled Mirror Lake Scenic Byway. Also, the sites here are larger and flatter than their local counterparts, so they're especially hospitable to tents, and tall conifers provide pleasant shade. Hikers can enjoy the nearby High Uintas Wilderness Area, and fishing is decent in the Lower Provo River, which is usually well stocked with rainbow trout.

*Season:* June through October.

## 80. SOAPSTONE

*Reference:* **In Wasatch National Forest near Kamas; map A2, grid g6.**

*Campsites, facilities:* There are 34 sites with picnic tables and fire pits. Water and vault toilets are available.

*Reservations, fee:* Some reservations are available; call the U.S. Forest Service National Reservation System at (800) 280-2267. Sites are $11, plus $5.50 for each additional vehicle.

*Contact:* Call the Kamas Ranger District at (801) 783-4338.

*Location:* From Kamas, drive 15.8 miles east on State Route 150. The campground is on the south side of the highway.

*Trip notes:* This is the first paved campground you come to when heading east on the Mirror Lake Scenic Byway. Located here are trailheads for four-wheel-drive roads to Wolf Creek Road, Soapstone Basin, and the Soapstone summer home area about a mile to the west. The relatively level campsites, shaded by conifers, face the Provo River, a good hiking and fishing spot. Other nice touches: several large, 16-foot picnic tables and ample parking space at each site.

*Season:* June 15 through September 15.

## 81. SHADY DELL

*Reference:* **In Wasatch National Forest near Kamas; map A2, grid g7.**

*Campsites, facilities:* There are 20 sites with picnic tables and fire pits. Water and vault toilets are available.

*Reservations, fee:* Sites are $11, plus $5.50 for additional vehicles, and are first come, first served.

*Contact:* Call the Kamas Ranger District at (801) 783-4338.

*Location:* From Kamas, drive 17.3 miles east on State Route 150. The campground is on the south side of the highway.

*Trip notes:* This campground on the Mirror Lake Scenic Byway has great views of the Uinta Mountains and highly fishable Provo River. Sites next to the river are in open country and surrounded by pine and aspen trees. Roads and sites are paved, with some pull-throughs and room for extra vehicles.

*Season:* June 8 through September 15.

## 82. COBBLEREST

*Reference:* **In Wasatch National Forest near Kamas; map A2, grid g7.**

*Campsites, facilities:* There are 18 sites with picnic tables and fire pits. Water and vault toilets are available.

*Reservations, fee:* Sites are $10, plus $5 per extra vehicle, and are first come, first served.

*Contact:* Call the Kamas Ranger District at (801) 783-4338.

*Location:* From Kamas, drive 19.1 miles east on State Route 150. The campground is on the south side of the highway.

*Trip notes:* Sites are paved and relatively level, but tightly spaced at this wooded campground on the Mirror Lake Scenic Byway. Many will accommodate long RVs. Each loop of the paved road offers visitors a number of pull-through sites. The campground's Provo River location makes for decent hiking and fishing.

*Season:* June 15 through September 15.

---

## 83. TRIAL LAKE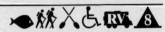

*Reference:* **In Wasatch National Forest near Kamas; map A2, grid g7.**

*Campsites, facilities:* There are 60 sites, with four pull-throughs, plus picnic tables and fire pits. Facilities include water and handicapped-accessible vault toilets.

*Reservations, fee:* For reservations, call the U.S. Forest Service National Reservation System at (800) 280-2267. Sites are $11, plus $5.50 for each extra vehicle.

*Contact:* Call the Kamas Ranger District at (801) 783-4338.

*Location:* From Kamas, drive 25.7 miles east on State Route 150. The campground is a quarter mile off the highway on the north side of the road.

*Trip notes:* The postcard setting—less than a stone's throw from Trial Lake on the Mirror Lake Scenic Byway—makes this a real find. High above the treeline, gray, majestic Bald Mountain overlooks the conifer-rimmed lake behind Trial Lake Dam. The main through-road is paved, and some of the camping is so close to the water that campers can fish from their site. Anglers can also use a lakeside parking lot near the campground entrance. The water is heavily stocked with rainbow trout (though it's also heavily fished), and the trail leading from here to other lakes is a favorite with hikers. Non-motorized boats are allowed. Visitors like to use inflatable rafts or canoes to fish or just enjoy the scenery. Due to the 10,000-foot elevation, this place opens late in the summer.

*Season:* June 26 through September 10.

---

## 84. LILLY LAKE

*Reference:* **In Wasatch National Forest near Kamas; map A2, grid g7.**

*Campsites, facilities:* There are 14 sites with picnic tables and fire pits. Water and vault toilets are available.

*Reservations, fee:* Sites are $10, plus $5 for extra vehicles, and are first come, first served.

*Contact:* Call the Kamas Ranger District at (801) 783-4338.

*Location:* From Kamas, drive 26.7 miles east on State Route 150. The campground is on the north side of the highway.

*Trip notes:* Located between small Lilly Lake and Teapot Lake, this loop campground on the Mirror Lake Scenic Byway has some sites overlooking the water, but most are up on higher ground. The campground, with a paved road and pads, is at 9,800 feet—almost treeline—so lake visitors have picture-perfect views of the surrounding tall conifers and the bare mountains looming dramatically to the east. Inflatable rafts and canoes are popular here; so is fishing the well-stocked waters from the shore.

*Season:* June 26 through September 10.

---

## 85. LOST CREEK

*Reference:* **In Wasatch National Forest near Kamas; map A2, grid f7.**

*Campsites, facilities:* There are 34 sites with picnic tables and fire pits. Water and vault toilets are available.

*Reservations, fee:* For reservations, call the U.S. Forest Service National Reservation System at (800) 280-2267. Sites are $10, plus $5 for extra vehicles.

*Contact:* Call the Kamas Ranger District at (801) 783-4338.

*Location:* From Kamas, drive 26.9 miles east on State Route 150. The campground is on the east side of the highway.

*Trip notes:* At 10,000 feet up, this campground on the Mirror Lake Scenic Byway is late to open, but you can't beat the scenery. Lost Creek flows past on the east, Lost Lake is to the west, and the sites are set amid tall conifer trees. The road is paved, and the loops are separated by pretty meadows. Local lake fishing is excellent, and there's plenty of hiking in the nearby High Uintas Wilderness Area.

*Season:* June 26 through September 10.

## 86. MOOSEHORN

*Reference:* **In Wasatch National Forest near Kamas; map A2, grid f7.**

*Campsites, facilities:* There are 33 sites with picnic tables and fire pits. Water and vault toilets are available.

*Reservations, fee:* For reservations, call the U.S. Forest Service National Reservation System at (800) 280-2267. Sites are $9 plus $4.50 for extra vehicles.

*Contact:* Call the Kamas Ranger District at (801) 783-4338.

*Location:* From Kamas, drive east for 30.8 miles on State Route 150. The campground is on the west side of the highway.

*Trip notes:* The view from here is superb: at a timberline elevation of 10,400, it's right at the base of majestic Bald Mountain, next to glacier-carved Moosehorn Lake. Both the road and sites are unpaved. This is one of the last campgrounds to open on the Mirror Lake Scenic Byway, and one of the coolest in summer.

*Season:* July 1 through September 7.

## 87. MIRROR LAKE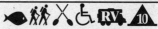

*Reference:* **In Wasatch National Forest near Kamas; map A2, grid f7.**

*Campsites, facilities:* This handicapped-accessible campground has 85 sites with picnic tables and fire pits, plus vault toilets, water, and a boat ramp.

*Reservations, fee:* For reservations, call the U.S. Forest Service National Reservation System at (800) 280-2267. Sites are $11, plus $5.50 for each extra vehicle.

*Contact:* Call the Kamas Ranger District at (801) 783-4338.

*Location:* From Kamas, drive east for 31.5 miles on State Route 150. The campground is on the east side of the lake, a quarter of a mile from the highway.

*Trip notes:* This cool, woodsy, high-country campground (elevation 10,200) is the largest on the Mirror Lake Scenic Byway, designed in a series of several loops not far from the lake itself. Surrounding the place are the high Uintas peaks, Bald Mountain, and Hayden Peak. Rafts, canoes, and nonmotorized boats are popular for fishing and scenery-watching, and a trail around the lake offers decent hiking. A small amphitheater occasionally hosts interpretive programs on weekends. Facilities for the disabled are the best in the area.

*Season:* July through November.

---

# 88. BUTTERFLY

*Reference:* **In Wasatch National Forest near Kamas; map A2, grid f7.**

*Campsites, facilities:* There are 20 sites with picnic tables and fire pits. Vault toilets and water are available.

*Reservations, fee:* Sites are $9, plus $4.50 for each additional vehicle, and are first come, first served.

*Contact:* Call the Kamas Ranger District at (801) 783-4338.

*Location:* From Kamas, drive 34.2 miles east on State Route 150. The campground is on the west side of the highway.

*Trip notes:* Some sites at this Mirror Lake Scenic Byway campground (elevation 10,300) overlook a pretty little lake; all are unpaved and nestled amid tall conifers. Many picnic tables are set far back from the road for more privacy; from that vantage point, campers can gaze up along Hayden Peak and the range leading north—an experience akin to looking down a row of giant pyramids. The Highline Trail, a major hiking artery of the High Uintas, takes off to the east just across the highway. Anglers can use a parking lot near the entrance. Rafts, canoes, and nonmotorized boats are allowed for fishing or recreation. Butterfly opens late because of the high elevation, but it's with the wait.

*Season:* July through November.

---

# 89. SULPHUR

*Reference:* **In Wasatch National Forest near Kamas; map A2, grid f7.**

*Campsites, facilities:* There are 26 sites with picnic tables and fire pits. Water and vault toilets are available.

*Reservations, fee:* Sites are $8 and are first come, first served.

*Contact:* Call the Evanston Ranger District at (307) 789-3194.

*Location:* From Kamas, drive 38.9 miles east on State Route 150. The campground is on the west side of the highway.

*Trip notes:* Since not very many campers venture past Mirror Lake, this remote campground on the Mirror Lake Scenic Byway is sometimes less crowded than the others. The sites are also farther apart here—a definite plus—with many flat areas for tents and some room for small groups. The setting has the feel of a high mountain meadow; the trees are not so dense, and the sites look out over grassy expanses and the Hayden Fork of the Bear River. Some campers come here to hike and fish, others just to take in the fantastic views of the high Uinta Mountains.

*Season:* June through October.

---

## 90. BEAVER VIEW

*Reference:* In Wasatch National Forest near Kamas; map A2, grid f7.

*Campsites, facilities:* There are 18 sites (including one group site) with picnic tables and fire pits. Water and vault toilets are available.

*Reservations, fee:* Sites are $8 and are first come, first served.

*Contact:* Call the Evanston Ranger District at (307) 789-3194.

*Location:* From Kamas, drive east for 41.9 miles on State Route 150. The campground is on the east side of the highway.

*Trip notes:* Beaver View is another secluded campground along the Mirror Lake Scenic Byway, with fairly well-spaced sites, a nice mix of forest and meadow scenery, and great views of the Hayden Fork of the Bear River. The river is a favored fishing and hiking spot, as is the campground's namesake Beaver Pond nearby. The road and sites are unpaved, with some gravel pull-throughs for RVs.

*Season:* June through October.

## 91. HAYDEN FORK

*Reference:* In Wasatch National Forest near Kamas; map A2, grid f7.

*Campsites, facilities:* There are nine sites with picnic tables and fire pits. Water and vault toilets are available.

*Reservations, fee:* Sites are $8 and are first come, first served.

*Contact:* Call the Evanston Ranger District at (307) 789-3194.

*Location:* From Kamas, drive east for 42.3 miles on State Route 150. The campground is on the east side of the highway.

*Trip notes:* While not recommended for RVs due to the steep and winding dirt access road, this campground on the Mirror Lake Scenic Byway is a nice place to bring a tent. Some sites are on the Hayden Fork of the Bear River, a favorite with anglers and hikers alike. The fire pits are above-ground stone stoves.

*Season:* June through October.

## 92. WOLVERINE ATV TRAILHEAD

*Reference:* In Wasatch National Forest near Kamas; map A2, grid f7.

*Campsites, facilities:* There are six sites with picnic tables, fire pits, and vault toilets, but *no water.*

*Reservations, fee:* Sites are free and are first come, first served.

*Contact:* Call the Evanston Ranger District at (307) 789-3194.

*Location:* From Kamas, drive east for 49.1 miles on State Route 150. Look for the marked turnoff to Forest Service Road 057. The campground is 1.5 miles up the mountain on the rough dirt road.

*Trip notes:* This is primarily a staging area for all-terrain vehicles, with ramps for loading and unloading, numerous dirt roads, and more than nine miles of developed ATV trails. The setting is mainly open terrain with a few young trees, but a tall forest surrounds it all.

*Season:* June through October.

## 93. CHRISTMAS MEADOWS

*Reference:* **In Wasatch National Forest near Kamas; map A2, grid f8.**

*Campsites, facilities:* There are 11 sites with picnic tables and fire pits. Water and vault toilets are available.

*Reservations, fee:* Sites are $8 and are first come, first served.

*Contact:* Call the Evanston Ranger District at (307) 789-3194.

*Location:* From Kamas, drive east on State Route 150. Just past Stillwater campground (see below), look for Forest Service Road 057, the turnoff to Christmas Meadows and Wolverine ATV campground. The campground is four miles down this relatively rough dirt road, which runs parallel to a summer home development.

*Trip notes:* True to its name, small Christmas Meadows campground is set in a beautiful high alpine meadow, with a few trees and spectacular views of the surrounding mountains. Anglers like to pass the time fishing the Stillwater Fork of the Bear River.

*Season:* June 15 through September 15.

## 94. STILLWATER

*Reference:* **In Wasatch National Forest near Kamas; map A2, grid f8.**

*Campsites, facilities:* There are 21 sites with picnic tables and fire pits. Water and vault toilets are available.

*Reservations, fee:* Sites are $8 and are first come, first served.

*Contact:* Call the Evanston Ranger District at (307) 789-3194.

*Location:* From Kamas, drive east 45.6 miles on State Route 150. The campground is on the east side of the highway.

*Trip notes:* Stillwater, on the deep and wide Bear River, is farther off the highway and has bigger sites than most other campgrounds along the Mirror Lake Scenic Byway. The road and sites are unpaved. Some of the sites are large enough for groups; most are relatively level and right by the water. Fishing and hiking are big attractions here.

*Season:* June through October.

## 95. BEAR RIVER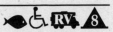

*Reference:* **In Wasatch National Forest near Kamas; map A2, grid e7.**

*Campsites, facilities:* There are four established campsites with picnic tables and fire pits. Water and handicapped-accessible vault toilets are available.

*Reservations, fee:* Sites are $8 and are first come, first served.

*Contact:* Call the Evanston Ranger District at (307) 789-3194.

*Location:* From Kamas, drive east for 48.3 miles on State Route 150. The campground is on the west side of the highway.

*Trip notes:* At this unpaved campground close to the end of the Mirror Lake Scenic Byway, all the sites are next to the fishable Bear River, amid a smattering of trees. The rest room is wheelchair accessible, but the rocky sites are not level.

*Season:* June through October.

## 96. EAST FORK

*Reference:* In Wasatch National Forest near Kamas; map A2, grid e7.

*Campsites, facilities:* There are seven sites, with picnic tables and fire pits. Water and vault toilets are available.

*Reservations, fee:* Sites are $8 and are first come, first served.

*Contact:* Call the Evanston Ranger District at (307) 789-3194.

*Location:* From Kamas, go 50 miles northeast on Highway 150 to the camp.

*Trip notes:* At East Fork—the last campground on the Mirror Lake Scenic Byway before you leave the forest and enter Evanston, Wyoming—all sites are on the river next to clumps of willows, in mostly open country with young conifers and aspens nearby. The road and sites are unpaved, and trailers are not recommended due to lack of turnaround room. A private gas station and store are just north of the campground.

*Season:* June through October.

## 97. LITTLE LYMAN LAKE

*Reference:* In Wasatch National Forest near Kamas; map A2, grid e7.

*Campsites, facilities:* There are 10 sites with picnic tables and fire pits. Water and vault toilets are available.

*Reservations, fee:* Sites are $8 and are first come, first served.

*Contact:* Call the Evanston Ranger District at (307) 789-3194.

*Location:* From Kamas, drive east on State Route 150. Take Forest Service Road 058 to the east, and look for the campground turnoff about 12 miles later. The campground is 65.6 miles from Kamas.

*Trip notes:* This campground is located between Big and Little Lyman Lakes, which are (anglers take note) the only stocked lakes on the Blacks Fork of the Bear River. The road and sites are gravel.

*Season:* June 15 through September 15.

## 98. CHINA MEADOWS

*Reference:* In Wasatch National Forest near Mountain View, Wyoming; map A2, grid e8.

*Campsites, facilities:* There are nine sites with picnic tables and fire pits. Water and vault toilets are available.

*Reservations, fee:* Sites are $6 and are first come, first served.

*Contact:* Call the Mountain View Ranger District at (307) 782-6555.

*Location:* Take Interstate 80 or State Highway 150 north to Evanston, Wyoming, then go 12 miles north on Interstate 80. Take the Fort Bridger exit and follow State Highway 412 south to Mountain View. From there, take State Route 410 south for seven miles and look for the junction with Uinta County Road 246. Go straight on Uinta County Road 246 for 8.2 miles to the Forest Service boundary, where it becomes Forest Service Road 072, and drive 11 miles to the China Meadows campground.

*Trip notes:* This high-country campground on China Meadows Lake is a favorite with folks who like to fish, hike, and horseback ride, though some simply take in the scenery on rafts, canoes, and boats (trolling motors only). Across the road, the China Meadows Trailhead campground (see below) provides access to Red Castle, a High Uintas scenic basin with alpine lakes.

*Season:* July through September.

## 99. CHINA MEADOWS TRAILHEAD

*Reference:* **In Wasatch National Forest near Mountain View, Wyoming; map A2, grid e8.**

*Campsites, facilities:* There are 12 sites with vault toilets and picnic tables, but *no water.*

*Reservations, fee:* Sites are $4 and are first come, first served.

*Contact:* Call the Mountain View Ranger District at (307) 782-6555.

*Location:* Take Interstate 80 or State Highway 150 north to Evanston, Wyoming, then go 12 miles north on Interstate 80. Take the Fort Bridger exit and follow State Highway 412 south to Mountain View. From there, take State Route 410 south for seven miles to the junction with Uinta County Road 246. Go straight on Uinta County Road 246 for 8.2 miles to the Forest Service boundary, where it becomes Forest Service Road 072, and go 11 miles to the wilderness trailhead. The trailhead campground is 26.2 miles from Mountain View, Wyoming, on partially paved, then gravel road.

*Trip notes:* With two horse-loading ramps and a six-stall corral, this campground is used as a trailhead for horse packing trips into the Uinta Wilderness. It's set at an elevation of 10,000 feet, so there's usually a later opening date. Road conditions limit RVs to those under 14 feet long.

*Season:* July through September.

## 100. MARSH LAKE

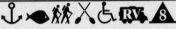

*Reference:* **In Wasatch National Forest near Mountain View, Wyoming; map A2, grid e8.**

*Campsites, facilities:* There are 34 sites, 33 with picnic tables (including one 16-foot-long table), plus vault toilets, water, stoves, grills and fire rings, and a boat ramp. One site is wheelchair accessible.

*Reservations, fee:* Reservations are accepted for a limited number of sites, including the wheelchair-accessible site; call the U.S. Forest Service National Reservation System at (800) 280-2267. Sites are $7.

*Contact:* Call the Mountain View Ranger District at (307) 782-6555.

*Location:* Take Interstate 80 or State Highway 150 north to Evanston, Wyoming, then go 12 miles north on Interstate 80. Take the Fort Bridger exit and follow State Highway 412 south to Mountain View. From there, take State Route 410 south for seven miles to the junction with Uinta County Road 246. Take Uinta County Road 246 for 8.2 miles, where it becomes Forest Service Road 072, and continue for another 8.7 miles to the campground. The campground is 23.9 miles from Mountain View, Wyoming.

*Trip notes:* Two forested loops overlook tree-lined Marsh Lake, where owners of rafts and canoes can fish and enjoy the tranquil beauty of the surroundings. Fly fishers like to try their luck from shore. At an elevation of 9,800,

this place stays open a little longer than high-country campgrounds like nearby China Meadows (see page 98).
*Season:* June through October.

---

## 101. BRIDGER LAKE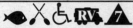

*Reference:* **In Wasatch National Forest near Mountain View, Wyoming; map A2, grid e8.**

*Campsites, facilities:* There are 30 sites with vault toilets, plus water and a boat ramp. One site is handicapped accessible.

*Reservations, fee:* Reservations are accepted for a limited number of sites, including the handicapped-accessible site; call the U.S. Forest Service National Reservation System at (800) 280-2267. Sites are $8.

*Contact:* Call the Mountain View Ranger District at (307) 782-6555.

*Location:* Take Interstate 80 or State Highway 150 north to Evanston, Wyoming, then go 12 miles north on Interstate 80. Take the Fort Bridger exit, and follow State Highway 412 south to Mountain View. Then take State Route 410 south for seven miles to the junction with Uinta County Road 246. Go straight on Uinta County Road 246 for 8.2 miles until it becomes Forest Service Road 072, and continue for 7.9 miles to Forest Service Road 126, which heads off to the east. Then take Road 126 to the campground on Bridger Lake.

*Trip notes:* Set in a woodsy area along the shore of Bridger Lake, this is a popular base camp for hikers or starting point for backpackers. Other campers just take their rafts, canoes, or boats with trolling motors onto the water, where they fish for planted trout or simply take in the scenery.

*Season:* June through October.

---

## 102. STATE LINE

*Reference:* **In Wasatch National Forest near Mountain View, Wyoming; map A2, grid e8.**

*Campsites, facilities:* There are 41 sites (one of them wheelchair accessible) with picnic tables, fire pits, water, and vault toilets. A boat ramp is available on State Line Reservoir.

*Reservations, fee:* For reservations, call the U.S. Forest Service National Reservation System at (800) 280-2267. Sites are $7.

*Contact:* Call the Mountain View Ranger District at (307) 782-6555.

*Location:* Take Interstate 80 or State Highway 150 north to Evanston, Wyoming. Then go 12 miles north on Interstate 80, take the Fort Bridger exit, and follow State Highway 412 south to Mountain View, Wyoming. Take State Route 410 south until it intersects with Uinta County Road 246, go straight on Uinta County Road 246 for 8.2 miles until it becomes Forest Service Road 072, and go 5.5 miles to the campground.

*Trip notes:* The sites are rather close together, but they're set in an alpine forest and face State Line Reservoir. Campers use the nearby boat ramp to take to the water with canoes and rafts.

*Season:* June through September.

---

# 103. HOOP LAKE

*Reference:* **In Wasatch National Forest near Mountain View, Wyoming; map A2, grid e8.**

*Campsites, facilities:* There are 44 sites with picnic tables and fire pits, a horse corral, and an adjacent trailhead for hiking or horseback riding. Water and vault toilets are available.

*Reservations, fee:* Sites are $6 and are first come, first served.

*Contact:* Call the Mountain View Ranger District at (307) 782-6555.

*Location:* Take Interstate 80 or State Highway 150 north to Evanston, Wyoming. Then go 12 miles north on Interstate 80, take the Fort Bridger exit, and follow State Highway 412 south to Mountain View, Wyoming. From there, take State Route 414 southeast for 23.6 miles, turn right off onto gravel Uinta County Road 264, and drive for 3.2 miles. Stay on that road, which turns into Forest Road 78, heading south for seven miles to the campground.

*Trip notes:* Like most of the high mountain lakes in Utah, Hoop Lake offers good fishing in a scenic locale. Anglers won't catch any lunkers here, but the fish are usually plentiful. The campground itself is in a pristinely beautiful alpine setting; don't be surprised if you spot a moose. Horseback riders and hikers can find plenty to explore in the nearby High Uintas Wilderness Area.

*Season:* June 15 through September 3.

# 104. SPRUCES

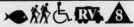

*Reference:* **In Big Cottonwood Canyon east of Salt Lake City; map A2, grid g3.**

*Campsites, facilities:* There are 86 individual sites and 20 group sites. Facilities include picnic tables, fire pits, wheelchair-accessible flush toilets, rest rooms with cold running water, hiking trails, softball diamonds, and an amphitheater. Dogs are not allowed.

*Reservations, fee:* For reservations, call the U.S. Forest Service National Reservation System at (800) 280-2267. Sites are $9.

*Contact:* Call the Salt Lake Ranger District at (801) 524-5042.

*Location:* From Salt Lake City, take Interstate 15 or Interstate 80 east and look for the signs for Big and Little Cottonwood Canyons. Take Big Cottonwood Canyon Road (State Highway 190) and head southeast from town for 13.7 miles to the campground, on the south (right) side of the road.

*Trip notes:* Though this is the largest of the Wasatch Front campgrounds, it also has some of the best sites, so it fills up fast. Set in a shaded area off the highway, it's serenaded by the constant soothing babble of Big Cottonwood Creek, which offers some remarkably good trout fishing in the open meadows nearby. A number of popular hiking trails, including the short trek to Donut Falls, lead out of the campground, but don't even think about bringing your dog into the canyon unless you want a citation. The elevation of 7,400 keeps it cool here in summer.

*Season:* June 5 through October 15.

## 105. REDMAN

*Reference:* In Big Cottonwood Canyon, east of Salt Lake City; map A2, grid g3.

*Campsites, facilities:* There are 37 individual sites and five group sites, with no hookups. Flush toilets, drinking water, picnic tables, and fire grills are available. Dogs are not allowed.

*Reservations, fee:* For reservations, call the U.S. Forest Service National Reservation System at (800) 280-2267. Individual sites are $9; group fees vary.

*Contact:* Call the Salt Lake Ranger District at (801) 524-5042.

*Location:* From Salt Lake City, follow the signs from Interstates 80, 15, or 215 to Big Cottonwood Canyon. Take Big Cottonwood Canyon Road (State Highway 190) southeast for 16.4 miles to the campground.

*Trip notes:* This pine-shrouded retreat is surprisingly peaceful for a campground located so close to a major city. The only sound is the agreeable trickle of flowing water from Big Cottonwood Canyon, and while the sites themselves are dusty and well used, nearby attractions abound: Silver Lake, at the top of the canyon, has a boardwalk trail and fishing piers, and there are several beautiful canyon hiking trails. (Dogs, however, are prohibited, because this area is city watershed.) At an elevation of 8,300, Redman sometimes opens later in June due to heavy snow.

*Season:* June 15 through October 15.

---

## 106. TANNERS FLAT

*Reference:* In Little Cottonwood Canyon, east of Salt Lake City; map A2, grid g3.

*Campsites, facilities:* There are 32 family sites and three group sites, with no hookups. Facilities include rest rooms with cold running water, drinking water, picnic tables, fire pits, a trailhead, and a view area. Dogs are not allowed.

*Reservations, fee:* For reservations, call the U.S. Forest Service National Reservation System at (800) 280-2267. Sites are $9; fees for group sites vary.

*Contact:* Call the Salt Lake Ranger District at (801) 524-5042.

*Location:* From Salt Lake City, take Interstate 15, 215, or 80 into the Salt Lake Valley and follow the signs to Little Cottonwood Canyon. Take Little Cottonwood Canyon Road for 11.7 miles southeast of town to the campground.

*Trip notes:* The pleasing trickle of water from Little Cottonwood Canyon is a natural buffer against noise from other campers or traffic, making this one of the better Wasatch Front campgrounds. At an elevation of 7,200 feet, the sites are shaded by pines; some are guarded by large slabs of granite or literally carved out of oak trees. Campers can enjoy the hiking and mountain-biking trails at nearby Snowbird ski resort or take the Snowbird tram to the top of Hidden Peak to view the spectacular summer wildflower displays. Note: Dogs are not allowed, as this area is city watershed.

*Season:* Memorial Day weekend through October, depending on the snow conditions.

---

# 107. ALBION

*Reference:* **In Little Cottonwood Canyon, east of Salt Lake City; map A2, grid g3.**

*Campsites, facilities:* There are 24 individual sites and two group sites, with no hookups. Facilities include vault toilets, picnic tables, drinking water, picnic tables, and trailheads. Dogs are not allowed.

*Reservations, fee:* For reservations, call the U.S. Forest Service National Reservation System at (800) 280-2267. Sites are $8.

*Contact:* Call the Salt Lake Ranger District at (801) 524-5042 for more information.

*Location:* Albion is 18.4 miles southeast of Salt Lake City. From Salt Lake City, take Interstate 15, 215, or 80 into the Salt Lake Valley and follow the signs to Little Cottonwood Canyon. Take Little Cottonwood Canyon Road (State Highway 210) to the top of the road; follow the pavement to the Alta ski resort, then use the dirt road into the campground.

*Trip notes:* There is no denying the beauty of this campground, with its breathtaking wildflower displays, alpine meadows, and views of granite, glacier-carved mountains. But private homes, ski lift towers, and power lines, coupled with road dust from the early-summer weekend crowds, detract from the splendor somewhat. Hiking trails leading to Cecret Lake and Sunset Peak are among the most popular on the Wasatch Front. When crowds fill up the parking spaces, expect to be stopped by an attendant and asked to park nearby at the Alta ski resort instead. Given the altitude (9,500 feet), the camping season can be short.

*Season:* Late June to mid-September.

# 108. LITTLE MILL

*Reference:* **In Uinta National Forest; map A2, grid g3.**

*Campsites, facilities:* There are 79 sites with picnic tables, fire pits, and grills. Rest rooms with flush toilets and drinking water are available.

*Reservations, fee:* For reservations, call the U.S. Forest Service National Reservation System at (800) 280-2267. Sites are $11.

*Contact:* Call the Pleasant Grove Ranger District at (801) 785-3563 for more information.

*Location:* From Salt Lake City, drive south on Interstate 15 until you reach exit 287. Take the exit and drive east on State Route 92 approximately 12 miles up American Fork Canyon. The campground is located on the south side of the road near a fork.

*Trip notes:* Large Little Mill campground, located on the banks of American Fork Creek in a steep canyon (elevation 6,000), is popular with Wasatch Front residents looking for a weekend retreat. Other big attractions in the area include the hike to Timpanogos Cave at the national monument just down the canyon, and whiling away the hours fishing on the creek below nearby Tibble Fork Reservoir.

*Season:* May through October.

## 109. GRANITE FLAT

*Reference:* **In the North Fork of American Fork Canyon; map A2, grid g3.**

*Campsites, facilities:* There are 44 single-family sites, eight double-family sites, and three group areas, with no hookups. Facilities include picnic tables, fire pits, drinking water, and flush toilets.

*Reservations, fee:* Reservations are taken for group sites only. Single-family sites are $13, double-family sites are $26, and group site fees vary.

*Contact:* Call the Pleasant Grove Ranger District at (801) 785-3563.

*Location:* Drive south from Salt Lake City on Interstate 15, taking exit 287. Go east on State Route 92 for approximately 15 miles, traveling up American Fork Canyon. Take North Fork Road (Forest Road 85) past Tibble Fork Reservoir to the campground.

*Trip notes:* Located in pines and aspens above scenic Tibble Fork Reservoir, Granite Flat has long been a local favorite. At an elevation of 6,800 feet, it offers a cool alternative to the sunbaked valley. Favorite summer pastimes here are rafting, canoeing, and fishing at the reservoir or Silver Flat Lake; hiking to Timpanogos Cave; or horseback riding or hiking into the Lone Peak Wilderness Area. Horse-unloading facilities are nearby.

*Season:* May 24 through September 30.

## 110. MOUNT TIMPANOGOS

*Reference:* **In Uinta National Forest; map A2, grid g3.**

*Campsites, facilities:* There are 27 sites with picnic tables, fire grills, drinking water, and flush toilets.

*Reservations, fee:* Eleven sites can be reserved; call the U.S. Forest Service National Reservation System at (800) 280-2267. Sites are $11.

*Contact:* Contact the Pleasant Grove Ranger District at (801) 785-3563.

*Location:* From Orem, drive east up U.S. 189. Look for the turnoff to the Sundance ski area on State Highway 92. Take that road to the north for just over three miles to the campground.

*Trip notes:* Campers who saw the movie Jeremiah Johnson should recognize the alpine splendor of this forested campground. Mount Timpanogos, one of the tallest peaks in the Wasatch range, guards the campground. Ambitious hikers make the 18-mile round-trip hike to the summit; others enjoy shorter walks to the nearby waterfalls in the Mount Timpanogos Wilderness Area. Horseback riders can ride from the stables at the nearby Sundance ski area. For another scenic outing, take a drive north to Forest Road 114 and visit Cascade Springs, a wonderful nature area where boardwalks lead past interpretive signs and spring-fed ponds filled with trout.

*Season:* June 1 through September 25.

## 111. TIMPANOKE

*Reference:* **In Uinta National Forest; map A2, grid g3.**

*Campsites, facilities:* There are 26 single-family and six double-family sites with picnic tables, fire grills, vault toilets, and drinking water.

*Reservations, fee:* Reservations are taken for 16 single-family and five double-family sites; call the U.S. Forest Service National Reservation System at (800) 280-2267. Single-family sites are $11 and doubles are $22.

*Contact:* Contact the Pleasant Grove Ranger District at (801) 785-3563.

*Location:* Drive south from Salt Lake City on Interstate 15 and take exit 287 to State Route 92. From the mouth of American Fork Canyon, drive nine miles to the campground, staying on State Route 92, now marked as the Alpine Loop.

*Trip notes:* Located at the pinnacle of the Alpine Loop at an elevation of 7,400 feet in forests of aspen and pine, this campground is a popular foliage-viewing spot in the fall. The Loop, in fact, might be the most-traveled scenic autumn drive along the Wasatch Front, so expect heavy traffic in the campground, which is located next to the road. Hiking and horseback riding are favorite activities on the nearby Great Western Trail.

*Season:* May 25 through October 31.

---

## 112. DEER CREEK STATE PARK

*Reference:* On Deer Creek Reservoir; map A2, grid g4.

*Campsites, facilities:* There are 32 sites, with no hookups. Facilities include picnic tables, fire grills, rest rooms with showers, a sewage disposal and fish-cleaning station, and a concrete boat-launching ramp and adjacent paved parking area. In the reservoir's day-use areas, two concessionaires offer a restaurant, boat rentals, gasoline, and camping supplies.

*Reservations, fee:* Reservations are available 120 days in advance for a nonrefundable $5 per site; call (800) 322-3770 Monday through Friday from 8 A.M. to 5 P.M. Sites are $10. Utah residents 62 years and older with a Special Fun Tag receive a $2 discount Sunday through Thursday, excluding holidays.

*Contact:* Call Deer Creek State Park at (801) 654-0171.

*Location:* From Heber City, take U.S. Highway 189 heading southwest and go seven miles. The park is located on the east side of the highway.

*Trip notes:* Apart from the abundant amenities at the campground, the Deer Creek Reservoir offers a wide range of recreational activities. Its north end, near the Island Boat Camp, is popular with sailboarders, and consistent winds make it a prime sailboating area. Anglers like to fish the waters for bass, walleye, and trout. And relatively warm summer water temperatures make Deer Creek a popular waterskiing park. The campground is set on a flat spot overlooking the reservoir, in the shadow of spectacular Mount Timpanogos.

*Season:* May 1 through October 1.

---

## 113. MOUNTAIN SPA

*Reference:* In Midway; map A2, grid g5.

*Campsites, facilities:* This RV campground is next to the cabins at the Mountain Spa Resort, where two mineral pools, a cafe, and a gift shop are open to campers for use. There are seven sites with full hookups and a grassy area for tents, plus rest rooms, showers, picnic tables, and a swing set. Pets are allowed on a leash.

---

*Reservations, fee:* For reservations and fees, call (801) 654-0721.

*Contact:* Call the campground at (801) 654-0721.

*Location:* From Salt Lake City, take Interstate 80 east to U.S. Route 40, and take Route 40 south toward Midway. Turn off on River Road and take it to 600 North, then take 600 North to 200 East. Turn onto 200 East, go two blocks, and turn right at the sign to Mountain Spa Resort.

*Trip notes:* There's not an awful lot to this campground per se; it's basically contained within a gravel parking area of the Mountain Spa Resort. Still, it has the feeling of being way out in the country, and the resort itself (which, unlike the campground, is open year-round) is an appealingly old-fashioned bathing spa with most activity centered around the bubbling hot springs. Golfers can perfect their game on courses at the Homestead Resort and in Wasatch Mountain State Park.

*Season:* Memorial Day through Labor Day.

---

## 114. OAK HOLLOW

*Reference:* **In Wasatch Mountain State Park; map A2, grid g5.**

*Campsites, facilities:* There are 40 sites, handicapped-accessible rest rooms with flush toilets, showers, water, sewage disposal, picnic tables, and fire pits.

*Reservations, fee:* Reservations are strongly recommended, since this is Utah's most popular state park; call (800) 322-3770. Sites are $11; Utah seniors with a Special Fun Tag get a $2 discount Sundays through Thursdays, excluding holidays.

*Contact:* Call the campground at (801) 654-1791.

*Location:* From Salt Lake City, take Interstate 80 east. Turn onto U.S. Route 40 and follow the signs to Wasatch Mountain State Park, turning onto River Road. Follow River Road as it turns into Burgi Lane. At another park sign, turn right on Pine Canyon Lane and continue to the park.

*Trip notes:* Oak Hollow is a campground set up for tent campers only, with a leveled, framed dirt pad at each site and picnic tables set on cement pads. Each site is surrounded by scrub oak, which serves as a vegetation screen. The surrounding Wasatch Mountain State Park is famous for its 27-hole golf course (popular with cross-country skiers and snowmobilers in winter), and nearby Deer Creek Reservoir is a prime spot for fishing and other types of water sports.

*Season:* May through October, depending on snow conditions.

---

## 115. MAHAGONY

*Reference:* **In Wasatch Mountain State Park; map A2, grid g5.**

*Campsites, facilities:* This RV-only campground has 35 sites, full hookups, RV disposal, showers, flush toilets, water, picnic tables, and fire pits. The rest rooms are handicapped accessible.

*Reservations, fee:* Reservations are strongly recommended; call (800) 322-3770. Sites are $15. Utah residents 62 and older with a Special Fun Tag get a $2 discount on Sundays through Thursdays, excluding holidays.

*Contact:* Call the campground at (801) 654-3961.

---

*Location:* From Salt Lake City, take Interstate 80 east. Turn onto U.S. Route 40 and follow the signs to Wasatch Mountain State Park, turning onto River Road. Follow River Road as it turns into Burgi Lane. At another park sign, turn right on Pine Canyon Lane and continue to the park.

*Trip notes:* The campground, one of four in Wasatch Mountain State Park, is built especially for RVs. The paved, level sites have full hookups, with back-ins and pull-throughs; the road is paved as well, and the picnic tables are set on cement pads. Many sites are in an open setting, in tall grass and sage-brush, with good views of the Heber Valley, Deer Creek Reservoir, and the surrounding mountains, and access to a pleasant stream. The park, a favorite getaway from Salt Lake City, has a 27-hole golf course. Fishing and other water sports are popular at Deer Creek Reservoir.

*Season:* May through October, depending on snow conditions.

## 116. COTTONWOOD

*Reference:* **In Wasatch Mountain State Park; map A2, grid g5.**

*Campsites, facilities:* This campground is divided into two sections: one for RVs only, with 31 sites and full hookups, and one for tents or self-contained campers, with 15 sites and no hookups. Picnic tables, fire rings, flush toilets, showers, water, and RV disposal are available. The rest rooms are handicapped accessible.

*Reservations, fee:* Reservations are recommended; call (800) 322-3770. Sites with full hookups are $15 on Friday, Saturday, and holidays, and $13 other days; sites without hookups are $12 on Friday, Saturday, and holidays, and $11 other days.

*Contact:* Call (801) 654-3961.

*Location:* From Salt Lake City, take Interstate 80 east. Turn onto U.S. Route 40 and follow the signs to Wasatch Mountain State Park, turning onto River Road. Follow River Road as it turns into Burgi Lane. At another park sign, turn right on Pine Canyon Lane and continue to the park.

*Trip notes:* The settings vary in this split campground for tent campers and RVs: some sites are back in the trees, others are out in the scrub oak and tall grass, and still others border the famed 27-hole golf course. All roads and sites are paved. No tents are allowed in the RV section. This area abounds with hiking trails; the park visitors center can provide information, maps, and travel tips.

*Season:* May through October.

## 117. DEER CREEK

*Reference:* **In Wasatch Mountain State Park; map A2, grid g5.**

*Campsites, facilities:* There are 17 sites with no hookups. Picnic tables, fire pits, water, and flush toilets are available. The rest rooms are handicapped accessible.

*Reservations, fee:* Reservations are recommended; call (800) 322-3770. Sites are $8. Utah seniors with a Special Fun Tag get a $2 discount on Sundays through Thursdays, excluding holidays.

*Contact:* Call (801) 654-3961.

*Location:* From Provo, drive east up Provo Canyon on U.S. 189 and take the Sundance turnoff. Take State Route 92 approximately six miles, then turn east toward Cascade Springs on Forest Road 114. Stay on that road, which takes a turn past Cascade Springs and then heads north, approximately eight miles, following the signs to Deer Creek.

*Trip notes:* This remote campground, although part of Wasatch Mountain State Park, is 17 miles southwest of the park's other campgrounds and its golf course. Yet it's not too far from Cascade Springs—a beautiful natural preserve with boardwalks, interpretive signs, bubbling pools and waterfalls, and spring-fed ponds full of trout (but no fishing is allowed). Located on Forest Road 114 approximately five miles south of the campground, it's a must-see and a special treat for families.

*Season:* April through November.

---

## 118. HEBER VALLEY RV PARK

*Reference:* **Next to the Jordanelle Reservoir; map A2, grid g5.**

*Campsites, facilities:* There are 34 sites with full RV hookups, 66 sites with water and electricity, and some tent sites and cabins.

*Reservations, fee:* Reservations are accepted. Sites with full hookups are $16.95, sites for RVs with no hookups are $12.95, sites with water and electricity are $14.95, and tent sites are $10.95.

*Contact:* Call the campground at (801) 654-4049.

*Location:* From Salt Lake City, take Interstate 80 east, turn off on U.S. Route 40, and go past the Jordanelle Dam. Take State Route 32 toward Francis about .4 miles, turn left on a dead-end road, and proceed 2.1 miles to the campground. The campground is 12 miles from the Kamas–Park City interchange.

*Trip notes:* This mostly RV campground is in a wonderfully scenic, remote spot, right below the dam holding back Jordanelle Reservoir. The terrain is spacious and open, with young trees and new facilities. And while the sites are close together, the place is not always full, so campers aren't so apt to feel crowded. Trout fishing is great on the Provo River and Jordanelle Reservoir.

*Season:* Open year-round.

---

## 119. WOLF CREEK

*Reference:* **In Uinta National Forest; map A2, grid g6.**

*Campsites, facilities:* There are three single-family and three group sites, with picnic tables, fire pits, drinking water, and vault toilets.

*Reservations, fee:* No reservations are accepted for the single-family units. Sites are $11.

*Contact:* Call the Heber Ranger District at (801) 342-5200.

*Location:* From Woodland, take State Route 35 east for 13 miles to reach the campground.

*Trip notes:* The big attractions here are the quiet and the scenery: a forested setting next to a dirt road at an elevation of 9,000 feet. There's also plenty of

---

fishing nearby on the North Fork of the Duchesne River and the Mill Hollow Reservoir. This is a beautiful area for an autumn drive.

*Season:* Late May through September.

## 120. MILL HOLLOW

*Reference:* **In the Uinta National Forest; map A2, grid g6.**

*Campsites, facilities:* There are 25 sites with picnic tables and fire pits; drinking water and vault toilets are available.

*Reservations, fee:* Sites are $11 and are first come, first served.

*Contact:* Call the Heber Ranger District at (801) 342-5200.

*Location:* From Woodland, drive 12 miles southeast on State Route 35, then turn south on Forest Road 504 and look for the sign to the campground.

*Trip notes:* Many come to this pine-shaded area to fish on the small reservoir at the campground's edge. Whether from shore, a raft, or a canoe, the rainbow trout (regularly stocked by the Utah Division of Wildlife Resources) are catchable through most of the summer. With an elevation of 8,800 feet, the nights can be cool.

*Season:* June through September.

## 121. AMERICAN CAMPGROUND

*Reference:* **In American Fork; map A2, grid g4.**

*Campsites, facilities:* There are 53 RV sites, most of them occupied by year-round residents, with 12 reserved for overnighters. Full hookups, rest rooms, showers, laundry facilities, RV disposal, picnic tables, and a public phone are available. Pets are welcome.

*Reservations, fee:* Reservations are accepted. Sites are $16.

*Contact:* American Campground, 418 East 620 South, American Fork, UT 84003; (801) 756-5502.

*Location:* From Provo, go north three miles on Interstate 15 and take exit 279 to Pleasant Grove. Take the first road to the left over the freeway, and turn left at the sign to the campground.

*Trip notes:* This campground is on gravel with small grass strips. But campers are shaded by tall cottonwoods, and there are pleasing touches such as flowers planted around the trees. The sites are close together and bordered by a field on one side and storage units on the other.

*Season:* Open year-round.

## 122. UTAH LAKE STATE PARK

*Reference:* **On Utah Lake; map A2, grid h3.**

*Campsites, facilities:* There are 71 sites with no hookups. Facilities include handicapped-accessible rest rooms, showers, a fish-cleaning station, a dump station, four boat-launching ramps, a marina, and a visitors center. The fishing pier is also handicapped accessible.

*Reservations, fee:* Reservations are available 120 days in advance for a nonrefundable $5 per site; call (800) 322-3770 Monday through Friday from

8 A.M. to 5 P.M. Sites are $10. Utah residents 62 years and older with a Special Fun Tag get a $2 discount Sunday through Thursday, excluding holidays.
*Contact:* Call the campground at (801) 375-0731.
*Location:* From Interstate 15 in Provo, take the West Center Street exit and drive five miles west to the campground.
*Trip notes:* For a campground next to a big city, this one has a surprisingly quiet feel. Many of the tree-shaded sites are grassy, and most are set along the Provo River. A short walk from the premises, anglers can fish the river for white bass and walleye. There's even an Olympic-sized ice rink next to the visitors center (though it's only open in winter). The state park provides access to 96,000-acre Utah Lake, which, while muddy and turbid enough to deter all but the hardiest swimmers or water-skiers, makes a good early-season boating spot.
*Season:* Open year-round.

## 123. HOPE

*Reference:* In Uinta National Forest; map A2, grid h4.
*Campsites, facilities:* There are 24 sites with picnic tables and fire grills. Drinking water and vault toilets are available.
*Reservations, fee:* Sites are $7 and are first come, first served.
*Contact:* Call the Pleasant Grove Ranger District at (801) 785-3563.
*Location:* From Orem, head east on U.S. 189 toward Provo Canyon for about two miles. Right after entering the mouth of the canyon, look for Squaw Creek Road, or Forest Road 027. Drive five miles south on this dirt road, which climbs quickly above the canyon.
*Trip notes:* One of the only public campgrounds in Provo Canyon, this scenic little spot called Hope (elevation 6,600) in Uinta National Forest offers visitors hiking on Squaw Peak and an overnight stopping place for anglers looking to try their luck in the popular Provo River. Families enjoy visiting nearby Bridal Veil Falls, where water cascades several hundred feet off the canyon walls.
*Season:* June through September.

## 124. LAKESIDE CAMPGROUND

*Reference:* In Provo; map A2, grid h4.
*Campsites, facilities:* There are 148 sites with full hookups and 12 sites for tents, with rest rooms, showers, laundry facilities, an RV disposal site, picnic tables, a game room, a swimming pool, a public phone, a convenience and gift store, a playground, a volleyball and a basketball court, and a horseshoe pit.
*Reservations, fee:* Reservations are suggested between June and October. Sites are $18 with full hookups, $15 with water and electricity, and $13 for tents, plus $2 for each additional person in groups of more than two.
*Contact:* Lakeside Campground, 4000 West Center Street, Provo, UT 84601; (801) 373-5267.

*Location:* In Provo, take Interstate 15 and get off at exit 258. Go west for two miles on Center Street to the campground at 4000 West Center Street.

*Trip notes:* This campground, next to the entrance to Utah Lake State Park, is a cut above the usual, with new facilities, attractive landscaping, and well-shaded, grassy sites. Even better, it sits in front of majestic Mount Timpanogos. And nearby Utah Lake is popular with anglers and boaters.

*Season:* Open year-round.

## 125. PROVO KOA

*Reference:* In Provo; map A2, grid h4.

*Campsites, facilities:* There are 95 sites; 45 have full hookups, 20 have water and electricity, and 30 are for tents. Amenities include rest rooms, showers, laundry facilities, RV disposal, picnic tables, a swimming pool, and a playground for the kids.

*Reservations, fee:* Reservations are accepted. Sites are $21 with full hookups, $19.50 with water and electricity, and $15.50 for tents.

*Contact:* Provo KOA Campground, 2050 West 320 North, Provo, UT 84601; (801) 375-2994.

*Location:* From Provo, take Interstate 15 and get off at exit 268. Go west on Center Street for about one mile to 2050 West. Turn right and go to 320 North. The campground is on the right side of the street at 2050 West 320 North.

*Trip notes:* The appeal of this semiurban campground, located two miles from boating and water sports at Utah Lake State Park, is its proximity to the Provo River Parkway, a riverside jogging and hiking path. The campground itself is in a residential area, but the vegetation provides privacy and some noise buffering. The road and sites are gravel and shaded by tall trees, and there's a grassy area for tents.

*Season:* Open year-round.

## 126. FRAZIER TRAILER PARK

*Reference:* In Provo Canyon near Provo; map A2, grid i4.

*Campsites, facilities:* There are 40 sites; eight have full hookups, 30 have water and electricity, and two are for tents. Amenities include a half-court for basketball and a jungle gym.

*Reservations, fee:* Reservations are recommended; call (801) 225-5346. Campsites are $15.

*Contact:* Frazier Trailer Park, 3362 East Provo Canyon Road, Provo, UT 84604; (801) 225-5346.

*Location:* From Provo, take U.S. 189 and travel up Provo Canyon for about five miles, to the point where the highway narrows into two lanes. The campground is on the right side of the highway.

*Trip notes:* Provo Canyon is a narrow canyon, with the campgrounds, river, and highway sometimes squeezed all together in one small space. At this shaded trailer park, the sites themselves are close together and situated on gravel, giving the feeling of being in a parking lot; some RV sites are right next to the highway. The canyon itself, however, is indisputably scenic, and the Provo River is famous for its fly-fishing. Kayak and tube rentals are available nearby, and just a quarter mile down the canyon is the historic Heber Creeper, a steam engine that takes tourists on a panoramic ride up the canyon to Heber Valley and back.

*Season:* March 20 through November 1.

## 127. DEER CREEK PARK

*Reference:* **In Provo Canyon near Provo; map A2, grid h4.**

*Campsites, facilities:* There are 100 sites, 65 with full hookups, plus a grassy area for tents. Amenities include chemical toilets, showers, picnic tables, barbecue grills, a public phone, and a small shop for snacks, firewood, and ice. Dogs are allowed on a leash.

*Reservations, fee:* Reservations are recommended on summer holidays. Sites with full hookups are $14.15; all others are $12.

*Contact:* Deer Creek Park, Rural Route 3 Box 620, Provo, UT 84604; (801) 225-9783.

*Location:* From Provo, take U.S. 189 north and travel up Provo Canyon 10 miles. The campground is right past Bridal Veil Falls and the turnoff to Sundance, in front of the Deer Creek Reservoir dam.

*Trip notes:* Set off the road a ways (a nice plus in such a narrow canyon), this campground offers great views of Mount Timpanogos, and decent, plentiful fishing on the Provo River. Deer Creek Reservoir is another popular place to fish as well as water-ski, and the fairly constant breeze makes it a favorite with sailors and windsurfers, too.

*Season:* May through September.

## 128. RIVER BEND TRAILER PARK

*Reference:* **In Provo Canyon near Orem; map A2, grid h5.**

*Campsites, facilities:* There are 13 overnight RV sites in a mostly residential summer RV park.

*Reservations, fee:* Reservations are accepted. Call the campground for fee information.

*Contact:* Call the RV park at (801) 225-1863.

*Location:* From Orem, take U.S. 189 up Provo Canyon to Bridal Veil Falls and continue for another two miles. The campground is on the north side of the canyon.

*Trip notes:* As with most Provo Canyon campgrounds, River Bend Trailer Park is squeezed in between the highway and river and the canyon walls. Set slightly off the highway in the trees, it has a paved road and paved sites that are terraced up the mountainside. The campground is also right across the street from the Vivian Park Cafe and the station for the Heber Creeper, the historical steam engine that takes tourists up the canyon into the Heber Valley and back—a spectacular trip to take in the fall. Anglers can try their luck at fly-fishing in the Provo River.

*Season:* April 15 through October 15.

# 129. LODGEPOLE

*Reference:* **In Daniels Canyon; map A2, grid h6.**

*Campsites, facilities:* There are 50 sites with picnic tables and fire pits, flush toilets, a dump station, and some wheelchair-accessible facilities.

*Reservations, fee:* Reservations are available for 25 sites; call the U.S. Forest Service National Reservation System at (800) 280-2267. Sites are $11.

*Contact:* Call the Heber Ranger District at (801) 342-5200.

*Location:* From Heber City, drive 16 miles southeast on U.S. 40 to the campground, which is on the west side of the road.

*Trip notes:* This is the kind of pretty canyon campground that can easily be overlooked by campers looking to be close to a lake. It's located at the bottom of Daniels Canyon at an elevation of 7,800 feet in a grove of aspen and pine. The paved loops lead to private sites tucked away in the trees. Anglers, in particular, appreciate the tranquil beauty of nearby Strawberry and Deer Creek Reservoirs. Though the place isn't fully wheelchair accessible, some sites and rest rooms have been modified to accommodate people with disabilities.

*Season:* June through October.

---

# 130. CURRANT CREEK

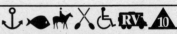

*Reference:* **Near Currant Creek Reservoir; map A2, grid h7.**

*Campsites, facilities:* There are 99 sites with picnic tables and fire grills, wheelchair-accessible rest rooms with flush toilets, a wheelchair-accessible fishing pier over the reservoir, a playground, running water, a boat ramp, a fish-cleaning station, and a dump station.

*Reservations, fee:* For reservations, call the U.S. Forest Service National Reservation System at (800) 280-2267. Sites are $11.

*Contact:* Call the Heber Ranger District at (801) 342-5200.

*Location:* From Heber City, drive 41 miles southeast on U.S. 40 to the Currant Creek Lodge, then 20 miles north on a rough dirt road around the reservoir. The campground is on the southwest side of the reservoir.

*Trip notes:* Few U.S. Forest Service campgrounds in Utah offer such extensive amenities, including some of the best facilities for the disabled in the state. Children like the western-themed tot lot, and Loop C, with its horse-unloading ramps, feeding troughs, and corrals, was clearly designed with riders in mind. Trout fishing on the reservoir can be excellent, though anglers shouldn't ignore the creek below the dam. The campground is tucked away amid the quaking aspens, with the paved sites spaced a nice distance apart.

*Season:* May 25 through October 31.

---

# 131. STRAWBERRY BAY

*Reference:* **On Strawberry Reservoir; map A2, grid h7.**

*Campsites, facilities:* There are 249 single-family sites without hookups, 26 sites (on Loop B) with hookups, and a few group sites, plus wheelchair-accessible rest rooms, sheltered picnic tables and fire grills, a day-use shelter,

---

fish-cleaning stations, a full-service marina with gasoline and boat rentals, a dump station, and a boat ramp.

*Reservations, fee:* Reservations are available through the U.S. Forest Service National Reservation System at (800) 280-2267. Sites are $11 for single or large families and $17 with full hookups. Group sites vary.

*Contact:* Call the Heber Ranger District at (801) 342-5200.

*Location:* From Heber, drive 23 miles southeast on U.S. Highway 40, then approximately five miles on Forest Road 131. Look for signs for the marina and campground. A small entrance station signals the start of the forest facilities.

*Trip notes:* This huge, modern facility is the hub of activity at Utah's most popular trout-fishing spot. Many of the paved sites, set largely in sagebrush-covered, open terrain, have views of the nearby Strawberry Reservoir. Sheltered picnic tables come in handy as wind and sun breaks. The marina store offers boat rentals, groceries, motel units, and a small cafe, making this an ideal spot for both boaters and anglers. At an elevation of 7,700 feet, the campground usually opens when the ice leaves the reservoir and closes when the snow flies.

*Season:* May through mid-to-late October.

---

## 132. RENEGADE POINT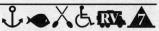

*Reference:* **On Strawberry Reservoir; map A2, grid i7.**

*Campsites, facilities:* There are 66 sites, plus picnic tables, fire grills, flush toilets, and drinking water. The rest rooms are handicapped accessible.

*Reservations, fee:* Sites are $11 and are first come, first served.

*Contact:* Call the Heber Ranger District at (801) 342-5200.

*Location:* Drive 23 miles southeast of Heber City on U.S. 40 and then south on Forest Road 131 about eight miles to the campground.

*Trip notes:* Anglers come to this place to pursue lunker, rainbow, and cutthroat trout in the shallower Meadows area of Strawberry Reservoir. There's a boat ramp in the area and some shore fishing as well. Renegade Point campground itself is a little more rustic and out-of-the-way than some Strawberry facilities.

*Season:* May 25 through October 31.

---

## 133. SOLDIER CREEK

*Reference:* **On Strawberry Reservoir; map A2, grid h7.**

*Campsites, facilities:* There are 163 sites with no hookups. Facilities include picnic tables, fire grills, handicapped-accessible rest rooms with flush toilets, drinking water, a small marina, a boat ramp, a fish-cleaning station, a covered group-use area, and a dump station.

*Reservations, fee:* For reservations, call the U.S. Forest Service National Reservation System at (800) 280-2267. Fees are $11.

*Contact:* Call the Heber Ranger District at (801) 342-5200.

*Location:* Drive 33 miles southeast of Heber City on U.S. 40, then turn south on Forest Road 480 and go 3.5 miles to the campground.

---

*Trip notes:* Strawberry Reservoir is one of the premier trout-fishing areas in the United States, regularly yielding cutthroat and rainbows up to 10 pounds. And this campground, located on a bay in the newer portion of the expanded reservoir, primarily caters to anglers. The property is paved, in somewhat open terrain, with a few picnic shelters. At an elevation of 7,600 feet, these are cooler waters, so water-skiers should consider pulling on their wet suits before taking off.

*Season:* May 25 through October 31.

## 134. ASPEN GROVE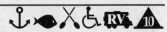

*Reference:* **On Strawberry Reservoir; map A2, grid i8.**

*Campsites, facilities:* There are 60 sites with no hookups. Facilities include picnic tables, fire grills, handicapped-accessible rest rooms with flush toilets, drinking water, and a nearby boat ramp.

*Reservations, fee:* Sites are $11 and are first come, first served.

*Contact:* Call the Heber Ranger District at (801) 342-5200.

*Location:* Drive 34 miles southeast of Heber City on U.S. 40 to Forest Road 482, then drive about seven miles on Road 482, past the Strawberry Dam to the campground.

*Trip notes:* Aspen Grove is the most remote, shaded, and scenic of the many campgrounds surrounding huge Strawberry Reservoir. The paved loops at the edge of a high-elevation alpine forest make it a popular weekend retreat during the summer, especially for anglers, boaters, and other water enthusiasts. While the fishing on the reservoir is fantastic, fly fishers shouldn't ignore the Strawberry River below the dam, one of Utah's few blue-ribbon trout streams.

*Season:* May 25 through October 31.

## 135. WHITING

*Reference:* **In Uinta National Forest; map A2, grid i5.**

*Campsites, facilities:* There are 16 sites for families, three sites for equestrians, and six double-family sites. Picnic tables, fire pits, flush toilets, drinking water, and equestrian facilities are available.

*Reservations, fee:* For reservations, call the U.S. Forest Service National Reservation System at (800) 280-2267. Single-family and horse sites are $11 and double-family sites are $22.

*Contact:* Call the Spanish Fork Ranger District at (801) 798-3571.

*Location:* To reach the campground, drive two miles east of the Utah County town of Mapleton on Forest Road 025.

*Trip notes:* This relatively small campground is in a timbered setting, with access to some nice forest hiking trails and a small, fishable stream. At an elevation of 5,400 feet, the place features some especially splendid views in the fall. Whiting is also popular with equestrians who ride on the extensive nearby trail system; three campsites are designed specifically for horse owners.

*Season:* May through October.

# 136. CHERRY

*Reference:* **In Hobble Creek Canyon; map A2, grid i5.**

*Campsites, facilities:* There are 10 single-family, four double-family, and four group sites, with drinking water, picnic tables, fire pits, and handicapped-accessible rest rooms with flush toilets.

*Reservations, fee:* For reservations, call (800) 280-2267. Fees are $11 for single-family sites and $22 for double sites.

*Contact:* Call the Spanish Fork Ranger District at (801) 798-3571.

*Location:* From Springville, drive east on State Route 79, which turns into Forest Road 058. The campground is 8.3 miles up the canyon from Springville on the south side of the road.

*Trip notes:* Though many campers like to fish the stream running through this beautiful forested canyon, the real draw is the nearby Hobble Creek Golf Course, one of Utah's more scenic links. The Springville Art Museum, one of the state's oldest visual arts centers, is also worth checking out. And with oaks and aspens so plentiful in the canyon, this is a great place to view the changing autumn leaves. The elevation of 5,200 feet means it stays fairly warm here late into the year.

*Season:* May 21 through October 31.

---

# 137. BALSAM

*Reference:* **In Hobble Creek Canyon; map A2, grid i5.**

*Campsites, facilities:* There are 24 single-family sites, one triple-family site, and one group site; amenities include picnic tables, fire grills, flush toilets, and drinking water.

*Reservations, fee:* For reservations, call the U.S. Forest Service National Reservation System at (800) 280-2267. Fees are $11 for single-family sites and $33 for the triple-family site; group prices vary.

*Contact:* Call the Spanish Fork Ranger District at (801) 798-3571.

*Location:* From Springville, head east on State Route 79, which turns into Forest Road 058. The campground is 13.1 miles up the canyon from Springville on the south side of the road.

*Trip notes:* Located at the end of a paved road in a gorgeous canyon setting, this remote campground is especially scenic in the fall. A small stream offers plenty of fishing, hiking trails are nearby, and there's golfing down the canyon at Hobble Creek Golf Course.

*Season:* May 25 through October 31.

---

# 138. PALMYRA

*Reference:* **In Diamond Fork Canyon; map A2, grid i5.**

*Campsites, facilities:* There are 11 single-family and four group sites, plus picnic tables, fire grills, drinking water, and vault toilets.

*Reservations, fee:* For reservations, call the U.S. Forest Service National Reservation System at (800) 280-2267. Sites are $6 for single-family sites; group prices vary.

---

*Contact:* Call the Spanish Fork Ranger District at (801) 798-3571.

*Location:* From Spanish Fork, drive 10 miles east on U.S. Highway 6 into Spanish Fork Canyon, and look for Diamond Fork Road, which heads north and east. The campground is five miles up that road on the east side.

*Trip notes:* Located off to the wayside, scenic Diamond Fork Canyon is often overlooked by the thousands of motorists visiting Spanish Fork Canyon each year. Yet this is a wonderfully quiet, shaded retreat next to a stream. Unfortunately, high stream flows can make fishing somewhat difficult. Check with the Spanish Fork Ranger District for information on the many excellent hiking trails in the area. And don't forget to watch for the wild turkeys that roam the canyon.

*Season:* May 15 through October 31.

## 139. DIAMOND

*Reference:* **In Diamond Fork Canyon; map A2, grid i5.**

*Campsites, facilities:* There are 32 single-family and three double-family sites with picnic tables, fire grills, drinking water, and vault toilets.

*Reservations, fee:* Fees are $6 for single-family and $12 for double-family sites. Campsites are first come, first served.

*Contact:* Call the Spanish Fork Ranger District at (801) 798-3571.

*Location:* From Spanish Fork, drive 10 miles east on U.S. Highway 6 into Spanish Fork Canyon, looking for Diamond Fork Road, which heads north and east. The campground is six miles up that road on the east side.

*Trip notes:* Located in a fairly open setting at an elevation of 5,200 feet, Diamond campground has a small stream that offers decent fishing at times. And if you don't manage to catch any fish, you're almost certain to catch glimpses of the abundant local wildlife, including turkeys, elk, deer, and even cougar and bear.

*Season:* May through October.

## 140. MAPLE BENCH

*Reference:* **In Payson Canyon; map A2, grid i3.**

*Campsites, facilities:* There are 10 sites with picnic tables and fire grills. Flush toilets and drinking water are available.

*Reservations, fee:* Sites are $7 and are first come, first served.

*Contact:* Call the Spanish Fork Ranger District at (801) 798-3571.

*Location:* From Payson, drive five miles south on Nebo Scenic Loop Road. The campground is on the west side of the road.

*Trip notes:* This small campground just off the road often serves as an overflow area when nearby campgrounds fill up early. Located close to a small reservoir that's frequently stocked with catchable trout, Maple Bench is a favorite with canoeing and rafting enthusiasts. The elevation is 5,800 feet and the setting is fairly open, with hiking trails leading out from the campground into the nearby forest. Horseback riding trails meander through the area as well.

*Season:* May through October.

# 141. PAYSON LAKES

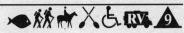

*Reference:* **In Payson Canyon; map A2, grid i4.**

*Campsites, facilities:* There are 82 single-family sites, 10 double-family sites, and three group sites, plus picnic tables and fire grills, drinking water, flush toilets, a paved trail around the lake, and a grassy area nearby. Some sites are wheelchair accessible.

*Reservations, fee:* Reservations are available for group sites, 26 of the single-family sites, and four of the double-family sites; call the U.S. Forest Service National Reservation System at (800) 280-2267. Fees are $11 for single-family and $22 for double-family sites. Group prices vary.

*Contact:* Call the Spanish Fork Ranger Station at (801) 798-3571.

*Location:* Drive 12 miles south of Payson on Nebo Scenic Loop Road, then turn southwest and follow the signs to the lake.

*Trip notes:* Long a favorite with Utah County residents, this fine National Forest Service campground (elevation 8,000) has a lot to offer. The paved spurs are nice, but the surroundings are even nicer: visitors enjoy fishing for trout on the small but well-stocked lake, strolling on the pavement near the water, or driving along Nebo Scenic Loop Road, with its views of towering Mount Nebo in the distance. Horseback riding trails are nearby.

*Season:* June through October.

# 142. TINNEY FLAT

*Reference:* **In Santaquin Canyon; map A2, grid j3.**

*Campsites, facilities:* There are 12 single-family sites, two double-family sites, and three group sites, plus picnic tables, fire grills, drinking water, and flush toilets.

*Reservations, fee:* For reservations, call the U.S. Forest Service National Reservation System at (800) 280-2267. Fees are $11 for single-family sites and $22 for double-family sites. Group prices vary.

*Contact:* Call the Spanish Fork Ranger District at (801) 798-3571.

*Location:* Driving south from Provo, take exit 248 (the Santaquin exit) and head east on Forest Road 014. The campground is nine miles east of the town of Santaquin.

*Trip notes:* Less crowded than nearby Payson Lakes campground (see above), this campground is set in an excellent side canyon that is great for exploring in the fall. A trailhead at the campground leads to the adjacent Mount Nebo Wilderness Area, popular with hikers and horseback riders, and the main road connects to Nebo Scenic Loop Road. There's a small fishable stream, and the sites are shielded by shade trees.

*Season:* June through October.

# 143. BLACKHAWK

*Reference:* **Near Payson; map A2, grid j4.**

*Campsites, facilities:* Sites are designed for horse owners. There are 12 single-family sites, three double-family sites, and three group sites, with picnic tables, fire grills, drinking water, toilets, and facilities for holding and unloading horses. The rest rooms are handicapped accessible.

*Reservations, fee:* For reservations, call the U.S. Forest Service National Reservation System at (800) 280-2267. Sites are $11 for single units and $22 for double units.

*Contact:* Call the Spanish Fork Ranger District at (801) 798-3571.

*Location:* From Payson, drive 16 miles south on Nebo Loop Scenic Road. The campground is about two miles south of the main road on Forest Road 175.

*Trip notes:* The former forest supervisor who helped design this relatively new campground was a horseback rider, and it shows. With cribs, unloading docks, and overnight holding space for horses, this is an ideal place for equestrians looking to explore the nearby woods and mountains of the Uinta National Forest. Blackhawk campground itself is at an elevation of 7,100 feet. Check with the Spanish Fork Ranger District for suggestions on trail rides in the surrounding area.

*Season:* June through October.

## 144. MOUNTAIN VIEW

*Reference:* **In Scofield State Park; map A2, grid j6.**

*Campsites, facilities:* There are 34 sites, plus picnic tables, fire grills, showers, handicapped-accessible rest rooms, a fish-cleaning station, a boat ramp, and a dump station.

*Reservations, fee:* Reservations are available 120 days in advance for a nonrefundable $5 per site; call (800) 322-3770 Monday through Friday from 8 A.M. to 5 P.M. Sites are $10. Utah residents 62 years and older with a Special Fun Tag get a $2 discount Sunday through Thursday, excluding holidays.

*Contact:* Call Scofield State Park at (801) 448-9449.

*Location:* From Spanish Fork, drive east on U.S. Highway 6, passing the tiny hamlet of Soldier Summit. Then drive 13 miles south on State Route 96 to the campground.

*Trip notes:* Though surrounded by forest, Scofield Reservoir is somewhat devoid of shade. The campground, located near the dam at an elevation of 7,600 feet, features grassy sites with paved parking areas terraced on the reservoir banks. Though this can be a good waterskiing spot, fishing for rainbow trout is the main attraction.

*Season:* May 15 through September 15.

## 145. MADSEN BAY

*Reference:* **On Scofield Reservoir; map A2, grid j6.**

*Campsites, facilities:* There are 37 sites, plus picnic tables, grills, modern rest rooms, a dump station, a boat ramp, and a group-use pavilion.

*Reservations, fee:* Reservations are available 120 days in advance for a nonrefundable $5 per site; call (800) 322-3770 Monday through Friday from 8 A.M. to 5 P.M. Sites are $8. Utah residents 62 years and older with a Special Fun Tag get a $2 discount Sunday through Thursday, excluding holidays.

*Contact:* Call Scofield State Park at (801) 448-9449.

*Location:* Drive east on U.S. Highway 6 from Spanish Fork until you pass the small hamlet of Soldier Summit. Look for the signs to Scofield Reservoir. Drive 13 miles south on State Route 96 to the campground.

*Trip notes:* The group-use pavilion makes this a popular local family reunion spot. The campground is located on the north end of Scofield Reservoir in a fairly open setting. Fishing for rainbow trout at the reservoir and fly-fishing on nearby streams can be excellent.

*Season:* May 15 through September 15.

## 146. GOOSEBERRY

*Reference:* In Manti–La Sal National Forest; map A2, grid j5.

*Campsites, facilities:* There are 10 sites, plus picnic tables, fire grills, vault toilets, and drinking water.

*Reservations, fee:* Sites are $5 and are first come, first served.

*Contact:* Call the Price Ranger District at (801) 637-2817.

*Location:* From the town of Fairview, drive east on State Route 31 about seven miles, looking for Forest Road 51. Travel north on that road and then slightly east for another two miles to the campground.

*Trip notes:* This campground offers some excellent fishing in the small stream running through it and at nearby Lower Gooseberry Reservoir. It's located in somewhat open country at an elevation of 8,600 feet, affording beautiful views of the surrounding mountain areas.

*Season:* June through September.

## 147. FLAT CANYON

*Reference:* On Boulger Reservoir; map A2, grid j6.

*Campsites, facilities:* There are 12 sites with no hookups. Picnic tables, fire grills, drinking water, and vault toilets are available.

*Reservations, fee:* Sites are $6 and are first come, first served.

*Contact:* Call the Price Ranger District at (801) 637-2817.

*Location:* From Fairview, take State Route 31 east for approximately six miles. Turn south and west on State Route 264 (Forest Road 057) to the campground, which is on the west side of the road.

*Trip notes:* This pretty little spot is in a wooded area at an elevation of 8,900 feet, a stone's throw from Boulger Reservoir. Though small, the reservoir is regularly stocked with catchable rainbow trout.

*Season:* May 15 through September 15.

## 148. OLD FOLKS FLAT

*Reference:* In Manti–La Sal National Forest; map A2, grid j7.

*Campsites, facilities:* There are nine sites, plus picnic tables, fire grills, drinking water, and handicapped-accessible toilets.

*Reservations, fee:* Sites are $6 and are first come, first served.

*Contact:* Call the Ferron Ranger District at (801) 384-2372.

*Location:* From Huntington, drive 21 miles northwest on State Route 31 to the campground, which is on the east side of the road.

*Trip notes:* This is one of the closest campgrounds to Electric Lake and Miller Flat Reservoir. Fly fishers especially like nearby Huntington Creek, one of the better fishing rivers in the area. Located in an alpine setting next to a paved road at an elevation of 8,100 feet, the campground is easily accessible and not too far from Skyline Drive, a popular four-wheel-drive scenic route in the fall.

*Season:* June 1 through September 15.

## 149. FORKS OF THE HUNTINGTON

*Reference:* **In Manti–La Sal National Forest; map A2, grid j6.**

*Campsites, facilities:* There are six sites, plus vault toilets, picnic tables, and fire pits, but *no water.*

*Reservations, fee:* Sites are $5 and are first come, first served.

*Contact:* Call the Ferron Ranger District at (801) 384-2372.

*Location:* Drive 18 miles northwest of Huntington on State Route 31 to the campground, which is on the west side of the road.

*Trip notes:* This small retreat is popular with locals for the superb alpine scenery, the fishing at Huntington Creek and nearby Electric Lake, and the easy paved access. The campground sits at an elevation of 7,700 feet.

*Season:* June through September.

## 150. INDIAN CREEK

*Reference:* **In Fishlake National Forest; map A2, grid j6.**

*Campsites, facilities:* There are 29 sites, plus picnic tables, fire grills, drinking water, and flush toilets.

*Reservations, fee:* Sites are $5 and are first come, first served.

*Contact:* Call the Ferron Ranger District at (801) 384-2372.

*Location:* From Orangeville, travel eight miles on State Route 29, looking for a road that heads north near a gravel pit. That road turns into Forest Road 40, which leads 11 miles to the campground.

*Trip notes:* At an elevation of 8,000 feet, this remote campground is in a timbered setting with a small, fishable creek. Its out-of-the-way location recommends it as a place to beat the big crowds. Alert campers can spot a more-than-occasional elk or mule deer in the area.

*Season:* June through September.

## 151. PRICE CANYON RECREATION AREA

*Reference:* **On Bureau of Land Management property near Price; map A2, grid j7.**

*Campsites, facilities:* There are 18 sites and one group site with picnic tables, fire grills, drinking water, vault toilets, and a nature trail nearby.

*Reservations, fee:* Reservations are accepted only for the group site. Campsites are $6.

*Contact:* Call the Bureau of Land Management at (801) 637-4584.

*Location:* Drive 15 miles north of Price on U.S. 6/50, then three miles west on a well-marked paved Bureau of Land Management road into Price Canyon.

*Trip notes:* Shaded by large ponderosa pines, this campground is a popular place to beat the heat. Nature lovers will appreciate the nearby short and easy Bristlecone Ridge Hiking and Nature Trail, which offers fascinating information on local flora and fauna, along with excellent vistas of the surrounding area.

*Season:* June through October.

---

# 152. NEPHI KOA

*Reference:* **East of Nephi; map A2, grid j2.**

*Campsites, facilities:* There are 87 sites; 28 have full hookups, 39 have water and electricity, and 20 are for tents. Cabins are also available. Amenities include picnic tables, barbecue grills, rest rooms, showers, laundry facilities, an RV disposal site, a game room, a public phone, a convenience/gift store, and a playground. Pets are allowed on a leash.

*Reservations, fee:* Reservations are strongly recommended. Sites are $19 with full hookups, $18 with water and electricity, and $14.50 for tents. Cabins are $26. Groups of more than two pay an additional $2.50 for each extra child over four and $3.50 for each extra adult over 18.

*Contact:* Nephi KOA, P.O. Box 309, Nephi, UT 84648; (801) 623-0811.

*Location:* From Provo, go south on Interstate 15 and take exit 225. Then follow State Route 132 east up Salt Creek Canyon for five miles to reach the campground.

*Trip notes:* This isolated spot high in a scenic canyon has lots of trees and grass to recommend it, along with the more dramatic attractions of the Uinta National Forest four miles away. Anglers can try their luck with the trout in smallish Salt Creek, which runs past the campground. For golfers, there's a city-owned course in Nephi.

*Season:* May 15 through October 1.

---

# 153. CHICKEN CREEK

*Reference:* **In Manti–La Sal National Forest; map A2, grid j3.**

*Campsites, facilities:* There are eight sites, plus picnic tables, fire grills, drinking water, and vault toilets.

*Reservations, fee:* Sites are $5 and are first come, first served.

*Contact:* Call the Sanpete Ranger District at (801) 283-4151.

*Location:* From Salt Lake City, take Interstate 15 south for 90 miles, exit at Nephi, and follow State Route 28 to Levan. From Levan, travel six miles to the east on Chicken Creek Canyon Road to the campground.

*Trip notes:* Before reaching the campground itself, anglers can find a nice, deep pond, regularly stocked with rainbow trout, behind a small dam. There's also pretty respectable fishing in Chicken Creek itself, which flows nearby. Located in a timbered setting, the campground is remote and quiet. Consider taking the road that heads east from the campground over the San Pitch Mountains into Sanpete County, for the spectacular views of the Wasatch Plateau to the east and the valley below.

*Season:* June 1 through September 10.

---

# 154. MAPLE CANYON

*Reference:* **In Manti–La Sal National Forest; map A2, grid j3.**

*Campsites, facilities:* There are 12 sites, plus picnic tables, fire grills, and vault toilets, but *no drinking water.*

*Reservations, fee:* Sites are $5 and are first come, first served.

*Contact:* Call the Sanpete Ranger District at (801) 283-4151.

*Location:* From Nephi, drive south and east on State Route 132 to Fountain Green. Look for State Route 30 and follow it south about 5.5 miles to the town of Freedom. Take a winding road north and east into Maple Canyon about three miles.

*Trip notes:* This is a fantastic spot in the fall when the canyon's eponymous maples begin to change. The campground is remote but extremely pretty, with large rocks sheltering the sites. A short hiking trail leads into some geologically interesting scenery in the canyon.

*Season:* June 1 through September 10.

## LEAVE NO TRACE TIPS

### Keep the wilderness wild.

• Treat our natural heritage with respect.
Leave plants, rocks, and historical artifacts as you found them.

• Good campsites are found, not made. Do not alter a campsite.

• Let nature's sounds prevail; keep loud voices and noises to a minimum.

• Do not build structures or furniture or dig trenches.

**MAP A3**

Map of Utah ........................ see page 46

Beyond This Region:

North ............................................ Idaho

East .......................................... Colorado

56 Campgrounds    South (Map B1) .............. see page 150

Pages 124–149    West (Map A2) ................... see page 56

| | Utah |
|---|---|
| A1 | A2 | A3 |
| B1 | B2 | B3 |

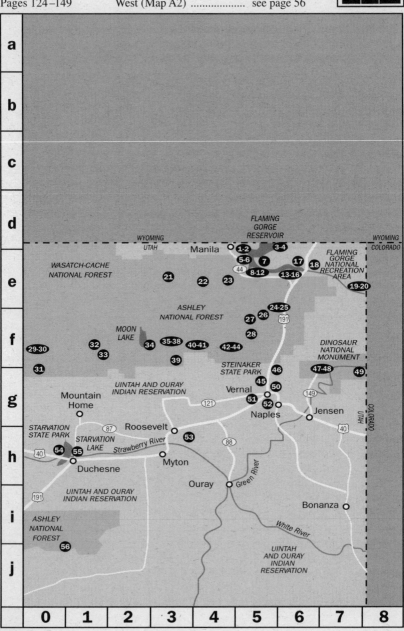

**Chapter A3 features:**

1. Vernal KOA
2. Carmel
3. Lucerne Valley
4. Gravel Pit/Stateline/Swim Beach
5. Kingfisher Island
6. Hideout Canyon
7. Antelope Flat
8. Canyon Rim
9. Gooseneck
10. Greens Lake
11. Skull Creek
12. Greendale West
13. Firefighters Memorial
14. Cedar Springs
15. Deer Run
16. Mustang Ridge
17. Jarvies Canyon
18. Dripping Springs
19. Bridge Hollow
20. Indian Crossing
21. Spirit Lake
22. Browne Lake
23. Deep Creek
24. Lodgepole
25. Red Springs
26. East Park
27. Oaks Park
28. Kaler Hollow
29. Iron Mine
30. Hades
31. Aspen Grove
32. Yellowpine
33. Upper Stillwater
34. Moon Lake
35. Swift Creek
36. Riverview
37. Reservoir
38. Bridge
39. Yellowstone
40. Wandin
41. Uinta Canyon
42. Pole Creek
43. Paradise Park
44. Whiterocks
45. Steinaker State Park
46. Red Fleet State Park
47. Split Mountain
48. Green River
49. Rainbow Park
50. Fossil Valley
51. Manila / Flaming Gorge KOA
52. Vernal Campground Dina
53. Pelican Lake
54. Mountain View
55. Lower Beach
56. Avintaquin

## 1. VERNAL KOA

*Reference:* **In Manila; map A3, grid d4.**

*Campsites, facilities:* There are 55 RV sites with full hookups and 35 tent sites, plus rest rooms, showers, laundry facilities, RV disposal, picnic tables, a game room, barbecue grills, a swimming pool, a public phone, a convenience and gift store, cable TV, and a playground. Miniature golf, volleyball, and horseshoe facilities are also available. Pets are welcome.

*Reservations, fee:* Reservations are recommended in the summer. Sites with full hookups are $18, and tent sites are $13.

*Contact:* Call the campground at (801) 789-8935.

*Location:* In Vernal, take U.S. 191 east and go 2.5 miles past the intersection with State Route 191. The KOA is on the west side of the road near the Westin Plaza.

*Trip notes:* This is a shaded, grassy oasis in an otherwise arid urban setting. Actually, the campground is at the edge of town, in a semirural residential section of Vernal surrounded by open fields. But the real bonus is all that's nearby: the Utah Field House of Natural History, Steinaker and Red Fleet

---

State Parks, Dinosaur National Monument, and Flaming Gorge National Recreation Area are all a short drive away.

*Season:* May 1 through September 3.

---

## 2. CARMEL

*Reference:* **In Flaming Gorge National Recreation Area; map A3, grid e4.**

*Campsites, facilities:* There are 15 sites with pit toilets and fire grills, but *no drinking water.*

*Reservations, fee:* Sites are free and are first come, first served.

*Contact:* Call the Flaming Gorge Ranger District at (801) 784-3445.

*Location:* From Vernal, drive north on U.S. 191 for 36 miles. Turn west on State Route 44, go 20 miles, and pick up Forest Service Road 218. Continue heading west for one mile to the campground, located on the north side of the road.

*Trip notes:* Due to flash-flood danger, the National Forest Service closes Carmel to camping during most of the warm-weather season, which means that unlike most Utah campgrounds, this is a fall-through-winter kind of place, located near an interesting geological area called Sheep Creek Canyon. Here, erosion has exposed the canyon geology to dramatic effect, revealing a tremendous array of formations from earlier eras amid a series of towering cliffs.

*Season:* October 1 through May 15.

---

## 3. LUCERNE VALLEY

*Reference:* **In Flaming Gorge National Recreation Area; map A3, grid d5.**

*Campsites, facilities:* There are 161 sites with picnic tables, fire pits, and water, plus a boat ramp, RV disposal, a public phone, a marina, and an amphitheater.

*Reservations, fee:* Reservations are accepted for group sites and some single sites. Single-family sites are $11, and group sites are $22.

*Contact:* Call the Flaming Gorge Ranger District at (801) 784-3445.

*Location:* From Vernal, take U.S. 191 north, and then take State Route 44 to Manila. In Manila, follow State Route 43 east for about four miles. Turn right on Forest Service Road 146, and continue for four miles to the campground.

*Trip notes:* Fishing is the big activity here. Flaming Gorge Reservoir is famous for producing trophy lake trout, and the Lucerne Marina is one of its most-favored launching areas. Swimming and waterskiing are popular pastimes, too; the reservoir is large enough to provide boaters with lots of opportunity to escape the crowds. Unfortunately, the campground—in a sagebrush setting with a only a few shade trees—tends to be hot and windy in the summer.

*Season:* Mid-April through October, though the water is turned off when the temperature is below freezing.

---

## 4. GRAVEL PIT/STATELINE/ SWIM BEACH

*Reference:* **On Flaming Gorge Reservoir; map A3, grid d5.**

*Campsites, facilities:* This place has undeveloped campsites, with a vault toilet at Gravel Pit and another at Swim Beach. There is *no drinking water.*

---

*Reservations, fee:* Sites are free and are first come, first served.

*Contact:* Call the Flaming Gorge Ranger District at (801) 784-3445.

*Location:* From Vernal, drive north on U.S. 191 to State Route 44. Take that route for four miles to Lucerne Valley. Gravel Pit is 2.1 miles down Lucerne Valley Road on the right, Stateline is 2.4 miles down the road on the left, and Swim Beach is 2.9 miles down on the left.

*Trip notes:* If you're looking to get rustic and close to the water, this place fits the bill, with expansive beaches and swimming options galore. But be warned: the dispersed camping is on the flats, so summers can be hot.

*Season:* Mid-May through mid-September.

## 5. KINGFISHER ISLAND

*Reference:* **In Flaming Gorge National Recreation Area; map A3, grid e4.**

*Campsites, facilities:* There are eight sites with pit toilets, picnic tables, and fire grills, but *no water.*

*Reservations, fee:* Sites are free and are first come, first served.

*Contact:* Call the Flaming Gorge Ranger District at (801) 789-1181.

*Location:* This campground is accessible by boat only. To get there, travel 17.5 miles up the reservoir from the Flaming Gorge Dam, or seven miles down the reservoir (south) from the Lucerne Valley or Antelope Flat boat ramps.

*Trip notes:* This is a boater's paradise, not to mention a rare chance to get away from car campers and experience the water at its most pristine. To reach the campsites, expect to climb a moderately steep slope from shore. The sites are terraced, providing nice views of the red rock formations, though the campground, in a sagebrush, juniper, and pinyon setting, is rocky and lacks shade. Alert campers can catch a glimpse of the osprey that nest and fish in the area.

*Season:* April 1 through December 31.

## 6. HIDEOUT CANYON

*Reference:* **In Flaming Gorge National Recreation Area; map A3, grid e4.**

*Campsites, facilities:* There are 18 sites with picnic tables and fire grills, plus flush toilets, water, and boat docks.

*Reservations, fee:* Reservations are available for some sites up to 120 days in advance, from July 1 through Labor Day; call the National Reservation System at (800) 280-2267. Sites are $17.

*Contact:* Call the Flaming Gorge Ranger District at (801) 784-3445.

*Location:* Access here is primarily by boat, though hikers can reach the campground via the lower two miles of the Hideout Trail, which starts near the Dowd Mountain Overlook (which can be reached by taking State Route 44 to Forest Road 94 and driving west for four miles). By water, travel 15.5 miles up Flaming Gorge Reservoir, nine miles down the reservoir (south) from the boat ramps at Lucerne Valley and Antelope Flat, or three miles east from the Sheep Creek Bay boat launch.

*Trip notes:* With sites on moderately steep, terraced land in a pinyon and juniper forest, this campground offers boat campers some nice amenities, better-than-normal shade, and relative solitude. There's good fishing for kokanee salmon, smallmouth bass, and rainbow and lake trout, and excellent water-skiing in the summer.

*Season:* Open year-round, but water is only available from mid-May through mid-September.

---

## 7. ANTELOPE FLAT

*Reference:* **In Flaming Gorge National Recreation Area; map A3, grid e5.**

*Campsites, facilities:* There are 121 single sites and four group sites, plus picnic tables and fire grills, water, and rest rooms with cold running water. An RV disposal site, a boat ramp, a public phone, a fish-cleaning station, an undeveloped swimming area, and a covered picnic pavilion are also available at Antelope Flat.

*Reservations, fee:* Reservations are available 120 days in advance; call the National Reservation System at (800) 280-2267. Sites are $9.

*Contact:* Call the Flaming Gorge Ranger District at (801) 784-3445.

*Location:* From Vernal, take U.S. Route 191 north to Flaming Gorge National Recreation Area. Then follow Forest Service Road 145 west for four miles to the campground.

*Trip notes:* Because this site is a little farther from the major marinas and less shaded than other area campgrounds, Antelope Flat tends to be less crowded than its neighbor. Campers who do venture here find a real treasure: the swimming beach, though on the primitive side, is one of Flaming Gorge's best, with antelope often wandering by. And the view of the gorge that gives the reservoir its name is a sight to remember. Shore fishing for smallmouth bass can be excellent.

*Season:* Mid-May through mid-September.

---

## 8. CANYON RIM

*Reference:* **In Flaming Gorge National Recreation Area; map A3, grid e5.**

*Campsites, facilities:* There are 18 sites with picnic tables, plus fire grills, drinking water, and vault toilets.

*Reservations, fee:* Sites are $9 and are first come, first served.

*Contact:* Call the Flaming Gorge Ranger District at (801) 784-3445.

*Location:* From Vernal, take U.S. Route 191 north to Flaming Gorge National Recreation Area. Follow State Route 44 east for about three miles. Turn north on Forest Service Road 095 and continue for about 1.5 miles to the campground.

*Trip notes:* Set in a lodgepole forest at an elevation of 7,400 feet, small Canyon Rim campground is blessed with a convenient location: visitors will discover that it's close to the Red Canyon Visitors Center, commercial Red Canyon Lodge, and Greens Lake. Take time to enjoy the various natural history exhibits at the visitors center, with its standout views of Flaming Gorge. Following the short nature walk that starts and ends near the center property is also a worthwhile activity.

*Season:* Mid-May through mid-September.

---

# 9. GOOSENECK

*Reference:* **In Flaming Gorge National Recreation Area; map A3, grid e5.**

*Campsites, facilities:* There are six sites with picnic tables, plus fire grills, and pit toilets, but *no water.*

*Reservations, fee:* Sites are free and are first come, first served.

*Contact:* Call the Flaming Gorge Ranger District at (801) 784-3445.

*Location:* This campground is only accessible by boat. Travel 8.5 miles up the reservoir from the Flaming Gorge Dam or 16 miles down the reservoir from the marinas at Lucerne Valley or Antelope Flat.

*Trip notes:* Solitude is the number-one selling point here; boaters don't often get the chance to enjoy their crafts in such beautiful seclusion. The canyon scenery is superb, and the campground has a nice shaded setting of large ponderosa pines with scattered juniper and pinyon trees. Expect a steep climb to the sites, and be aware that at this altitude (elevation 6,040), the reservoir does freeze up some winters.

*Season:* Open year-round.

---

# 10. GREENS LAKE

*Reference:* **In Flaming Gorge National Recreation Area; map A3, grid e5.**

*Campsites, facilities:* There are 19 sites with picnic tables and fire grills, plus water, vault toilets, a group area, and trash pickup. The Red Canyon Visitors Center and Nature Trail are nearby, and the trailhead for the Canyon Rim hiking trail is at the campground entrance.

*Reservations, fee:* For reservations, call the National Reservation System at (800) 280-2267. Sites are $9.

*Contact:* Call the Flaming Gorge Ranger District at (801) 784-3445.

*Location:* From Vernal, take U.S. Route 191 north to Flaming Gorge National Recreation Area. Follow State Route 44 west for about four miles to Forest Service Road 095, known as Red Canyon Road. Turn north and proceed about a mile to the campground on Greens Lake.

*Trip notes:* Campers won't lack for things to do at this shaded haven perched at 7,400 feet in the ponderosa pines. Greens Lake, at the campground's edge, has plenty of decent fishing for planted rainbow trout, as well as opportunities for swimming and exploring in small rowboats and canoes. The Red Canyon Nature Trail and the walk on the Canyon Rim are a bonanza for hikers, with views of a red-rock gorge and of Flaming Gorge Reservoir 1,360 feet below the rim. And the Red Canyon Visitors Center has some interesting exhibits on the area's geology, cultural history, and plant and animal life, along with great views of the gorge.

*Season:* May 17 through November 1.

---

# 11. SKULL CREEK

*Reference:* **In Flaming Gorge National Recreation Area; map A3, grid e5.**

*Campsites, facilities:* There are 17 sites with picnic tables and fire pits, plus water and two vault toilets.

---

*Reservations, fee:* For reservations, call the Flaming Gorge Natural History Association at (801) 885-3305. Sites are $8.

*Contact:* Call the Flaming Gorge Ranger District at (801) 784-3445.

*Location:* From Vernal, take U.S. Route 191 north to the Flaming Gorge National Recreation Area, and follow State Route 44 west for three miles. The campground is on the north side of the highway.

*Trip notes:* This retreat in the ponderosa pines has a creek trickling melodiously nearby. There's also a trailhead for the Canyon Rim hiking trail, which offers some nice views of Flaming Gorge Reservoir. At the sites, the spurs are somewhat short, suitable for trailers or RVs up to 20 feet. At an elevation of 7,600 feet, this campground is cooler than many.

*Season:* Memorial Day weekend through Labor Day weekend.

---

## 12. GREENDALE WEST

*Reference:* In Flaming Gorge National Recreation Area; map A3, grid e5.

*Campsites, facilities:* There are eight campsites with picnic tables and fire pits; drinking water and vault toilets are available.

*Reservations, fee:* Sites are $9 and are first come, first served.

*Contact:* Call the Flaming Gorge Ranger District at (801) 784-3445.

*Location:* From Vernal, take U.S. 191 north to Flaming Gorge Dam. From there, drive four miles south, staying on the highway. The campground is on the west side of the road near Flaming Gorge Lodge.

*Trip notes:* Set in a fairly open part of the national recreation area at an elevation of 6,950 feet, this campground is within walking distance of Flaming Gorge Lodge, which, along with a motel, has a store, a restaurant, and raft rentals for exploring the Green River below the Flaming Gorge Dam. On some summer weekends, campfire programs are available at the nearby Bootleg Amphitheater. This is a good central location for anyone planning to enjoy Green River rafting or water sports on the reservoir itself.

*Season:* May 20 through December 31.

---

## 13. FIREFIGHTERS MEMORIAL

*Reference:* In Flaming Gorge National Recreation Area; map A3, grid e5.

*Campsites, facilities:* There are 94 sites with picnic tables and fire pits, plus water, flush toilets, and an amphitheater.

*Reservations, fee:* For reservations, call the National Reservation System at (800) 280-2267. Sites are $11.

*Contact:* Call the Flaming Gorge Ranger District at (801) 784-3445.

*Location:* From Vernal, take U.S. 191 north to Flaming Gorge National Recreation Area. After the Flaming Gorge Dam, go another 3.5 miles. The campground is right off the highway, just north of Flaming Gorge Lodge.

*Trip notes:* For RVers looking for ponderosa-shaded sites with large parking spurs, this is the spot. The only drawback: you'll have to drive to the aquatic attractions of Flaming Gorge Reservoir. Still, this is a nice, fairly quiet retreat—conveniently close to all the amenities of Flaming Gorge Lodge.

---

Families, especially, will like the self-guided tours of nearby Flaming Gorge Dam. Some visitors like to walk the trail that leads along the Green River from the dam, fly-fishing for trout as they go. The elevation is 6,900 feet.
*Season:* May 17 through September 12.

## 14. CEDAR SPRINGS

*Reference:* **In Flaming Gorge National Recreation Area; map A3, grid e5.**
*Campsites, facilities:* There are 23 sites with picnic tables and fire grills, plus water, vault toilets, RV disposal, a boat ramp, and a marina.
*Reservations, fee:* For reservations, call the U.S. Forest Service National Reservation System at (800) 280-2267. Sites are $9.
*Contact:* Call the Flaming Gorge Ranger District at (801) 784-3445.
*Location:* From Vernal, drive north on U.S. 191. About 1.5 miles south of Flaming Gorge Dam, look for a turnoff to Cedar Springs Marina, heading north. The campground is just over a mile north of the highway.
*Trip notes:* This is one of the better area campgrounds for serious boaters, since it's right near the full-service Cedar Springs Marina, which offers boat rentals, boat launching, and overnight boat trailer parking. But despite some tall pinyon and juniper trees, summers can be scorching. Luckily, swimmers and water-skiers can cool off in the reservoir.
*Season:* May 17 through September 12.

## 15. DEER RUN

*Reference:* **In Flaming Gorge National Recreation Area; map A3, grid e5.**
*Campsites, facilities:* There are 15 single sites and four group areas, along with picnic tables, fire grills, vault toilets, drinking water, and access to the Cedar Springs Marina.
*Reservations, fee:* For reservations, call the National Reservation System at (800) 230-2267. Rates are $9 for single sites and $18 for group sites.
*Contact:* Call the Flaming Gorge Ranger District at (801) 784-3445.
*Location:* From Vernal, drive north toward Flaming Gorge Dam on U.S. 191, then go 1.5 miles south of the dam on the same highway. Look for the turnoff to the Cedar Springs Marina.
*Trip notes:* This is a nice central location for boat trips on Flaming Gorge Reservoir, raft trips on the Green River below the dam, or tours of the dam and its visitors center. And there's overnight boat trailer parking (plus boat rentals) at Cedar Springs Marina. Still, the campground can get hot in the summer, even though it's surrounded by 10- to 20-foot pinyon and juniper trees.
*Season:* April 20 through September 12.

## 16. MUSTANG RIDGE

*Reference:* **In Flaming Gorge National Recreation Area; map A3, grid e5.**
*Campsites, facilities:* There are 54 single sites, most built for large trailers and RVs, and 19 group sites, with picnic tables and fire grills, drinking water, and vault toilets. A nearby paved boat ramp, an undeveloped swimming area, and boat trailer parking are also available.

*Reservations, fee:* To reserve campsites one through 39, call the U.S. Forest Service National Reservation System at (800) 280-2267. Rates are $11 for single sites and $22 for group sites.

*Contact:* Call the Flaming Gorge Ranger District at (801) 784-3445.

*Location:* From Vernal, take U.S. Route 191 north to Flaming Gorge National Recreation Area. Just past Dutch John Service Station, a prominently located gas station, turn left on Forest Service Road 184 (State Route 260), and continue for just under four miles to the campground.

*Trip notes:* This is one of the only area campgrounds with a view of Flaming Gorge Dam. That, along with the decent swimming beach, good fishing, and shaded sites carved out of a pinyon-and-juniper forest, also make it one of the most popular. Reservations are strongly suggested on weekends. Fishing for smallmouth bass is especially good on the rocky points near the boat ramp. At an elevation of 6,200 feet, the water is cold, even in summer, but that doesn't discourage folks from venturing in.

*Season:* May 17 through September 12.

---

## 17. JARVIES CANYON

*Reference:* **In Flaming Gorge National Recreation Area; map A3, grid e6.**

*Campsites, facilities:* There are eight sites with picnic tables, fire grills, and pit toilets, but *no water.*

*Reservations, fee:* Sites are free and are first come, first served.

*Contact:* Call the Flaming Gorge Ranger District at (801) 784-3445.

*Location:* This campground on Flaming Gorge Reservoir is accessible by boat only. Go 4.5 miles upstream from Flaming Gorge Dam or 20 miles from the Lucerne Valley or Antelope Flat boat ramps.

*Trip notes:* The best thing about this little canyon spot is its remoteness. In a sagebrush, pinyon, and juniper setting, far from the car-camping crowds, boaters can water-ski or gaze at the stellar scenery in relative solitude. The sites are terraced, so expect to walk uphill with your camping equipment. And be aware that at this 6,040-foot elevation, the reservoir does freeze some winters.

*Season:* Open year-round.

---

## 18. DRIPPING SPRINGS

*Reference:* **In Flaming Gorge National Recreation Area; map A3, grid e6.**

*Campsites, facilities:* There are 19 single sites, four group sites, and two double sites, plus picnic tables, fire grills, drinking water (from Memorial Day through Labor Day weekend), and vault toilets.

*Reservations, fee:* For reservations, call the U.S. Forest Service National Reservation System at (800) 280-2267. Sites are $11 from Memorial Day through Labor Day weekend, and free (but without water) the rest of the year.

*Contact:* Call the Flaming Gorge Ranger District at (801) 784-3445.

*Location:* From Vernal, take U.S. Route 191 north to Flaming Gorge National Recreation Area. At Dutch John Service Station, turn right on Forest Service Road 075. Go about two miles on the dirt road to the campground.

---

*Trip notes:* Fishing is so popular on the Green River that this place probably fills more quickly than any other campground in Flaming Gorge National Recreation Area. Set in a spectacular gorge and full of large, hungry trout, the Green is known for having some of the best fishing in the western United States, and hence draws fly anglers from all over the world. Rafters also like the river access. The campground, in a pinyon and juniper forest, is also three miles from the Little Hole boat ramp, which is about seven miles from the boat ramp near Flaming Gorge Dam. But be warned: it can get a little windy here.

*Season:* Open year-round.

## 19. BRIDGE HOLLOW

*Reference:* **On Bureau of Land Management property; map A3, grid e7.**

*Campsites, facilities:* There are 13 sites with picnic tables and fire pits. Vault toilets and drinking water are available.

*Reservations, fee:* Sites are $4 and are first come, first served.

*Contact:* Call the Vernal District Office of the Bureau of Land Management at (801) 789-1362.

*Location:* From Vernal, take U.S. 191 north to the town of Dutch John and continue three miles north. Then drive east for 20 miles on Clay Basin Road. Look for a turnoff into Jesse Ewing Canyon, drive five miles south through the canyon, and cross the Green River. The campground is near the bridge.

*Trip notes:* Located next to the Green River in the midst of willows and cottonwood trees, this is a great place for anglers to end their float trips, should they elect to raft past Little Hole while floating from Flaming Gorge Dam. Also, the nearby Browne's Park State Waterfowl Management Area is a good place to see all types of migrating birds. And the John Jarvie Historic Site is on the banks of the river (see page 134). Road conditions can be iffy in bad weather, so check out the situation first in Vernal or Dutch John during the off-season.

*Season:* Open year-round.

## 20. INDIAN CROSSING

*Reference:* **On Bureau of Land Management property; map A3, grid e7.**

*Campsites, facilities:* There are 13 sites with picnic tables and fire pits. Vault toilets and drinking water are available.

*Reservations, fee:* Sites are $2 and are first come, first served.

*Contact:* Call the Vernal District Office of the Bureau of Land Management at (801) 789-1362.

*Location:* From Vernal, take U.S. 191 north to Dutch John. Go three more miles, then head east on winding Clay Basin Road for 20 miles, which eventually takes you five miles south into Jesse Ewing Canyon. Cross the bridge over the Green River, then drive west for two miles. The campground is just past the Jarvie Historic Ranch.

*Trip notes:* This Green River campground is popular among anglers and rafters coming from Little Hole, a boat ramp and picnic area (accessible by road from Dutch John) in Flaming Gorge National Recreation Area. Tours of the nearby John Jarvie Historic Site, a ranch once visited by outlaw Butch Cassidy himself, are available during much of the spring, summer, and fall tourist season. Mr. Jarvie, an innkeeper and ranch owner, was murdered by a pair of transient workers in 1909; today, the property consists of the stone house and dugout that served as his home, along with a blacksmith shop and corrals.

*Season:* Open year-round.

## 21. SPIRIT LAKE

*Reference:* **In Ashley National Forest; map A3, grid e3.**

*Campsites, facilities:* There are 24 family sites with picnic tables, fire grills, and vault toilets, but *no drinking water.*

*Reservations, fee:* Sites are $5 and are first come, first served.

*Contact:* Call the Flaming Gorge Ranger District at (801) 784-3445.

*Location:* From Vernal, take U.S. 191 north to Greendale Junction, then head west on State Route 44 and drive 14.6 miles to Sheep Creek Canyon Road. Follow this road for three miles to the Deep Creek/Spirit Lake junction, then take Spirit Lake Road (which is Forest Road 001) for 10.4 miles to the Spirit Lake turnoff. The campground entrance is 6.25 miles from the turnoff.

*Trip notes:* The U.S. Forest Service describes this area as "mountainous, lakefront terrain with plenty of shade and lots of mosquitoes." They're not kidding about the mosquitoes: anyone going into this part of the Uinta Mountains is definitely going to run into them, so come prepared. Though a bit on the rustic side, the campground is a good place to start a day hike or a backpacking trip into the High Uintas Wilderness Area, Utah's largest. Spirit Lake itself is a pretty spot, with adequate fishing for stocked trout; a commercial lodge there provides cabins, horse rentals, boat and canoe rentals, a cafe, and a guide service. Due to the 10,000-foot altitude, the campground has a fairly short season, so check the weather before you come.

*Season:* June through Labor Day weekend, depending on snow conditions.

## 22. BROWNE LAKE

*Reference:* **In Ashley National Forest; map A3, grid e4.**

*Campsites, facilities:* There are eight sites with picnic tables, fire grills, and vault toilets, but *no drinking water.*

*Reservations, fee:* Sites are free and are first come, first served.

*Contact:* Call the Flaming Gorge Ranger District at (801) 784-3445.

*Location:* From Vernal, drive north on U.S. 191 to Greendale Junction. Take State Route 44 west for about 10 miles to State Route 218. Follow it approximately three miles to a dirt road, Forest Road 221; take this road west about four miles to Forest Road 96, which leads southeast for about one mile to Browne Lake.

*Trip notes:* Browne Lake is a pretty little spot with some trees and open spaces, at an elevation of 8,200 feet. Though remote and a bit tricky to reach (it's a rough ride for most trailers and RVs, though some do make the trip), this place can be popular, largely due to the trout fishing. History buffs can explore the nearby Ute Mountain fire lookout, a restored historic fire tower. Guided tours are offered at certain times of year; consult the Flaming Gorge Ranger District for details.

*Season:* May through September.

---

## 23. DEEP CREEK

*Reference:* **In Ashley National Forest; map A3, grid e4.**

*Campsites, facilities:* There are 17 sites, plus vault toilets, picnic tables, and fire grills, but *no water.*

*Reservations, fee:* Sites are free and are first come, first served.

*Contact:* Call the Flaming Gorge Ranger District at (801) 784-3445.

*Location:* From Vernal, take U.S. 191 north to Greendale Junction. Then take State Route 44 for 11.4 miles to the Deep Creek Road junction. The campground is located 2.4 miles to the southwest on that road.

*Trip notes:* Many anglers like to fish the namesake creek near this nicely shaded campground; the water flows through the rolling and steep reaches of the surrounding terrain. Sites here are not far from Browne Lake or from trailheads into the High Uintas Wilderness Area (popular with horseback riders). The elevation is 7,800 feet.

*Season:* June 1 through October 1.

---

## 24. LODGEPOLE

*Reference:* **In Ashley National Forest; map A3, grid e5.**

*Campsites, facilities:* There are 35 sites; five are pull-throughs and 30 are pull-ins. The RV limit is 22 feet. Facilities include picnic tables, fire pits, water, flush toilets, and a dumpster.

*Reservations, fee:* To reserve sites 1 through 3 and 5 through 11, call the National Reservation System at (800) 280-2267. Campsites are $11.

*Contact:* Call the Vernal Ranger District at (801) 789-1181.

*Location:* From Vernal, take U.S. 191 north for 30.5 miles. The campground is on the east side of the road.

*Trip notes:* Away from the visitor traffic of Flaming Gorge Reservoir, this pretty spot nestled in the quaking aspens and lodgepole pines offers a quieter kind of camping. Yet it's conveniently situated so that boaters and anglers can still enjoy Flaming Gorge to the north, as well as Red Fleet and Steinaker Reservoirs to the south. Hiking, riding, swimming, and waterskiing are all popular at nearby Flaming Gorge National Recreation Area.

*Season:* April 25 through October 31.

---

## 25. RED SPRINGS

*Reference:* **In Ashley National Forest; map A3, grid e5.**

*Campsites, facilities:* There are 13 sites with picnic tables, fire pits, and vault toilets, plus drinking water from May through September.

*Reservations, fee:* Sites are $8 and are first come, first served.

*Contact:* Call the Vernal Ranger District at (801) 789-1181.

---

*Location:* From Vernal, take U.S. 191 north for 26 miles. The campground is on the west side of the road.

*Trip notes:* On busy weekends, campers arriving too late to snag a site at Flaming Gorge Reservoir often look to this place next. Set in a forest of quaking aspen and lodgepole pine, it's just a few miles from the reservoir, though boaters, swimmers, water-skiers, and anglers shouldn't ignore the less-crowded Red Fleet Reservoir to the south.

*Season:* April 25 through September 30.

## 26. EAST PARK

*Reference:* **In Ashley National Forest; map A3, grid f5.**

*Campsites, facilities:* There are 21 sites; five are pull-throughs and 16 are pull-ins. The RV length limit is 22 feet. Facilities include picnic tables, fire grills, and vault toilets, with drinking water from June through September.

*Reservations, fee:* Sites are $8 and are first come, first served.

*Contact:* Call the Vernal Ranger District at (801) 789-1181.

*Location:* From Vernal, drive north on U.S. 191 for 20 miles, looking for Red Cloud Loop Road (Forest Road 018) to the northwest. Take that road, following the pavement for about nine miles to the end before turning right on East Park Campground Road (Forest Road 020). Drive on the gravel for one mile to the campground.

*Trip notes:* Located in a somewhat open setting surrounded by lodgepole pines, this campground sits right next door to East Park Reservoir. Anglers will find this small reservoir regularly stocked with fish, though they may have better luck coaxing rainbow, cutthroat, and brook trout from the nearby streams. Hiking trails lead north and west from the reservoir through the Ashley National Forest. And there's some enticing alpine scenery along nearby Red Cloud Loop Road.

*Season:* June through October.

## 27. OAKS PARK

*Reference:* **In Ashley National Forest; map A3, grid f5.**

*Campsites, facilities:* There are 11 single sites with picnic tables, fire grills, and vault toilets. Water is available from mid-June through September from a pump-handle well in an undeveloped area north of the campground.

*Reservations, fee:* Sites are $6 and are first come, first served.

*Contact:* Call the Vernal Ranger District at (801) 789-1181.

*Location:* From Vernal, take U.S. 191 north for 20 miles, then head west on Red Cloud Loop Road (Forest Road 018) for 13 miles. Turn off at the Oaks Park sign, and proceed another mile to the campground.

*Trip notes:* The elevation of 9,200 feet makes for a short season, but this pretty alpine campground is a great place for a woodsy summer retreat. There's catchable rainbow trout in adjacent Oaks Park Reservoir, along with decent stream fishing from small area creeks. The reservoir, though not large, is fine for rafts, canoes, and small boats.

*Season:* June through September.

# 28. KALER HOLLOW

*Reference:* **In Ashley National Forest; map A3, grid f5.**

*Campsites, facilities:* There are four tables with fire rings at this largely undeveloped site, with one vault toilet, but *no water.*

*Reservations, fee:* Sites are free and are first come, first served.

*Contact:* Call the Vernal Ranger District at (801) 789-1181.

*Location:* From Vernal, take U.S. 191 north to Red Cloud Loop Road (Forest Road 018) and head west. The campground is located at the junction of the loop road and Taylor Mountain Road.

*Trip notes:* Group camping is the norm and fishing is the prime pastime at this small campground in the quaking aspens and lodgepole pines. Local streams yield plenty of trout, as do the nearby Oak Park and East Park Reservoirs. Another good diversion is the Red Cloud Loop, a scenic stretch of pavement and dirt that basically starts and ends in Vernal. Pick up a "Drive Through the Ages" brochure at the downtown Vernal Visitors Center to learn about the geological history of the area along Highway 191.

*Season:* June 1 through October 31.

---

# 29. IRON MINE

*Reference:* **In Ashley National Forest; map A3, grid f0.**

*Campsites, facilities:* There are 22 single sites, two double sites, and one group site, with picnic tables, fire grills, vault toilets, and dumpsters. The RV length limit is 22 feet. Water is available from Memorial Day through Labor Day.

*Reservations, fee:* For reservations, call the National Reservation System at (800) 280-2267. Single sites are $6, doubles are $10, and the group site is $25.

*Contact:* Call the Duchesne Ranger District at (801) 738-2482.

*Location:* From Duchesne, drive west on U.S. 40 for approximately 17 miles. Turn north on State Route 208 and go nine miles. Then head west on State Route 35 through the tiny hamlets of Tabiona and Hanna, looking for Forest Road 144 to the north. Take that road north and go another seven miles to the campground.

*Trip notes:* The number-one bonus of this lovely mountain spot is the trout fishing on the North Fork of the Duchesne River; the campground is right on the banks. Surrounded by fir, quaking aspen, and pine at an elevation of 7,200 feet, it's also convenient to the horseback rentals of nearby Defas Dude Ranch. The Grandview Trailhead, providing hiking and horseback access into the High Uintas Wilderness Area, is just six miles away.

*Season:* Memorial Day to Labor Day, and open without water during the fall hunting season.

---

# 30. HADES

*Reference:* **In Ashley National Forest; map A3, grid f0.**

*Campsites, facilities:* There are 17 sites, 10 of them suitable for RVs up to 22 feet, with picnic tables, fire grills, drinking water, and pit toilets.

*Reservations, fee:* Sites are $6 and are first come, first served.

---

*Contact:* Call the Duchesne Ranger District at (801) 738-2482.

*Location:* From Duchesne, drive west on U.S. 40 for approximately 17 miles. Turn north on State Route 208 and go another nine miles. Then head west on State Route 35 through the hamlets of Tabiona and Hanna, looking for Forest Road 144 to the north. Drive five miles north on that road; the campground is on the west side near Defas Dude Ranch.

*Trip notes:* This is one of the more remote areas in Utah—and, despite the name, one of the prettiest, especially in fall when the aspen leaves begin to change. For those who make the extra effort to get here, the rewards are great: there's ample fishing in the nearby North Fork of the Duchesne River and in the High Uintas Wilderness Area lakes, which you can reach by horseback or on foot.

*Season:* April 25 through September 10.

---

# 31. ASPEN GROVE

*Reference:* In Ashley National Forest; map A3, grid f0.

*Campsites, facilities:* There are 33 sites, 26 of them appropriate for RVs up to 22 feet, with picnic tables, fire pits, drinking water, and pit toilets.

*Reservations, fee:* Sites are $6 and are first come, first served.

*Contact:* Call the Duchesne Ranger District at (801) 738-2482.

*Location:* From Duchesne, drive west on U.S. 40 for approximately 17 miles. Turn north on State Route 208 and go nine miles. Then head west on State Route 35 through the hamlets of Tabiona and Hanna, looking for Forest Road 144 to the north. Drive 2.5 miles north on that road; the campground is on the west side.

*Trip notes:* Set in the quaking aspens in another of northern Utah's most gorgeous hideaways, this remote, high-country campground offers hiking and horseback trails that lead to the high mountain lakes of the nearby High Uintas Wilderness Area. And there's all the trout fishing you could want on the North and West Forks of the Duchesne River (the North Fork is adjacent to the campground).

*Season:* June 25 through September 10.

---

# 32. YELLOWPINE

*Reference:* In Ashley National Forest; map A3, grid f1.

*Campsites, facilities:* There are 20 single sites, seven double sites, and two triple-family sites, with picnic tables, fire grills, handicapped-accessible flush toilets, drinking water, dumpsters, and an RV disposal site.

*Reservations, fee:* To reserve sites 1 through 10, call the National Reservation System at (800) 280-2267. Rates are $10 for single sites, $16 for doubles, and $30 for triples.

*Contact:* Call the Duchesne Ranger District at (801) 738-2482.

*Location:* From Duchesne, head north on Highway 87. When you reach Mountain Home, take the road that heads north and west, which becomes Forest Road 134. The campground is about 20 miles from Mountain Home along that road.

*Trip notes:* Adjacent to Rock Creek in a wooded setting of lodgepole, quaking aspen, and ponderosa pine, this is another favored fishing spot. Anglers try their luck in both the creek and the nearby Upper Stillwater Reservoir, five miles up the canyon. A hiking and horseback trail along Rock Creek begins a quarter-mile away from the campground.

*Season:* Memorial Day through Labor Day, and open without water in the fall.

---

## 33. UPPER STILLWATER

*Reference:* **In Ashley National Forest; map A3, grid f1.**

*Campsites, facilities:* This is one of the state's newest campgrounds, with 14 single sites, six double sites, and one triple site. The RV length limit is 22 feet. Picnic tables, fire pits, running water, and wheelchair-accessible flush toilets are available.

*Reservations, fee:* Sites are $10 for singles, $16 for doubles, and $30 for the triple, and are first come, first served.

*Contact:* Call the Duchesne Ranger District at (801) 738-2482.

*Location:* From Duchesne, head north on Highway 87. When you reach Mountain Home, take the road that heads north and west, which becomes Forest Road 134. The campground is about 19 miles from Mountain Home along that road.

*Trip notes:* This relatively new facility in a setting of lodgepole, quaking aspen, and ponderosa pine provides good access to the High Uintas Wilderness Area; a hiking trail leads right there from the campground. Fishing can be decent at Upper Stillwater Reservoir, a relatively new part of the Central Utah Project (a massive effort to bring water from the Colorado River basin to the Wasatch Front), though bank access is somewhat difficult. Anglers also report success on Rock Creek in the area where it flows into the reservoir and where it leaves the dam.

*Season:* Memorial Day through Labor Day.

---

## 34. MOON LAKE

*Reference:* **On Moon Lake in Ashley National Forest; map A3, grid f2.**

*Campsites, facilities:* There are 56 single sites, two group sites, and one double site, with picnic tables and fire grills, flush toilets, running water, and a dumpster. The RV length limit is 22 feet.

*Reservations, fee:* Only the two group sites can be reserved; call the National Reservation System at (800) 280-2267. Fees are $10 for single sites, $20 for the double, and $40 for the group sites.

*Contact:* Call the Roosevelt Ranger District at (801) 722-5018.

*Location:* From Duchesne, drive north on State Route 87 for 33 miles to the campground. Once in the forest, the road turns into Forest Road 131.

*Trip notes:* Situated next to a rustic old lodge in the midst of lodgepole pines, this popular campground also sits right up against scenic Moon Lake, a man-made reservoir on the edge of the High Uintas Wilderness Area. There's good rainbow trout fishing here and on the streams flowing in and out of the reservoir (but be careful not to cross into the Ute Indian Reservation down-

---

stream without a special Ute license). At an elevation of 8,100 feet, the campground is also a trailhead for horseback riding and hikes into the High Uintas.
*Season:* May through September.

## 35. SWIFT CREEK

*Reference:* **In Ashley National Forest; map A3, grid f3.**

*Campsites, facilities:* There are 13 single sites with picnic tables and fire grills.
Drinking water and vault toilets are available.

*Reservations, fee:* Sites are $6 and are first come, first served.

*Contact:* Call the Roosevelt Ranger District at (801) 722-5018.

*Location:* The campground is 32 miles north of Duchesne. From Duchesne,
take State Route 87 for 21 miles and turn onto Forest Road 119, a dirt road
leading to the campground.

*Trip notes:* This is one of the horse-friendliest campgrounds in the area, with
16 stalls and two unloading ramps at the Swift Creek Trailhead. The trailhead
itself leads to some fishable waters in the scenic High Uintas Wilderness
Area. Closer by, the Yellowstone River offers decent trout fishing. The campground is in a setting of flat-to-rolling canyon bottom with conifer, aspen,
and sagebrush, at an elevation of 8,200 feet.

*Season:* May through September.

## 36. RIVERVIEW

*Reference:* **In Ashley National Forest; map A3, grid f3.**

*Campsites, facilities:* There are 19 single sites with picnic tables and fire grills;
drinking water and vault toilets are available.

*Reservations, fee:* Sites are $6 and are first come, first served.

*Contact:* Call the Roosevelt Ranger District at (801) 722-5018.

*Location:* The campground is 31 miles north of Duchesne. From Duchesne,
take State Route 87 for 21 miles to Forest Road 119, a dirt road leading to
the campground.

*Trip notes:* Situated on the Yellowstone River at an elevation of 8,000 feet, this
is a pleasant and remote place to relax in an alpine setting. Rainbow trout
fishing on the Yellowstone River can be good, as is hiking the nearby High
Uintas Wilderness Area. Backpackers like to take trails to Timothy Lake or, if
they're ambitious, up to 13,528-foot King's Peak, the highest point in Utah.

*Season:* May 17 through September 12.

## 37. RESERVOIR

*Reference:* **In Ashley National Forest; map A3, grid f3.**

*Campsites, facilities:* There are five single sites with an RV length limit of 22
feet, plus vault toilets, picnic tables, and fire grills. There is *no water.*

*Reservations, fee:* Sites are free and are first come, first served.

*Contact:* Call the Roosevelt Ranger District at (801) 722-5018.

*Location:* The campground is 31 miles north of Duchesne. From Duchesne,
take State Route 87 for 21 miles to Forest Road 119, a dirt road leading to
the campground.

*Trip notes:* The reservoir in question here is tiny but full of rainbow trout, and the nearby Yellowstone River isn't bad for angling either. Nestled in a flat and rolling canyon bottom amid conifers, aspens, and sagebrush, this high-country spot (elevation 8,000) is a place to enjoy camping on the cool side. Hiking and horse-packing trips lead from here into the High Uintas Wilderness Area, Utah's largest.

*Season:* May through September.

## 38. BRIDGE

*Reference:* **In Ashley National Forest; map A3, grid f3.**

*Campsites, facilities:* There are five tent sites with picnic tables and fire pits. Drinking water and vault toilets are available.

*Reservations, fee:* Sites are $6 and are first come, first served.

*Contact:* Call the Roosevelt Ranger District at (801) 722-5018.

*Location:* The campground is about 28 miles north of Duchesne. From Duchesne, take State Route 87 for 21 miles to Forest Road 119, a dirt road leading to the campground.

*Trip notes:* This campground, in a mixed pine, aspen, and conifer forest at an elevation of 7,800 feet, is not far from the hiking trails and horseback riding areas of Ashley National Forest. Trout fishing can be quite productive in the Yellowstone River as well as in nearby Water Lily Lake, so don't forget your fishing pole.

*Season:* May through September.

## 39. YELLOWSTONE

*Reference:* **In Ashley National Forest; map A3, grid f3.**

*Campsites, facilities:* There are 16 single sites with an RV length limit of 22 feet. Picnic tables, fire grills, vault toilets, and drinking water are available.

*Reservations, fee:* Sites are $6 and are first come, first served.

*Contact:* Call the Roosevelt Ranger District at (801) 722-5018.

*Location:* The campground is 28 miles north of Duchesne. From Duchesne, take State Route 87 for 21 miles to Forest Road 119, a dirt road leading to the campground.

*Trip notes:* Because this place is somewhat off the beaten byways, there's some better-than-average fishing in the small canyon reservoir, the scenic Yellowstone River, and nearby Water Lily Lake. The campground itself is in a mixed pine, conifer, aspen, and sagebrush forest at the edge of the High Uintas Wilderness Area.

*Season:* May through September.

## 40. WANDIN

*Reference:* **In Ashley National Forest; map A3, grid f3.**

*Campsites, facilities:* There are six single sites with picnic tables, fire grills, and vault toilets, but *no water.* The RV length limit is 22 feet.

*Reservations, fee:* Sites are $5 and are first come, first served.

*Contact:* Call the Roosevelt Ranger District at (801) 722-5018.

*Location:* From Roosevelt, drive 16 miles north on State Highway 121. The road becomes Forest Road 118, a dirt road that leads north; take it nine more miles to the campground.

*Trip notes:* Located on flat-to-rolling terrain in a mixed conifer forest, this small campground sits right on the edge of the Uinta River at an elevation of 7,800 feet. Trout fishing in the river and hiking or horseback riding in the canyon are the chief lures for visitors here.

*Season:* June through September.

## 41. UINTA CANYON

*Reference:* **In Ashley National Forest; map A3, grid f3.**

*Campsites, facilities:* There are 24 single sites with picnic tables and fire grills, drinking water, vault toilets, and a dumpster. The RV limit is 22 feet.

*Reservations, fee:* Reservations are accepted. Sites are $5.

*Contact:* Call the Roosevelt Ranger District at (801) 722-5018.

*Location:* Drive 16 miles north of Roosevelt on State Route 121, which turns into Forest Road 118; take it north for nine more miles to the campground.

*Trip notes:* This campground is set in a lovely alpine meadow at an elevation of 7,600 feet, surrounded by aspen and ponderosa pine. There's fishing for small trout on the Uinta River (which is really more of a creek) and plenty of hiking and horseback riding in the nearby High Uintas Wilderness Area, a rugged expanse of glacier-carved mountain terrain that's the largest such area in the state.

*Season:* May through September.

## 42. POLE CREEK

*Reference:* **In Ashley National Forest; map A3, grid f4.**

*Campsites, facilities:* There are 18 single sites with picnic tables, fire grills, and pit toilets, but *no water.*

*Reservations, fee:* Sites are $5 and are first come, first served.

*Contact:* Call the Roosevelt Ranger District at (801) 722-5018.

*Location:* From Roosevelt, take State Highway 121 north for 16 miles. Go four miles northeast on Forest Road 118, a dirt road, then turn on Forest Road 117 and climb for another seven miles to the campground.

*Trip notes:* As the rugged uphill drive here might suggest, this is one of the state's highest campgrounds, at an elevation of 10,200 feet. It's a spectacularly secluded setting of mixed conifers on flat-to-rolling terrain, right next to the highly fishable Pole Creek Lake. Hikers can take one- to two-mile treks to Upper, Middle, and Lower Rock Lakes, just east and south of the High Uintas Wilderness Area boundary.

*Season:* July through September.

## 43. PARADISE PARK

*Reference:* **In Ashley National Forest; map A3, grid f4.**

*Campsites, facilities:* There are 15 pull-in sites with picnic tables, fire grills, and vault toilets, but *no water.*

*Reservations, fee:* Sites are $6 and are first come, first served.

*Contact:* Call the Vernal Ranger District at (801) 789-1181.

*Location:* From Vernal, follow State Route 121 to a junction east of Lapoint. Turn north and follow the signs on Forest Road 104, continuing on the dirt road for another 11 miles to the campground.

*Trip notes:* Located next to the small Paradise Reservoir, this is a much-visited boating, swimming, and fishing spot. Hiking and horse trails lead to nearby alpine lakes in the High Uintas Wilderness Area, where brook and cutthroat trout are the main prey. At an elevation of 10,000 feet, the campground is a good place to beat the summer heat.

*Season:* June through October.

## 44. WHITEROCKS

*Reference:* **In Ashley National Forest; map A3, grid f4.**

*Campsites, facilities:* There are 19 single sites and two group sites with picnic tables, fire grills, two double vault toilets, and drinking water. The RV length limit is 22 feet.

*Reservations, fee:* Sites are $8 and are first come, first served.

*Contact:* Call the Vernal Ranger District at (801) 789-1181.

*Location:* The campground is 31 miles northwest of Vernal. From Vernal, drive west on State Route 121. Just past Lapoint, look for a sign on an unnamed road leading to the town of Whiterocks on the Uinta and Ouray Indian Reservation. From Whiterocks, drive north for four miles to the graveled Forest Road 492. Follow that road for another eight miles.

*Trip notes:* Set at the bottom of a steep-walled canyon in a forest of blue spruce, aspen, and Ponderosa and lodgepole pine, this is clearly a place for folks who like their camping remote. The nearby Whiterocks River offers good trout fishing, and hikers can access a trail a little farther up the canyon.

*Season:* May through September.

## 45. STEINAKER STATE PARK

*Reference:* **On Steinaker Reservoir; map A3, grid g5.**

*Campsites, facilities:* There are 31 sites with picnic tables, fire grills, modern rest rooms, a boat ramp, two group-use pavilions, and a dump station.

*Reservations, fee:* Reservations are available 120 days in advance; call (800) 322-3770 Monday through Friday from 8 A.M. to 5 P.M. Sites are $8.

*Contact:* Call Steinaker State Park at (801) 789-4432.

*Location:* From Vernal, drive seven miles north on U.S. 191, turning to the west after passing the Steinaker Reservoir.

*Trip notes:* The warm water at this relatively low-altitude reservoir (5,500 feet) is a special enticement for water-skiers, boaters, and swimmers; the sandy beaches are popular, too. The reservoir also offers some decent fishing for stocked rainbow trout and largemouth bass. The surrounding terrain is largely open, though there are shady spots near the campground.

*Season:* April through November.

## 46. RED FLEET STATE PARK

*Reference:* **On Red Fleet Reservoir; map A3, grid g5.**

*Campsites, facilities:* There are 29 sites near the water, with 32 covered picnic tables, two modern rest rooms (with no showers), a sandy beach, a boat ramp, a fish-cleaning station, and a sewage dump station.

*Reservations, fee:* Reservations are available 120 days in advance for a non-refundable $5 per site; call (800) 322-3770 Monday through Friday from 8 A.M. to 5 P.M. Sites are $8. Utah residents 62 years and older with a Special Fun Tag receive a $2 discount Sunday through Thursday.

*Contact:* Call Red Fleet State Park at (801) 789-4432.

*Location:* From Vernal, drive 10 miles north on U.S. 191 and turn east at the state park sign. Follow the road to the park for about five miles.

*Trip notes:* One of the best parts of visiting scenic Red Fleet Reservoir (apart from the first-rate fishing and boating) is the drive from Vernal. Before heading out of town, pick up a "Drive Through the Ages" brochure at the visitors information center on Main Street and use it to trace the interesting geologic history of the route to Flaming Gorge Reservoir. Inside the park boundary is a dinosaur trackway dating back 200 million years.

*Season:* Open year-round, though winter camping is not recommended due to cold weather.

---

## 47. SPLIT MOUNTAIN

*Reference:* **In Dinosaur National Monument; map A3, grid g6.**

*Campsites, facilities:* There are 35 sites, including tent sites, with picnic tables and fire pits. Also available are drinking water, modern rest rooms, some pit toilets, firewood for sale, and a ramp for launching boats or rafts onto the Green River.

*Reservations, fee:* Sites are $5 and are first come, first served.

*Contact:* Call Dinosaur National Monument Headquarters in Colorado at (303) 374-2216 or the Dinosaur Quarry Visitors Center in Utah at (801) 789-2115.

*Location:* From Vernal, drive east on U.S. 40 for 13.4 miles to Jensen, then drive 6.5 miles north on State Route 149 to the Dinosaur Quarry Visitors Center. The campground is four miles east of the quarry on State Route 149.

*Trip notes:* This is the first campground you come to after entering the Dinosaur National Monument area from the west. Featuring some open and some wooded sites, it's set right on the Green River, with impressive views of the rock formations on either side (hence the Split Mountain name). A nature trail with interpretive signs leads from the campground into the surrounding rugged sandstone terrain. At the Dinosaur Quarry, where remains of *Stegosaurus, Apatosaurus,* and *Allosaurus* are on view, fossils are preserved just as they were found (some were removed in the past, but no longer). The visitors center, open daily except New Year's Day, Thanksgiving, and Christmas, offers information on river rafting and fishing as well.

*Season:* Open year-round.

---

## 48. GREEN RIVER

*Reference:* **In Dinosaur National Monument; map A3, grid g6.**

*Campsites, facilities:* There are 100 sites for RVs and tents, with picnic tables and fire pits, drinking water, modern rest rooms, and pit toilets.

*Reservations, fee:* Sites are $5 and are first come, first served.

*Contact:* Call Dinosaur National Monument headquarters in Colorado at (303) 374-2216 or the Dinosaur Quarry Visitors Center in Utah at (801) 789-2113.

*Location:* From Vernal, drive west on U.S. 40 for 13.4 miles to Jensen, then north for 6.5 miles to the Dinosaur Quarry Visitors Center. The campground is five miles east of the Quarry.

*Trip notes:* Though the Dinosaur Quarry is the big draw at this Green River campground, the area features some other nice side trips and hiking trails. Just down Cub Creek Road, for example, there's the historic Josie Morris Ranch, commemorating one of the area's first settlers, along with a short walk to some petroglyphs. The campground itself, in a mostly desertlike setting, has some lovely river views.

*Season:* Memorial Day through Labor Day.

## 49. RAINBOW PARK

*Reference:* **In Dinosaur National Monument; map A3, grid g7.**

*Campsites, facilities:* There are four tent sites with picnic tables, fire pits, and pit toilets, but *no drinking water.* A boat ramp also provides Green River launch access for rafts.

*Reservations, fee:* Sites are free and are first come, first served.

*Contact:* Call Dinosaur National Monument headquarters in Colorado at (303) 374-2216 or the Dinosaur Quarry Visitors Center in Utah at (801) 782-2115.

*Location:* From Vernal, go east on U.S. 40 for 13.4 miles to Jensen. Then drive four miles to Brush Creek Road and take it for 4.8 miles to the northwest, looking for an unnamed dirt road that heads north. Take this unlabeled road for 2.2 miles until it intersects with Island Park Road, and take that dirt road for 13.8 miles to the campground. Note: These rugged dirt roads are impassable when wet, and trailers are not recommended.

*Trip notes:* This area is mainly used by boaters taking day trips down the Green River to Split Mountain, but the cottonwood-shaded campground is a nice place to spend the night. Nearby, the federally managed Jones Hole Fish Hatchery makes for an interesting visit. Trout fishing on Jones Hole Creek below the hatchery can be challenging: fly fishers can see big fish in the pools, but getting them to bite may be another story.

*Season:* May 1 through November 30.

## 50. FOSSIL VALLEY

*Reference:* **In Vernal; map A3, grid g6.**

*Campsites, facilities:* There are 45 sites with full hookups and five tent sites, plus picnic tables, rest rooms, showers, laundry facilities, RV disposal, and a public phone. Cable TV is available for $1 a night. Pets are welcome.

*Reservations, fee:* Reservations are recommended in summer. Sites are $18 for full hookups and $9 for tents, plus an additional $2 for each extra person over age six in groups of more than two.

*Contact:* Fossil Valley, 999 West U.S. 40, Vernal, UT 84078; (801) 789-6450.

*Location:* The campground is right in Vernal, on U.S. Route 40, two miles into town.

*Trip notes:* This is a city RV park, with little more to recommend it than decent hookups and some grass and trees. It's next to several grocery stores and restaurants.

*Season:* April through October.

---

## 51. MANILA/FLAMING GORGE KOA

*Reference:* In Manila; map A3, grid g5.

*Campsites, facilities:* There are 47 RV sites and 23 tent sites, with picnic tables, barbecue grills, rest rooms, showers, laundry facilities, RV disposal, a game room, a swimming pool, a public phone, and a convenience/gift store. Pets are allowed.

*Reservations, fee:* Reservations are strongly recommended; some sites are booked a year in advance. Tent sites are $14. RV sites are $15 with no hookups; $16 with electricity; $17 with water and electricity; $18 with water, electricity, and sewer; and $20 with full hookups plus cable TV. Cabins are $26.

*Contact:* Manila/Flaming Gorge KOA, P.O. Box 157, Manila, UT 84046; (801) 784-3184.

*Location:* In Manila, take State Route 43 west for three blocks to the sign for the campground.

*Trip notes:* Manila's shaded, grassy KOA is in a rural area, on a hill five miles above Flaming Gorge Reservoir. This private facility has hookups, whereas area U.S. Forest Service facilities do not, making it popular with boaters and anglers looking for a more civilized camping experience. Manila, though small, is the largest Utah town near the reservoir.

*Season:* Mid-April through mid-October.

---

## 52. VERNAL CAMPGROUND DINA

*Reference:* In Vernal; map A3, grid g5.

*Campsites, facilities:* There are 150 RV sites with full hookups, plus a 10-acre grassy area for tents. Some of the pull-throughs are big enough for extra-wide trailers. Facilities include rest rooms, showers, cable TV, a swimming pool, a convenience/gift shop, a covered picnic pavilion, a playground, miniature golf, and a game-room area. Pets are allowed.

*Reservations, fee:* Reservations are recommended in June and July. Sites with full hookups are $17.40; sites with water and electricity are $16.40; and tent sites are $6 for each adult. Prices for hookup sites increase by $2 for every adult in groups of more than two, and all sites charge $1 extra per child, ages seven to 15.

*Contact:* Vernal Campground Dina, 930 North Vernal Avenue, Vernal, UT 84078; (801) 789-2148 or (800) 245-2148.

---

*Location:* The campground is on U.S. 191 in Vernal, nine blocks north of the city center. (The highway becomes Vernal Avenue in town.)

*Trip notes:* This urban RV park caters to groups, and it hosts trailer rallies each year. Vernal is the gateway to Dinosaur National Monument, with lots of city amenities; alas, it also has the city ambience to go with 'em, meaning business and highway noise all around.

*Season:* May 1 through November 30, though nine hookup sites are open through the winter.

---

## 53. PELICAN LAKE

*Reference:* **On Bureau of Land Management property at Pelican Lake; map A3, grid h3.**

*Campsites, facilities:* There are 12 sites with picnic tables and pit toilets, but *no drinking water.*

*Reservations, fee:* Sites are free and are first come, first served.

*Contact:* Call the Vernal District Office of the Bureau of Land Management at (801) 789-1362.

*Location:* From Vernal, take U.S. 191 and head south and west to State Route 88. Turn south and proceed for about 15 miles to Pelican Lake.

*Trip notes:* Don't expect big crowds at this small desert pond, set in largely open farmland. Pelican Lake once had a reputation as one of the West's best bluegill fisheries, but a variety of water-quality problems has caused fishing to drop off; accordingly, camping has, too. In spring and summer, birders may enjoy driving south on State Route 88 to view migrating winged species at the Ouray National Wildlife Refuge. In fact, there are good numbers of feathered creatures, including red-winged and yellow-headed blackbirds, at Pelican Lake itself.

*Season:* Open year-round.

---

## 54. MOUNTAIN VIEW

*Reference:* **On Starvation Reservoir; map A3, grid h0.**

*Campsites, facilities:* There are 30 sites with no hookups. Facilities include modern rest rooms, showers, a nice playground, a group use area, and a sewage dump station. A few of the campsites are handicapped accessible.

*Reservations, fee:* Reservations are available from three to 120 days in advance; call (800) 322-3770 Monday through Friday from 8 A.M. to 5 P.M. Sites are $10.

*Contact:* Call Starvation State Park at (801) 738-2326.

*Location:* From the west end of Duchesne, take the well-marked paved road to the state park and follow it northwest for four miles.

*Trip notes:* This campground is situated above a 3,500-acre desert reservoir, providing nice views of the buff-colored rock all around. Scattered shade trees give welcome relief from the sun, and boating and water sports help keep campers cool, too. Ask the ranger about the nearby off-highway vehicle riding area.

*Season:* May 1 through October 15.

---

# 55. LOWER BEACH

*Reference:* **On Starvation Reservoir; map A3, grid h1.**

*Campsites, facilities:* There are 24 sites with no hookups. Facilities include modern rest rooms, showers, a nice playground, a group use area, and a sewage dump station. A few of the campsites are handicapped accessible.

*Reservations, fee:* Reservations are available from three to 120 days in advance; call (800) 322-3770 Monday through Friday from 8 A.M. to 5 P.M. Sites are $9 Monday through Thursday and $10 Friday, Saturday, and holidays.

*Contact:* Call Starvation State Park at (801) 738-2326.

*Location:* From the west end of Duchesne, take the paved, well-marked road that leads to the state park and drive northwest for four miles.

*Trip notes:* Beach lovers clamor for the grassy sites right next to the water at this 3,500-acre reservoir. And while boating and water sports are prime pastimes, the reservoir isn't as crowded as many along the Wasatch Front, so it's worth the drive to beat the crowds.

*Season:* May 1 through October 15.

# 56. AVINTAQUIN

*Reference:* **In Ashley National Forest; map A3, grid j0.**

*Campsites, facilities:* There are 13 RV sites and two tent sites, with picnic tables, fire grills, and pit toilets, but *no water.*

*Reservations, fee:* Sites are $5 and are first come, first served.

*Contact:* Call the Duchesne Ranger District at (801) 738-2482.

*Location:* From Duchesne, drive 32.7 miles southwest on State Route 33. Then go about one mile west on Forest Road 047 to the campground.

*Trip notes:* There's no fishing in this forest campground—a rarity in Utah. That makes it a nice, quiet place to get away from the angling crowds for a simple weekend of hiking or horseback riding. The campground is at an elevation of 8,800 feet in a remote alpine setting of aspen and pine; in the surrounding rolling meadows, wildlife—especially mule deer—is a common sight.

*Season:* April 25 through September 10.

## LEAVE NO TRACE TIPS

### Minimize use and impact of fires.

• Campfires can have a lasting impact on the backcountry. Always carry a lightweight stove for cooking, and use a candle lantern instead of building a fire whenever possible.

• Where fires are permitted, use established fire rings only. Do not scar large rocks or overhangs.

• Gather sticks for your campfire that are no larger than the diameter of your wrist. Do not scar the natural setting by snapping the branches off live, dead, or downed trees.

• Completely extinguish your campfire and make sure it is cold before departing. Remove all unburned trash from the fire ring and scatter the cold ashes over a large area well away from any camp.

# MAP B1

Map of Utah .......................... see page 46
Beyond This Region:
North (Map A1) ................... see page 48
East (Map B2) .................... see page 188
South ........................................... Arizona
West ............................................ Nevada

81 Campgrounds
Pages 150–187

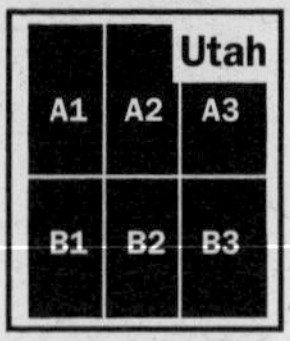
Utah
A1
A2
A3
B1
B2
B3

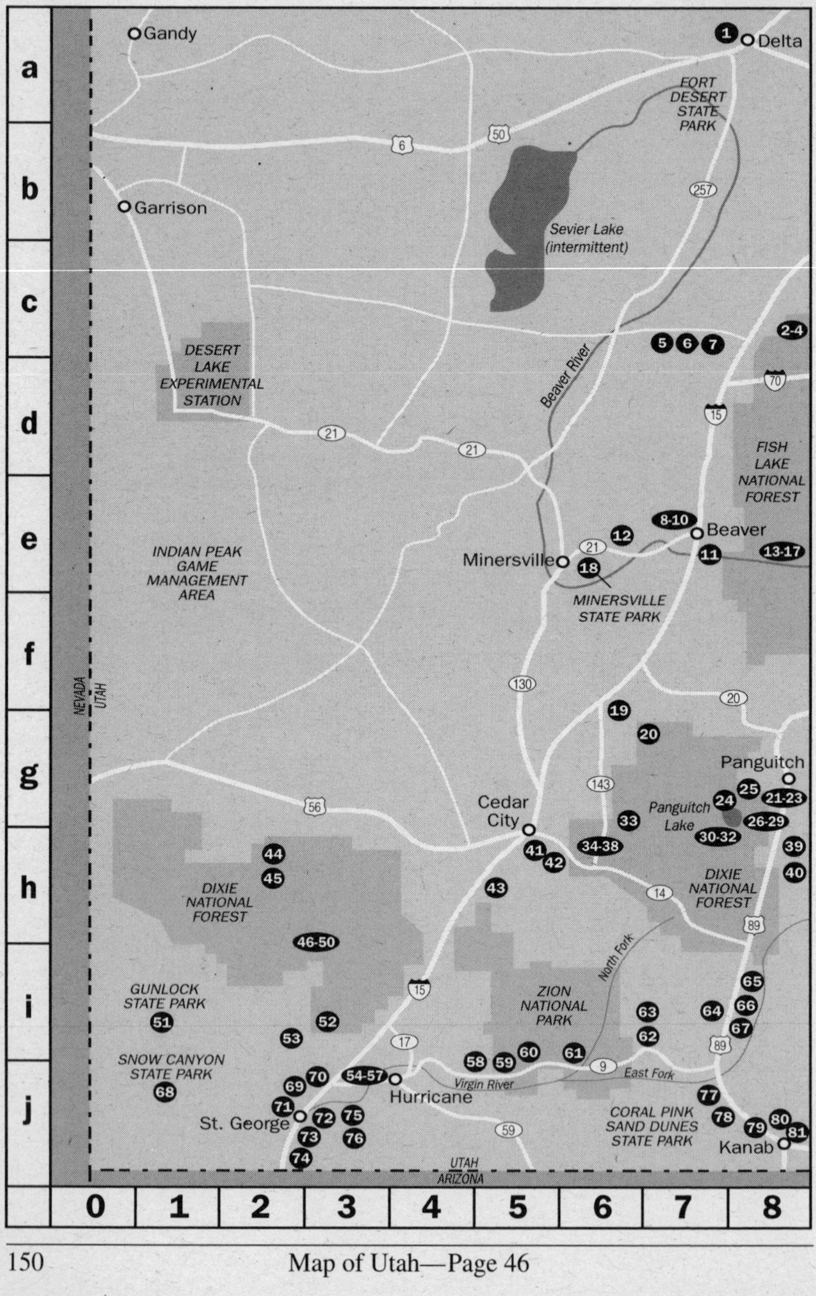
a
b
c
d
e
f
g
h
i
j
0
1
2
3
4
5
6
7
8
Gandy
Delta
1
FORT DESERT STATE PARK
6
50
257
Garrison
Sevier Lake (intermittent)
DESERT LAKE EXPERIMENTAL STATION
Beaver River
5
6
7
2-4
70
15
21
21
FISH LAKE NATIONAL FOREST
8-10
Beaver
12
21
Minersville
18
11
13-17
INDIAN PEAK GAME MANAGEMENT AREA
MINERSVILLE STATE PARK
130
NEVADA
UTAH
20
19
20
Panguitch
143
Cedar City
25
24
21-23
Panguitch Lake
26-29
30-32
33
34-38
56
44
45
41
42
39
40
43
14
DIXIE NATIONAL FOREST
DIXIE NATIONAL FOREST
89
46-50
North Fork
15
65
GUNLOCK STATE PARK
ZION NATIONAL PARK
63
64
66
51
52
53
17
62
67
89
SNOW CANYON STATE PARK
58
59
60
61
9
68
69
70
54-57
Hurricane
Virgin River
East Fork
77
71
72
75
CORAL PINK SAND DUNES STATE PARK
78
80
St. George
73
76
59
79
81
Kanab
74
UTAH
ARIZONA

## Chapter B1 features:

1. Antelope Valley RV Park
2. Oak Creek Canyon
3. Maple Hollow
4. Adelaide
5. Fillmore KOA
6. R and R
7. Wagons West
8. Beaver KOA
9. Delano Motel and RV Park
10. United Beaver Camperland
11. Beaver Canyon Campground
12. Rock Corral
13. Little Cottonwood
14. Kents Lake
15. Mahogany Cove
16. Little Reservoir
17. Anderson Meadow
18. Minersville State Park
19. Pit Stop
20. Vermillion Castle
21. Sportsman's Paradise Park and Campground
22. Red Canyons RV Park
23. Panguitch KOA
24. Hitch-N-Post RV Park and Campground
25. White Bridge Campground
26. Lake View Resort
27. Panguitch Lake Resort
28. Panguitch Lake North
29. Panguitch Lake South
30. General Store Gift Shop and RV Park
31. Rustic Lodge
32. Deer Trail Lodge
33. Point Supreme
34. Cedar Canyon
35. Te-Ah
36. Navajo Lake
37. Spruces
38. Duck Creek
39. Riverside Campground
40. Mountainridge
41. Cedar City KOA
42. Country Aire
43. Red Ledge Campground
44. Honeycomb Rocks
45. Pine Park
46. Blue Spring
47. Equestrian
48. North Juniper Park
49. South Juniper Park
50. Pines
51. Gunlock State Park
52. Oak Grove
53. Baker Dam
54. Silver Springs RV Park
55. Quail Lake RV Park
56. Willow Park
57. Brentwood Utah RV Park
58. Zion Canyon Campground
59. Watchman
60. South
61. Lava Point
62. Mukuntuweep RV Park and Campground
63. Zion Ponderosa Resort
64. Zion/Bryce KOA
65. Bauer's Canyon Ranch
66. Tortoise and Hare Trailer Court
67. East Zion Trailer Park
68. Shivwits Campground
69. Leeds RV Park
70. Harrisburg Lakeside RV Resort
71. Settlers RV Park
72. McArthur's Temple View RV Resort
73. St. George Campground and RV Park
74. Redlands RV Park
75. Quail Creek State Park
76. Dixie Red Cliffs
77. Coral Pink Sand Dunes State Park
78. Ponderosa Grove
79. Crazy Horse Campark
80. Kanab RV Corral
81. Hitch 'N Post

# 1. ANTELOPE VALLEY RV PARK

**RV 3**

*Reference:* **Near Delta; map B1, grid a8.**

*Campsites, facilities:* There are 96 RV sites with full hookups, plus rest rooms, showers, laundry facilities, a public phone, and a playground.

*Reservations, fee:* Reservations are accepted. Sites are $18.

*Contact:* Call the RV park at (801) 864-1813.

*Location:* From Delta, take U.S. 50 west for a quarter of a mile; the campground is just west of the overpass. Delta is located 89 miles southeast of Provo along Highway 6, and 87 miles east of the Nevada border along Highway 50/6.

*Trip notes:* This is a 5.5-acre park just outside of Delta, population 3,000. Delta, the largest town in the Great Basin area, is home to some interesting rock shops as well as the Great Basin History Museum. The campground is dotted with more than 40 full-grown trees, though the campsites are in open desert with little shade.

*Season:* Open year-round.

# 2. OAK CREEK CANYON

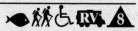 **RV 8**

*Reference:* **In Fishlake National Forest; map B1, grid c8.**

*Campsites, facilities:* This campground has 19 single sites and four group sites, plus picnic tables, fire grills, vault toilets, running water, a covered picnic pavilion, and an amphitheater. One group site has a wheelchair-accessible rest room.

*Reservations, fee:* Reservations are only accepted for the group site with a wheelchair-accessible rest room. Sites are $5.

*Contact:* Call the Fillmore Ranger District at (801) 743-5721.

*Location:* The campground is 4.5 miles northeast of Oak City on State Route 125. From Delta, drive seven miles east on State Route 125 and then turn east to the campground.

*Trip notes:* This campground is next to a small stream planted with rainbow trout in a canyon filled with oak and maple trees, so it's especially lovely in fall. The sites sit in a circle on a gravel road. Short hiking trails crisscross the area. Covered picnic tables and horseshoe and volleyball areas make it an ideal family reunion spot.

*Season:* April 21 through September 30.

# 3. MAPLE HOLLOW

**RV 4**

*Reference:* **In Fishlake National Forest; map B1, grid c8.**

*Campsites, facilities:* There are 10 sites with picnic tables and fire pits. Water and pit toilets are available.

*Reservations, fee:* Sites are free and are first come, first served.

*Contact:* Call the Fillmore Ranger District at (801) 743-5721.

*Location:* From Beaver, drive north on Interstate 15 for 57 miles and take the Fillmore turnoff, exit 163. In Fillmore, follow U.S. Route 91 north for about six miles, and turn east on Maple Hollow Road. When the road hits the

Forest Service boundary, it becomes Forest Service Road 098; the campground is about a mile inside the boundary on the north side of the road.

*Trip notes:* This campground is a popular canyon getaway for locals. It's not high enough on the mountain to actually be called alpine, but it is forested and in the shade, so it's a good cooling-off spot in the summer. Anglers can fish for trout in nearby Kents and Puffer Lakes, while hikers can set off for the trails around Delano Peak and Mount Holly.

*Season:* May 21 through October 30.

## 4. ADELAIDE

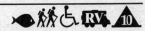

*Reference:* **In Fishlake National Forest; map B1, grid c8.**

*Campsites, facilities:* This handicapped-accessible campground has eight sites, most large enough to handle several cars or RVs, plus picnic tables and fire pits, vault and flush toilets, drinking water, a covered pavilion, and an amphitheater.

*Reservations, fee:* Sites are $5 and are first come, first served.

*Contact:* Call the Fillmore Ranger District at (801) 743-5721.

*Location:* Take Interstate 15 south from Fillmore or north from Beaver, and look for the Kanosh exit. Drive into Kanosh and follow Forest Road 106 east up Corn Creek Canyon for six miles to the campground.

*Trip notes:* Don't be fooled by the diminutive size of the stream that flows through this campground: Corn Creek can produce some mighty big fish. The campground itself, built in the Civilian Conservation Corps era, exudes nostalgia; the bandstand-like pavilion with a rock foundation is still a fine place to sit and talk. The sites are nestled under huge trees in a red-rock canyon that's particularly pretty in the fall. Nearby is the Paiute ATV Trail, one of the longest motorized trails of its kind in the United States.

*Season:* April 21 through October 30.

## 5. FILLMORE KOA

*Reference:* **In Fillmore; map B1, grid c7.**

*Campsites, facilities:* There are 54 RV sites with full hookups, a tent camping area with covered picnic tables, and several one- and two-room camping cabins. A rest room, a shower, laundry facilities, a convenience and gift store with RV supplies, a swimming pool, a game room, a playground, and RV disposal are available. Pets are welcome on a leash.

*Reservations, fee:* Reservations are accepted. Sites are $17.50 for full hookups, $16.50 for water and electricity, and $13.50 for tents; cabins are $24 for one room and $28 for two rooms. Off-season rates are slightly lower.

*Contact:* Fillmore KOA, HC 61 Box 26, Fillmore, UT 84631; (801) 743-4420.

*Location:* From Beaver, go north on Interstate 15 for 57 miles. Take exit 163 and go east for one-tenth of a mile to the KOA sign. Turn right and proceed half a mile to the campground.

*Trip notes:* This is a newer KOA, meaning it's mostly out in the open with some small shade trees; the grassy tent sites are set amid sagebrush, and the area is served by a gravel road. The place offers a nice combo of amenities

and out-of-the-way location, with views of the Pavant Mountains to the east and the volcanic cinder cones of the valley to the west. There's direct access to the Paiute ATV Trail, used by horses and dune buggies alike, with ATV and horse rentals and tours available from vendors in town, not to mention tours to favorite area rockhounding spots. And history buffs, take note: in Fillmore, Utah's first capital, the old capitol building is now a museum.
*Season:* March 1 through December 10.

## 6. R AND R

*Reference:* **In Fillmore; map Utah 2, grid c7.**
*Campsites, facilities:* There are 18 RV sites with full hookups, and one rest room, but no showers.
*Reservations, fee:* Reservations are accepted. Sites are $5.
*Contact:* R and R, P.O. Box 1166, Fillmore, UT 84631; (801) 743-6131.
*Location:* From Beaver, take Interstate 15 north for 57 miles to Fillmore. Take exit 163 and head for Main Street. R and R is on Main Street.
*Trip notes:* This is hardly a campground; it's basically a gravel spot with hook-ups behind an old service station. The service station will repair RVs, however, as well as arrange ATV or fishing tours.
*Season:* Open year-round.

## 7. WAGONS WEST

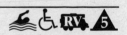

*Reference:* **In Fillmore; map B1, grid c7.**
*Campsites, facilities:* There are 42 RV sites with full hookups, and eight tent camping sites. Rest rooms, showers, picnic tables, laundry facilities, cable TV, and RV supplies are available. Pets are allowed.
*Reservations, fee:* Reservations are accepted. Sites are $16 for full hookups and $11 for tents.
*Contact:* Wagons West, P.O. Box 901, Fillmore, UT 84631; (801) 743-6188.
*Location:* From Beaver, take Interstate 15 north for 57 miles to Fillmore (exit 163), and head for Main Street. Wagons West is at 545 North Main Street.
*Trip notes:* This campground is in downtown Fillmore, which was the territorial capital of Utah; its red sandstone capitol building is now a museum that's well worth touring. The campground itself is shaded and grassy and next to a private pioneer-era house. It's also close to the Paiute ATV Trail, popular with horseback riders and ATV users alike. ATV riders can access the trail directly from the campground, while horseback riders must transport their horses to the nearby canyons.
*Season:* Open year-round.

## 8. BEAVER KOA

*Reference:* **In Beaver; map B1, grid e7.**
*Campsites, facilities:* This handicapped-accessible campground has 65 RV sites, 27 with full hookups; 10 tent camping sites; and another group area for tents. Also available are rest rooms, showers, laundry facilities, a disposal site, a swimming pool, a grocery and gift shop, fire pits, and a public phone.

*Reservations, fee:* Reservations are accepted. Sites are $17 with full hookups, $16 for water and electricity, and $13.50 for tents.

*Contact:* Beaver KOA, P.O. Box 1437, Beaver, UT 84731; (801) 438-2924.

*Location:* Follow Interstate 15 to Beaver and take exit 122, on the north end of town. Turn left and go one mile north on Manderfield Road. The campground is visible from the freeway, on the west side of Manderfield Road.

*Trip notes:* This KOA is a little roomier than most, with unusually well-spaced sites and an open farmland setting. And though it's not far from the freeway, it's far enough to have a somewhat rural feel. Most sites are shaded and grassy, with gravel patches and interior roads; a fence shields the shaded tent area from the road. There's even a view of the towering Tushar Mountains a few miles to the east.

*Season:* March through November.

---

## 9. DELANO MOTEL AND RV PARK

*Reference:* In Beaver; map B1, grid e7.

*Campsites, facilities:* There are 28 RV sites with pull-throughs and hookups, plus rest rooms, showers, and laundry facilities. Pets are allowed.

*Reservations, fee:* Reservations are accepted. Sites are $8.50.

*Contact:* Delano Motel and RV Park, 480 North Main Street, Beaver, UT 84713; (801) 438-2418.

*Location:* Take Interstate 15 to Beaver, get off at either of the two exits, and head for Main Street. Delano RV Park is at 480 North Main Street, behind the Delano Motel.

*Trip notes:* This is basically a parking-lot RV spot in the middle of a small town: a gravel area off Main Street, behind a motel, with some rough picnic tables and a handful of small trees. Beaver *is* close to Elk Meadows Ski Resort, however, so the campground is a low-cost winter lodging alternative. Golfing, fishing, and hunting possibilities abound nearby in Beaver Canyon, which can be reached via a scenic highway (State Route 153).

*Season:* Open year-round.

---

## 10. UNITED BEAVER CAMPERLAND

*Reference:* In Beaver; map B1, grid e7.

*Campsites, facilities:* There are 85 sites with full hookups, plus rest rooms, showers, laundry facilities, and an RV disposal site. Facilities are all set on one level for wheelchair access.

*Reservations, fee:* Reservations are accepted. Sites are $13.95 for two people, plus $2 for each additional person.

*Contact:* United Beaver Camperland, P.O. Box 1060, Beaver, UT 84713; (801) 438-2808.

*Location:* Take Interstate 15 to Beaver and get off at exit 109. Turn right on Campground Road and go to the campground at 1603 South.

*Trip notes:* Visible from the highway in a farmland setting at the end of town, this campground has some good views of the Tushar Mountains to the east. There are some shaded and grassy sites, and the tent section is on partially

---

open terrain. Heat is usually not a problem, though, because Beaver is at an elevation of 6,000 feet. For winter sports buffs, the Elk Meadows Ski Resort is nearby.

*Season:* Open year-round.

## 11. BEAVER CANYON CAMPGROUND

*Reference:* **East of Beaver, map B1, grid e7.**

*Campsites, facilities:* There are 31 sites with full hookups, 25 with water and electricity only, and 50 tent sites. Rest rooms, showers, laundry facilities, a public phone, a playground, fire pits, and firewood are available. Pets are allowed. A Mexican restaurant on the premises offers homemade tamales and chilis rellenos daily.

*Reservations, fee:* Reservations are accepted. Sites are $12 with full hookups, $10 with water and electricity, and $10 for tents.

*Contact:* Beaver Canyon Campground, P.O. Box 1528, Beaver, UT 84713; (801) 438-5654.

*Location:* Take Interstate 15 to Beaver and get off at exit 112 or 109; either way, you'll end up on Main Street. Go to the center of town, pick up State Route 153 heading east, and continue for 1.25 miles until you reach the campground.

*Trip notes:* This country campground looks right up at the Tushar Mountains and has a funky Old West feel. In fact, pioneer paraphernalia and artifacts abound. There's a log fort, old wagons and wagon wheels, and a Western-themed children's playground on the property. Even the covered picnic tables in the tent section are made from logs. Most of the campsites are gravel, with little grass or greenery. The Beaver public golf course is located just up the road.

*Season:* April 15 through November 10.

## 12. ROCK CORRAL

*Reference:* **On Bureau of Land Management property; map B1, grid e6.**

*Campsites, facilities:* This is a rather primitive area with just a few picnic tables, two fire pits, and pit toilets, but *no water.*

*Reservations, fee:* Camping is free and sites are first come, first served.

*Contact:* Call the Cedar City District Office of the Bureau of Land Management at (801) 586-2401.

*Location:* From Milford, go south for half a mile on State Route 21. Take a marked turnoff to the east for Rock Corral, and drive another 10 miles to the campground.

*Trip notes:* Though in a remote part of Utah's western desert, this dispersed-camping spot in an oak-brush, pinyon, and juniper forest offers lots of interesting things to do. The granite rock formations make it one of the area's most scenic campgrounds; rock climbing is also catching on in these parts. And rockhounders and hikers can find plenty of geologic fascination in the nearby Mineral Mountains.

*Season:* Open year-round.

# 13. LITTLE COTTONWOOD

*Reference:* **In Fishlake National Forest; map B1, grid e8.**

*Campsites, facilities:* There are eight sites with flush toilets, picnic tables, and fire pits. Three of the sites are handicapped accessible.

*Reservations, fee:* Sites are $6 and are first come, first served.

*Contact:* Contact the Beaver Ranger District at (801) 438-2436.

*Location:* From Beaver, drive six miles east on State Route 153. The campground is on the right side of the road, with sites situated along the Beaver River.

*Trip notes:* Accessible by a paved road, this campground has several features for the disabled, including three specially designed sites, roomy rest rooms, and a special ramp leading to the river for fishing. Sites are right next to the Beaver River in a forest of cottonwood and ponderosa pine; the nearby woods have shorter mountain mahogany and juniper trees as well.

*Season:* May through November.

# 14. KENTS LAKE

*Reference:* **In Fishlake National Forest; map B1, grid e8.**

*Campsites, facilities:* There are 31 sites and one group-use site with picnic tables and fire grills. Drinking water, vault toilets, and a covered picnic pavilion are also available. The RV length limit is 60 feet.

*Reservations, fee:* Sites are $4 and are first come, first served.

*Contact:* Call the Beaver Ranger District of Fishlake National Forest at (801) 438-2436.

*Location:* From Beaver, drive east on State Route 153 approximately nine miles. Look for a road marker to Forest Road 137. Drive south on this dirt road for approximately three miles; the campground is on the north side.

*Trip notes:* At 8,800 feet, this high-country campground has a somewhat abbreviated season (with water typically available for about four months). The primary pastime is trout fishing on the high alpine lake, where anglers are allowed to launch small boats. And for hikers, there's ready access to area trails.

*Season:* June through September.

# 15. MAHOGANY COVE

*Reference:* **In Fishlake National Forest; map B1, grid e8.**

*Campsites, facilities:* There are seven sites with picnic tables and fire pits. Drinking water and vault toilets are available. The RV length limit is 24 feet.

*Reservations, fee:* Sites are $4 and are first come, first served.

*Contact:* Call the Beaver Ranger District of Fishlake National Forest at (801) 438-2436.

*Location:* From Beaver, take State Route 153 southeast for 11.2 miles into Beaver Canyon. The campground is on the north side of the highway.

*Trip notes:* Easy access, an alpine setting (elevation 7,500), and impressive views of the nearby Tushar Mountains are the big pluses here. Locals also like being close to the amenities of nearby Elk Meadows Ski Resort and the

---

trout fishing in area streams, lakes, and the Beaver River a one-mile walk away. Half the campground is shaded by ponderosa pine, while the other half is covered with shorter mountain mahogany. In summer, a leisurely scenic drive over the top of the Tushar Mountains into Piute County on the eastern side of the Tushars affords some panoramic glimpses of both sides of the range.

*Season:* Late May through mid-October.

---

## 16. LITTLE RESERVOIR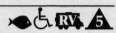

*Reference:* **In Fishlake National Forest; map B1, grid e8.**

*Campsites, facilities:* There are five family sites and two group sites, plus picnic tables, fire grills, drinking water, vault toilets, and wheelchair access for fishing near the dam. There's also a wheelchair-accessible rest room, though the doorway is small. The RV length limit is 40 feet.

*Reservations, fee:* Sites are $5 and are first come, first served.

*Contact:* Call the Beaver Ranger District of Fishlake National Forest at (801) 438-2436.

*Location:* From Beaver, take State Highway 153 southeast for 11.2 miles up Beaver Canyon; the campground is on the south side of the road.

*Trip notes:* The accessible location and pretty alpine scenery (elevation 7,350) make Little Reservoir one of Beaver Canyon's most popular campgrounds. It's set right next to a fishing lake in a forest of juniper, scrub oak, and ponderosa pine. Little Reservoir is regularly stocked by the Utah Division of Wildlife Resources with catchable rainbow trout and has a wheelchair-accessible dam.

*Season:* May through mid-October.

---

## 17. ANDERSON MEADOW

*Reference:* **In Fishlake National Forest; map B1, grid e8.**

*Campsites, facilities:* There are 10 sites with picnic tables and fire grills. Drinking water and vault toilets are available. The RV length limit is 24 feet.

*Reservations, fee:* Sites are $4 and are first come, first served.

*Contact:* Contact the Beaver Ranger District of Fishlake National Forest at (801) 438-2436.

*Location:* From the town of Beaver just off Interstate 15, take State Route 153 east for approximately nine miles into Beaver Canyon, looking for a marked turnoff to Forest Road 137. Drive south on this dirt road for approximately five miles to the campground.

*Trip notes:* This small alpine campground (elevation 9,500), set in an aspen and mixed conifer forest, is on the edge of Anderson Meadow Reservoir and is somewhat removed from the traffic of Beaver Canyon. Trout fishing is the primary activity here, though the exceptional setting alone is worth the trip. Pick up a hiking guide to the area at the ranger station in Beaver. The altitude limits water availability—and the season—to about four months of the year.

*Season:* June through September.

---

# 18. MINERSVILLE STATE PARK

*Reference:* **On Minersville Reservoir; map B1, grid e6.**

*Campsites, facilities:* There are 29 sites with electric hookups, modern rest rooms with showers, a sewage dump station, and a fish-cleaning station. Boat docks and a launching ramp are nearby.

*Reservations, fee:* Reservations are available 120 days in advance for a nonrefundable $5 per site; call (800) 322-3770 Monday through Friday from 8 A.M. to 5 P.M. Sites are $11. Utah residents 62 years and older with a Special Fun Tag get a $2 discount Sunday through Thursday.

*Contact:* Call Minersville State Park at (801) 438-5472.

*Location:* To reach the campground, drive 12 miles west of Beaver off State Route 21.

*Trip notes:* Electrical hookups being a rarity on Utah reservoirs, this is a popular place. The Utah Division of Wildlife Resources manages Minersville as a source of trophy trout; flies and lures are the only tackle allowed. Drawdowns in late summer, which come close to draining the reservoir at times, can make boating difficult; otherwise, the 1,130-acre reservoir is a good boating and waterskiing park. The campground itself has a little landscaped shade, though there's a somewhat desolate feel to the area.

*Season:* April through November.

---

# 19. PIT STOP

*Reference:* **In Parowan; map B1, grid g6.**

*Campsites, facilities:* There are 21 sites with full hookups, plus a few picnic tables, a small store, rest rooms, showers, a disposal site, and a public phone. Facilities have ramps for wheelchair access. Pets are allowed.

*Reservations, fee:* Reservations are recommended for summer weekends. Sites are $11 for two people, plus 50 cents for each additional person over age 13.

*Contact:* Pit Stop, P.O. Box 888, Parowan, UT 84761; (801) 477-3714.

*Location:* Parowan is about 31 miles south of Beaver and about 28 miles north of Cedar City, off Interstate 15. From the interstate, take the Parowan turnoff (exit 78) and go west onto Main Street. The Pit Stop is on the west side of the street, just past the Best Western Motel.

*Trip notes:* This is the only RV campground in Parowan, the nearest town to Brian Head Ski Resort. It is located behind the Pit Stop Restaurant.

*Season:* Open year-round.

---

# 20. VERMILLION CASTLE

*Reference:* **In Dixie National Forest east of Parowan; map B1, grid g7.**

*Campsites, facilities:* There are 20 sites, plus picnic tables, fire grills, flush and vault toilets, drinking water, and two group sites.

*Reservations, fee:* For reservations, call the U.S. Forest Service National Reservation System at (800) 280-2267. Sites are $7.

*Contact:* Call the Cedar City Ranger District at (801) 865-3700.

*Location:* From Cedar City, drive north on Interstate 15 for 15 miles. Take the

---

Parowan turnoff (exit 75). In Parowan, follow State Route 143 south for four miles. Then turn east and go one mile on Forest Road 049 to the campground.

*Trip notes:* The scenery here is an appealing mix of high-altitude alpine forest and the red rock that makes southern Utah famous. At an elevation of 7,000 feet, the campground usually opens in early May—long before the snow has melted at nearby Cedar Breaks National Monument—making this a good early-season base for trips to the Cedar Breaks overlooks, about 14 miles to the south. Lately the Dixie National Forest crew has been marking new mountain-bike trails, which, together with the cool weather, makes this an ideal summer biking spot. Note: While Bowery Creek at the campground is not regularly stocked with fish, you can find good angling and some boating at Yankee Meadows Reservoir, six miles east. Two mile-long hiking trails, Noah's Ark and Vermillion Castle, lead from the campground into alpine and red rock terrain.

*Season:* May 15 through October 15.

## 21. SPORTSMAN'S PARADISE PARK AND CAMPGROUND

*Reference:* **In Panguitch; map B1, grid g8.**

*Campsites, facilities:* There are 50 RV sites with full hookups, 33 of these pull-throughs; 16 RV sites with water and electricity, five of these pull-throughs; and 25 to 50 tent camping sites in a grassy area. Also available are picnic tables, fire pits, rest rooms, showers, a playground, laundry facilities, and a disposal site, as well as a restaurant, video rentals, a recreation hall, and a weight room. The campground has some handicapped-accessible facilities.

*Reservations, fee:* Reservations are accepted. Sites are $12 with full hookups, $10 with water and electricity, and $8 for tents.

*Contact:* Sportsman's Paradise Park and Campground, P.O. Box 655, Panguitch, UT 84759; (801) 676-8348.

*Location:* Take U.S. 89 north from Glendale, or south from Junction, for about 11 miles to Panguitch. The campground is in town on the west side of the highway, across the street from the Sevier River.

*Trip notes:* This place is nowhere near as scenic as campgrounds on nearby Panguitch Lake: it's out in the open, in a flat valley of farms and sagebrush, with gravel sites and roads and not much grass. Still, the location is decent: Panguitch is 24 miles from Bryce Canyon National Park, 30 miles from Cedar Breaks National Monument, and 45 miles from Zion National Park. The campground itself is spread over 10 acres. Anglers can try their luck at Panguitch Lake and in small streams in the area.

*Season:* April 15 through November 15.

## 22. RED CANYONS RV PARK

*Reference:* **East of Panguitch on State Route 12; map B1, grid g8.**

*Campsites, facilities:* There are 40 RV sites, all with full hookups, plus a large grassy area with room for 20 tents. New rest rooms and showers, covered picnic tables, a convenience store, and an RV disposal site are also available.

***Reservations, fee:*** Reservations are accepted. Sites are $14 with full hookups, $12 with water and electricity, and $9 for tents, plus $1 for each additional person in groups of more than two.

***Contact:*** Red Canyons RV Park, P.O. Box 717, Panguitch, UT 84759; (801) 676-2243.

***Location:*** From Panguitch, take U.S. 89 south toward Kanab to the Bryce Canyon turnoff (State Route 12), and travel east for one more mile to the campground.

***Trip notes:*** This rural campground has sites in the open, but with covered picnic tables. Campers can view the russet cliffs of Red Canyon in the distance. Mountain bikers will find some good trails in the area, and anglers can head for the small lakes in the surrounding forest, including Pine Lake and Tropic Reservoir.

***Season:*** March 1 through November 1.

---

## 23. PANGUITCH KOA

***Reference:*** **South of Panguitch on Highway 143; map B1, grid g8.**

***Campsites, facilities:*** There are 35 sites with full hookups, 20 sites with water and electricity, 14 tent sites, five cabins, and three group sites. Picnic tables, barbecue grills, rest rooms, showers, laundry facilities, a convenience store, a game room, a swimming pool, a playground, and a half-court for basketball are also available. Pets are allowed everywhere but in the cabins.

***Reservations, fee:*** Reservations are recommended from Memorial Day through Labor Day. Sites are $20 with full hookups, $19 with water and electricity, $16 for tents, and $29 for cabins.

***Contact:*** Panguitch KOA, Box 384, Panguitch, UT 84759; (801) 676-2225.

***Location:*** In Panguitch, drive south through town; then, instead of following U.S. 89 east, take State Route 143 south for five blocks. The KOA is 16 miles before Panguitch Lake.

***Trip notes:*** In a rural, sagebrush-covered valley outside town, this campground looks right up at the mountains of Dixie National Forest. The grassy sites are basically in the open with a few small shade trees. This KOA is in a good location for visitors to the Panguitch Lake area, as well as nearby Bryce Canyon National Park and Cedar Breaks National Monument, both within an hour's drive from the campground.

***Season:*** April 1 through November 1.

---

## 24. HITCH-N-POST RV PARK AND CAMPGROUND

***Reference:*** **On Panguitch Lake; map B1, grid g8.**

***Campsites, facilities:*** There are 19 sites with full hookups and 15 sites with water and electricity, plus two tent camping areas. Picnic tables, rest rooms, showers, laundry facilities, an RV disposal site, and an RV-and-car wash are also available. Pets are allowed on a leash.

---

*Reservations, fee:* Reservations are accepted. Sites are $10 and up for RVs and $10 for tents.

*Contact:* Hitch-N-Post RV Park and Campground, P.O. Box 368, Panguitch, UT 84759; (801) 676-2436 or (800) 282-9633.

*Location:* In Panguitch, take Main Street to the campground at 420 North Main Street.

*Trip notes:* Sites at urban Hitch-N-Post campground are shaded with medium-sized trees; there are two grassy areas in back for tents. The roads and RV sites are gravel. In a nutshell, this site is not as nice as many camping spots on Panguitch Lake, but it's closer to Bryce Canyon. The campground is 10 miles east of Panguitch Lake and 24 miles west of Bryce Canyon National Park.

*Season:* Open year-round.

## 25. WHITE BRIDGE CAMPGROUND

*Reference:* In Dixie National Forest; map B1, grid g7.

*Campsites, facilities:* There are 28 sites, plus picnic tables and fire grills, drinking water, vault toilets, and a dump station.

*Reservations, fee:* For reservations, call the U.S. Forest Service National Reservation System at (800) 280-2267. Sites are $9.

*Contact:* Call the Cedar City Ranger District at (801) 865-3700.

*Location:* From Panguitch, drive south on South Canyon Road, which turns into Forest Road 36. The campground is on the north side of the road, 10 miles out of town.

*Trip notes:* Though a few miles from Panguitch Lake itself, this is a popular spot. The well-shaded sites are along a pretty little stream (with good fishing), the lush vegetation lending a nice sense of privacy.

*Season:* June 1 through October 1.

## 26. LAKE VIEW RESORT

*Reference:* On Panguitch Lake in Dixie National Forest; map B1, grid g8.

*Campsites, facilities:* The resort has 20 sites with full hookups; housekeeping cabins are also available. Facilities include picnic tables, fire pits, rest rooms, showers, laundry facilities, a public phone, a playground, a convenience store, a restaurant, boat rentals, a boat dock, and gasoline.

*Reservations, fee:* Reservations are accepted. RV sites are $15 and tent sites are $10.

*Contact:* Lake View Resort, Box 397, Panguitch, UT 84759; (801) 676-2650.

*Location:* From Panguitch, drive 17 miles west on State Route 143. The resort is across the road on the east side of the lake.

*Trip notes:* Nestled among the large conifers of Dixie National Forest, this campground has the pleasant feel of an old-fashioned boat camp. Some sites are in the aspens and ponderosa pines and others are in the open; all have a great view of Panguitch Lake, one of Utah's top rainbow trout producers. Note: The dirt road to the sites is rough and steep.

*Season:* June through August.

## 27. PANGUITCH LAKE RESORT

*Reference:* **On Panguitch Lake; map B1, grid g8.**

*Campsites, facilities:* All 65 RV sites have full hookups. The resort has rest rooms, showers, picnic tables, a public phone, a fish cleaning station, and a convenience store. Pets are allowed.

*Reservations, fee:* Sites are $18.50 and are first come, first served.

*Contact:* Panguitch Lake Resort, P.O. Box 567, Panguitch, UT 84759; (801) 676-2657.

*Location:* From Panguitch, take State Route 143 to Panguitch Lake. Look for a sign for Panguitch Lake Resort on the north side of the road. Go down this road .25 miles to the resort on the south side of the lake.

*Trip notes:* The sites at this campground are best for RVs, since they're right next to each other and out in the open behind the resort. Panguitch Lake, complete with boat tie-ups, is 500 feet away. Views of the lake and mountains are somewhat obstructed.

*Season:* April through October.

## 28. PANGUITCH LAKE NORTH

*Reference:* **On Panguitch Lake; map B1, grid g8.**

*Campsites, facilities:* This campground with 39 sites offers campers flush and vault toilets, running water, picnic tables, fire grills, a group area, a trailer dump station, an amphitheater, and a ranger station.

*Reservations, fee:* Reservations for some sites can be made by calling the U.S. Forest Service National Reservation System at (800) 280-2267. Rates are $9, $11, or $18, depending on the size of the campsite.

*Contact:* Call the Cedar City Ranger District at (801) 865-3200.

*Location:* The campground is located 19 miles southwest of Panguitch. From U.S. 89 in Panguitch, take South Canyon Road/State Route 143 to Panguitch Lake. A large sign in the middle of Panguitch directs travelers to the lake. Drive past the southern edge of Panguitch Lake. The campground is on the north side of the road, south and slightly west of Panguitch Lake on Forest Road 80.

*Trip notes:* Nestled among tall ponderosa pines and wildflowers with a view of Panguitch Lake, this is one of the nicer campgrounds in Utah, and it has the best seat on the lake. Anglers flock to the waters here, one of the state's premier trout fishing spots. Sites are level and far apart, and the road and spurs are paved.

*Season:* June 1 through September 15.

## 29. PANGUITCH LAKE SOUTH

*Reference:* **On Panguitch Lake; map B1, grid g8.**

*Campsites, facilities:* This campground with 19 sites features vault toilets, picnic tables, drinking water, a trailer dump station, and fire grills.

*Reservations, fee:* Sites are $7 and are first come, first served.

*Contact:* Call the Cedar City Ranger District at (801) 865-3200.

*Location:* The campground is located 19 miles southwest of Panguitch. From U.S. 89 in Panguitch, take South Canyon Road/State Route 143 to Panguitch Lake. A large sign in the middle of Panguitch directs travelers to the lake. Drive past the southern shore of Panguitch Lake. The campground is on the south side of the road, south and slightly west of Panguitch Lake.

*Trip notes:* This campground with gravel roads and sites is across the lake from Panguitch Lake North (see page 163). Though less developed than its northern sister, the sites are still far apart and nestled in the trees, and all of them have nice views of the water. Some sites are next to the highway. Panguitch Lake and nearby streams keep trout anglers happy.

*Season:* June 1 through September 15.

## 30. GENERAL STORE GIFT SHOP AND RV PARK

*Reference:* **On Panguitch Lake; map B1, grid g7.**

*Campsites, facilities:* There are 14 RV sites with full hookups. Pit toilets and drinking water are available. Laundry facilities are located at the store, which sells groceries, sporting goods, and gift items.

*Reservations, fee:* Reservations are accepted. Sites are $16.

*Contact:* General Store Gift Shop and RV Park, P.O. Box 688, Panguitch, UT 84759; (801) 676-2464.

*Location:* From Panguitch, take State Route 143 to Panguitch Lake. The General Store and RV Park are on the south side of the lake, on the left side of the highway when coming from Panguitch.

*Trip notes:* This campground is for totally self-contained RVs only, since there are no rest rooms other than pit toilets and no showers. Campsites are on the aspen-covered hill behind the store, so campers have a view of the store and trout-filled Panguitch Lake.

*Season:* Open year-round.

## 31. RUSTIC LODGE

*Reference:* **On Panguitch Lake; map B1, grid g7.**

*Campsites, facilities:* The campground has 26 graveled sites, all with full hookups, plus sites for tent camping. Showers, rest rooms, laundry facilities, and fire rings are available. The resort also has a restaurant and cabins.

*Reservations, fee:* Reservations are recommended. Rates are $16 for RVs, $10 for tents, and $60 to $80 for cabins.

*Contact:* Rustic Lodge, P.O. Box 373, Panguitch, UT 84759; (801) 676-2627.

*Location:* From Panguitch, take State Route 143 to Panguitch Lake. Turn right off State Route 143 onto West Shore Road and look for the sign to Rustic Lodge on the left side of the road.

*Trip notes:* This year-round resort offers excellent fishing on Panguitch Lake in the spring, summer, and fall, and cross-country skiing, snowmobiling, and ice fishing in the winter. The primitive but pleasant campground is located in a grove of trees, across the street from the lake.

*Season:* Open year-round.

## 32. DEER TRAIL LODGE

*Reference:* **On the west side of Panguitch Lake on Clear Creek; map B1, grid g8.**

*Campsites, facilities:* There are 10 sites surrounding Deer Trail Lodge. Tents and small RVs only are recommended. Campers can use the showers in the cabins maintained by the lodge when the cabins are not occupied.

*Reservations, fee:* Reservations are accepted. Campsites are $7.50.

*Contact:* Deer Trail Lodge, Box 647, Panguitch, UT 84759; (801) 676-2211.

*Location:* From Panguitch, take State Highway 143 to Panguitch Lake. Turn right off State Route 143 onto West Shore Road. Look for Clear Creek Canyon Road off West Shore Road on the west side of the lake. The resort is .25 miles up this road on Clear Creek.

*Trip notes:* This campground should be considered more or less an overflow area in case the other campgrounds on Panguitch Lake are full. The primitive campsites are little more than bare areas around the lodge.

*Season:* May through October.

---

## 33. POINT SUPREME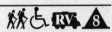

*Reference:* **In Cedar Breaks National Monument; map B1, grid h6.**

*Campsites, facilities:* This campground has 30 sites, all appropriate for RVs, plus drinking water, picnic tables, fire grills, and handicapped-accessible rest rooms with cold running water.

*Reservations, fee:* Campsites are $8 and are first come, first served.

*Contact:* Call Cedar Breaks National Monument at (801) 586-9451.

*Location:* Take State Highway 14 east from Cedar City for 23 miles. Point Supreme is a mile north of the Cedar Breaks National Monument Visitors Center.

*Trip notes:* The camping season is short at Cedar Breaks National Monument, thanks to a 10,000-foot elevation that often leaves the area blanketed by snow into June. The National Park Service tries to open the campground by mid-June, but call in advance just in case the weather isn't cooperating. When summer does finally break through, Cedar Breaks features Bryce Canyon–like amphitheaters, short hiking trails, and scenic overlooks. Wildflower displays in the high alpine meadows in July and August are stunning.

*Season:* Mid-June through late September.

---

## 34. CEDAR CANYON

*Reference:* **In Dixie National Forest; map B1, grid h6.**

*Campsites, facilities:* This campground has 19 sites, vault toilets, picnic tables, drinking water, and fire pits.

*Reservations, fee:* Sites are $7 and are first come, first served.

*Contact:* Call the Cedar City Ranger District office of Dixie National Forest at (801) 865-3700.

*Location:* From Cedar City, drive 13 miles southeast on State Highway 14. Look for the campground on the north side of the road.

---

*Trip notes:* At an elevation of 8,100 feet, this campground sits in the midst of red rock and forest, offering a cool alternative to the summer heat of the valley below. Campsites are shaded by tall trees and next to a nonfishable stream. Fishing is available nearby at Navajo and Panguitch Lakes. Cedar Canyon is a great base for campers who come to nearby Cedar City for the annual Utah Shakespearean Festival held every summer from the first week of July through the first week of September. The festival features professional actors, an outdoor replica of Shakespeare's Globe Theatre, and a free Green Show with period music and dance. The campground is also located near Milt's Stage Stop, one of the best steak houses in southern Utah. Other activities in the vicinity include an archery range and a children's fishing pond at Iron County–owned Woods Ranch. The 32-mile Virgin River Rim Trail also begins at Woods Ranch, and horseback riders can explore the nearby forest.

*Season:* May 25 through September 18.

## 35. TE-AH

*Reference:* **In Dixie National Forest; map B1, grid h6.**

*Campsites, facilities:* This campground with 42 sites features drinking water, picnic tables, flush toilets, a trailer dump station, and fire grills.

*Reservations, fee:* Reservations are accepted; call the U.S. Forest Service National Reservation System at (800) 280-2267. Sites are $9.

*Contact:* Call the Cedar City Ranger District at (801) 865-3700.

*Location:* From Cedar City, drive 28 miles east on State Route 14, then seven miles on Navajo Lake Road. The campground is located just over two miles west of Navajo Lake itself.

*Trip notes:* Since it's not set right on the lake, Te-Ah tends to fill up later on busy weekends than other Navajo Lake campgrounds. It's also the only campground on the lake that takes reservations in advance, and planning ahead might be a good idea in this popular recreation area. At an elevation of 9,200 feet, the season at this cool, alpine campground is relatively short, usually running from June through mid-September, depending on the weather. Most of the campsites are set in an aspen forest. The road and sites are paved. Hikers should note that the half-mile Pinks Trail, so named because of the path it takes through pink cliffs, begins at the upper portion of the campground. The longer 32-mile Virgin River Rim Trail, which offers great views of the Virgin River Basin and Zion National Park, can also be accessed from the campground. Look for deer and wild turkey in the area.

*Season:* June through mid-September.

## 36. NAVAJO LAKE

*Reference:* **In Dixie National Forest; map B1, grid h6.**

*Campsites, facilities:* This campground with 34 sites has flush toilets, drinking water, picnic tables, fire grills, and a public boat ramp for access to Navajo Lake. Roads and sites are paved.

*Reservations, fee:* Campsites are $9 and are first come, first served.

*Contact:* Call the Cedar City Ranger District at (801) 865-3200.

*Location:* The campground is located 25 miles east of Cedar City. Take State Route 14 from Cedar City for approximately 20 miles. Continue past Navajo Lake to Navajo Lake Road, and take it three miles south and west to the campground, which is on the southern shore of the lake.

*Trip notes:* Set high in the pines at an elevation of 9,600 feet, this popular campground on the shore of Navajo Lake fills up quickly, so try to find a spot early in the day, especially on weekends. Anglers will find better places in the state to fish, including nearby Panguitch Lake, but the Utah Division of Wildlife Resources stocks Navajo Lake with rainbow trout on a regular basis, which certainly helps your chances of catching dinner. Nearby, Navajo Lake Lodge offers boating, cabins, a restaurant, and a grocery store. Hiking, biking, and horseback riding can all be found on a trail leading from the campground to the 32-mile Virgin River Rim Trail.

*Season:* May 25 through September 18.

## 37. SPRUCES

*Reference:* **In Dixie National Forest; map B1, grid h6.**

*Campsites, facilities:* This campground with 28 sites offers drinking water, flush toilets, picnic tables, and fire grills. Roads and sites are paved.

*Reservations, fee:* Campsites are $9 and are first come, first served.

*Contact:* Call the Cedar City Ranger District at (801) 865-3700.

*Location:* From Cedar City, drive 25 miles east on State Route 14. Take Navajo Lake Road 2.5 miles west and south. The campground is located on the southeastern shore of Navajo Lake.

*Trip notes:* The high 9,200-foot elevation, towering pine trees, and lush alpine nature of Spruces campground make it a southern Utah favorite that can fill quickly during the busy summer months. Anglers can fish for rainbow trout at Navajo Lake, and boat rentals are available nearby at Navajo Lake Lodge. Hiking, biking, and horseback riding are popular on the trail from the campground that connects to the 32-mile Virgin River Rim Trail. The views of the Virgin River Valley and Zion National Park from this trail are excellent.

*Season:* June 15 through September 15.

## 38. DUCK CREEK

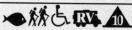

*Reference:* **In Dixie National Forest; map B1, grid h6.**

*Campsites, facilities:* This campground with 79 sites features drinking water, handicapped-accessible rest rooms with flush toilets, picnic tables, a group site, a dump station, an amphitheater, fire grills, and a ranger station. Nearby Duck Creek Village offers a restaurant, laundry facilities, a grocery store, and a gas station.

*Reservations, fee:* Reservations are accepted for sites in Loop B and the four group areas; call the U.S. Forest Service National Reservation System at (800) 280-2267. Sites are $9.

*Contact:* Call the Cedar City Ranger District at (801) 865-3700.

*Location:* Drive 29 miles east of Cedar City on State Route 14. The campground is located on the north side of the road.

*Trip notes:* This campground at Duck Creek is one of the better public facilities in the area, thanks to its setting amid verdant meadows and pine trees and its easy access to trout fishing on the creek, pond, and Navajo and Panguitch Lakes. At an elevation of 8,600 feet, this is also a great place to beat the often scorching summer heat of the southern Utah deserts. In the vicinity is Cedar Breaks National Monument, home to excellent hiking opportunities, a small visitors center, and overlooks into a red rock amphitheater. Bicycling is also popular in the area.

*Season:* June 15 through September 15.

## 39. RIVERSIDE CAMPGROUND

*Reference:* **Near Red Canyon; map B1, grid h8.**

*Campsites, facilities:* There are 47 sites with full hookups and 15 with partial hookups, plus 15 tent sites. Other facilities include a laundry room, showers, a restaurant, two picnic pavilions, a disposal station, a recreation hall and field, a public phone, and fire grates.

*Reservations, fee:* Reservations are accepted. Campsites with full and partial hookups are $16.67, while tent sites are $13.08.

*Contact:* Riverside Campground, 594 U.S. 89, Hatch, UT 84735; call (801) 735-4223.

*Location:* From Panguitch, travel 15 miles south to Hatch. The campground is one mile north of Hatch on U.S. 89.

*Trip notes:* While you won't find trees at this campground set at an elevation of 7,000 feet, you will find grassy campsites on a hill off the highway and weather that's generally cool and breezy, not to mention nice views of the Sevier River (which flows through the campground) and the orange sandstone cliffs of the Paungausant Plateau to the east. Swimming and fishing for rainbow and brown trout are popular river activities here. Rock shops in such nearby towns as Orderville sell some interesting jewelry. Also close by and worth a visit is the Utah Division of Wildlife Resources fish hatchery. A little farther afield are Bryce Canyon National Park (21 miles), Zion National Park (51 miles), and Cedar Breaks National Monument (37 miles).

*Season:* May through October.

## 40. MOUNTAINRIDGE

*Reference:* **In Hatch; map B1, grid h8.**

*Campsites, facilities:* There are 18 RV sites with full hookups and room for about 10 tents in a grassy area. The campground has rest rooms, showers, laundry facilities, picnic tables, groceries, a playground, and a public phone. Pets are allowed.

*Reservations, fee:* Reservations are taken. RV sites are $12 and tents are $10.

*Contact:* Mountainridge, P.O. Box 454, Hatch, UT 84735; (801) 735-4258.

*Location:* The campground is located on U.S. 89 in Hatch, a small rural town 15 miles south of Panguitch.

*Trip notes:* Set in rural Utah, this campground has a parklike feel, thanks to the grass and trees. Views are of the small town of Hatch, the Sevier River, and the orange cliffs of Paungausant Plateau. Next door is a motel and Grandma Grunt's gas station.
*Season:* April 1 through October 31.

---

# 41. CEDAR CITY KOA

*Reference:* **In Cedar City; map B1, grid h5.**
*Campsites, facilities:* This handicapped-accessible KOA has 94 RV sites (37 with full hookups and the rest with water and electricity), plus 35 tent camping sites. Also here are rest rooms, showers, laundry facilities, an RV disposal site, picnic tables, some barbecue grills, a swimming pool, a public phone, a game room, a playground, and a convenience store. Cable TV is available for the higher nightly rate.
*Reservations, fee:* Reservations are recommended. RV sites with full hookups range from $19 to $21, while sites with water and electricity are $17. Tent sites are $16.
*Contact:* Cedar City KOA, 1121 North Main Street, Cedar City, UT 84720; (801) 586-9872.
*Location:* When coming south from Beaver on Interstate 15, take exit 62. Turn south onto State Route 130 and drive for two miles to the campground. When coming north on Interstate 15, take exit 57. Turn north on State Route 130 and continue for four miles to the campground. State Route 130 becomes Main Street in Cedar City.
*Trip notes:* This RV park at the north end of Cedar City is located in a business district, and though it's landscaped with grass and trees, it definitely feels more urban than rural. Colorful Dixie National Forest mountains surrounding the city do create a nice backdrop, and the swimming pool provides relief on warm days. Cedar City is a central location for trips to Cedar Breaks National Monument and Brian Head Ski Resort, which is open year-round for summer and winter recreation. Zion National Park and Bryce Canyon National Park are an hour away, and the Grand Canyon is two hours away. Cedar City itself is home to the annual Utah Shakespearean Festival, which presents Shakespearean plays in an outdoor replica of the Globe Theatre and modern plays in the Randall Jones Theatre, plus a free nightly Green Show with period music and dances and puppet shows. The festival is held every summer from the first week of July through the first week of September.
*Season:* Open year-round.

---

# 42. COUNTRY AIRE

*Reference:* **In Cedar City; map B1, grid h5.**
*Campsites, facilities:* The 54 RV sites at this handicapped-accessible campground have full hookups; 28 of the sites are pull-throughs. Roads and campsites are paved. Amenities include rest rooms, showers, laundry facilities, a convenience store, a swimming pool, a playground, and a public phone.
*Reservations, fee:* Reservations are accepted. Campsites are $19.

---

*Contact:* Country Aire, 1700 North Main Street, Cedar City, UT 84720; (801) 586-2550.

*Location:* North of St. George, take exit 63 off of Interstate 15 and turn right, following the road as it turns into Main Street. The campground is 1.5 miles from the exit on the east side of the street.

*Trip notes:* A location on a side road on the edge of Cedar City helps give this suburban RV park more of a country feeling. One side of the campground faces a residential area, the other fields. The park is landscaped with flower beds, and views are of the red hills surrounding the city.

*Season:* Open year-round.

---

## 43. RED LEDGE CAMPGROUND

*Reference:* **In Kanarraville; map B1, grid h5.**

*Campsites, facilities:* This campground has 22 RV sites with full hookups; six are pull-throughs. Roads and campsites are gravel. Amenities include rest rooms, showers, laundry facilities, a convenience store, and a public phone.

*Reservations, fee:* Reservations are accepted. Campsites range from $15 to $17.

*Contact:* Red Ledge Campground, P.O. Box 420130, Kanarraville, UT 84742; (801) 586-9150.

*Location:* From Cedar City, drive 11 miles south on Interstate 15 and take the Kanarraville exit. Turn left and continue to the campground, which is located in the middle of town at 15 North.

*Trip notes:* Set next to a small city park, Red Ledge is about the only business in the town of Kanarraville. Shade trees and grass help keep campers cool. Kanarraville is less than 10 miles from the Kolob Canyon entrance to Zion National Park, which gets fewer visitors than the rest of the park.

*Season:* Open year-round.

---

## 44. HONEYCOMB ROCKS

*Reference:* **In Dixie National Forest near Enterprise; map B1, grid h2.**

*Campsites, facilities:* The campground features 21 sites with flush toilets, drinking water, and picnic tables.

*Reservations, fee:* Campsites are $9 and are first come, first served.

*Contact:* Call the Pine Valley Ranger District at (801) 652-3100.

*Location:* To reach the campground from Enterprise, drive west on State Highway 120 for about seven miles, and then take Pine Creek Road/Forest Road 006 south for approximately four miles to the campground.

*Trip notes:* Honeycomb Rocks campground is nestled between Upper and Lower Enterprise Reservoirs in a fairly remote part of the state. Campsites are set on a sagebrush plain, surrounded by hills. The relatively low 5,700-foot elevation makes for a long season, running from mid-May through the end of October most years. Trout fishing on the reservoirs can be good, and swimmers enjoy the warm lake waters. The campground gets its name from an unusual light rock formation nearby that is full of holes like a honeycomb.

*Season:* May 15 through October 31.

---

# 45. PINE PARK

*Reference:* **In Dixie National Forest near Pine Valley; map B1, grid h2.**

*Campsites, facilities:* This campground with 11 sites has vault toilets, picnic tables, and fire grills, but *no drinking water.*

*Reservations, fee:* Campsites are free and are first come, first served.

*Contact:* Call the Pine Valley Ranger District at (801) 652-3100.

*Location:* The campground is located 22.5 miles west of Enterprise. Drive about 15 miles west of Enterprise on State Highway 120, where it turns into Shoal Creek and then Forest Road 300. Take Forest Road 001 southeast for approximately seven more miles to the campground.

*Trip notes:* Reaching this rather primitive campground next door to Bureau of Land Management property means a long drive on a twisty dirt road that eliminates trailer use. It's set in a pinyon juniper forest with a few small patches of pines. The campsites themselves are so rarely used that it's hard to tell where they start. Hiking and horseback riding are available nearby in Barn Pole Hollow and Clay Wash.

*Season:* May 20 through October 31.

# 46. BLUE SPRING

*Reference:* **In Dixie National Forest near Pine Valley; map B1, grid h3.**

*Campsites, facilities:* This campground has 19 sites, plus drinking water, picnic tables, flush toilets, fire grills, a group area, and an RV disposal site.

*Reservations, fee:* Reservations are accepted; call the U.S. Forest Service National Reservation System at (800) 280-2267. Campsites are $9.

*Contact:* Call the Pine Valley Ranger District at (801) 652-3100.

*Location:* To reach this campground east of Pine Valley, drive 19 miles north of St. George on State Highway 18 to Veyo. Continue six miles north to Central, turning east and driving seven more miles to Pine Valley. The campground is less than a mile down the road.

*Trip notes:* Located at an elevation of 6,800 feet near the Santa Clara River, this campground dotted with pine trees is part of the Pine Valley Recreation complex, which includes a number of campgrounds and a small lake, where campers can canoe and fish. A hiking trail leads into the nearby Pine Valley Wilderness Area, where horseback riding is also popular (horses can be rented at Pine Valley Lodge). Campers can use the single- or multiple-family sites. It's best to reserve in advance, since the campsites usually fill up on weekends and holidays.

*Season:* June 1 through September 15.

# 47. EQUESTRIAN

*Reference:* **In Dixie National Forest near Pine Valley; map B1, grid h3.**

*Campsites, facilities:* This campground with 16 sites has picnic tables, flush toilets, fire pits, drinking water, and a group site.

*Reservations, fee:* Campsites are $9 and are first come, first served.

*Contact:* Call the Pine Valley Ranger District at (801) 652-3100.

*Location:* The campground is located two miles east of Pine Valley. To reach Pine Valley, drive 19 miles north of St. George on State Highway 18 to Veyo. Continue six miles north to Central, turning east and driving seven more miles to Pine Valley and the campground.

*Trip notes:* As the name of this facility suggests, this is a campground geared toward horseback riding in the alpine splendor of the surrounding Pine Valley Mountains. Several nice trails lead from the campground into the nearby mountains. Horses can also be rented from Pine Valley Lodge, located two miles to the west.

*Season:* June 20 through October 31.

## 48. NORTH JUNIPER PARK

*Reference:* **In Dixie National Forest near Pine Valley; map B1, grid h3.**

*Campsites, facilities:* This campground with 12 sites has a dump station, flush toilets, drinking water, picnic tables, and fire grills.

*Reservations, fee:* Campsites are $9 and are first come, first served.

*Contact:* Call the Pine Valley Ranger District at (801) 652-3100.

*Location:* The campground is located three miles east of Pine Valley. To reach Pine Valley, drive 19 miles north of St. George on State Highway 18 to Veyo. Continue six miles north to Central, turning east and driving seven more miles to Pine Valley and the campground.

*Trip notes:* North Juniper Park, elevation 6,800 feet, is one of a number of campgrounds surrounding a small forest lake that is regularly stocked with catchable rainbow trout by the Utah Division of Wildlife Resources. Pine trees shade the sites. The campground also serves as a trailhead into the nearby Pine Valley Mountains, where hikers and horseback riders will find trails aplenty.

*Season:* June 20 through October 31.

## 49. SOUTH JUNIPER PARK

*Reference:* **In Dixie National Forest near Pine Valley; map B1, grid h3.**

*Campsites, facilities:* This campground with 11 sites has flush toilets, drinking water, fire pits, and picnic tables.

*Reservations, fee:* Campsites are $9 and are first come, first served.

*Contact:* Call the Pine Valley Ranger District at (801) 652-3100.

*Location:* The campground is located three miles east of Pine Valley. To reach Pine Valley, drive 19 miles north of St. George on State Highway 18 to Veyo. Continue six miles north to Central, turning east and driving seven more miles to Pine Valley. Look for a sign just after North Juniper Park campground that points right off the highway to South Juniper Park campground.

*Trip notes:* Regular plantings of rainbow trout make for fine fishing at the small lake here. The campground, which has shaded sites, is located at the base of the Pine Valley Wilderness Area, which is popular with hikers and horseback riders looking to beat the heat. The elevation is 6,800 feet. One of the oldest Mormon churches in Utah is located nearby in the town of Pine Valley.

*Season:* June 20 through October 31.

## 50. PINES

*Reference:* **In Dixie National Forest near Pine Valley; map B1, grid h3.**

*Campsites, facilities:* This campground with 13 sites has flush toilets, drinking water, a trailer dump station, picnic tables, and fire pits.

*Reservations, fee:* Campsites are $9 and are first come, first served.

*Contact:* Call the Pine Valley Ranger District at (801) 652-3100.

*Location:* The campground is located three miles east of Pine Valley. To reach Pine Valley, drive 19 miles north of St. George on State Route 18 to Veyo. Continue six miles north to Central, turning east and driving seven more miles to Pine Valley and the campground.

*Trip notes:* Pines is another in the string of campgrounds surrounding a small, trout-filled lake at the base of the Pine Valley Mountains. Shade from pine trees helps give desert travelers a forest respite from the heat. Hiking and horseback-riding trails crisscross the area as well. The elevation is 6,800 feet.

*Season:* June 20 through October 31.

## 51. GUNLOCK STATE PARK

*Reference:* **On Gunlock Reservoir; map B1, grid i1.**

*Campsites, facilities:* This is a primitive campground with a few picnic tables and pit toilets. There is *no drinking water.* A boat ramp is available for launching.

*Reservations, fee:* Campsites are free and are first come, first served.

*Contact:* Call Snow Canyon State Park at (801) 628-2255.

*Location:* Drive 15 miles northwest of St. George on State Route 18 to Veyo and then head south to the tiny town of Gunlock. The campground is just south of town on the east bank of Gunlock Reservoir.

*Trip notes:* Set in a dry and often warm part of Utah on 240-acre Gunlock Reservoir, this primitive camping area offers guests a place to enjoy a swim when the weather heats up. The reservoir is also a popular early-season water-skiing area. Anglers enjoy fishing for bass and crappie.

*Season:* Open year-round.

## 52. OAK GROVE

*Reference:* **In Dixie National Forest; map B1, grid i3.**

*Campsites, facilities:* This campground with 10 sites has drinking water, vault toilets, picnic tables, and fire grills.

*Reservations, fee:* Campsites are $5 and are first come, first served.

*Contact:* Call the Pine Valley Ranger District at (801) 652-3100.

*Location:* Drive north of St. George on Interstate 15 for 11 miles to the town of Leeds. Take the Leeds exit and drive to the north end of town, looking for signs to Silver Reef ghost town. Take Forest Road 32 for nine miles up a dirt road to the campground.

*Trip notes:* It takes a bit of effort to reach this small alpine campground set in a grove of oak trees, but the extra time is worth it if you want to be close to all the hiking and horseback riding opportunities in the Pine Valley Wilderness Area.

*Season:* Late May through October.

---

## 53. BAKER DAM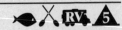

*Reference:* **On Bureau of Land Management property west of St. George; map B1, grid i2.**

*Campsites, facilities:* This campground with 20 sites has vault toilets, picnic tables, fire grills, and drinking water.

*Reservations, fee:* Campsites are $5 and are first come, first served.

*Contact:* Call the Cedar City District Office of the Bureau of Land Management at (801) 586-2401.

*Location:* To reach the campground, drive 25 miles north of St. George on State Route 18. Look for the small brown Bureau of Land Management sign for Baker Reservoir on the right side of the road. Turn here and follow the road to the campground.

*Trip notes:* A pinyon forest surrounds each campsite at this primitive campground. The big draw is trout fishing in the reservoir and nearby stream. Anglers should check with the Utah Division of Wildlife Resources in Cedar City for information on when the reservoir was last stocked with fish.

*Season:* Open year-round.

---

## 54. SILVER SPRINGS RV PARK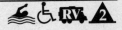

*Reference:* **In La Verkin; map B1, grid j3.**

*Campsites, facilities:* This handicapped-accessible campground has 55 RV sites, all with full hookups. A grassy area can accommodate up to 50 tents. Amenities include rest rooms, showers, laundry facilities, an RV disposal site, picnic tables, barbecue grills, swings, a swimming pool, cable TV, and a convenience store. Pets are welcome with overnight visitors.

*Reservations, fee:* Reservations are recommended for holidays. RV sites are $15 and tent sites are $12.

*Contact:* Call the campground at (801) 635-7340.

*Location:* From St. George, drive north on Interstate 15 approximately 10 miles and exit east on State Route 9. Go another 10 miles to La Verkin. The campground is at the north end of town.

*Trip notes:* This RV park in La Verkin, a rural Utah town close to Zion National Park and year-round golf in St. George, has shade and trees. Many of the RV park residents are permanent.

*Season:* Open year-round.

---

## 55. QUAIL LAKE RV PARK

*Reference:* **In Hurricane; map B1, grid j3.**

*Campsites, facilities:* This campground has 15 RV sites with full hookups. Roads are gravel, and sites are gravel with cement pads. Amenities include rest rooms, showers, laundry facilities, a swimming pool, a public phone, and cable television ($1 a night). No pets are allowed.

---

*Reservations, fee:* Reservations are accepted. Campsites are $14.

*Contact:* Quail Lake RV Park, 4400 North State Street, Hurricane, UT 84737; (801) 635-9960.

*Location:* From Interstate 15, take State Route 9 east toward Hurricane for nine miles. The RV park is in town at 4400 West State Street.

*Trip notes:* Located in Hurricane next to a convenience store, this large RV park was built with sunbirds in mind—folks who flock here in the winter to take advantage of the sunny, dry climate. The owners have added such touches as a small fountain and a rock garden in front, not to mention a swimming pool, to try to give the park the feel of a resort. There are few trees, but the views of the high plateau country surrounding Hurricane are nice.

*Season:* Open year-round.

---

## 56. WILLOW PARK

*Reference:* **In Hurricane; map B1, grid j3.**

*Campsites, facilities:* This campground has 95 RV sites with full hookups. A grassy, shaded area can accommodate about 25 tents, making this a good bet for groups of tent campers. Roads are gravel, but the sites have cement pads. The park has rest rooms, showers, laundry facilities, an RV disposal site, barbecue pits, two public phones, cable TV, and picnic tables (though not at every site). There is a five-acre pet run.

*Reservations, fee:* Reservations are recommended in the spring and fall. Sites with full hookups are $18 for the first two people and $1 a person thereafter. Tent sites are $12 for the first two people and $1 a person thereafter.

*Contact:* Willow Park, 1151 West 80 South, Hurricane, UT 84737; call (801) 635-4154.

*Location:* From Interstate 15, take State Route 9 east toward Hurricane for nine miles. The park is at the west end of Hurricane, across from Lin's Supermarket.

*Trip notes:* This well-manicured RV park across the street from the supermarket (the largest business in Hurricane) has grass and trees and a view of the fields and sandstone walls that mark the entrance to Zion National Park some 30 miles away. The tent camping area is mostly out in the open.

*Season:* Open year-round.

---

## 57. BRENTWOOD UTAH RV PARK

*Reference:* **In Hurricane; map B1, grid j3.**

*Campsites, facilities:* This handicapped-accessible campground has 189 RV sites with full hookups, plus grassy spaces for 15 tents. Amenities include rest rooms, showers, laundry facilities, some moveable picnic tables, a game room, a bowling alley, a waterslide park, indoor miniature golf, an indoor swimming pool, and cable TV. Pets are allowed. There is a nine-hole pitch-and-putt golf course on site. The park also boasts a tennis court.

*Reservations, fee:* Reservations are accepted. RV sites are $16 and tent sites are $12. Groups with more than four people are charged an additional $2 per person.

---

*Contact:* Brentwood Utah RV Park, 150 North 3700 West, Hurricane, UT 84737; (801) 635-2320.

*Location:* Take the Hurricane exit off Interstate 15 north of St. George, and then drive east on State Route 9 for five miles. Brentwood is on the north side of the road, about four miles west of Hurricane.

*Trip notes:* This well-maintained resort is perhaps the nicest RV park near the entrance to Zion National Park, which is located about 30 miles away. Sites are shaded by tall mulberry trees. Activities, including swimming and golf, are just outside your door (or tent flap). The Virgin River, which runs through Zion Canyon, is also nearby. The tent camping area is fenced off and separate from the RV area.

*Season:* Open year-round.

---

## 58. ZION CANYON CAMPGROUND

*Reference:* **In Springdale; map B1, grid j5.**

*Campsites, facilities:* This handicapped-accessible campground has 100 RV sites with full hookups, plus 50 tent camping sites. Amenities include rest rooms, showers, laundry facilities, an RV disposal site, picnic tables, and a large grocery and gift store. Barbecue grills are available upon request. There is an extra charge for cable television. Pets are allowed with RV campers only.

*Reservations, fee:* Reservations are recommended from Easter weekend through October. Advance reservations are accepted by mail only. Write to P.O. Box 99, Springdale, UT 84767. RV sites are $19 and tent sites are $15. For groups of more than two people, $3.50 is charged for individuals over 16 and $2 is charged for children under 15.

*Contact:* Zion Canyon Campground, P.O. Box 99, Springdale, UT 84767; (801) 772-3237.

*Location:* The campground is off Highway 9 in Springdale. It is on the east side of the street across from Flanigan's Restaurant. The south entrance to Zion National Park is half a mile away.

*Trip notes:* This campground in the town of Springdale is adjacent to a motel operated by the same owners. Sites are under large shade trees; some are grassy while others are in sand. A few of the tent camping sites are next to the Virgin River, where many guests like to swim. The river can be a slow stream in late summer or a raging torrent in early spring, and relatively clear or cloudy red. Springdale, home to quite a few artisans, is a great place to browse through the many craft and souvenir shops. The town also has some eclectic restaurants.

*Season:* Open year-round.

---

## 59. WATCHMAN

*Reference:* **In Zion National Park; map B1, grid j5.**

*Campsites, facilities:* The handicapped-accessible campground has 229 sites, 140 of which are appropriate for RVs. Facilities include picnic tables, rest rooms with cold running water, drinking water, a group area, and a dump station.

---

*Reservations, fee:* Campsites are $8 and are first come, first served.

*Contact:* Call Zion National Park at (801) 772-3256.

*Location:* The campground is located near Zion National Park's south entrance on State Highway 9, about 21 miles east of Hurricane.

*Trip notes:* This campground, nestled next to the Virgin River and shaded by old cottonwood trees, is the only one in Zion National Park that is open year-round. The town of Springdale is next door, and traffic whizzing by on State Highway 9 can be somewhat noisy, but the sound of the flowing river and rustling trees helps to mute the noise. Within walking distance are the Zion Visitors Center and Zion Nature Center, which offers an excellent junior ranger program for children. Nearby hiking trails and a paved bicycle route are added amenities. Horse rentals are available further up the canyon. The river is swimmable in the warmer months.

*Season:* Open year-round.

## 60. SOUTH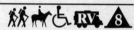

*Reference:* **In Zion National Park; map B1, grid i5.**

*Campsites, facilities:* This handicapped-accessible campground consists of 140 sites, all appropriate for RVs. Amenities include picnic tables, fire grills, rest rooms with cold running water, a dump station, and drinking water. Zion National Park's only group area is located here.

*Reservations, fee:* Campsites are $8 and are first come, first served.

*Contact:* Call Zion National Park at (801) 772-3256.

*Location:* The campground is located just east of the Zion National Park's south entrance on State Highway 9, about 21 miles east of Hurricane.

*Trip notes:* Set amid cottonwood trees near the Virgin River, this campground can be one of the coolest places in the park when temperatures begin to hover near the 100s in the summer months. Hiking and bicycling trails add to the popularity of this spot, so try to arrive early during the peak summer season. Horses can be rented at the nearby lodge.

*Season:* April 15 through September 15, depending on use, so call in advance.

## 61. LAVA POINT

*Reference:* **In Zion National Park; map B1, grid i6.**

*Campsites, facilities:* This primitive campground with six sites has vault toilets, picnic tables, and fire grills. *No water* is available.

*Reservations, fee:* Campsites are free and are first come, first served.

*Contact:* Call Zion National Park at (801) 772-3256.

*Location:* Drive 26 miles north from Virgin off Highway 9, turning west to the campground just before reaching Blue Springs Reservoir.

*Trip notes:* Lava Point is located in one of the more remote parts of Zion National Park, making it a good, if primitive, alternative to the hustle and bustle of the larger park campgrounds near the park's south entrance. Be sure to bring your own water supply when camping here. Nearby Kolob Reservoir offers good fishing in the summer and fall. Hiking trails from the campsites will take you deep into the park. Arrive early, since the sites fill up quickly.

The 7,900-foot elevation limits the camping season to the summer and early fall months.

*Season:* June through mid-October, depending on snow conditions.

---

## 62. MUKUNTUWEEP RV PARK AND CAMPGROUND

*Reference:* **Near Mount Carmel Junction; map B1, grid i7.**

*Campsites, facilities:* This campground has 30 RV sites with full hookups; 20 of these are pull-throughs. A grassy area can accommodate about 140 tents. Amenities include rest rooms, showers, laundry facilities, an RV disposal site, a game room, barbecue pits, a playground, and a convenience and gift store. Pets are allowed. There is also a Mexican restaurant on site.

*Reservations, fee:* Reservations are accepted. RV sites are $15 and tent sites are $12.50. For groups of more than two, an additional $3 is charged per person.

*Contact:* Call the campground at (801) 644-5445.

*Location:* The campground is located 13 miles west of Mt. Carmel Junction and half a mile from the east entrance to Zion National Park. Mt. Carmel Junction is 17 miles north of Kanab on Highway 9. The campground is on the south side of the highway, across the street from a Mexican restaurant.

*Trip notes:* While the campground itself isn't that exciting, the scenery surrounding it is spectacular, namely the massive sandstone walls of Zion National Park. The RV area has small trees, which provide some shade. The tent area is in a grassy spot under juniper trees. This campground is a good alternative to the more crowded national park and Springdale facilities. Hiking and horseback riding are available minutes away from the campground inside the park.

*Season:* April through October.

---

## 63. ZION PONDEROSA RESORT

*Reference:* **East of Zion National Park; map B1, grid i7.**

*Campsites, facilities:* This campground has 20 gravel tent sites. Facilities include flush toilets, showers, picnic tables, and fire pits. The campground is five miles from a more developed resort that offers swimming, a playground, log cabins, and a small gift shop.

*Reservations, fee:* Reservations are recommended. Sites are $10.

*Contact:* Call the campground at (801) 581-9817 or (800) 293-4444.

*Location:* Drive 1.5 miles past the east entrance of Zion National Park. Turn north on North Fork Road and drive five miles to the resort. Two of the five miles are on gravel road.

*Trip notes:* This campground, one of the newest resorts in the Zion National Park area, is in the midst of a ponderosa-scrub oak forest with views of Zion's tall peaks. Horseback riding and hay rides are popular activities here, and the resort serves as the trailhead for the well-known Zion Narrows hike. Zion has strict limitations on overnight camping and some day-use rules, and high water can make the Narrows hike dangerous, so check with park

---

headquarters before attempting the hike. After a long day of hiking, campers can soak in a hot tub back at the resort.
*Season:* May through October.

# 64. ZION/BRYCE KOA

*Reference:* **In Glendale; map B1, grid i7.**
*Campsites, facilities:* This handicapped-accessible campground has 59 RV sites, 19 of which have full hookups, plus 22 tent camping sites. All sites are grass and gravel. Amenities include rest rooms, showers, laundry facilities, an RV disposal site, picnic tables, a game room, barbecue grills, a public phone, a playground, and a convenience and gift store. Pets are allowed.
*Reservations, fee:* Reservations are recommended between June and September. Campsites are $18.50 for full hookups, $17 for RV sites, and $15 for tent sites. For groups of more than two, an additional $3 is charged per person.
*Contact:* Call the campground at (800) 648-2035.
*Location:* Glendale is located about 41 miles south of Panguitch and 26 miles north of Kanab. The KOA itself is five miles north of Glendale on U.S. 89, and a quarter of a mile north of the state rest area on the west side of the highway.
*Trip notes:* Located on a ranch in a mountain valley, this KOA rates a nine for scenery but a seven overall because of its flat, open landscape and closely spaced campsites. Trees surround the ranch, but there are none in the campground, so the place really heats up in the summer. Since it's a bit off the highway, it's quieter than some campgrounds in the area. Guided horseback rides organized by the KOA go up a side canyon the locals call Little Bryce because it has the characteristic sculpted red rock formations found in Bryce Canyon National Park. Rides cost $15 per person for an hour; riders must be over eight years of age. Hiking is popular in this area as well.
*Season:* May 1 through October 15.

# 65. BAUER'S CANYON RANCH

*Reference:* **In Glendale; map B1, grid i8.**
*Campsites, facilities:* This handicapped-accessible campground has 20 RV sites, all with full hookups. There is a grassy area for tents. The park has rest rooms, showers, laundry facilities, picnic tables, an RV disposal site, and a public phone. Pets are allowed.
*Reservations, fee:* Reservations are accepted. RV sites are $13.50 and tent sites are $8.50.
*Contact:* Bauer's Canyon Ranch, Box 65, Glendale, UT 84729; (801) 648-2564.
*Location:* The ranch is in the middle of Glendale, which is 20 miles from Zion National Park. It's on the west side of U.S. 89, the main road through this small town.
*Trip notes:* This campground in the rural town of Glendale sits on 1,000 acres in a valley, next to a creek and across the highway from a country store, a cider mill, and an apple orchard. While the scenery looking back at Zion National Park is great, the campsites are mostly out in the open, a hot prospect

in the summer, and the road and parking spots are gravel. The RV sites are grassy and the tent area is grassy and shaded.

*Season:* March 1 through November 1.

---

## 66. TORTOISE AND HARE TRAILER COURT

*Reference:* **In Orderville, east of Zion National Park; map B1, grid i8.**

*Campsites, facilities:* The 15 RV sites all have full hookups. There are rest rooms, showers, laundry facilities, picnic tables, and a gift store.

*Reservations, fee:* Reservations are accepted. Sites are $11 for two people and $1 for each additional person.

*Contact:* Tortoise and Hare Trailer Court, P.O. Box 161, Orderville, UT 84758; (801) 648-2312.

*Location:* The campground is located on the east side of Orderville right on U.S. 89. Orderville is 22 miles north of Kanab between Glendale and Mt. Carmel. It's 16 miles from the east entrance to Zion National Park.

*Trip notes:* This campground with gravel sites is in the quaint, rural town of Orderville and near Zion National Park (16 miles), Coral Pink Sand Dunes State Park (25 miles), Cedar Breaks National Monument (35 miles), and Bryce Canyon National Park (55 miles). There are several rock shops in town.

*Season:* April through November.

---

## 67. EAST ZION TRAILER PARK

*Reference:* **In Mt. Carmel Junction; map B1, grid i8.**

*Campsites, facilities:* The 20 RV sites all have full hookups. Roads and sites are dirt. Facilities include picnic tables, an RV disposal site, a public phone, and a small grocery store.

*Reservations, fee:* Reservations are accepted. Sites are $12.

*Contact:* East Zion Trailer Park, Junction U.S. 89 and Utah 9, Orderville, UT 84758; (801) 648-2326.

*Location:* The campground is located in Mt. Carmel Junction, at the intersection of U.S. 89 and State Route 9, about 11 miles from the east entrance to Zion National Park.

*Trip notes:* Though this RV park is little more than a large gravel area with limited services, it is a convenient 11 miles from Zion National Park. The view of the Zion formations from Mt. Carmel is impressive.

*Season:* March through November.

---

## 68. SHIVWITS CAMPGROUND

*Reference:* **In Snow Canyon State Park; map B1, grid j1.**

*Campsites, facilities:* This handicapped-accessible campground has 14 sites with full hookups and 21 sites with no hookups. Amenities include showers, modern rest rooms with hot and cold running water, a dump station, a covered group use area, and such recreational facilities as volleyball courts and horseshoe pits.

*Reservations, fee:* Reservations can be made 120 days in advance by calling (800) 322-3770 Monday through Friday from 8 A.M. to 5 P.M. A $5 nonre-

---

fundable reservation fee is charged for each site reserved. Campsites with hookups are $15, while sites with no hookups are $11. Utah residents 62 years and older who have a Special Fun Tag receive a $2 discount Sunday through Thursday.

*Contact:* Call Snow Canyon State Park at (801) 628-2255.

*Location:* The campground is about 11 miles northwest of St. George on State Highway 18.

*Trip notes:* This campground is located in stunning Snow Canyon State Park, where the red and tan Navajo sandstone and black lava rock are a study in colorful contrasts. Campers can explore lava tubes, hike along a nature trail near the campground, or take longer hiking adventures through the red-rock landscape. Children enjoy playing in the shifting coral pink sand dune and crawling around on the rocks in the campground. Because of mild winter temperatures, this is an especially popular off-season camping area. In fact, Snow Canyon's off season is usually in the summer when temperatures regularly top more than 100 degrees Fahrenheit. The tent camping sites are among the best in this part of the state. A horseback riding concession is available in the park.

*Season:* Open year-round.

## 69. LEEDS RV PARK

*Reference:* In Leeds; map B1, grid j2.

*Campsites, facilities:* This campground has 43 RV sites with full hookups, plus eight tent sites. Roads and campsites are gravel. Amenities include rest rooms, showers, picnic tables, and a public phone.

*Reservations, fee:* Reservations are accepted. RV sites with full hookups are $15 and tent sites are $10.

*Contact:* Leeds RV Park, P.O. Box 461149, Leeds, UT 84746; (801) 879-2450.

*Location:* From St. George, drive about 15 miles north on Interstate 15. Take the Leeds exit and follow the signs through the small town to reach Leeds RV Park.

*Trip notes:* This campground with grass and trees is a rural alternative to staying in the town of St. George. The grassy tent area is separate from the RV area. Quail Creek State Park, Zion National Park, and the Dixie Red Cliffs Recreation Area are all close by. Leeds is a historic town with several sandstone buildings dating from early pioneer days. Stop by the Silver Reef Museum to learn more about its pioneer and mining history.

*Season:* Open year-round.

## 70. HARRISBURG LAKESIDE RV RESORT

*Reference:* In Leeds; map B1, grid j3.

*Campsites, facilities:* This RV park has 150 RV sites, all with full hookups. Amenities include showers, a rest room, laundry facilities, a swimming pool, a convenience store, a gas station, picnic tables, a barbecue grill, an RV disposal site, and a clubhouse.

*Reservations, fee:* Reservations are accepted. Campsites are $20.01. Cable TV is extra.

*Contact:* Harrisburg Lakeside RV Resort, P.O. Box 2146, St. George, UT 84771; (801) 879-2312.

*Location:* From Cedar City, take exit 23 off of Interstate 15. From St. George, take exit 22 off of Interstate 15. The resort is two miles south of Leeds on the frontage road.

*Trip notes:* Though most of the guests at this resort are club members, overnighters are welcome. The resort is just outside of Quail Creek State Park and overlooks the historic old town of Harrisburg, an early Mormon pioneer settlement. Quail Creek Reservoir, a short walk from the campground when full of water, is a popular boating and fishing destination. The campground has grass and trees, though it is primarily developed for RVs. Hikers can head for the many trails available nearby at the Dixie Red Cliffs Recreation Area.

*Season:* Open year-round.

## 71. SETTLERS RV PARK

*Reference:* In St. George; map B1, grid j2.

*Campsites, facilities:* This campground has 160 RV sites, all with full hookups. Sites are gravel with cement patios. Also here are rest rooms, showers, picnic tables, laundry facilities, a game room, barbecue grills, a swimming pool, a public phone, cable TV, and a playground.

*Reservations, fee:* Reservations are recommended, especially during the winter. Campsites are $18.59.

*Contact:* Settlers RV Park, 1333 East 100 South, St. George, UT 84790; (801) 628-1624.

*Location:* From Interstate 15, take exit 8 to St. George and turn east on St. George Boulevard. Turn south on River Road and drive to 100 South. Look for the Settlers RV Park sign by Shoneys Restaurant.

*Trip notes:* As with other RV parks in St. George, this is definitely a winter-oriented urban facility, since summer temperatures often top the 100-degree mark—making the swimming pool the place to be on hot days. The park is neat and clean, with a few trees and cement patios. Some spaces are used by permanent residents, but overnighters are welcome. St. George is home to eight public golf courses.

*Season:* Open year-round.

## 72. McARTHUR'S TEMPLE VIEW RV RESORT

*Reference:* In St. George; map B1, grid j3.

*Campsites, facilities:* This large, handicapped-accessible campground has 260 sites with full hookups, including 50 pull-throughs and a grassy area for tents. RV sites are gravel and cement. Amenities include a heated swimming pool and Jacuzzi, a clubhouse, a game room, billiards, a dance floor, shuffleboard, a TV room, volleyball, and laundry facilities.

*Reservations, fee:* Reservations are accepted. RV sites are $20.95 for two people and tent sites are $15.95 for two people. Each additional person is $2. The weekly rate is $125.70.

*Contact:* McArthur's Temple View RV Resort, 975 South Main Street, St. George, UT 84770; (800) 776-6410.

*Location:* In St. George, take exit 6 off Interstate 15, then go two blocks north on Main Street to the campground on the east side of the road.

*Trip notes:* This urban campground is landscaped with palm trees and shrubs, and is a short walk away from St. George's city park, shopping district, and fast food restaurants. The view from the resort—beyond the business area— is of the colorful lava-topped mesa that guards the city. The warm climate and year-round golfing opportunities make this a popular winter destination. Snow Canyon State Park (19 miles away) and the Jacob Hamblin Home (five miles away) are nearby attractions. Jacob Hamblin was a Mormon pioneer who was active in negotiations with the Native Americans in the 1800s. Snow Canyon has great hiking, including a hike down a lava tube. Kids will like the amusement park, within walking distance of the campground, with car rides, miniature golf, and batting cages.

*Season:* Open year-round.

---

# 73. ST. GEORGE CAMPGROUND AND RV PARK

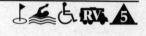

*Reference:* **In St. George; map B1, grid j3.**

*Campsites, facilities:* The 120 RV sites all have full hookups. Also here are rest rooms, showers, laundry facilities, barbecue grills, cable TV, a swimming pool, and a small store. Pets are welcome. Some of the facilities are handicapped accessible.

*Reservations, fee:* Reservations aren't necessary during the summer (off-season) months. In the winter, sites are given on a first-come, first-served basis. Sites are $15 for hookups and $12 without hookups. Seniors 55 and older are given a $1 discount.

*Contact:* St. George Campground, RV Park, 2100 North Middleton Drive, St. George, UT 84770; (801) 673-2970.

*Location:* In St. George, take exit 10 off Interstate 15. The north frontage road leads to Middleton Drive. The campground is at 2100 North Middleton Drive.

*Trip notes:* This campground and RV park in a residential section of St. George has lots of permanent residents, but space for overnighters as well. It is nicely landscaped with a lawn and shade trees, plus a swimming pool for taking a dip on all those hot days. More vegetation around the perimeter of the park provides a buffer from Interstate 15. Red Cliffs Mall is across the freeway.

*Season:* Open year-round.

---

# 74. REDLANDS RV PARK

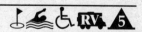

*Reference:* **Near St. George; map B1, grid j3.**

*Campsites, facilities:* This large, handicapped-accessible, 200-site campground has 120 pull-throughs. Because each site is grassy, tent campers can use them as well. Also here are rest rooms, laundry facilities, showers, cable TV, a recreation hall, shuffleboard, a swimming pool, a therapy pool, an RV and car wash, and a grocery store that sells RV supplies.

*Reservations, fee:* Reservations are recommended for the winter months. Fees are $19.75 for RV campers and $14.50 for tent campers. An additional $2 is charged per person for groups of over two people.

*Contact:* Redlands RV Park, P.O. Box 2000, Washington, UT 84780; (800) 553-8269.

*Location:* From just north of St. George, take exit 10 off Interstate 15. Turn south on Green Springs Drive and continue to Telegraph Street. Turn west on Telegraph Street and head to the campground at 650 West Telegraph Street.

*Trip notes:* This RV park two miles north of St. George looks and feels like a resort, thanks to its fancy clubhouse and swimming pool. Some overnighters are placed side by side in a gravel lot shaded by trees, so ask for one of the more generously spaced sites. Each campsite has two mature trees and lots of grass. Views are of the red desert and sandstone hills surrounding St. George. The park is a mile from a golf course and just down the street from a shopping mall. The Pine Valley Mountains are about 15 miles north, and Zion National Park is 40 miles away.

*Season:* Open year-round.

## 75. QUAIL CREEK STATE PARK

*Reference:* **On Quail Creek Reservoir; map B1, grid j3.**

*Campsites, facilities:* This handicapped-accessible campground with 23 sites has modern rest rooms but no showers, a fish cleaning station, and two covered group-use areas.

*Reservations, fee:* Reservations can be made 120 days in advance by calling (800) 322-3770 Monday through Friday from 8 A.M. to 5 P.M. A $5 nonrefundable reservation fee is charged for each site reserved. Campsites are $8. Utah residents 62 years and older who have a Special Fun Tag receive a $2 discount Sunday through Thursday.

*Contact:* Call the park at (801) 879-2378.

*Location:* Driving north from St. George, head three miles east of the Interstate 15/Hurricane exit on State Route 9. The campground is well marked.

*Trip notes:* Located on State Route 9 leading to Zion National Park, this campground in Quail Creek State Park is somewhat exposed, but views of the reservoir surrounded by red rock help compensate for the lack of shade. The reservoir is home to a rare combination of rainbow trout and largemouth bass, making it a popular year-round fishing and boating destination. Campsites are along the reservoir. Swimming and waterskiing are favorite warm-weather activities. Hiking is available at the Bureau of Land Management's Dixie Red Cliffs Recreation Area. The Silver Reef ghost town area, about two miles west, has a restored museum that's worth a look. Golfers can head three miles away to any of eight public golf courses in St. George.

*Season:* Open year-round.

# 76. DIXIE RED CLIFFS

*Reference:* **Near Quail Creek Reservoir; map B1, grid j3.**

*Campsites, facilities:* This handicapped-accessible campground with 10 sites has picnic tables, drinking water, and vault toilets.

*Reservations, fee:* Campsites are $4 and are first come, first served.

*Contact:* Call the Bureau of Land Management at (801) 673-4654.

*Location:* Drive on Interstate 15 for approximately 11 miles north of St. George to the town of Leeds. Take the Leeds exit and follow the signs 4.5 miles southwest to the campground and recreation area.

*Trip notes:* This small campground is a real find, set as it is in scenic southern Utah under cottonwood trees, with Quail Creek flowing through the middle of the picnic area. The campsites, surrounded by the red cliffs which give the place its name, are spaced a good distance apart. One hiking trail leads to waterfalls and swimming holes (be careful of broken glass when wading!), while another crosses slickrock to an overlook of an old ghost town. A third takes hikers to an ancient Anasazi ruin. Golf is available nearby in St. George and Washington, as is boating, fishing, and waterskiing at Quail Creek State Park.

*Season:* Open year-round.

# 77. CORAL PINK SAND DUNES STATE PARK

*Reference:* **Near the Utah-Arizona border; map B1, grid j7.**

*Campsites, facilities:* This campground with 22 sites has picnic tables, fire grills, drinking water, rest rooms with showers, sewage disposal, and a picnic area.

*Reservations, fee:* Reservations can be made 120 days in advance by calling (800) 322-3770 Monday through Friday from 8 A.M. to 5 P.M. A $5 nonrefundable reservation fee is charged for each site reserved. Campsites are $11. Utah residents 62 years and older who have a Special Fun Tag receive a $2 discount Sunday through Thursday.

*Contact:* Call the park at (801) 874-2408.

*Location:* Drive 22 miles northwest of Kanab on U.S. 89. Look for the park sign leading to a turnoff to the south. Turn and follow the road 12 miles to the campground.

*Trip notes:* True to its name, Coral Pink Sand Dunes State Park is home to beautiful coral-pink sand dunes. Sunrise and sunset on the dunes are pretty spectacular, so don't forget your camera. And if you have children in tow, be sure to bring buckets, shovels, and other sand toys so they can frolic on the dunes. But parents should be aware that the sand dunes are popular with dune buggies and all-terrain vehicles. The park also has a short nature trail, as well as an area that is off-limits to vehicles. The campground itself is located far from the nearest roads in a pinyon-juniper forest, with nicely spaced sites.

*Season:* Open year-round.

## 78. PONDEROSA GROVE

*Reference:* **Near Coral Pink Sand Dunes State Park; map B1, grid j7.**

*Campsites, facilities:* This campground has seven campsites with a maximum RV length of 20 feet, plus vault toilets, picnic tables, and fire grills. *No water* is available.

*Reservations, fee:* Campsites are free and are first come, first served.

*Contact:* Call the Cedar City District Office of the Bureau of Land Management at (801) 586-2401.

*Location:* Drive 14 miles northwest of Kanab on U.S. 89, taking the county road to Coral Pink Sand Dunes State Park and then following the signs to the campground.

*Trip notes:* Though primitive and lacking the facilities of the nearby Coral Pink Sand Dunes State Park campground (see page 185), which does offer water and showers, this is a good overflow area. It is popular with off-highway vehicle owners who enjoy taking all-terrain vehicles and specially designed dune buggies across the sand. Photographers should consider getting up early to take advantage of great lighting conditions on the dunes themselves, which feature fine, shifting, coral pink sands.

*Season:* May through November.

## 79. CRAZY HORSE CAMPARK

*Reference:* **In Kanab; map B1, grid j8.**

*Campsites, facilities:* There are 50 RV sites with full hookups, and 22 with water and electricity, plus eight designated tent camping sites with a grassy area for additional tents. Amenities include rest rooms, showers, laundry facilities, picnic tables, an RV disposal site, a game room, barbecue grills, a swimming pool, and a convenience store and gift shop. Cable TV is available in the sitting area. Pets are allowed on a leash.

*Reservations, fee:* Reservations are recommended in the summer months. Sites with full hookups are $16.48, sites with water and electricity are $14.83, and tent sites are $10.44. An additional fee of $1.09 is charged for more than two people if they are over six years old.

*Contact:* Crazy Horse Campark, 625 East 30 South, Kanab, UT 84741; (801) 644-2782.

*Location:* Drive east on U.S. 89 through the town of Kanab. The campground is on the north side of the road.

*Trip notes:* Kanab, home of Crazy Horse Campark, is a small Utah town with a colorful past. A number of old Westerns were filmed here, including the TV show *Gunsmoke*. Visitors can tour the Johnson Canyon Movie Set, where this long-running series was shot. Also in Kanab is Lopeman's Frontier Movie Town, a recreation of an old frontier town. The Campark picks up this Western theme in its game room, with everything from an old movie set to Old West storefronts and a general store. Half the sites at the Campark are shaded with tall trees, a rarity in this hot part of the world. The campsites are mostly the native red sand or gravel. Tent camping sites are in the sand. Views from

the Campark are of the red cliffs behind Kanab and the neighboring golf course. Kanab is close to Lake Powell (60 miles), the North Rim of the Grand Canyon (75 miles), and Bryce Canyon National Park (77 miles).
*Season:* Open year-round.

---

# 80. KANAB RV CORRAL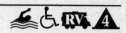
*Reference:* **In Kanab; map B1, grid j8.**
*Campsites, facilities:* This handicapped-accessible campground has 40 RV sites with full hookups and 20 tent camping sites. Amenities include rest rooms, showers, laundry facilities, an RV disposal site, picnic tables, and a swimming pool. Pets are allowed.
*Reservations, fee:* Reservations are accepted. RV sites are $20 and tent sites are $16.
*Contact:* Kanab RV Corral, 483 South 100 East, Kanab, UT 84741; call (801) 644-5330.
*Location:* In Kanab, go south on U.S. 89A (Main Street) for less than a block. The campground is by a fire station.
*Trip notes:* This campground is on Main Street in the middle of Kanab, surrounded by businesses and homes, which means it can be a bit noisy. A strip of trees forms the perimeter of the campground, and the sites are red cinder with narrow plots of grass. This is more of an RV park than a place to pitch a tent. Kanab is close to Lake Powell (60 miles) and Coral Pink Sand Dunes State Park (22 miles). It's also a jumping-off point to Zion National Park, Bryce Canyon National Park, Cedar Breaks National Monument, and Grand Canyon National Park, all within 100 miles.
*Season:* Open year-round.

---

# 81. HITCH 'N POST
*Reference:* **In Kanab; map B1, grid j8.**
*Campsites, facilities:* This campground has 50 sites, all with full hookups. Roads and campsites are gravel. There is a separate grassy area for tent camping, plus rest rooms, showers, fire rings, picnic tables on cement pads, and an RV disposal site.
*Reservations, fee:* Reservations are accepted. Sites with full hookups are $18 and tent sites are $10. An additional $2 is charged for each person in groups with more than two people.
*Contact:* Hitch 'N Post, 196 East 300 South, Kanab, UT 84741; (801) 644-2142 or (800) 458-3516.
*Location:* The campground is in the middle of Kanab, half a block east of the junction of U.S. 89 and U.S. 89A.
*Trip notes:* This campground set under tall shade trees is in the middle of the business section of Kanab, with a Laundromat across the street and several fast food restaurants within walking distance. Views are of the red cliffs surrounding town.
*Season:* Open year-round.

---

Map of Utah ........................ see page 46
Beyond This Region:
North (Map A2) ................... see page 56
East (Map B3) .................... see page 224
South ............................ Arizona
West (Map B1) ................... see page 150

| | Utah |
|----|----|----|
| A1 | A2 | A3 |
| B1 | B2 | B3 |

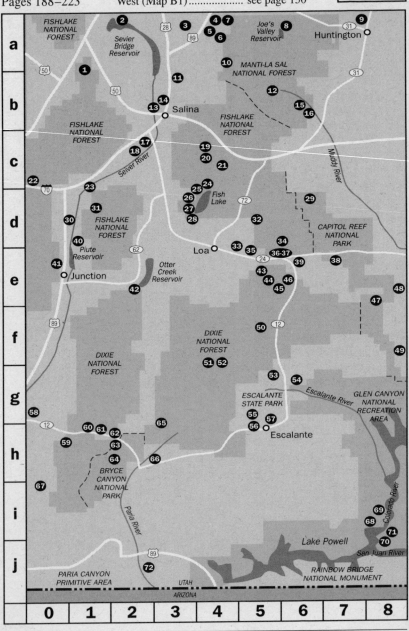

## Chapter B2 features:

1. Maple Grove
2. Yuba Lake State Park
3. Ponderosa
4. Yogi Bear's Jellystone Park
5. Palisade State Park
6. Manti Community
7. Lake Hill
8. Joe's Valley
9. Huntington State Park
10. Twelvemile Flat
11. Lund's Campground
12. Ferron Reservoir
13. Butch Cassidy Campground
14. Salina Creek RV and Campground
15. Ferron Canyon
16. Millsite State Park
17. JR Munchies Campground
18. Richfield KOA
19. Gooseberry
20. Tasha
21. Frying Pan
22. Castle Rock
23. Flying U Campground
24. Bowery Haven
25. Bowery
26. Fish Lake Lodge and Lakeside Resort
27. Mackinaw
28. Doctor Creek
29. Cathedral Valley
30. Wildflower RV
31. Monroe Mystic Hot Springs
32. Elkhorn
33. Sunglow
34. Aquarius Mobile and RV
35. Thousand Lakes RV Park
36. Chuckwagon Campground
37. Rim Rock Ranch Motel and RV Park
38. Fruita
39. Boulder Mountain Homestead
40. Piute State Park
41. Double W Campground
42. Otter Creek State Park
43. Singletree
44. Pleasant Creek
45. Oak Creek
46. Lower Bown
47. Cedar Mesa
48. Lonesome Beaver
49. McMillan Springs
50. Blue Spruce
51. Barker Reservoir
52. Posy Lake
53. Calf Creek Falls Recreation Area
54. Deer Creek Recreation Area
55. Escalante Petrified Forest State Park
56. Moqui Motel and Campground
57. Triple S RV Park and Campground
58. Red Canyon
59. Red Canyon RV Park and Campground
60. Bryce Canyon Pines Country Store & Campground, RV Park & Motel
61. Pink Cliffs Village
62. Ruby's Inn RV Campground
63. North Campground
64. Sunset Campground
65. Pine Lake
66. Kodachrome Basin State Park
67. Kings Creek
68. Bullfrog RV Park
69. Bullfrog
70. Hall's Crossing RV Park
71. Hall's Crossing
72. White House

# 1. MAPLE GROVE

*Reference:* **In Fishlake National Forest; map B2, grid b1.**

*Campsites, facilities:* This handicapped-accessible campground has 11 individual campsites and 11 group sites. Drinking water, picnic tables, and vault toilets are available.

**Reservations, fee:** Reservations are accepted for group sites only. Individual sites are $5.

**Contact:** Call the Fillmore Ranger District at (801) 743-5721.

**Location:** Driving south from Nephi on Interstate 15, take the Scipio exit and turn east onto State Route 50, following it through Scipio. Drive east 16 miles to a sign for the campground and then turn west. Stay on the paved road, which turns left near the foothills and then right over a cattle guard on paved but slightly rough Forest Road 101.

**Trip notes:** Rustic, remote Maple Grove campground is well worth the drive for the peace and quiet. It's popular with local groups and families looking for a place to hold a reunion. There is some fishing available in the small stream that flows next to some of the campsites. Camping spots are generously spaced with some tucked back into a forest well off the road. A pretty, dark-colored cliff guards the camp. This is a staging area for the Paiute ATV Trail.

**Season:** April 21 through October 30.

---

# 2. YUBA LAKE STATE PARK

**Reference:** On Yuba Reservoir; map B2, grid a2.

**Campsites, facilities:** There are 27 sites, plus picnic tables, fire grills, drinking water, showers, a dump station, and a group-use pavilion.

**Reservations, fee:** Reservations are available for a nonrefundable $5 per site; call (800) 322-3770 Monday through Friday from 8 A.M. to 4 P.M. Sites are $10. Utah residents 62 and older with a Special Fun Tag get a $2 discount Sundays through Thursdays, excluding holidays.

**Contact:** Call Yuba Lake State Park at (801) 758-2611.

**Location:** Drive 30 miles south of Nephi on Interstate 15, taking the Yuba Lake State Park exit to the east.

**Trip notes:** Because of its low elevation and relatively long season, Yuba Reservoir is popular with boaters and swimmers; in fact, this place can get pretty crowded on summer holiday weekends. There are also some off-road-vehicle trails in the area. The campground is out in the open and can be somewhat hot in the summer, though the picnic shelters on some sites provide shade. Fishing for perch and walleye is generally on the slow side.

**Season:** Open year-round.

---

# 3. PONDEROSA

**Reference:** Near Payson; map B2, grid a3.

**Campsites, facilities:** There are 22 single-family sites, plus picnic tables, fire grills, vault toilets, and drinking water.

**Reservations, fee:** For reservations, call the U.S. Forest Service National Reservation System at (800) 280-2267. Sites are $11.

**Contact:** Call the Spanish Fork Ranger District at (801) 798-3571.

**Location:** From Nephi, drive east on Highway 132 and look for Nebo Scenic Loop Road (Forest Road 15). Take this road north for seven miles, turn onto Forest Road 48, and look for the campground just off that road.

---

*Trip notes:* With its timbered setting at 6,200 feet, this is not just a good place to see some brilliant autumn hues; thanks to a nearby trailhead, it's also a prime spot to start a trek to the top of Mount Nebo, the tallest peak in the Wasatch area (allow all day for the 18-mile hike). Also try hiking around Devils Kitchen, locally dubbed Little Bryce Canyon because of the eroded red spires of earth that contrast sharply with the alpine surroundings. The fishing in these parts is fairly decent, too.

*Season:* May through October.

## 4. YOGI BEAR'S JELLYSTONE PARK

*Reference:* **In Manti; map B2, grid a4.**

*Campsites, facilities:* There are 20 RV sites with full hookups, 34 back-ins with water and electricity, and 16 tent camping sites. The campground, which is part of a national chain of the same name, has rest rooms, showers, an RV disposal site, laundry facilities, a gift shop and small store, a video game room, fire pits, a swimming pool, and a playground. Pets are allowed for an additional $1 a night.

*Reservations, fee:* Reservations are accepted. Fees are $20 for campsites with full hookups, $18 for those with water and electricity, and $16 for tent camping sites. Each additional person over four years old in groups of more than two is charged an extra $2.50 a night.

*Contact:* Call the campground at (801) 835-2267.

*Location:* This campground is located on U.S. 89 in Manti, a quarter of a mile north of the Manti Mormon Temple.

*Trip notes:* This campground with plenty of grass and shade has an activities director who plans hay rides, nature hikes for kids, pool games, and other activities all summer; catered birthday parties for groups with reservations are also available. This is a good place to stay during the annual Manti Mormon Miracle Pageant in late summer. The popular pageant draws Mormon faithful from all over the West. Canoeing, rafting, fishing, and golfing opportunities await just a few miles southeast of the campground in Palisade State Park.

*Season:* April through October.

## 5. PALISADE STATE PARK

*Reference:* **On Palisade Reservoir; map B2, grid a4.**

*Campsites, facilities:* This handicapped-accessible campground has 53 sites, plus a nine-hole golf course, picnic tables, fire grills, modern rest rooms with hot showers, a group camping area, and a covered group-use pavilion.

*Reservations, fee:* Reservations can be made 120 days in advance by calling (800) 322-3770 Monday through Friday from 8 A.M. to 5 P.M. A $5 nonrefundable reservation fee is charged for each site reserved. Campsites are $11. Utah residents 62 years and older who have a Special Fun Tag receive a $2 discount Sunday through Thursday, excluding holidays.

*Contact:* Call Palisade State Park at (801) 835-7275.

*Location:* From Manti, drive nine miles south on U.S. 89 to Sterling. Look for the sign to Palisade State Park, turn east, and follow the road for two miles to the campground.

*Trip notes:* This campground is set near a sandy beach on 70-acre Palisade Reservoir. Since the lake is small, only nonmotorized sailboats and canoes are allowed, making it a haven for swimmers and anglers. Some campers like the proximity of the golf course, which is walking-distance away. Other popular nearby attractions are the off-highway vehicle riding area at Six-Mile Canyon, the four-wheel drive road on Skyline Drive across the top of Manti Mountain, and the hiking trails in Manti–La Sal National Forest.

*Season:* Open year-round.

## 6. MANTI COMMUNITY

*Reference:* **On Yearns Reservoir; map B2, grid a4.**

*Campsites, facilities:* This campground has seven sites, plus drinking water, picnic tables, a small amphitheater, vault toilets, and fire grills.

*Reservations, fee:* Reservations are accepted for group and family sites only. Individual sites are $5 and group sites are $10.

*Contact:* Call the Sanpete Ranger District in Ephraim at (801) 283-4151.

*Location:* Drive seven miles east of Manti on Manti Canyon Road to the campground, which is on the south side of the road.

*Trip notes:* Yearns Reservoir provides good fishing for planted rainbow trout and a quiet place for a canoe trip. Nearby Skyline Drive at the top of the canyon offers some of the state's most scenic views for four-wheel-drive enthusiasts. The tree-shaded campsites are a short walk from the reservoir.

*Season:* June through October.

## 7. LAKE HILL

*Reference:* **In Manti–La Sal National Forest; map B2, grid a4.**

*Campsites, facilities:* This campground with 12 sites has drinking water, vault toilets, picnic tables, and fire grills.

*Reservations, fee:* Reservations are accepted for group and family units only. Individual sites are $5, and group sites are $10.

*Contact:* Call the Sanpete Ranger District in Ephraim at (801) 283-4151.

*Location:* Drive 8.5 miles southeast of Ephraim in Ephraim Canyon to the campground, which is on the south side of the road.

*Trip notes:* The small reservoir next to this campground offers visitors a place to fish for stocked trout and a good spot to enjoy a canoe trip. Campsites are in an alpine forest setting.

*Season:* June through October.

## 8. JOE'S VALLEY

*Reference:* **On Joe's Valley Reservoir; map B2, grid a6.**

*Campsites, facilities:* This 46-site campground offers handicapped-accessible rest rooms, drinking water, a cement boat-launching ramp, picnic tables, and fire grills.

*Reservations, fee:* Reservations are accepted through the U.S. Forest Service National Reservation System at (800) 280-2267. Fees are $6 for individual sites and $10 for multiple-family sites.

*Contact:* Call the Ferron Ranger District at (801) 384-2372.

*Location:* Drive 17.6 miles west from Orangeville on State Route 29 to Joe's Valley Reservoir. Signs point the way to the campground at the west end of the reservoir.

*Trip notes:* This campground is located somewhat out in the open on Joe's Valley Reservoir, surrounded by buff- and tan-colored cliffs. Nearby streams and small reservoirs provide good fishing, and the reservoir itself is popular with boaters and water skiers. A small store, snack bar, and gas station are part of the marina complex.

*Season:* Memorial Day through mid-October.

## 9. HUNTINGTON STATE PARK

*Reference:* **On Huntington Reservoir; map B2, a7.**

*Campsites, facilities:* This handicapped-accessible campground has 22 sites, plus showers, a picnic area, a covered group-use area, modern rest rooms, a boat ramp, and a sewage disposal station.

*Reservations, fee:* Reservations can be made 120 days in advance by calling (800) 322-3770 Monday through Friday from 8 A.M. to 5 P.M. A $5 nonrefundable reservation fee is charged for each site reserved. Campsites are $10, and $8 in the winter when the showers are no longer available. Utah residents 62 years and older who have a Special Fun Tag receive a $2 discount Sunday through Thursday, excluding holidays.

*Contact:* Call Huntington State Park at (801) 687-2491.

*Location:* The park is located two miles north of Huntington on State Route 10.

*Trip notes:* Sites at this campground in Huntington State Park are located in a grassy area near the shore of a reservoir. Fishing, boating, waterskiing, and swimming are prime activities in the park, and off-highway vehicle users and hikers enjoy the San Rafael Swell, which is about 25 miles away. Wasatch Plateau, 17 miles away, is the place to go for cooler weather in the summer; it has good fishing, mountain biking, and hiking areas on U.S. Forest Service–managed areas. The museum of San Rafael in Castle Dale focuses on the local area, featuring dinosaur, natural history, and Native American exhibits.

*Season:* Open year-round.

## 10. TWELVEMILE FLAT

*Reference:* **In Manti–La Sal National Forest; map B2, grid a4.**

*Campsites, facilities:* This campground with 13 sites has picnic tables, vault toilets, drinking water, and fire grills.

*Reservations, fee:* Reservations are accepted for family sites only through the ranger district office. Individual sites are $5 a night and family sites are $10 a night.

*Contact:* Call the Sanpete Ranger District of Manti–La Sal National Forest in Ephraim at (801) 283-4151.

*Location:* From Mayfield, located three miles south of U.S. 89, head east on the county road. At the Manti–La Sal National Forest boundary, the road becomes Forest Road 022; follow it to the campground near the top of Wasatch Plateau.

*Trip notes:* Located at an elevation of 10,000 feet, this campground offers a cool alpine respite during the hot summer months—and since it's off the beaten path, campers can enjoy the solitude, too. The area is especially pretty in the fall, when the oaks and aspens change color. Anglers can try their luck in the small reservoirs.

*Season:* July through September.

---

## 11. LUND'S CAMPGROUND

*Reference:* **In Gunnison; map B2, grid b3.**

*Campsites, facilities:* This 15-site RV park has full hookups, rest rooms, showers, picnic tables, and a public phone. Pets are allowed.

*Reservations, fee:* Reservations are accepted. Campsites are $12.

*Contact:* Lund's Campground, 240 South Main Street, Gunnison, UT 84634; (801) 528-3366.

*Location:* The campground is located at 240 South Main Street in Gunnison, on the west side of the road.

*Trip notes:* Gunnison is a quiet place full of small-town pleasures, including old-fashioned shakes and malts at one of several drive-through restaurants in town. Expect parking-lot camping on gravel sites with some shade. Yuba Reservoir and the Painted Rocks Recreation Area are approximately five miles to the north.

*Season:* March through November.

---

## 12. FERRON RESERVOIR

*Reference:* **On Ferron Reservoir; map B2, grid b5.**

*Campsites, facilities:* This 32-site campground has drinking water, vault toilets, picnic tables, and fire grills.

*Reservations, fee:* Campsites are $5 and are first come, first served.

*Contact:* Call the Ferron Ranger District at (801) 384-2372.

*Location:* To reach the campground, take Forest Road 22 west of Ferron for 28 miles. (Forest Road 22 connects the towns of Ferron on the east side of Manti Mountain and Mayfield on the west).

*Trip notes:* Due to the 9,500-foot elevation, the camping season is short but sweet at Ferron Reservoir. The dam has undergone recent repairs to help improve this pine-shrouded lake as a fishery. There are good views of Emery and Sanpete Counties from the top of Manti Mountain, which is part of Skyline Drive, a four-wheel drive road that stretches across the top of Manti Mountain from Salina to Spanish Fork Canyon. Campsites are nestled in the trees within walking distance of the reservoir. Horses can be rented nearby.

*Season:* June through September.

---

## 13. BUTCH CASSIDY CAMPGROUND

*Reference:* **In Salina; map B2, grid b3.**

*Campsites, facilities:* There are 60 level, gravel RV sites with full hookups (most of them pull-throughs), plus two grassy acres for tents. Amenities include rest rooms, showers, picnic tables, an RV disposal station, a swimming pool, a game room, laundry facilities, a grocery and gift shop, and a playground.

*Reservations, fee:* Reservations are recommended in June and July. Campsites with full hookups are $16.75 a night. Tent sites are $6 a night. These rates are based on two-person occupancy. An additional $2 a person for adults and $1 for children ages seven to 15 is charged for groups of more than two. The rates for campsites increase during the June, July, and August summer season.

*Contact:* Butch Cassidy Campground, 1100 South State Street, Salina, UT 84654; (801) 529-7400 or (800) 551-6842.

*Location:* Take the Salina exit off of Interstate 70 and head north on State Street about a block. The campground is on the west side of the road at 1100 South State Street.

*Trip notes:* Though located along a busy road, this campground offers shaded RV sites, a swimming pool, and a nice, grassy area for tents. Nearby activities abound, including Salina Canyon and the start of Skyline Drive, a four-wheel-drive road that winds its way across the top of the Wasatch Plateau for about 100 miles to Spanish Fork Canyon. The Paiute ATV and Great Western Trails provide good access for all-terrain vehicles and horseback, mountain, and dirt-bike riding.

*Season:* April through October.

## 14. SALINA CREEK RV AND CAMPGROUND

*Reference:* **Near Salina; map B2, grid b3.**

*Campsites, facilities:* This campground has 21 pull-through RV sites with full hookups, but no tent camping areas. Amenities include rest rooms, showers, laundry facilities, a grocery and gift store, and a public phone. Pets are allowed.

*Reservations, fees:* Reservations are accepted. Campsites are $15.50.

*Contact:* Salina Creek RV and Campground, 1385 South State Street, Salina, UT 84654; (801) 529-3711.

*Location:* Take the Salina exit off of Interstate 70, and drive north on State Street. The campground is in a parking lot behind a gas station and convenience store on the west side of the road.

*Trip notes:* The freeway location makes this a convenient overnight stop for campers coming from the east along Interstate 70 from Arches National Park into Bryce Canyon and Zion National Parks. The facility is basically a gravel parking lot behind a gas station with hookups and level places for RVs. There is only one shaded picnic table.

*Season:* Open year-round.

## 15. FERRON CANYON

*Reference:* **In Ferron Canyon; map B2, grid b6.**

*Campsites, facilities:* There are three campsites and a group picnic area. Amenities include vault toilets, fire grills, and picnic tables, but *no drinking water.*

*Reservations, fee:* Campsites are free and are first come, first served.

*Contact:* Call the Ferron Ranger District of Manti–La Sal National Forest in Ferron at (801) 384-2372.

*Location:* Take Forest Road 22 about nine miles northwest of Ferron to reach the campground.

*Trip notes:* While officially a picnic area, overnight camping is allowed at this forested site along Forest Road 22. Millsite State Park, which is located approximately four miles to the east, is the place to go for golfing, boating, and fishing.

*Season:* June 15 through September 20.

## 16. MILLSITE STATE PARK

*Reference:* **On Millsite Reservoir; map B2, grid b6.**

*Campsites, facilities:* This handicapped-accessible campground with 22 sites has two covered group-use areas, modern rest rooms with showers, picnic tables, and fire grills. A boat-launching ramp, nine-hole golf course, and sandy beach are located nearby.

*Reservations, fee:* Reservations can be made 120 days in advance by calling (800) 322-3770 Monday through Friday from 8 A.M. to 5 P.M. A $5 nonrefundable reservation fee is charged for each site reserved. Campsites are $6 to $10, depending on the season. Utah residents 62 years and older who have a Special Fun Tag receive a $2 discount Sunday through Thursday, excluding holidays.

*Contact:* Call Millsite State Park at (801) 687-2491.

*Location:* Drive four miles west of State Route 10 near the Emery County town of Ferron, and follow the signs to the campground.

*Trip notes:* Located at the mouth of Ferron Canyon, 435-acre Millsite Reservoir is surrounded by buff- and tan-colored cliffs. Fishing, golf, and water sports are the most popular activities. The park is four miles from the alpine splendor of Manti Mountain, where four-wheel-drive enthusiasts enjoy driving up the canyon and across the famed Skyline Drive in the fall. The golf course is especially scenic and usually uncrowded.

*Season:* May 15 to October 15, and open without water the rest of the year.

## 17. JR MUNCHIES CAMPGROUND

*Reference:* **In Richfield; map B2, grid c2.**

*Campsites, facilities:* This campground has 21 sites with full hookups, plus rest rooms, showers, laundry facilities, an RV disposal site, a public phone, a store, and a gas station. Pets are allowed.

*Reservations, fee:* Reservations are accepted. Campsites are $14.

*Contact:* JR Munchies Campground, P.O. Box 387, Richfield, UT 84701; (801) 896-9340.

*Location:* The campground is located at the south end of Richfield at 745 South Main Street.

*Trip notes:* This campground is basically a parking area for RVs, with fencing and small trees offering only a bit of shade. However, it is close to Richfield's public golf course and the Paiute ATV Trail. And Fremont State Park, with its archaeological museum, Indian rock art, and hiking trails, is located on Interstate 70 a few miles southwest of Richfield.

*Season:* Open year-round.

## 18. RICHFIELD KOA

*Reference:* **In Richfield; map B2, grid c2.**

*Campsites, facilities:* This campground has 83 RV sites with full hookups available, but campers only pay for the services they desire. Also here are approximately 50 tent sites on a large lawn area. Amenities include rest rooms; showers; laundry facilities; a store with groceries, gifts, and RV supplies; a game room; an RV disposal site; a playground; a swimming pool; a public phone; and a fire pit for large groups. Pets are allowed.

*Reservations, fee:* Reservations are accepted. Campsites are $15 for two people. Each additional adult is $3, and children ages three to 17 are $1.50. Additional fees are charged for using water ($1), sewer ($1), and electricity ($2).

*Contact:* Call the campground at (801) 896-6674.

*Location:* Take Interstate 70 to Richfield and get off on exit 37 or 40. From Main Street, turn west on 600 South Street into a residential area. Drive through two stop signs. The front entrance to the KOA passes through a permanent trailer park.

*Trip notes:* This well-kept private campground has nicely spaced campsites and plenty of grass and shade, plus a swimming pool. The perimeter is surrounded by vegetation, which adds to the peaceful feeling of the place. Nearby attractions include Richfield's public golf course and the Paiute ATV and Great Western Trails.

*Season:* March through October, with limited facilities the rest of the year.

## 19. GOOSEBERRY

*Reference:* **On Gooseberry Creek; map B2, grid c4.**

*Campsites, facilities:* This campground has five campsites and one group area. Amenities include picnic tables, fire grills, drinking water, and vault toilets.

*Reservations, fee:* Individual campsites are free and are first come, first served. Call the ranger district about the group site.

*Contact:* Call the Richfield Ranger District at (801) 896-9233.

*Location:* From Salina, take Interstate 70 southeast for seven miles to exit 61. Turn and head south for 11 miles to the campground.

*Trip notes:* The campground with shaded, generously spaced campsites is located on the banks of Gooseberry Creek and near a number of small reservoirs which provide fishing for stocked trout in the summer months. The nearby

Great Western Trail makes this an ideal base for horseback, off-highway-vehicle, and mountain-bike riding.

*Season:* June 15 through September 15.

## 20. TASHA

*Reference:* **Near Johnson Reservoir, map B2, grid c4.**

*Campsites, facilities:* Designed for campers with horses, this campground has 10 family campsites and one group area. Facilities include picnic tables, fire grills, and drinking water, but no rest rooms.

*Reservations, fee:* Campsites are free and are first come, first served.

*Contact:* Call the Loa Ranger District of Fishlake National Forest at (801) 836-2811.

*Location:* The campground is located north and west of Johnson Reservoir. To reach it, drive about 15 miles north of State Route 24 on State Route 25, following the signs to the camp.

*Trip notes:* This is a popular spot with elk and deer hunters, as well as horse owners who enjoy riding in the nearby forests. Campsites overlook Johnson Reservoir and are near a meadow.

*Season:* May through October.

## 21. FRYING PAN

*Reference:* **Near Johnson Reservoir; map B2, grid c4.**

*Campsites, facilities:* There are 11 family campsites and one group site, plus vault toilets, picnic tables, drinking water, and fire grills.

*Reservations, fee:* Reservations are only accepted for the group site, which can be reserved by calling the U.S. Forest Service National Reservation System at (800) 280-2267. Campsites are $6.

*Contact:* Call the Loa Ranger District at (801) 836-2811.

*Location:* The campground is located west of Johnson Reservoir. To reach it, drive about 13 miles north of State Route 24 on State Route 25.

*Trip notes:* Anglers and water sports enthusiasts will find plenty to do at this campground near Johnson Reservoir. The trout fishing is good in the reservoir, and there are also a number of small streams in the area. A herd of moose also calls these parts home. The campsites are somewhat out in the open, but they have nice views of the reservoir and the southern end of the Wasatch Plateau.

*Season:* May 27 through September 30.

## 22. CASTLE ROCK

*Reference:* **In Fishlake National Forest, operated by Fremont Indian State Park; map B2, grid c0.**

*Campsites, facilities:* This campground with 31 sites has picnic tables and a picnic area, fire grills, a group camping area, modern rest rooms, and drinking water, plus a large visitors center and museum.

*Reservations, fee:* Reservations can be made 120 days in advance by calling (800) 322-3770 Monday through Friday from 8 A.M. to 5 P.M. A $5 nonre-

fundable reservation fee is charged for each site reserved. Campsites are $7.
Utah residents 62 years and older who have a Special Fun Tag receive a $2
discount Sunday through Thursday, excluding holidays.

*Contact:* Call Fremont Indian State Park at (801) 527-4631.

*Location:* To reach the campground, drive 21 miles southwest of Richfield off
Interstate 70. Directions are well marked off freeway exits.

*Trip notes:* This campground is a popular spot for all-terrain vehicle users who
can access hundreds of miles of marked trails on the nearby Paiute ATV and
Great Western Trails. Hikers will enjoy the trails leading to ancient Native
American rock art sites. The visitors center and museum offer modern displays geared to challenge the imaginations of youngsters. A restored pithouse
is located near the visitors center parking area. Campers can fish in the creek
flowing through the campground.

*Season:* April through October.

## 23. FLYING U CAMPGROUND

*Reference:* **In Joseph; map B2, grid c1.**

*Campsites, facilities:* This RV park has eight campsites with full hookups, plus
rest rooms, laundry facilities, groceries, a public phone, and an RV disposal
site. Pets are allowed.

*Reservations, fee:* Reservations are accepted. Campsites are $7 to $10.

*Contact:* Flying U Campground, 45 South State Street, Joseph, UT 84739; (801)
527-4758.

*Location:* Driving south on Interstate 70 from Richfield, take exit 26 and head
east on Main Street. The campground is located on the east side of the road
in the middle of town.

*Trip notes:* Flying U Campground is little more than a gravel parking lot with
hookups and a few trees. Fremont Indian State Park, located about 10 miles
away, offers good hiking trails to Native American rock art sites, not to mention an excellent museum. There is also a small farm implements "museum"
adjacent to the campground with displays of old farm equipment that was
once used in the area.

*Season:* May 15 through October 30.

## 24. BOWERY HAVEN

*Reference:* **On Fish Lake; map B2, grid d4.**

*Campsites, facilities:* This campground has 69 RV sites with full hookups; 24
of these are pull-throughs. Also here are rest rooms, showers, picnic tables,
laundry facilities, groceries (including fishing tackle), and fire pits, plus a
large field for recreational activities. Horseshoes can be rented. The marina
has a boat ramp.

*Reservations, fee:* Reservations are accepted. Campsites are $14.

*Contact:* Bowery Haven, 1500 North Highway 25, Fish Lake, UT 84701; (801)
638-1040.

*Location:* From Richfield, drive north on Interstate 70. Take the Sigurd exit
and head southeast on Highway 24 for 46 miles until the junction with State

Route 25. Drive just over nine miles north to the northwest corner of Fish Lake and the campground.

*Trip notes:* Located next to Fish Lake, this resort campground offers boat rentals and launching, plus fishing for trout and yellow perch in the lake. One of the area's best restaurants is located at the lodge. Anglers who catch a nice trout or two can have the chef prepare the fish for dinner. The campsites have good views of the scenic lake. Hiking and horseback riding trails can be found throughout the area.

*Season:* May through September.

## 25. BOWERY

*Reference:* **On Fish Lake; map B2, grid d4.**

*Campsites, facilities:* This campground has 31 family campsites and 12 group sites, as well as drinking water, picnic tables, fire grills, and vault toilets.

*Reservations, fee:* For reservations, call the U.S. Forest Service National Reservation System at (800) 280-2267. Campsites are $6.

*Contact:* Call the Loa Ranger District at (801) 836-2811.

*Location:* From Richfield, drive north on Interstate 70 to the Sigurd exit. Drive 46 miles southeast on State Route 24, looking for the junction to State Route 25. Turn north on State Route 25 and drive nine miles to Fish Lake. The campground is on the west side of Fish Lake.

*Trip notes:* As the name implies, the big draw at this campground is the fishing at Fish Lake. Rainbow trout, lake trout, and yellow perch make this natural lake one of Utah's most popular summer destinations. A paved trail on the west side of the lake offers good hiking opportunities. The campground, located in a mixed forest of pine and aspen, overlooks the lake in a beautiful setting. Don't be surprised to see deer wander through the campground in the early morning.

*Season:* May through October.

## 26. FISH LAKE LODGE AND LAKESIDE RESORT

*Reference:* **On Fish Lake; map B2, grid d3.**

*Campsites, facilities:* There are 11 pull-through RV sites and 13 back-in RV sites, all with full hookups. The resort has a full-service marina with gas, groceries, and tackle and boat rental. Rest rooms, showers, laundry facilities, and a public phone are available.

*Reservations, fee:* Reservations are accepted. The fee is $14.

*Contact:* Fish Lake Lodge and Lakeside Resort, 10 East Center Highway 25, Fish Lake, UT 84701; (801) 638-1000.

*Location:* From Richfield, drive north on Interstate 70. Take the Sigurd exit and drive 24 miles southeast on State Route 24. Look for the signs to Fish Lake and drive about eight miles northeast on State Route 25 to the resort, which is on the west side of the lake.

*Trip notes:* Set beside lovely Fish Lake, this log-cabin resort has the feel of an old Yellowstone Park lodge. Pine trees surround the campsites. The forested

Fish Lake area, including nearby Johnson Reservoir, encompasses 13,700 acres, with 3,000 acres of lakes and reservoirs. Moose and mule deer roam through the region. Anglers can boat or raft onto the water and cast for plentiful yellow perch and trout; several commercial lodges on the lake offer boat rentals and guides. Equestrians enjoy exploring the open meadows and hills, and hikers can follow a paved, two-mile hiking trail that leads along the lake's western edge.

*Season:* May through October.

---

## 27. MACKINAW

*Reference:* **On Fish Lake; map B2, grid d3.**

*Campsites, facilities:* There are 53 campsites and 15 group areas. Facilities include vault toilets, picnic tables, fire grills, and drinking water. When the temperature dips below zero in late September, the water may be turned off.

*Reservations, fee:* Call the U.S. Forest Service National Reservation System at (800) 280-2267 to reserve a site. The fee is $6 when the water is turned on. Camping is free when the water is off.

*Contact:* Call Loa Ranger District of Fishlake National Forest at (801) 836-2811.

*Location:* From Richfield, drive north on Interstate 70. Take the Sigurd exit and drive about 24 miles southeast on State Route 24, looking for the signs to Fish Lake. Drive about eight miles north on State Route 25 to the campground, which is on the west side of the lake.

*Trip notes:* If you're looking for a cool climate on the way from Bryce Canyon or Zion National Park to Capitol Reef National Park, this alpine campground is a wonderful place to spend the night. Mackinaw is set on a beautiful hill in the midst of pine and aspen forest and meadows overlooking Fish Lake. Fishing for trout and yellow perch is excellent at Fish Lake. Several commercial lodges on the lake offer anglers boat rentals and guides. Keep an eye out for moose and mule deer in the area. A hiking trail traverses the lake's western edge, and the rolling open country makes for enjoyable off-trail horseback riding.

*Season:* May through September, although the camp's water may be turned off when the temperature dips below freezing.

---

## 28. DOCTOR CREEK

*Reference:* **Near Fish Lake; map B2, grid d3.**

*Campsites, facilities:* There are 29 campsites and two group areas. Facilities include vault toilets, picnic tables, fire grills, and drinking water. When the temperature dips below zero in late September, the water may be turned off. There is an RV disposal station at the group area.

*Reservations, fee:* Call the U.S. Forest Service National Reservation System at (800) 280-2267 to reserve a site. The fee is $6 when the water is on. Camping is free when the water is turned off.

*Contact:* Call Loa Ranger District of Fishlake National Forest at (801) 836-2811.

*Location:* From Richfield, drive north on Interstate 70. Take the Sigurd exit and drive about 24 miles southeast on State Route 24, looking for the signs

---

to Fish Lake. Drive about six miles north on State Route 25 to the campground, which is just south of the lake.

*Trip notes:* Just a short drive from the Fish Lake shoreline, this campground is a little more secluded than some of the others in the area. Surrounded by pine and aspen, it's especially pretty in the fall when the leaves change color. Located at the outlet end of Fish Lake, Doctor Creek is more of a slough than a true creek. For details on boating, fishing, and hiking recreation at Fish Lake, see Mackinaw on page 201.

*Season:* May through September, although the water may be turned off when the temperature dips below freezing.

---

## 29. CATHEDRAL VALLEY

*Reference:* **In Capitol Reef National Park; map B2, grid d6.**

*Campsites, facilities:* There are five campsites with vault toilets, picnic tables, and fire grills. No drinking water is available.

*Reservations, fee:* There is no fee. All sites are first come, first served. Backcountry camping is permitted in much of the park; obtain a free permit from park headquarters.

*Contact:* Call park headquarters at (801) 425-3791.

*Location:* From Torrey, drive 23 miles east on State Route 24. Look for a turnoff to the unpaved Cathedral Valley Road, just before reaching the town of Caineville. Drive 28 miles north into Cathedral Valley. The dirt road can be rugged; four-wheel drive is recommended.

*Trip notes:* You can escape the crowds at this quiet, primitive camp. Remote Cathedral Valley lies on the back side of Capitol Reef National Park, offering sweeping views of the high sandstone plateaus to the south that most visitors see up close. The "cathedrals" are towering plateaus and buttes that stand like lonely fortresses in a rugged red-rock desert. From Cathedral Valley campground, a quarter-mile (one-way) hiking trail leads to the top of a plateau and dead-ends at a cliff, where you can enjoy a 360-degree panorama of the sprawling terrain. Other scenic hikes, four-wheel-drive tours, and mountain-biking routes can be found throughout the park. One popular four-wheel-driving tour, the challenging Cathedral Valley Loop, begins just off of State Route 24, at River Ford Road, approximately 12 miles east of the visitors center.

*Season:* Open year-round.

---

## 30. WILDFLOWER RV

*Reference:* **In Marysville; map B2, grid d1.**

*Campsites, facilities:* There are six RV sites with full hookups. Rest rooms, showers, and a playground are available. Pets are allowed.

*Reservations, fee:* Reservations are accepted. The fee is $8.

*Contact:* Wildflower RV, P.O. Box 183, Marysville, UT 84750; (801) 326-4301.

*Location:* From the town of Marysville, drive four miles north on Highway 89 to the campground.

*Trip notes:* From this RV park in Marysville, it's approximately 10 miles boating and fishing recreation at Piute Reservoir. Rainbow trout grow to two and

---

three pounds here, but be forewarned: during dry summers, local farmers can draw the lake down to little more than a stream. When the water's up, both this lake and Otter Creek Reservoir (25 miles from Marysville) make good spots for waterskiing and canoeing. Otter Creek Reservoir also has a boat ramp.

*Season:* April through October.

## 31. MONROE MYSTIC HOT SPRINGS

*Reference:* **In Monroe; map B2, grid d1.**

*Campsites, facilities:* There are 35 RV campsites with full hookups, plus two tepees, one camping cabin, and a large grassy area for tent camping. Picnic tables, a playground, a small store, rest rooms, and mineral hot springs are available.

*Reservations, fee:* Reservations are accepted. The fee is $15 for full-hookup sites, $10 for tent sites, and $35 for tepees and the camping cabin. Hot springs are free to campers. Sevier County residents can use a hot tub for $3; non-residents pay $5.

*Contact:* Monroe Mystic Hot Springs, 475 East 100 North, Monroe, UT 84754; (801) 527-3286.

*Location:* From Richfield, take Interstate 70 south to the town of Monroe. In Monroe, turn east on 100 North. The campground is in three blocks, at the end of a gravel road.

*Trip notes:* This quiet, grassy rural campground is well off the beaten path. Tall trees shade the campsites, and kids get a playground with a trampoline. The hot tubs here are pretty primitive.

*Season:* Open year-round.

## 32. ELKHORN

*Reference:* **In Fishlake National Forest; map B2, grid d5.**

*Campsites, facilities:* There are six campsites and one group site. Vault toilets, drinking water, picnic tables, and fire grills are available.

*Reservations, fee:* Campsites are free and are first come, first served.

*Contact:* Call the Loa Ranger District of Fishlake National Forest at (801) 836-2811.

*Location:* From Loa, drive 11 miles northeast on State Route 72. Turn south on Forest Road 206 and drive nine miles to the campground.

*Trip notes:* Popular with folks enjoying a four-wheel-driving trip into Capitol Reef National Park's Cathedral Valley, which is 40 minutes away, this remote campground offers peace and quiet away from the crowds. Fishing opportunities abound, including the small Neff Reservoir and Round Lake, both of which are stocked with rainbow trout. Anglers can also visit Forsythe Reservoir, Mill Meadow Reservoir, and the Fremont River, but in the recent past they have been closed to fishing as resident trout have been found to carry whirling disease. Get in touch with the Utah Division of Wildlife Resources, (801) 538-4700, for the latest conditions.

*Season:* May 27 through September 30.

## 33. SUNGLOW

**Reference: In Fishlake National Forest; map B2, grid d4.**

*Campsites, facilities:* There are five family campsites and three group areas. Drinking water, picnic tables, and vault toilets are available.

*Reservations, fee:* Campsites are $5 and are first come, first served.

*Contact:* Call the Loa Ranger District of Fishlake National Forest at (801) 836-2811.

*Location:* From Bicknell, drive a half mile south on State Route 24. Follow Forest Road 143 approximately 11.5 miles east to the campground.

*Trip notes:* Though small, this scenic mountain campground can be a fine alternative to nearby Capitol Reef National Park. It's set on a graveled road amid red-rock canyons. Large cottonwood trees shade the sites and a stream runs near the camp. Although you won't find trails, you may enjoy hiking up the narrow canyon or scrambling up rocks to watch the sunset. Visit the nearby Perry Egan Fish Hatchery to see large brood stock trout, which grow up to six pounds and provide eggs for other Utah hatcheries. Anglers can fish trout in the many tiny alpine lakes that dot Boulder Mountain, a 10-mile drive from the campground.

*Season:* May 15 through October 30.

---

## 34. AQUARIUS MOBILE AND RV

**Reference: In Bicknell; map B2, grid e5.**

*Campsites, facilities:* There are 12 RV sites with full hookups. An RV disposal site is available. Pets are allowed.

*Reservations, fee:* Reservations are accepted. Campsites are $7.50.

*Contact:* Aquarius Mobile and RV, P.O. Box 304, Bicknell, UT 84715; (801) 425-3835.

*Location:* Follow State Route 24 into Bicknell; in town, it becomes Main Street. The campground is located at 294 West Main Street.

*Trip notes:* Even though this rural RV park is in the middle of the town of Bicknell, it doesn't get too loud. The camp's approximately 15 miles from Capitol Reef National Park and numerous hiking trails. Horseback riding is available at the Rim Rock Ranch Motel and RV Park in Torrey (see page 206). Nearby is the Perry Egan Fish Hatchery, a brood stock facility for the Utah Division of Wildlife Resources. Here you can see workers prepare eggs for shipment to other hatcheries in the facility; some of the trout raised here grow to more than six pounds. Visit the Sunglow Café to sample its pickle, pinto bean, or oatmeal pie. The restaurant at the Aquarius Motel also serves good down-home fare.

*Season:* Open year-round.

---

## 35. THOUSAND LAKES RV PARK

**Reference: Near Torrey; map B2, grid e5.**

*Campsites, facilities:* There are 36 sites with full hookups, 13 sites with water and electric hookups, nine tent sites, and two camping cabins. Thousand

---

Lakes RV Park also provides visitors with rest rooms, showers, laundry facilities, a pool, picnic tables, an RV disposal site, a public phone, a grocery and gift shop, a horseshoe pit, and a playground. For a fee, wagon rides are offered on weekends in the summer, as is a Dutch-oven Western dinner. Barbecue grills and four-wheel-drive vehicles are also available for rental from the campground.

**Reservations, fee:** Reservations are accepted. Sites with full and partial hookups cost $13.50 to $16.50, and tent sites on the grassy area are $10.50. Camping cabins are $26.

**Contact:** Thousand Lakes RV Park, P.O. Box 750070, Torrey, UT 84775; (801) 425-3500.

**Location:** The campground is located one mile west of Torrey on State Route 24.

**Trip notes:** With its summertime wagon rides and old-fashioned Dutch-oven dinners on weekends, this campground preserves a real Western flavor. And how's this for a nice touch? Each guest receives a homemade muffin in the morning. You can rent a four-wheel-drive vehicle and take a trip from Thousand Lakes Mountain into Capitol Reef National Park, which is one mile away. Here you can enjoy a 3.5-mile round-trip hike out to the monolithic Chimney Rock formation, which is located just east of the park entrance. Anglers fish for trout at many small alpine lakes on Boulder Mountain to the south.

**Season:** April through October.

## 36. CHUCKWAGON CAMPGROUND 🐟🎿🐎 RV 5

**Reference:** In Torrey; map B2, grid e6.

**Campsites, facilities:** There are five RV sites with full hookups. Amenities include rest rooms, showers, picnic tables, an RV disposal site, laundry facilities, a public phone, and a general store with camping supplies, a snack bar, and video rentals.

**Reservations, fee:** Reservations are recommended during the month of July. For full-hookup sites, Chuckwagon charges visitors $15. For sites with no hookups, the fee is $8.

**Contact:** Chuckwagon Campground, 12 West Main Street, Torrey, UT 84775; (801) 425-3288.

**Location:** Follow State Route 24 into the town of Torrey. In Torrey, State Route 24 becomes Main Street. Visitors should follow this road to Chuckwagon Campground, which is located at 12 West Main Street.

**Trip notes:** This small RV park sits beside a general store in the middle of the sleepy, rural town of Torrey. Just to the east you'll find Capitol Reef National Park, and numerous hiking and four-wheel-driving routes. One of the easier and more scenic foot trails is the 2.25-mile (one-way) trek through Capitol Gorge. It's a relatively flat walk through a narrow canyon. Anglers can drive approximately 20 minutes to fish at the dozens of small alpine lakes on Boulder Mountain.

**Season:** March through October.

## 37. RIM ROCK RANCH MOTEL AND RV PARK

*Reference:* **In Torrey; map B2, grid e6.**

*Campsites, facilities:* There are 35 RV sites with full hookups. Tent campers are accommodated around the perimeter of the park. Rest rooms, showers, laundry facilities, a public phone, a restaurant, a gift shop, and a pool are available. There is an enclosure to protect tents on windy days.

*Reservations, fee:* Reservations are not accepted. The fee is $15 for RV sites and $10 for tent sites.

*Contact:* Call the campground at (801) 425-3843.

*Location:* The campground is in Torrey, on State Route 24, one mile from the entrance to Capitol Reef National Park, and six miles from the park's visitors center.

*Trip notes:* This campground affords views over Capitol Reef National Park's impressive red-rock terrain, as well as Boulder Mountain to the southwest and the Henry Mountains far to the east. The national park features many short hiking trails. Anglers can drive 10 miles to Boulder Mountain's numerous alpine lakes and reservoirs, including Bown Reservoir.

*Season:* Open year-round.

## 38. FRUITA

*Reference:* **In Capitol Reef National Monument; map B2, grid e7.**

*Campsites, facilities:* There are 71 campsites. Rest rooms with cold running water, picnic tables, an amphitheater, fire grills, and an RV disposal station are available. One rest room is heated for winter use. Group areas are available, and can accommodate up to 100 people.

*Reservations, fee:* Campsites are $7 and are first come, first served. Backcountry camping is permitted in much of the park; obtain a free permit from park headquarters.

*Contact:* Call park headquarters at (801) 425-3791.

*Location:* Drive 11 miles east from Torrey on State Route 24 to the park visitors center. From there, drive 1.3 miles south on the marked road to the campground.

*Trip notes:* Capitol Reef National Park's Fruita campground is, in fact, set in the midst of an old fruit orchard, which was first planted in the nineteenth century by Mormon settlers. Apple, peach, cherry, mulberry, and Potawatamee plum trees grow here, and when the fruit ripens in midsummer, visitors can pick it fresh. If you want to pick a whole basket, however, you'll have to pay for it. Several good hiking trails, including a 1.75-mile (one-way) trek to Cohab Canyon and a 1.25-mile (one-way) walk to the Fremont River Overlook, begin at the campground. In the winter, deer and chukar partridge frequent the area. Near the camp you can visit several "living history" displays, including an old blacksmith shop and the Fruita School House, which has been refurbished with time-worn desks, a wood-burning stove, and old-fashioned school books.

*Season:* Open year-round.

# 39. BOULDER MOUNTAIN HOMESTEAD

*Reference:* **Near Torrey; map B2, grid e6.**

*Campsites, facilities:* There are 10 RV sites with water and electric hookups. Picnic tables and fire pits are available. Pets are allowed.

*Reservations, fee:* Reservations are accepted; you can call as early as March to reserve a spot. The fee is $13.

*Contact:* Call the campground at (801) 425-5374 or (800) 769-4644.

*Location:* The RV park is four miles south of Torrey on State Route 12.

*Trip notes:* The town of Torrey offers a good base for four-wheel-driving tours. This campground is a convenient locale for visits to Capitol Reef National Park and Boulder Mountain. You can cast for large brook trout at many Boulder Mountain alpine lakes and reservoirs, including Blind Lake and Donkey Lake.

*Season:* April through November.

# 40. PIUTE STATE PARK

*Reference:* **On Piute Reservoir; map B2, grid e0.**

*Campsites, facilities:* Primitive dispersed camping is available. Limited facilities consist of pit toilets, picnic tables, and a small cement boat ramp.

*Reservations, fee:* Campsites are free and are first come, first served.

*Contact:* Call Otter Creek State Park at (801) 624-3268.

*Location:* From Marysville, drive 12 miles south on U.S. 89. Turn east onto the dirt road to the reservoir.

*Trip notes:* This campground doesn't get too crowded, and when you see it you'll understand why. It's extremely primitive and the few facilities show signs of disrepair. The terrain is mostly open, dotted with a few small trees and sagebrush. Piute Reservoir offers wide open expanses of water when it's full, making this an excellent place to boat, raft, and water-ski. When the water is low, however, boat launching can be a problem. The reservoir is stocked regularly with rainbow trout, so fishing can be good. In the fall, this camp attracts many duck hunters.

*Season:* Open year-round.

# 41. DOUBLE W CAMPGROUND

*Reference:* **In Circleville; map B2, grid e1.**

*Campsites, facilities:* There are 18 RV sites, 12 with water and electric hookups and six with full hookups. Rest rooms, showers, laundry facilities, picnic tables, an RV disposal station, and two barbecue grills are available. Leashed pets are allowed off the lawn.

*Reservations, fee:* Reservations are accepted. Full-hookup sites are $10, and sites with water and electricity are $8.

*Contact:* Call the campground at (801) 577-2527.

*Location:* The campground is located at the south end of Circleville, on the east side of U.S. 89.

*Trip notes:* With its open gravel terrain, this campground resembles . . . well, a parking lot. It's like you've pulled into an old drive-in theater, with a view of the Tushar Mountains replacing the movie screen. Fishing in the area is the big draw here. Anglers can try for trout at Piute Reservoir, eight miles away, or at Otter Creek Reservoir, 12 miles away. Some small streams nearby also offer fishing prospects.

*Season:* June through October.

---

## 42. OTTER CREEK STATE PARK

*Reference:* **On Otter Creek Reservoir; map B2, grid e2.**

*Campsites, facilities:* There are 30 campsites. Modern rest rooms with showers, picnic tables, fire grills, a fish-cleaning station, and an RV disposal station are available. A boat dock and courtesy dock are located nearby.

*Reservations, fee:* Reservations, which are strongly recommended on summer weekends, can be made 120 days in advance by calling (800) 322-3770 Monday through Friday from 8 A.M. to 5 P.M. A $5 nonrefundable reservation fee is charged for each site reserved. The campsite fee is $10. Utah residents 62 years and older who have a Special Fun Tag receive a $2 discount Sunday through Thursday, excluding holidays.

*Contact:* Call the park at (801) 624-3268.

*Location:* From the town of Antimony, drive four miles northwest on State Route 22 to the state park.

*Trip notes:* Locals say the rainbow trout at Otter Creek Reservoir grow fast and grow big—some up to six pounds. Angling is the thing at this clean and comfortable campground. There's a dock to launch your boat or raft onto the water and a fish-cleaning station for whatever you catch. Campsites are mostly paved, but you'll find some grassy lawn area as well. Bryce Canyon National Park is approximately an hour's drive away. Take the scenic 56-mile drive that leads from Otter Creek into the town of Antimony and then over to State Route 12 and the park entrance. Hikers can trek around Otter Creek Reservoir.

*Season:* Open year-round.

---

## 43. SINGLETREE

*Reference:* **In Dixie National Forest; map B2, grid e5.**

*Campsites, facilities:* There are 26 individual campsites and some group sites. Drinking water, picnic tables, fire grills, and vault toilets are available.

*Reservations, fee:* Reservations can be made through the U.S. Forest Service National Reservation System by calling (800) 280-2267. Campsites are $7.

*Contact:* Call the Teasdale Ranger District of Dixie National Forest at (801) 425-3702.

*Location:* From Teasdale, drive 17 miles southeast on State Route 12 to the campground.

*Trip notes:* What you see is what you get at this high-alpine camp, and what you see can be spectacular. At an elevation of 8,200 feet, the panoramic

---

views encompass the Waterpocket Fold, Capitol Reef National Park, and the Henry Mountains to the east. Most of the campsites are shaded by large pine trees. A short hike brings you to Singletree Falls, providing glimpses of Capitol Reef's scenic terrain below. Other trails through the dense forest are ideal for hiking or horseback riding. Anglers find terrific opportunities to cast for large brook trout at Boulder Mountain's many decent-sized lakes and reservoirs. A particularly good bet for fishing is nearby Bown Reservoir.
*Season:* Memorial Day to mid-September.

## 44. PLEASANT CREEK

*Reference:* **In Dixie National Forest; map B2, grid e5.**
*Campsites, facilities:* There are 17 campsites. Picnic tables, vault toilets, drinking water, and fire grills are available.
*Reservations, fee:* Campsites are $7 and are first come, first served.
*Contact:* Call the Teasdale Ranger District of Dixie National Forest at (801) 425-3702.
*Location:* From Teasdale, drive 22 miles southeast on State Route 12 to the campground.
*Trip notes:* This is a good, cooler summer alternative to campgrounds at Capitol Reef National Park, which is 25 miles away. It's an older facility, however, and some of the campsites show signs of wear and tear. Set on Boulder Mountain at 8,700 feet, the campground is close to some decent fishing lakes and streams; check with the Teasdale Ranger Station for suggestions on where the brook trout are biting. The thick alpine forest is criss-crossed with fine hiking routes, four-wheel-drive roads, and horse trails.
*Season:* Memorial Day through mid-September.

## 45. OAK CREEK

*Reference:* **In Dixie National Forest; map B2, grid f5.**
*Campsites, facilities:* There are 10 campsites. Picnic tables, vault toilets, drinking water, and fire grills are available.
*Reservations, fee:* Campsites are $7 and are first come, first served.
*Contact:* Call the Teasdale Ranger District of Dixie National Forest at (801) 425-3702.
*Location:* From Teasdale, drive 24 miles southeast on State Route 12 to the campground.
*Trip notes:* This campground is located near the top of Boulder Mountain in a nice grove of pine trees. Set at 8,800 feet, a chill sets in here in the fall. The camp has a well-used look, and it becomes quite dusty in the summer. Small alpine lakes dot Boulder Mountain. Anglers can cast for some of the state's largest brook trout and a few planted rainbow trout. Pick up a forest map at the Teasdale Ranger Station, which shows hiking and horse trails. A scenic 13-mile drive to the south takes visitors to Anasazi State Park, which features a museum and the ruins of a twelfth-century Native American village.
*Season:* Memorial Day through mid-September.

## 46. LOWER BOWN

*Reference:* **On Lower Bown Reservoir; map B2, grid e6.**

*Campsites, facilities:* There are three sites for RVs and tents. Vault toilets, picnic tables, and fire grills are available, but there is *no drinking water.*

*Reservations, fee:* Campsites are free and are first come, first served.

*Contact:* Call the Teasdale Ranger District of Dixie National Forest at (801) 425-3702.

*Location:* From Teasdale, drive 22 miles southeast on State Route 12. Look for Forest Road 181 just past Pleasant Creek campground. Take that road approximately five miles east to the campground.

*Trip notes:* Though primitive, this Boulder Mountain campground stays quiet because it's off the main highway. Pine and pinyon-juniper trees provide some shade, but the terrain is more open than elsewhere in the area. Bown Reservoir is a smaller-sized lake that offers good fishing when the water is high. It's an ideal spot for anglers to launch a raft and cast for large brook trout. During some years, however, the quality can vary when the reservoir is drawn down for irrigation purposes. In late fall, the camp may be quite chilly, especially when the snow flies.

*Season:* Memorial Day through early October.

---

## 47. CEDAR MESA

*Reference:* **In Capitol Reef National Park; map B2, grid f7.**

*Campsites, facilities:* There are five campsites. A pit toilet, picnic tables, and fire grills are available, but there is *no water.*

*Reservations, fee:* Campsites are free and are first come, first served. Backcountry camping is permitted in much of the park; obtain a free permit from park headquarters.

*Contact:* Call the park headquarters at (801) 425-3791.

*Location:* From Torrey, drive 20 miles east on State Route 24. Look for a signed road to the tiny hamlet of Notom. Follow this dirt road about five miles south to Muley Twist Canyon and the campground.

*Trip notes:* Set in the remote southern end of Capitol Reef National Park, this primitive desert campground is close to spectacular backcountry hiking in nearby Muley Twist Canyon. Here hikers and four-wheelers can explore seldom-visited washes and narrow slot canyons, and gaze upon panoramic views of the surrounding Henry Mountains and Waterpocket Fold. It's a rugged, undeveloped corner of this national park that tends to be relatively uncrowded, except on busy weekends. If you decide to stay here, come prepared to rough it.

*Season:* Open year-round.

---

## 48. LONESOME BEAVER

*Reference:* **In the Henry Mountains; map B2, grid e8.**

*Campsites, facilities:* There are five campsites for tents and RVs. Vault toilets, picnic tables, fire grills, and drinking water are available.

---

*Reservations, fee:* Campsites are $4 and are first come, first served.

*Contact:* Call the Bureau of Land Management office in Hanksville at (801) 542-3461.

*Location:* From Hanksville, drive 33 miles south on signed dirt roads to the Sawmill Basin and the campground. Roads are unnamed; for precise directions, stop at the Hanksville BLM office before heading out.

*Trip notes:* Spruce, fir, and aspen trees shade this campground in the beautiful but rugged Henry Mountains. Set at an elevation of 8,000 feet, it can get cold here in the fall and the snow usually flies by late October. From camp, hikers can access the Mount Ellen Trail, one of the best trails in southern Utah. It winds 1.25 miles one-way along a boulder-strewn ridge to the 11,506-foot peak. From the top, you get a 360-degree view of Lake Powell, Canyonlands National Park, and the Waterpocket Fold.

*Season:* May through late October.

## 49. McMILLAN SPRINGS

*Reference:* **In the Henry Mountains; map B2, grid f8.**

*Campsites, facilities:* There are five sites for tents and RVs. Drinking water, picnic tables, and vault toilets are available.

*Reservations, fee:* Campsites are free and are first come, first served.

*Contact:* Call the Bureau of Land Management office in Hanksville at (801) 542-3461.

*Location:* From Hanksville, drive 33 miles south on signed dirt roads to the west side of the Henry Mountains, following signs to the campground. Roads are unnamed; for precise directions, stop at the Hanksville BLM office before heading out.

*Trip notes:* You might catch a glimpse of a wild bison herd that wanders through the Henry Mountains. Set in a ponderosa pine and pinyon-juniper grove, the remote camp is a good place to enjoy peace and quiet. Sites are spaced far apart, affording privacy. The 2.5-mile round-trip Mount Ellen Trail is nearby; see Lonesome Beaver on page 210. From the peak of Mount Ellen, hikers are treated to excellent views over the Waterpocket Fold and Canyonlands National Park.

*Season:* May through November.

## 50. BLUE SPRUCE

*Reference:* **In Dixie National Forest; map B2, grid f5.**

*Campsites, facilities:* There are six campsites. Drinking water, picnic tables, fire grills, and vault toilets are available.

*Reservations, fee:* Campsites are $5 and are first come, first served.

*Contact:* Call the Escalante Ranger District office of Dixie National Forest at (801) 826-5400.

*Location:* From Escalante, drive 17 miles north on Forest Road 153 to the campground.

*Trip notes:* Although the desert surrounding Escalante can get scorching hot in the summer months, this alpine area provides a cool alternative to the low-lying regions. The elevation is 7,800 feet. Anglers can try to catch rainbow trout at nearby Posy and Tule Lakes.

*Season:* June through mid-September.

## 51. BARKER RESERVOIR

*Reference:* **Near Escalante; map B2, grid g4.**

*Campsites, facilities:* There are seven campsites for tents and RVs. Picnic tables, fire pits, and vault toilets are available, but there is *no drinking water*.

*Reservations, fee:* Campsites are free and are first come, first served.

*Contact:* Call the Escalante Ranger District office of Dixie National Forest at (801) 826-5400.

*Location:* From Escalante, drive five miles west on State Route 12. Head north approximately 11 miles on Forest Road 149 to the campground.

*Trip notes:* The forested campground gets mighty cold in the fall, especially when the first snow hits. It's set at 9,550 feet beside a small reservoir. With panoramic views over the red-rock desert surrounding Escalante, campers will feel as though they are on the top of the world. Anglers can launch a raft onto the water and fish for rainbow trout.

*Season:* June through mid-September, depending on snow conditions.

## 52. POSY LAKE

*Reference:* **Near Escalante; map B2, grid g4.**

*Campsites, facilities:* There are 23 campsites for tents and RVs. Drinking water, picnic tables, fire grills, and vault toilets are available.

*Reservations, fee:* Campsites are $5 and are first come, first served.

*Contact:* Call the Escalante Ranger District office of Dixie National Forest at (801) 826-5400.

*Location:* From Escalante, drive 11 miles north on Forest Road 153. Turn west on Forest Road 154 and drive one mile to the campground.

*Trip notes:* When the desert lowlands surrounding Escalante heat up, it's time to head for the cool forest. This alpine camp sits beside tiny Posy Lake, where you can paddle a raft out to the deeper water and hope to catch a rainbow trout for dinner. It's a pleasant drive from the buff red-rock desert to the cool greens of the higher elevations.

*Season:* June through mid-September, depending on snow conditions.

## 53. CALF CREEK FALLS RECREATION AREA

*Reference:* **Near Escalante; map B2, grid g5.**

*Campsites, facilities:* There are 14 campsites. Picnic tables, fire grills, running water, and vault toilets are available.

*Reservations, fee:* Campsites are $7 and are first come, first served.

*Contact:* Call the Bureau of Land Management office in Escalante at (801) 826-4291.

*Location:* From Escalante, drive 16 miles east on State Route 12 to the recreation area.

*Trip notes:* Campsites are arrayed along a pretty little river that offers a pleasant spot to swim in the hot summer months. The big draw is the self-guided, 2.75-mile one-way nature walk up a sandy trail to Lower Calf Creek Falls, one of southern Utah's more famous landmarks. The waterfall tumbles several stories from a high sandstone cliff into a cool turquoise pool below. You can fish the creek for brown trout, or head over to Escalante Petrified Forest State Park to try for stocked rainbow trout. Anasazi State Park, approximately 12 miles away in Boulder, offers restored Native American ruins and a museum that are well worth a visit.

*Season:* Mid-April through November.

## 54. DEER CREEK RECREATION AREA

*Reference:* **Near Boulder; map B2, grid g6.**

*Campsites, facilities:* There are four sites with picnic tables and fire grills. The campground has one vault toilet. *No drinking water* is available.

*Reservations, fee:* Campsites are free and are first come, first served.

*Contact:* Call the Bureau of Land Management at (801) 826-4291.

*Location:* From Boulder, drive on the Burr Trail six miles east to reach the recreation area.

*Trip notes:* Surrounded by high sandstone walls in a narrow red-rock canyon, this campground/picnic area looks like a miniature Zion National Park. It's remote and spectacular country. From here, you can head into the Escalante River backcountry for off-trail exploration of the Deer Creek and Boulder Creek drainages. Expect to do some wading if you're taking a serious day hike or backpacking trip. Be sure to visit Boulder's Anasazi State Park, which features a fascinating museum and restored Native American ruins.

*Season:* Mid-March through November.

## 55. ESCALANTE PETRIFIED FOREST STATE PARK

*Reference:* **On Wide Hollow Reservoir; map B2, grid g5.**

*Campsites, facilities:* There are 22 campsites for tents and RVs. A modern rest room with showers, an RV disposal station, and a visitors center are available.

*Reservations, fee:* Reservations can be made 120 days in advance by calling (800) 322-3770 Monday through Friday from 8 A.M. to 5 P.M. A $5 nonrefundable reservation fee is charged for each site reserved. The campsite fee is $10. Utah residents 62 years and older who have a Special Fun Tag receive a $2 discount Sunday through Thursday, excluding holidays.

*Contact:* Call the park at (801) 826-4466.

*Location:* Drive on State Route 12 one mile west of the town of Escalante.

*Trip notes:* This park has something for everyone, and all of it's good. The campground is nestled in a small cove of Wide Hollow Reservoir at the base of a red-rock plateau. At the center of the camp is a large grassy lawn, where kids can play football or toss a Frisbee. Short, self-guided interpretive hiking trails begin at the campground and lead to large deposits of petrified wood. In the spring, Wide Hollow Reservoir offers decent fishing for stocked rainbow trout, and year-round you can enjoy swimming, rafting, boating, and waterskiing here. The best thing about the reservoir is that its shallow wetlands are the home for thousands of shorebirds. The park also makes a fine base for exploring the nearby Escalante Canyons, which are part of the newly designated, 1.7-million-acre Escalante–Grand Staircase National Monument.

*Season:* Open year-round.

## 56. MOQUI MOTEL AND CAMPGROUND

*Reference:* **In Escalante; map B2, grid h5.**

*Campsites, facilities:* This small, six-site RV campground with hookups has rest rooms, showers, an RV disposal station, and a public phone. Pets are allowed. The park is open year-round, but water is available only from the spring through the fall.

*Reservations, fee:* Reservations are accepted. The fee is $12.

*Contact:* Call the campground at (801) 826-4210.

*Location:* Follow State Route 12 into Escalante. In town, State Route 12 becomes Main Street. The campground is located at 80 West Main Street.

*Trip notes:* This nondescript RV park adjacent to a motel will suffice for a one-night stopover. Hikers and four-wheel-driving enthusiasts can head to the Bureau of Land Management's Deer Creek and Calf Creek Falls Recreation Areas. Water recreation and fishing for trout are available at nearby Wide Hollow Reservoir in Escalante Petrified Forest State Park.

*Season:* Open year-round, but water is only available from the spring through the fall.

## 57. TRIPLE S RV PARK AND CAMPGROUND

*Reference:* **In Escalante; map B2, grid h5.**

*Campsites, facilities:* There are 21 pull-through RV sites with full hookups and 20 tent sites. The campground has rest rooms, showers, picnic tables, laundry facilities, barbecue pits, a public phone, and a rock shop specializing in petrified wood and dinosaur bones. Pets are allowed.

*Reservations, fee:* Reservations are recommended on holiday weekends. RV sites are $12 and tent sites are $8.50.

*Contact:* Triple S RV Park and Campground, P.O. Box 505, Escalante, UT 84726; (801) 826-4959.

*Location:* Drive to Escalante on State Route 12. In town, State Route 12 becomes Main Street. The campground is four blocks west of the town center, at 495 South Main Street.

*Trip notes:* Located between Bryce Canyon and Capitol Reef National Parks, this campground is set in a quiet, rural setting in the midst of some of the more spectacular Bureau of Land Management and U.S. Forest Service country in the state. Consider taking a short drive out to the BLM's Devil's Garden Natural Area on Hole-in-the-Rock Road; the dirt road begins five miles east of Escalante off of State Route 12. Here you'll find a small, pretty sandstone natural arch and plenty of unusual rock formations. Boating, waterskiing, swimming, and fishing for planted rainbow trout are good one mile west of Escalante at Escalante Petrified Forest State Park's Wide Hollow Reservoir.

*Season:* Open year-round.

---

## 58. RED CANYON

*Reference:* **Near Panguitch; map B2, grid g0.**

*Campsites, facilities:* There are 40 campsites for tents and RVs. Picnic tables, drinking water, vault toilets, and fire grills are available.

*Reservations, fee:* For reservations, call the U.S. Forest Service National Reservation System at (800) 280-2267. The fee is $8.

*Contact:* Call the Powell Ranger District of Dixie National Forest in Panguitch at (801) 676-6815.

*Location:* From Panguitch, drive seven miles south on U.S. 89. Turn east on State Route 12 and then continue driving for approximately four miles to the campground.

*Trip notes:* With high spires, hoodoos, and pillars colored an almost fluorescent red, beautiful Red Canyon is like a miniature Bryce Canyon National Park. Huge ponderosa pines guard the U.S. Forest Service campground here. Trails venture into this region and surrounding canyons, offering spectacular routes for hikers, mountain bikers, and equestrians.

*Season:* Mid-May through October.

---

## 59. RED CANYON RV PARK AND CAMPGROUND

*Reference:* **Near the entrance to Red Canyon; map B2, grid h1.**

*Campsites, facilities:* There are 45 sites, of which 20 are pull-throughs, and six camp cabins. Facilities include new rest rooms, showers, a public phone, a small grocery store, and a picnic area.

*Reservations, fee:* Reservations are strongly recommended during the summer season. RV sites are $13.50 and tent sites are $9.81 for two people. Each additional person is $1 extra. Children under 10 are free. Cabins with showers cost $38.15 and rustic cabins are $24 for two.

*Contact:* Call the campground at (801) 676-2690.

*Location:* From Panguitch, drive seven miles south on U.S. 89. Turn east on State Route 12 and drive one mile to the campground.

*Trip notes:* You'll find some shaded and grassy campsites here, but it may be a little noisy as the park is located near the junction of two busy highways. The strongest selling point is its proximity to Red Canyon in Dixie National Forest, which offers excellent hiking, horseback-riding, and mountain-biking opportunities. If fishing's your pleasure, you can head to Tropic Reservoir approximately 15 miles away. Bryce Canyon National Park lies 15 miles to the east.

*Season:* April through October, depending on weather conditions.

---

## 60. BRYCE CANYON PINES COUNTRY STORE & CAMPGROUND, RV PARK & MOTEL

*Reference:* **Near Bryce Canyon National Park; map B2, grid h1.**

*Campsites, facilities:* There are 45 campsites, of which 17 are pull-throughs and 25 offer full hookups. Facilities include rest rooms with showers, a disposal station, a public phone, laundry facilities, and a small grocery store with ice, snacks, and supplies. Sites have fire grills. A game room, a horseshoe pit, and a playground are available.

*Reservations, fee:* Reservations are accepted. RV sites are $17 and tent sites are $10 for two people. Each additional person over age 6 is $1.

*Contact:* Bryce Canyon Pines Country Store & Campground, RV Park & Motel, P.O. Box 64005, Bryce, UT 84764; (801) 834-5441.

*Location:* From Bryce Canyon National Park, take State Route 63 six miles north to State Route 12. Turn west and drive to the campground.

*Trip notes:* The name of this quiet camp is a little deceptive: you are offered pleasant views of the towering pines that shade many of the campsites, but you won't catch a glimpse of Bryce Canyon itself. The national park and its many hiking opportunities are a short drive away. The owners offer horseback rides into the scenic, pine-shrouded country near the campground. While Bryce Canyon National Park is the big draw here, you can also drive 24 miles to beautiful Kodachrome Basin State Park or take a nature hike in Red Canyon to the west. Fish the private ponds at Ruby's Inn (see page 217), or head to Pine Lake in Dixie National Forest, which is approximately six miles away.

*Season:* April through November.

## 61. PINK CLIFFS VILLAGE

*Reference:* **Near Bryce Canyon National Park; map B2, grid h2.**

*Campsites, facilities:* There are 28 RV sites with full hookups and 50 tent sites. Pink Cliffs Village offers rest rooms with showers; laundry facilities; picnic tables; fire pits; an RV disposal station; a grocery and gift shop; a swimming pool; a field where you can play volleyball, badminton, and horseshoes; and a service station. Pets are allowed. Telephone and cable TV hookups are available.

*Reservations, fee:* Reservations are recommended in the summer. RV sites are $15 and tent sites are $7.

*Contact:* Pink Cliffs Village, Box 640006, Bryce, UT 84764; (801) 834-5351.

*Location:* The resort is three miles from Bryce Canyon National Park and one mile from Ruby's Inn. It is located at the junction of State Routes 12 and 63.

*Trip notes:* An abundance of large pine trees make this a pretty spot. Currently the resort offers guided horseback rides on its 156 acres; the owners hope to guide rides into Bryce Canyon National Park itself, pending National Park Service approval. Hikers can explore many trails in Bryce Canyon. If you want to fish, head to nearby Tropic Reservoir, or take the one-hour drive to

Boulder Mountain and its many small alpine lakes in the Escalante region. Although this camp is open all year, it gets very cold during the winter months.
*Season:* Open year-round.

---

## 62. RUBY'S INN RV CAMPGROUND

*Reference:* **Near Bryce Canyon National Park; map B2, grid h2.**

*Campsites, facilities:* There are 110 RV sites, of which 43 have full hookups and 67 have water and electric hookups, and 50 dispersed tent sites. Ruby's Inn has gift shops, an art gallery, a bakery, a barber and beauty shop, and two swimming pools. The campground offers a hot tub, a small grocery store, rest rooms, showers, a security phone, two Laundromats, and an arcade.

*Reservations, fee:* Reservations are strongly recommended in the summer. Full-hookup sites are $22, partial hookups are $20, and tent sites are $13.

*Contact:* Ruby's Inn RV Campground, P.O. Box 22, Bryce, UT 84764; (801) 834-5341.

*Location:* From Panguitch, drive seven miles south on U.S. 89. Turn east on State Route 12 and drive 13 miles east to State Route 63. The campground is on State Route 63, just south of the junction.

*Trip notes:* Although Ruby's Inn is a large motel and restaurant complex, the campground here feels surprisingly separate from the development. The owners have wisely segregated the area from the rest of the inn. The tall pines shading the camp give it an air of seclusion. You can fish for trout in a small private pond on the grounds, or head to Pine Lake in nearby Dixie National Forest. This is the closest private campground to Bryce Canyon National Park, but Ruby's Inn offers a slew of recreational options in addition to what's available at the national park. In the winter, it grooms cross-country ski trails and rents snowmobiles. In the summer, campers can enjoy a nightly rodeo (except on Sundays), helicopter flights, mountain-biking trails, horseback riding, gold panning, wagon rides, and hoedowns. Across from the inn, Ruby's has even recreated an old-fashioned Western town full of charming little shops. In the off-season, campers should check in at the motel lobby.

*Season:* April through October.

---

## 63. NORTH CAMPGROUND

*Reference:* **In Bryce Canyon National Park; map B2, grid h2.**

*Campsites, facilities:* There are 107 campsites for tents and RVs. Picnic tables, fire grills, drinking water, flush toilets with cold running water, and an RV disposal station are available. A general store, laundry facilities, and showers are located at Sunset Point, 1.5 miles from North Campground.

*Reservations, fee:* All sites are first come, first served. The fee is $7; campsites are half price with a Golden Age and Golden Access pass.

*Contact:* Call Bryce Canyon National Park at (801) 834-5322.

*Location:* From Panguitch, drive seven miles south on U.S. 89. Turn east on State Route 12 and drive 13 miles east. Drive two miles south on State Route

---

63 to reach the campground, which is just east of park headquarters near the entrance station.

*Trip notes:* Thanks to its high elevation, Bryce Canyon is one of the best of Utah's five national parks to visit in the summer. Temperatures tend to be 20 degrees cooler than nearby Zion or Capitol Reef National Parks. The park's centerpiece is a beautiful natural amphitheater filled with arches, hoodoos, spires, and strangely shaped eroded rocks in shades of buff, tan, and crimson. At sunset, the rocks seem to glow an almost fluorescent red. Several excellent hiking trails lead into the area. Try the 1.25-mile (one-way) Navajo Loop Trail into the Bryce Amphitheater; it begins at Sunset Point, 1.5 miles from the campground, and descends 521 feet into the canyon. A quarter mile from the campground, you can find breathtaking views at Sunrise Point Overlook. Many campsites are shaded by pines. In the busy summer months, North Campground can fill up, so arrive as early in the day as possible. Guided horseback tours of the park are available; check at the Bryce Canyon Lodge for details. Bring your own wood as wood gathering is not allowed in the park.

*Season:* April through November, though one loop of the campground is winterized and open year-round, when funding permits.

---

# 64. SUNSET CAMPGROUND

*Reference:* In Bryce Canyon National Park; map B2, grid h1.

*Campsites, facilities:* There are 111 campsites for tents and RVs. Rest rooms with cold running water, drinking water, picnic tables, and fire grills are available. A general store, laundry facilities, and showers are at Sunset Point, which is less than a mile from the campground. An RV disposal station is available at North Campground (see page 217).

*Reservations, fee:* All campsites are available on a first come, first served basis. The fee is $7; campsite rates are half price with a Golden Age and Golden Access pass.

*Contact:* Call Bryce Canyon National Park at (801) 834-5322.

*Location:* From Panguitch, drive seven miles south on U.S. 89. Turn east on State Route 12 and drive 13 miles east. Drive south on State Route 63 to the park. The campground is two miles south of park headquarters on the west side of the road.

*Trip notes:* Sunset Campground is slightly closer to Bryce Amphitheater and its fascinating red-rock formations than North Campground. Sites are shaded by pine trees, and you'll see nice displays of wildflowers here in late spring and early summer. Hikes in and around Bryce Canyon can be spectacular; check with the park's visitors center for guided interpretive strolls. The Queen's Garden Trail/Navajo Loop Trail combination, a 1.8-mile loop, is among the best hikes in southern Utah. Guided horseback tours of the park are available; inquire at the Bryce Canyon Lodge. If you want to build a campfire, bring your own wood; no wood gathering is allowed in the park.

*Season:* Late April through November, depending on the weather conditions in Bryce Canyon.

---

# 65. PINE LAKE

*Reference:* **Near Red Canyon; map B2, grid h3.**

*Campsites, facilities:* There are 26 campsites. Vault toilets, picnic tables, fire grills, drinking water, and a small boat ramp are available.

*Reservations, fee:* Call the U.S. Forest Service National Reservation System at (800) 280-2267 for reservations. The fee is $7.

*Contact:* Call the Escalante Ranger District of Dixie National Forest at (801) 826-5400.

*Location:* Drive through Red Canyon on State Route 12. Instead of turning south into Bryce Canyon National Park, look for Forest Road 16, a dirt road heading to the northeast near the junction with State Route 63. Drive eight miles north on Forest Road 16, then drive four miles south on Forest Road 132 to the campground.

*Trip notes:* Little Pine Lake offers good angling for stocked rainbow trout. A ramp is suitable for launching small boats, or you can just paddle a raft onto the water and cast for your supper. Campsites here are shaded by pine trees near the lake. It's conveniently close to Bryce Canyon National Park and Kodachrome Basin State Park, but you're guaranteed to avoid the crowds those places draw. Excellent hiking and horseback-riding options are available at Bryce Canyon; see North Campground on page 217 for details.

*Season:* Mid-June through mid-September.

# 66. KODACHROME BASIN STATE PARK

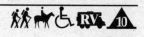

*Reference:* **Near Cannonville; map B2, grid h3.**

*Campsites, facilities:* There are 26 campsites for tents and RVs and a group-use area. Facilities include modern rest rooms with showers, drinking water, an RV disposal station, and picnic tables on concrete with fire grills. A concessionaire operates a small store inside the park.

*Reservations, fee:* Reservations can be made 120 days in advance by calling (800) 322-3770 Monday through Friday from 8 A.M. to 5 P.M. A $5 nonrefundable reservation fee is charged for each reserved site. The site fee is $10. Utah residents 62 years and older who have a Special Fun Tag receive a $2 discount Sunday through Thursday, excluding holidays.

*Contact:* Call park headquarters at (801) 679-8562.

*Location:* From Bryce Canyon National Park, drive two miles north on State Route 63. Head east on State Route 12 until reaching Cannonville, and then follow signs nine miles south on a paved road to the state park.

*Trip notes:* This ranks among Utah's best campgrounds. Set in a pinyon-juniper forest, with campsites spaced far apart for privacy, the camp boasts impressive views of this red-rock wonderland's massive stone towers, called "chimneys." Hiking trails, appropriate for children and most less than three miles long, lead from the campground into the pink and white sandstone basin. Try the quarter-mile (one-way) trail to the Shakespeare Arch, one of the last discovered natural bridges in the area. Or follow the one-mile (one-way)

Grand Parade Trail, which passes the monolithic spires that make this place unique. A horseback-riding and stagecoach concession allow disabled persons and seniors to visit the backcountry. For a side trip, drive 10 miles east of the park to Grosvenor Arch, a huge buff-colored double-arch formation.
*Season:* Open year-round.

## 67. KINGS CREEK

*Reference:* **On Tropic Reservoir; map B2, grid i1.**
*Campsites, facilities:* The 40-site campground has vault toilets, a boat ramp, picnic tables, drinking water, and fire grills.
*Reservations, fee:* Campsites are $7 and are first come, first served.
*Contact:* Call the Powell Ranger District office of Dixie National Forest at (801) 676-6815.
*Location:* Drive through Red Canyon on State Route 12, looking for Forest Road 087, which is just east of the canyon. Drive approximately six miles south to the campground.
*Trip notes:* At an elevation of 8,000 feet, the campground sits in the midst of a pretty alpine forest beside Tropic Reservoir. It's quite popular with locals and can get crowded. Paddle a raft or launch a boat onto the small reservoir to fish for trout. It's close to Bryce Canyon National Park and its many scenic hikes; see North Campground on page 217 for suggestions. Horseback riding is fun throughout the forested area. Horse rentals and guided tours are available at Bryce Canyon Lodge and Ruby's Inn.
*Season:* June through mid-September.

## 68. BULLFROG RV PARK

*Reference:* **Near Lake Powell; map B2, grid i8.**
*Campsites, facilities:* There are 22 RV sites with full hookups. Showers, rest rooms, picnic tables, a public phone, and cable TV are available. Groceries, laundry facilities, and a full-service marina are close by.
*Reservations, fee:* Reservations are accepted. The fee is $22.
*Contact:* Bullfrog RV Park, Box 56909, Phoenix, AZ 85079; (801) 684-2233 or (800) 528-6154.
*Location:* From Hanksville, drive approximately 30 miles south on State Route 95 to its junction with State Route 276. Drive approximately 24.5 miles south on State Route 276 to the campground.
*Trip notes:* This camp is approximately a half mile from massive, manmade Lake Powell, one of Utah's premier boating destinations. It can get scorching hot here in the summer, with temperatures easily exceeding 100 degrees Fahrenheit. Shade trees guard some of the campsites. If you want to hike in the area, head to U.S. Forest Service trails in the nearby Henry Mountains. Campers who wish to continue on State Route 276 towards Hall's Crossing and the Four Corners Monument can take a 20-minute ride on the *John Atlantic Burr* ferry, which leaves from the Bullfrog Marina. You'll find a good restaurant at the Bullfrog Lodge motel.
*Season:* Open year-round.

# 69. BULLFROG

*Reference:* **Near Lake Powell; map B2, grid i8.**

*Campsites, facilities:* The 86-unit campground offers flush toilets, drinking water, picnic tables, fire grills, and an RV disposal station. A beach and a boat ramp onto Lake Powell are situated nearby, as are showers and laundry facilities.

*Reservations, fee:* Campsites are $10 and are first come, first served.

*Contact:* Call the campground at (801) 684-2233.

*Location:* From Hanksville, drive approximately 30 miles south on State Route 95 to its junction with State Route 276. Drive approximately 25 miles south on State Route 276 to the campground.

*Trip notes:* Few areas in the United States offer better boating than Lake Powell, Utah's 186-mile-long manmade reservoir. Whether you want to water-ski on open water, paddle a canoe among narrow side canyons, cruise in a houseboat, fish for largemouth or striped bass, or take a cooling dip near the shore, the lake provides an idyllic setting. Located two blocks from the lake, this campground has good views of the beautiful blue water and majestic sandstone cliffs. Campsites are shaded and some have grassy lawn, a plus during hot summer months. It's well off the highway and can be quiet during the off-season. When the lake draws lots of visitors, this camp sometimes attracts a crowd that likes to party, so it can get noisy. From here it's a short walk to a sand and pebble beach along the lake.

*Season:* Open year-round.

# 70. HALL'S CROSSING RV PARK

*Reference:* **Near Lake Powell; map B2, grid j8.**

*Campsites, facilities:* There are 32 RV sites with full hookups. The campground has rest rooms, showers, picnic tables, laundry facilities, a grocery store, a public phone, and barbecue grills. An RV disposal station is located across the street.

*Reservations, fee:* Reservations are accepted. The fee is $22.

*Contact:* Call the campground at (801) 684-2261.

*Location:* From Blanding, drive west on State Route 95. Turn southwest on State Route 276 and drive 29 miles to the RV park.

*Trip notes:* Because of its remoteness, Hall's Crossing is one of the more laid-back marinas on Lake Powell, making this a quiet place to camp. The park is set on a small ridge with views over the water. Ample fishing and boating opportunities are available nearby at Lake Powell, which is the second largest manmade reservoir in the United States (the largest reservoir is Lake Mead, in Arizona and California). Spend a day taking a 50-mile boat ride from Hall's Crossing to Rainbow Bridge National Monument. The largest natural bridge in the world, Rainbow Bridge spans 275 feet and stands 290 feet high.

*Season:* Open year-round.

# 71. HALL'S CROSSING

*Reference:* **Near Lake Powell, in Glen Canyon National Recreation Area; map B2, grid j8.**

*Campsites, facilities:* There are 65 campsites. Picnic tables, fire pits, and rest rooms with cold water and flush toilets are available. An RV disposal station is nearby. Showers are available at Hall's Crossing RV Park for a small fee.

*Reservations, fee:* Campsites are $8.50 and are first come, first served.

*Contact:* Call Glen Canyon National Recreation Area at (801) 684-2261.

*Location:* From Blanding, drive west on State Route 95. Turn southwest on State Route 276 and drive 29 miles to the campground.

*Trip notes:* Set a short walk from the water, this campground makes a good base for exploring Lake Powell. The manmade reservoir offers 186 miles of surface water and 1,960 miles of shoreline—more shoreline, in fact, than spans the western United States' coast from California to Washington. It's truly a boater's paradise, with power boats speeding alongside sail boats, slow-roaming houseboats, and rafts. Anglers will find excellent fishing for crappie, striped bass, largemouth bass, smallmouth bass, bluebell, and wall-eye. The camp itself is largely out in the open desert, making it vulnerable to summer temperatures that exceed 100 degrees Fahrenheit most days. Because most visitors travel by boat to the more primitive and private side canyons on the lake, the campground rarely fills up.

*Season:* Open year-round.

# 72. WHITE HOUSE

*Reference:* **Near the Paria River; map B2, grid j2.**

*Campsites, facilities:* There are three campsites with picnic tables and vault toilets. *No water* is available.

*Reservations, fee:* Campsites are free and are first come, first served.

*Contact:* Call the Bureau of Land Management in Kanab at (801) 644-2672.

*Location:* From Kanab, drive 42 miles east on U.S. 89. Look for a sign to a dirt road heading south. Drive one mile south to the campground.

*Trip notes:* Few places can match the rugged beauty of the narrow slot canyons you'll find in Paria Canyon. The lower portion of the canyon, which stretches almost 40 miles to Lee's Ferry at the edge of the Grand Canyon, makes a terrific four-day backpacking trip. Day hikes into the area are also rewarding. Be prepared, though: flash floods can occur and are especially dangerous because of the narrowness of the canyon. Check with the Bureau of Land Management office in Kanab for weather details, especially in late July and August, when thunderstorms can be a major problem. The small BLM campground is set in a relatively flat area at the edge of the wash. It's very open desert and can be extremely hot in the summer months. One block away is the Paria River, which often dries to less than a trickle during scorching summers.

*Season:* April through October.

## Leave No Trace Tips

**Travel and camp with care.**

*On the trail:*

• Stay on designated trails.

• Do not take shortcuts on switchbacks.

• When traveling cross-country where there are no trails,
follow animal trails or spread out your group so no new routes are created.
Walk along the most durable surfaces available,
such as rock, gravel, dry grasses, or snow.

• Use a map and compass to eliminate the need for
rock cairns, tree scars, or ribbons.

• If you encounter pack animals, step to the downhill side
of the trail and speak softly to avoid startling them.

*At camp:*

• Choose an established, legal site that will not be damaged by your stay.

• Restrict activities to areas where vegetation is compacted or absent.

• Keep pollutants out of the water by camping at least 200 feet
(about 70 adult steps) from lakes and streams.

• Control pets at all times, or leave them at home
with a sitter. Remove dog feces.

# MAP B3

Map of Utah ........................ see page 46

Beyond This Region:
North (Map A3) ................. see page 124
East .......................................... Colorado
South ......................................... Arizona
West (Map B2).................. see page 188

**57 Campgrounds**
**Pages 224–253**

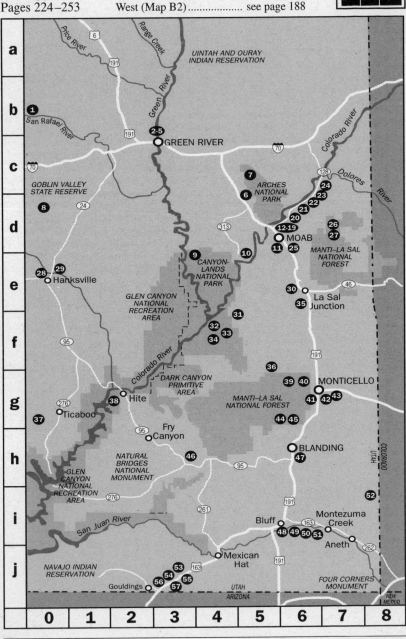

**Chapter B3 features:**

1. San Rafael
2. Green River KOA
3. Green River State Park
4. Shady Acres
5. United Campground
6. Arch View Campground
7. Devil's Garden
8. Goblin Valley State Park
9. Willow Flat
10. Dead Horse Point State Park
11. Kane Springs Campground
12. Portal RV Park and Fishery
13. Slickrock Campground
14. Moab Valley RV and Campark
15. Spanish Trail RV Park and Campground
16. Canyonlands Campark
17. Up the Creek Camp Park
18. Pack Creek Campground
19. Moab KOA
20. Hal Canyon
21. Oak Grove
22. Big Bend
23. Hittle Bottom
24. Dewey Bridge
25. Sand Flats
26. Warner Lake
27. Oohwah Lake
28. Jurassic Park
29. Red Rock Restaurant and Campground
30. Hatch Point
31. Needles Outpost
32. Indian Creek
33. Hamburger Rock
34. Squaw Flat
35. Windwhistle
36. Newspaper Rock
37. Starr Springs
38. Hite
39. Buckboard
40. Dalton Springs
41. Westerner RV Park
42. Monticello KOA
43. Mountain View RV Park
44. Nizhoni
45. Devil's Canyon
46. Natural Bridges
47. Blanding Kampark
48. Sand Island
49. Cadillac Ranch
50. K and C RV Park
51. Turquoise
52. Square Tower Campground
53. Goosenecks State Park
54. Burches Trading Post
55. Valles Trailer Park
56. Mitten View Campground
57. Goulding's Monument Valley Campground

## 1. SAN RAFAEL

*Reference:* **In the San Rafael Swell; map B3, grid b0.**

*Campsites, facilities:* There are eight sites with vault toilets, picnic tables, and fire grills. *No drinking water* is available.

*Reservations, fee:* Campsites are $5 and are first come, first served.

*Contact:* Call the Bureau of Land Management in Price at (801) 637-4584.

*Location:* In the Emery County town of Cleveland, look for a signed dirt road leading to the San Rafael Swell and the campground. Follow the marked backcountry road 25 miles southeast from Cleveland to the camp.

*Trip notes:* Just southeast of the geographic center of Utah, the San Rafael Swell is a wild region of sandstone cliffs and slot canyons, with few developed roads or marked trails. Roughly 65 miles long and 35 miles wide, it's a popular area for horseback riding, hiking, and four-wheel-drive exploration. Equestrians will enjoy exploring the area known as "the Wedge" or "Little

Grand Canyon," a deep, red-rock gorge with fascinating side canyons and rock art sites. Beyond the small campground, the BLM allows free dispersed camping in many side canyons off the main route. Be careful to observe signs designating Wilderness Study Areas, however; vehicles are prohibited here. Five miles north of the campground, visit the Buckhorn Wash rock art panel, home to prehistoric Native American pictographs and ghostlike petroglyphs. Recent preservation efforts have led to the removal of some modern graffiti that marred the site.

*Season:* Open year-round.

## 2. GREEN RIVER KOA

*Reference:* **In Green River; map B3, grid c2.**

*Campsites, facilities:* There are 77 RV sites with full hookups, 42 sites with water and electricity hookups, 30 tent sites, and three camping cabins. The campground has rest rooms, showers, laundry facilities, a pool, barbecue grills, picnic tables, a playground, a public phone, and a grocery store. Pets are allowed.

*Reservations, fee:* Reservations are recommended in early September, during the Melon Days celebration. Full hookup sites are $19.50, sites with water and electricity are $17.50, and tent sites are $15. Camping cabins are $29.50.

*Contact:* Green River KOA, P.O. Box 14, Green River, UT 84525-0014; (801) 564-3651.

*Location:* Follow Interstate 70 to the town of Green River. Drivers approaching from the west should take exit 158 and follow Main Street, looking for the sign to Green River State Park on the south side of the road. Entering Green River from the east, take exit 162. The camp is a block south from the entrance to the state park, at 550 South Green River Boulevard.

*Trip notes:* Campers get shaded sites on a pleasant green lawn in a relatively secluded spot between Interstate 70 and Green River's business district. The Green River State Park Golf Course is across the street. The gentle-flowing Green River is ideal for canoeing and rafting; commercial outfitters in town can help you arrange a one-day trip in Desolation Canyon upstream or a four-to five-day excursion to the Mineral Canyon takeout in Canyonlands National Park. In late summer and early fall, stop at one of the nearby fruit stands and pick up locally grown cantaloupe, honeydew, or watermelons. They're some of the best eating anywhere! In early September, Green River hosts its annual Melon Days Festival, with a parade and other fun-filled activities.

*Season:* April through mid-October.

## 3. GREEN RIVER STATE PARK

*Reference:* **In Green River; map B3, grid c2.**

*Campsites, facilities:* There are 42 campsites. Facilities include a golf course, hot showers, a boat-launching ramp, modern rest rooms, a group-use area, and an amphitheater.

*Reservations, fee:* Reservations can be made 120 days in advance by calling (800) 322-3770 Monday through Friday from 8 A.M. to 5 P.M. A $5 nonrefundable reservation fee is charged for each site reserved. Campsites are $10. Utah residents 62 years and older with a Special Fun Tag receive a $2 discount Sunday through Thursday, excluding holidays.

**Contact:** Call Green River State Park at (801) 564-3633.

**Location:** Follow Interstate 70 to the town of Green River. Drivers approaching from the west should take exit 158 and follow Main Street, looking for the sign to Green River State Park on the south side of the road. Entering Green River from the east, take exit 162. The park is on South Green River Boulevard, two blocks south of Main Street, beside the Green River.

**Trip notes:** Huge cottonwood trees shade most of the campsites in Green River State Park. A fairly large facility, the park offers grassy lawns, a day-use picnic area, a boat-launching ramp, and a recently completed nine-hole public golf course. All told, this is one of the better tent-camping areas in southeastern Utah. While the campground often fills up on holiday weekends, at other times it provides a less-crowded alternative to Moab camps flooded with visitors to Arches and Canyonlands National Parks, both approximately 45 minutes away. The Green River itself, a fine stretch of floater-friendly water, is about a half block from the camp. Local outfitters can arrange a one- or multi-day rafting trip down the Green. Four blocks from the park, visit the John Wesley Powell River Running Museum, home of the Utah River Runner's Hall of Fame. Exhibits detail the history of river-running in the state, including some replicas of early wooden boats and rafts. The museum also celebrates the life of Major John Wesley Powell, who conducted the first scientific exploration of the Green and Colorado Rivers in the mid-1800s. The friendly museum staff is knowledgeable about travel in the area, and many free brochures provide information on local attractions.

**Season:** Open year-round.

## 4. SHADY ACRES

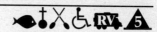

**Reference:** In Green River; map B3, grid c2.

**Campsites, facilities:** There are 92 RV sites with full hookups, some of which are pull-throughs and others back-in sites, and 14 tent sites. The campground has rest rooms, showers, laundry facilities, an RV disposal station, a grocery store, barbecue grills, a public phone, a playground, and cable TV hookups. Pets are allowed.

**Reservations, fee:** Reservations are accepted. Pull-through sites are $17, back-in sites are $15, and tent sites are $13.

**Contact:** Call the campground at (801) 564-8292.

**Location:** Follow Interstate 70 to the town of Green River. Drivers approaching from the west should take exit 158. Entering Green River from the east, take exit 162. The park is located at 360 Main Street, with its back to the Green River State Park Golf Course.

**Trip notes:** Although much of the land surrounding the town of Green River is treeless and desolate, this camp is shaded by fairly large cottonwood trees. From here, it's a short, two-block stroll to the John Wesley Powell River Running Museum, with its excellent multimedia exhibits about the history

---

of river-running in Utah. Or, you can rent a raft or canoe in town and make a little history running the river yourself.

*Season:* Open year-round, with water available from March through October.

---

## 5. UNITED CAMPGROUND    ♦X🏊⛵♿ RV 5

*Reference:* **In Green River; map B3, grid c2.**

*Campsites, facilities:* There are 65 sites with full hookups and 15 sites for tents. The campground has rest rooms, showers, picnic tables, laundry facilities, barbecue grills, a gift shop, a public phone, a pool, a playroom, cable TV, and an RV disposal station. Pets are allowed.

*Reservations, fee:* Reservations are accepted. Full hookups are $16 and tent sites are $13.

*Contact:* Call the campground at (801) 564-8195.

*Location:* Take Interstate 70 to the town of Green River. Drivers approaching from the west should take exit 158. Entering Green River from the east, take exit 162. The park is located at 910 Main Street, across from the John Wesley Powell River Running Museum. The campground is situated on the south side of the road.

*Trip notes:* One of the larger private campgrounds in Green River, United Campground offers gravel sites and less shade cover than other area camps. The pool, however, provides a welcome respite during hot summer months. Nearby Green River State Park offers river access. Just across the way is the John Wesley Powell River Running Museum, which details the history of river-running in Utah. If campsite cooking's not to your liking, visit the Tamarisk Restaurant at the Best Western Motel for good food and views over the Green River.

*Season:* Open year-round.

---

## 6. ARCH VIEW CAMPGROUND    🚶‍♂️♿ RV 8

*Reference:* **Near Moab; map B3, grid d4.**

*Campsites, facilities:* There are 44 RV sites with full hookups and 33 tent sites. Rest rooms, showers, laundry facilities, a game room, a grocery and gift shop, barbecue pits, and a public phone are available.

*Reservations, fee:* Reservations are accepted. RV sites are $18.95 and tent sites are $14.50.

*Contact:* Arch View Campground, P.O. Box 1406, Moab, UT 84532; (801) 259-7854 or (800) 813-6622.

*Location:* From Moab, drive eight miles north on U.S. 191. The camp is on the east side of the road, near the junction of U.S. 191 and State Route 313.

*Trip notes:* You won't get much shade at this campground—although newly planted trees are starting to grow—but you'll enjoy the great views of Klondike Bluff in Arches National Park, four miles away, and the surrounding La Sal Mountains. In addition to its proximity to Arches, the camp is only 23 miles from Canyonlands National Park. Mountain bikers enjoy many routes in the vicinity, including one trail that begins in the parking area across from the camp and leads into red-rock country. Pick up a free mountain biker's guide

---

at the campground, the Moab Information Center, or the John Wesley Powell River Running Museum in Green River. Also near the camp, off a spur road, hikers can take a short, 100-yard trek to view exposed dinosaur bones at the Bureau of Land Management's Mill Creek Canyon site; obtain directions at the campground or pick up a brochure at the Moab Information Center.
*Season:* February through October.

## 7. DEVIL'S GARDEN

*Reference:* **In Arches National Park; map B3, grid c5.**
*Campsites, facilities:* The 52-site campground has rest rooms with cold running water, drinking water, picnic tables, fire grills, group areas, and an amphitheater for evening programs. There is a seven-day stay limit, and the maximum RV length is 35 feet. Vault toilets are only available during the winter months.
*Reservations, fee:* All individual sites are first come, first served. Group sites can be reserved in advance. From October through March, when water is not available, fees are $5. During the warmer months, when water is available, fees are $8.
*Contact:* Contact the park headquarters at (801) 259-5279.
*Location:* From Moab, take U.S. 191 five miles north to the park's visitors center. Drive 18 miles north to reach the campground on the park's only paved road.
*Trip notes:* Home to the largest concentration of natural arches in the world, Arches National Park is a land of towering sandstone cliffs and fins, narrow slot canyons, and gravity-defying balanced rocks. It's spectacular terrain, and it's no surprise that Devil's Garden, the park's only campground, is one of Utah's most popular camping destinations. With spacious sites set among a juniper forest, it fills up almost every night of the year. Make certain to get here early, before 9 A.M., if you hope to camp. Right in the middle of the campground you'll find a pretty amphitheater guarded by the Skyline Arch, one of the more magical settings for an outdoor evening program in the entire National Park System. Hikers can venture three miles round-trip on the moderately difficult trail to Delicate Arch, possibly the park's best-known landmark. (It graces countless postcards, book covers, and even Utah state license plates.) Rangers also lead daily hikes into the mazelike Fiery Furnace, an easy place to lose your way among slot canyons and dead-end turnoffs; sign up for the guided trip at the park's visitors center early in the day.
*Season:* Open year-round, with water available from April through September.

## 8. GOBLIN VALLEY STATE PARK

*Reference:* **Near Hanksville; map B3, grid d0.**
*Campsites, facilities:* There are 21 campsites. Amenities include picnic tables, fire grills, a modern rest room with showers, a dump station, and a picnic shelter.
*Reservations, fee:* Reservations can be made 120 days in advance by calling (800) 322-3770 Monday through Friday from 8 A.M. to 5 P.M. Campsites are

$10, plus a nonrefundable $5 reservation fee. Utah residents 62 years and older with a Special Fun Tag receive a $2 discount Sunday through Thursday, excluding holidays.

*Contact:* Park information can be obtained by calling Green River State Park at (801) 564-3633.

*Location:* From Green River, drive about eight miles west on Interstate 70. Take exit 147 and drive about 25 miles south on State Route 24. The turnoff to Goblin Valley State Park is well marked. Follow road, which is dirt at times, about 15 miles to the park.

*Trip notes:* This is a great camp for children! Kids' imaginations will get a real workout at this 3,654-acre park as they wander among the valley's wonderfully bizarre sandstone formations. They're sure to have a great time playing hide-and-go-seek with the hundreds of goblins and ghouls hidden among the rocks. The campground itself is tucked away on a paved loop off the park's main road, with some tent sites well hidden from the road. Two well-marked trails, the 1.5-mile (one-way) Carmel Canyon Trail and the three-mile (one-way) Curtis Bench Trail, wind through Goblin Valley. One mile west of the park, the San Rafael Swell offers additional hiking adventures among its numerous slot canyons. Set at an elevation of 5,200 feet, the park can be on the cold side in winter and hot in the summer.

*Season:* Open year-round.

---

## 9. WILLOW FLAT

*Reference:* **In Island in the Sky District, Canyonlands National Park; map B3, grid e4.**

*Campsites, facilities:* This primitive facility has 12 sites with picnic tables and vault toilets. *No drinking water* is available.

*Reservations, fee:* All campsites are free and are first come, first served. Backcountry camping is allowed in designated areas; a limited number of permits are issued to backpackers, mountain bikers, and four-wheel-drive enthusiasts. Reserve these sites through park headquarters well in advance.

*Contact:* Call park headquarters at (801) 259-7164.

*Location:* From Moab, drive 12 miles north on U.S. 191 to State Route 313. Follow State Route 313 approximately 30 miles southwest to Willow Flat campground in Canyonland's Island in the Sky District.

*Trip notes:* With 527 square miles of rugged wilderness divided into four distinct "districts," Canyonlands National Park ranks among the more remote national parks in the lower 48. This primitive camp is just off the pavement on the top of a plateau in the park's most accessible district, set in a pinyon-juniper forest. The camp does tend to fill up, so arrive early in the day to secure a spot. Nearby you'll find panoramic views over Canyonlands' broad mesas and vertigo-inducing canyons. One of the best overlooks, Mesa Arch, is a half-mile hike from Willow Flat. The arch frames a deep canyon gorge with vistas of the often snow-capped La Sal Mountains in the distance. Other hiking trails lead to popular destinations such as Grandview Point, Whale Rock, and Upheaval Dome. Mountain bikers and four-wheel-drive enthusiasts enjoy the 100-mile White Rim Trail, which ventures into the red-rock canyon country that gives the park its name. Make sure to bring plenty of your own water. That's a scarce commodity in this part of Canyonlands National Park.

*Season:* Open year-round.

## 10. DEAD HORSE POINT STATE PARK

*Reference:* **Near Canyonlands National Park; map B3, grid d5.**

*Campsites, facilities:* There are 21 campsites with shaded picnic tables and tent pads. Facilities include a visitors center with a small museum, rest rooms with hot and cold running water but no showers, a sewage disposal station, a group camping area, a pavilion, and a large overlook shelter.

*Reservations, fee:* Reservations can be made 120 days in advance by calling (800) 322-3770 Monday through Friday from 8 A.M. to 5 P.M. A $5 nonrefundable reservation fee is charged for each site reserved. Campsites are $9. Utah residents 62 years and older who have a Special Fun Tag receive a $2 discount Sunday through Thursday, excluding holidays.

*Contact:* Call the park at (801) 259-2614.

*Location:* From Moab, drive 12 miles north on U.S. 191 to State Route 313. Follow State Route 313 approximately 22 miles southwest to reach the park entrance.

*Trip notes:* Dead Horse Point State Park is relatively small, but it provides a fine jumping-off point to the hiking, four-wheeling, and mountain biking trails in the northern part of Canyonlands National Park. Set 2,000 feet above the Colorado River on a pointed plateau surrounded by cliffs, it's a scenic spot in its own right, with overlooks providing views of the canyon below. According to park rangers, cowboys used to round up and corral wild mustangs on this jut of land; a few leapt to their deaths rather than being caught, thus earning the area its colorful name. The quarter-mile Dead Horse Point Nature Trail offers sweeping panoramas of the Canyonlands area and interpretive signs about the cliffrose, pygmy forest, desert varnish, stone staircases, and Mormon tea you'll encounter along the rim. Keep a close eye on children on the trail—drop-offs are steep. Since there's no water at Canyonlands National Park's Willow Flat campground, Dead Horse Point is a good alternative. Water is limited, however, so park managers ask RV owners to fill their water tanks before arriving.

*Season:* Open year-round.

## 11. KANE SPRINGS CAMPGROUND

*Reference:* **Near Moab; map B3, grid d5.**

*Campsites, facilities:* There are 30 campsites, with no developed facilities at present. In 1997, RV hookups, a modern rest room, and showers are scheduled to be added. Group sites accommodating up to 50 people also will be available.

*Reservations, fee:* Reservations are accepted. Campsites are $8. Sites with RV hookup will cost $12 when completed.

*Contact:* Call the campground at (801) 259-7821 or (801) 259-8844.

*Location:* From Moab, drive four miles north on Kane Springs Road along the Colorado River. The camp is located in Red Rock Canyon at the end of the paved road.

*Trip notes:* Cottonwoods shade campsites beside the small, flowing Kane Creek, which occasionally runs dry. The camp is snuggled against a tall, red-rock cliff. Nine miles away is the BLM-managed Hurrah Pass area, and mountain bikers enjoy following the steep, winding dirt road from the campground to the pass. Along the way, they're treated to views of the Colorado River and ancient Native American rock writings.

*Season:* April through October.

## 12. PORTAL RV PARK AND FISHERY

*Reference:* In Moab; map B3, grid d5.

*Campsites, facilities:* There are 36 pull-through RV sites with full hookups and 10 shaded tent sites. Rest rooms, showers, laundry facilities, an RV disposal site, and a convenience store are available. Ponds on the premises are stocked with trout.

*Reservations, fee:* Reservations are accepted. Full hookups with 50-amp service are $20, and sites with 30-amp service are $17. Sites with water and electricity cost $14, and tent sites are $12.

*Contact:* Portal RV Park and Fishery, 1261 North Highway 191, Moab, UT 84532; (801) 259-6108 or (800) 574-2028.

*Location:* From Moab, drive three-quarters of a mile north on U.S. 191. The camp is adjacent to Matheson Wetlands Preserve.

*Trip notes:* At sunset, the pretty views to the west of this campground take in the Nature Conservancy's 800-acre Matheson Wetlands Preserve and a red-rock canyon cut by the Colorado River. In the midday sun, however, the young trees here don't provide much shade. The mostly open terrain is well landscaped with grassy lawn, and ponds here are stocked with rainbow trout for catch-and-release fly fishing. The fee is $10 per hour, no state license is required, and you can rent a fishing rod at the park's convenience store. From a nearby parking area, a boardwalk leads to self-guided nature trails through the Matheson Wetlands Preserve, providing glimpses of its plentiful bird and wildlife. Bald eagles frequent the area in winter, and a surprising variety of ducks, cranes, and songbirds live here year-round.

*Season:* Open year-round.

## 13. SLICKROCK CAMPGROUND

*Reference:* In Moab; map B3, grid d5.

*Campsites, facilities:* There are 197 sites, 120 of which have full hookups, 87 tent sites, and 14 camping cabins. The campground has three sets of rest rooms and showers, laundry facilities, an RV disposal site, picnic tables, a grocery and gift store, barbecue grills, a pool, three hot tubs, a public phone, and cable TV. Pets are allowed.

*Reservations, fee:* Reservations are accepted. Full hookups are $19.75 for two people, plus $3 for each additional person. Tent sites are $14.50, plus $5 for each additional person over 18. Camping cabins are $27.

*Contact:* Slickrock Campground, 1301½ North Highway 191, Moab, UT 84532; (801) 259-7660.

*Location:* The camp is at the north end of Moab, along U.S. 191. It is across from the Butch Cassidy Water Park, next to Buck's Grill House, on the west side of the road.

*Trip notes:* How close is too close? When it comes to campsites, it's when you can hear your neighbor snoring in the next tent—and that's about how close together the sites are at this park. Well, at least it's got a pool and hot tubs to keep the kids occupied after the sun goes down, and plenty of nearby recreation during the day. Arches National Park, with dozens of great hiking trails, is only three miles away. Five miles to the south, golfers can visit the 18-hole, public Spanish Valley Golf Course. The campground's staff also books four-wheel-drive, mountain biking, river-rafting, and airplane trips out of Moab.

*Season:* Open year-round.

## 14. MOAB VALLEY RV AND CAMPARK

*Reference:* In Moab; map B3, grid d5.

*Campsites, facilities:* There are 50 RV sites, 40 of which have full hookups, and 55 tent sites. Rest rooms, showers, laundry facilities, an RV disposal site, barbecue pits, a public phone, and cable TV are available.

*Reservations, fee:* Reservations are accepted. RV sites are $18 and tent sites are $14.

*Contact:* Moab Valley RV and Campark, 1773 North Highway 191, Moab, UT 84532; (801) 259-4469.

*Location:* The camp is at the north end of Moab, at 1773 North U.S. 191, near the Butch Cassidy Water Park and Matheson Wetlands Preserve.

*Trip notes:* This grassy campground is close to Arches National Park, making it a good alternative when Devil's Garden campground fills up. From the camp, you get pleasant sunset views of a red-rock canyon formed by the Colorado River. Also nearby is Matheson Wetlands Preserve, an excellent spot for birding. Golfers can get in 18 holes at the public Spanish Valley Golf Course. Moab's commercial outfitters offer half- and full-day rafting excursions on the Colorado, and hiking and mountain biking options abound on surrounding national park, BLM, and U.S. Forest Service lands. Pick up free mountain biker's and hiker's guides at the Moab Information Center.

*Season:* March through October.

## 15. SPANISH TRAIL RV PARK AND CAMPGROUND

*Reference:* In Moab; map B3, grid d5.

*Campsites, facilities:* There are 55 RV sites with full hookups and 26 tent sites. Rest rooms, showers, laundry facilities, an RV disposal site, cable TV, and a public phone are available. Pets are allowed on a leash. Owners are required to clean up after their pets.

*Reservations, fee:* RV sites are $19.50 and tent sites are $15.50 for two people. Each additional person at an RV site is $2, and $3 at a tent site. Reservations are accepted.

*Contact:* Spanish Trail RV Park and Campground, 2980 South Highway 191, Moab, UT 84532; (801) 259-2411.

*Location:* In Moab, follow U.S. 191 to the campground at 298 South.

*Trip notes:* Located in the middle of Moab, near the business district, this newer park has little shade. It's convenient to restaurants, stores, and the Slickrock Bike Trail, which is three miles to the east. For more information on other recreational options in the Moab area, see Moab Valley RV and Campark on page 233.

*Season:* Open year-round.

## 16. CANYONLANDS CAMPARK

*Reference:* **In Moab; map B3, grid d5.**

*Campsites, facilities:* There are 108 RV sites, of which 70 sites have full hookups, 32 sites have water and electricity, and six have no hookups. There are also 40 tent sites. Rest rooms, showers, laundry facilities, a grocery and gift shop, a game room, barbecue grills, an RV disposal site, a playground, a public phone, cable TV, and a pool are available. Pets are allowed.

*Reservations, fee:* Reservations are accepted. Full hookup sites are $19, sites with water and electricity are $19, and tent sites are $14 for two people. Each additional person costs $2.

*Contact:* Canyonlands Campark, 555 South Main Street, Moab, UT 84532; (801) 259-6848 or (800) 522-6848.

*Location:* Follow U.S. 191 into Moab. The park is on the south side of Moab, at 555 South Main Street.

*Trip notes:* Set in downtown Moab, this RV campground doesn't offer much of a wilderness experience, but it's close to shopping and restaurants. The pool and shaded sites make this an attractive choice during the hot summer months. For more information on other recreational options in the Moab area, see Moab Valley RV and Campark on page 233.

*Season:* Open year-round.

## 17. UP THE CREEK CAMP PARK

*Reference:* **In Moab; map B3, grid d5.**

*Campsites, facilities:* There are seven tent sites with picnic tables. Rest rooms, showers, and a public phone are available.

*Reservations, fee:* Campsites are $7 and are first come, first served.

*Contact:* Call the campground at (801) 259-2213.

*Location:* Follow U.S. 191 into downtown Moab, then turn east on 300 South. The campground is located at 210 East 300 South, behind City Market. The tent sites are walk-in only.

*Trip notes:* Here's a rarity—a park where campers can set up a tent for the night on a shaded, grassy spot without a single recreational vehicle in sight. If it's quiet you're seeking, this may be the place for you. Campsites are hike-in only, set alongside Mill Creek. The trailhead to the Slickrock Bike Trail is about two miles away. For more information on other recreational options in the Moab area, see Moab Valley RV and Campark on page 233.
*Season:* March 20 through October 31.

## 18. PACK CREEK CAMPGROUND

*Reference:* In Moab; map B3, grid d5.
*Campsites, facilities:* There are 36 RV sites with full hookups and 17 tent sites. The campground has rest rooms, picnic tables, showers, laundry facilities, an RV disposal site, and a playground.
*Reservations, fee:* Reservations are accepted. RV sites cost $16.50 and tent sites are $10.
*Contact:* Pack Creek Campground, 1520 Murphy Lane #10, Moab, UT 84532; (801) 259-2982.
*Location:* Driving north on U.S. 191, turn left on Spanish Trail Drive, and then left on Murphy Lane. The campground is in a quiet, residential part of town at 1520 Murphy Lane.
*Trip notes:* If you want to take a rugged mountain-biking trip or enjoy a relaxing round of golf, this is the camp for you. It's set in-between Moab's Spanish Valley Golf Course and the Slickrock Bike Trail. The camp's off Moab's main drag, so it tends to be quieter than other area campgrounds. Tall old trees shade the sites. You can amble along Pack Creek, which runs through the property. For more information on other recreational options in the Moab area, see Moab Valley RV and Campark on page 233.
*Season:* Open year-round.

## 19. MOAB KOA

*Reference:* In Moab; map B3, grid d5.
*Campsites, facilities:* There are 58 RV sites, of which 38 have full hookups, and 45 tent sites. Picnic tables, camping cabins, fire grills, laundry facilities, showers, an RV dump site, a swimming pool, and a miniature golf course are available.
*Reservations, fee:* Reservations are accepted. Campsites are $17 to $31.95.
*Contact:* Moab KOA, 3225 South Highway 191, Moab, UT 84532; (801) 259-6682.
*Location:* Follow U.S. 191 to the southern outskirts of Moab. The park is located at 3225 South Highway 191.
*Trip notes:* This well-established, older campground is quiet, shaded, and one step removed from the hustle and bustle of the city. Nearby you'll find Moab's public, 18-hole Spanish Valley Golf Course and Ken's Lake, a popular fishing area stocked regularly with rainbow trout by the Utah Division of Wildlife Resources. For one of the most spectacular driving tours in the state, campers should take the nearby La Sal Mountain Loop. Partially paved but

negotiable by passenger cars, this 65-mile road takes you from red-rock desert through pinyon-forested foothills and into a cool alpine wonderland guarded by 12,000-foot-high peaks. Views of the sandstone cliffs and green Moab Valley below are truly a sight to behold.

*Season:* March through September.

## 20. HAL CANYON

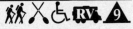

*Reference:* **Near Moab, on the Colorado River; map B3, grid d6.**

*Campsites, facilities:* There are seven sites. Vault toilets, picnic tables, and fire grills are available. There is *no drinking water.*

*Reservations, fee:* Campsites are $5 and are first come, first served.

*Contact:* Call the Bureau of Land Management at (801) 259-8193.

*Location:* From Moab, drive south on U.S. 191. Follow State Route 128 seven miles east, then north along the Colorado River to Hal Canyon.

*Trip notes:* Oak and cottonwood trees shade this pleasant Bureau of Land Management camp near the Colorado River. A popular area with mountain bikers, this is an inexpensive alternative to the private campgrounds in Moab. A few small rapids liven up this otherwise gentle-flowing stretch of the Colorado. In places the current can be strong, so be careful when swimming. Life jackets are a must for children. Four miles south of the camp, hikers should explore Negro Bill Canyon, where a little stream cuts through a red-rock wonderland. The well-traveled trail here ventures two miles to Morning Glory Bridge for an approximately four-hour round-trip hike. Additional hiking is available at Arches National Park, which is 10 miles from the camp.

*Season:* Open year-round.

## 21. OAK GROVE

*Reference:* **Near Moab, on the Colorado River; map B3, grid d6.**

*Campsites, facilities:* There are three sites with picnic tables, vault toilets, and fire grills. *No drinking water* is available.

*Reservations, fee:* Campsites are $5 and are first come, first served.

*Contact:* Call the Bureau of Land Management at (801) 259-8193.

*Location:* From Moab, drive south on U.S. 191. Follow State Route 128 seven miles east, then north along the Colorado River. The camp is adjacent to Hal Canyon.

*Trip notes:* Shaded campsites along the Colorado River are guarded on both sides by red sandstone cliffs. Like Hal Canyon next door, Oak Grove is a decent, inexpensive alternative to the numerous private camps in Moab. For details on river conditions and nearby Negro Bill Canyon, see the Hal Canyon campground above.

*Season:* May 20 through October 31.

## 22. BIG BEND

*Reference:* **Near Moab, on the Colorado River; map B3, grid d6.**

*Campsites, facilities:* There are 29 sites that can accommodate RVs up to 34 feet in length. No drinking water is available, but there are picnic tables, fire

grills, and vault toilets. Rest rooms are wheelchair accessible, but gravel at
the campsites could cause some wheelchair problems.

**Reservations, fee:** Campsites are $5 and are first come, first served.

**Contact:** Call the Bureau of Land Management at (801) 259-8193.

**Location:** From Moab, drive south on U.S. 191. Follow State Route 128 eight
miles east, then north along the Colorado River to the camp.

**Trip notes:** The Bureau of Land Management opened this camp in the early
1990s, while trying to curtail undeveloped camping along the Colorado River.
Some cottonwood trees provide shade. The stretch of the river along the
camp is relatively gentle, with a few small rapids popular with day-trip rafters
and kayakers. Four miles north of the camp on the east side of U.S. 191
you'll find Fisher Towers, which rise 1,500 feet from the desert floor. Little
visited, the BLM-managed spot offers a picnic area and a short hiking trail.
For details on nearby Negro Bill Canyon, see Hal Canyon on page 236.

**Season:** Open year-round.

## 23. HITTLE BOTTOM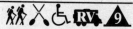

**Reference: Near Moab, on the Colorado River; map B3, grid d6.**

**Campsites, facilities:** There are eight sites with picnic tables, vault toilets, and
fire grills. *No drinking water* is available.

**Reservations, fee:** Campsites are $5 and are first come, first served.

**Contact:** Call the Bureau of Land Management at (801) 259-8193.

**Location:** From Moab, head south on U.S. 191. On State Route 128 drive 23
miles east, then north along the Colorado River to the camp.

**Trip notes:** At this camp, another scenic spot along the Colorado River, tall
cottonwood trees shade some of the sites. On a rainy summer day, you may
see tiny waterfalls tumble over the surrounding sandstone cliffs. The campground is especially popular with mountain bikers. Fisher Towers and Negro
Bill Canyon are both approximately 10 minutes away. For details about Fisher
Towers, see Big Bend on page 236, and for information about Negro Bill
Canyon, see Hal Canyon on page 236. It can be cold here in winter.

**Season:** Open year-round.

## 24. DEWEY BRIDGE

**Reference: Near Moab, on the Colorado River; map B3, grid c6.**

**Campsites, facilities:** There are seven campsites. Vault toilets, picnic tables,
and fire grills are available, but there is *no drinking water.*

**Reservations, fee:** Campsites are $5 and are first come, first served.

**Contact:** Call the Bureau of Land Management at (801) 259-8193.

**Location:** From Moab, head south on U.S. 191. On State Route 128 drive 30
miles east, then north along the Colorado River to the camp.

**Trip notes:** As you travel north along the Colorado River from Moab, the terrain
becomes increasingly expansive. This wide-open camp is set along the historic, one-lane Dewey Bridge. An old suspension bridge built in 1916, it's on
the National Register of Historic Places and currently is only open to foot
and bicycle traffic. The bridge is a popular put-in and takeout for river-rafting

---

trips. One of the Moab area's best two- to three-day white-water adventures begins many miles upstream in Westwater Canyon, near the Colorado-Utah border; Dewey Bridge is the first place rafters can exit the water. Day trips rafting downstream from the bridge can also be enjoyable. Fans of Native American petroglyphs can take the day trip to Sego Canyon, near the town of Thompson, about 50 miles from the camp along Interstate 70. Rock carvings here date back between 800 and 1300 years.

*Season:* Open year-round.

## 25. SAND FLATS

*Reference:* **Near Moab; map B3, grid e6.**

*Campsites, facilities:* There are 125 designated campsites with vault toilets. *No drinking water* is available.

*Reservations, fee:* All sites are first come, first served. The fee is $4 per vehicle for two people. Each additional person is $1.

*Contact:* Call the Bureau of Land Management in Moab at (801) 259-8193.

*Location:* From Moab, drive three miles east on Sand Flats Road to the Sand Flats Recreation Area and the camp.

*Trip notes:* This mostly open, primitive campground is next to the entrance to the Moab Slickrock Bike Trail, one of the nation's premier mountain-biking paths. The 10-mile marked loop is extremely difficult, but rewards physically fit bikers with scenic views over the Colorado River, beautiful red-rock canyons, and the surrounding La Sal Mountains. Before attempting the trail, try the two-mile practice loop to see if you're ready for the longer route. Juniper trees guard many of the sites here; others are nestled in small alcoves among the area's sandstone cliffs and petrified sand dunes.

*Season:* Open year-round.

## 26. WARNER LAKE

*Reference:* **In Manti–La Sal National Forest; map B3, grid d7.**

*Campsites, facilities:* There are 20 sites. Picnic tables, fire grills, vault toilets, and drinking water are available.

*Reservations, fee:* Campsites are $5 and are first come, first served.

*Contact:* Contact the Moab Ranger District of Manti–La Sal National Forest at (801) 259-7155.

*Location:* From Moab, drive eight miles south on U.S. 191, looking for the sign to the La Sal Loop. Take the paved and then graveled road 16 miles east to the Warner Lake turnoff and continue six miles east to the campground.

*Trip notes:* Here's one of the prettiest campgrounds you'll find anywhere in the fall. Set at an elevation of 9,400 feet, lovely little Warner Lake is surrounded by quaking aspens. In summer, its waters are well stocked with rainbow trout, offering anglers a decent place to cast a reel. Campsites are quiet and shaded; some sites overlook the lake, and all are only a quick hike from the water. Other short marked hiking trails lead through forest to Oohwah Lake and Burro Pass high in the La Sal Mountains. Horses and mountain bikes are welcome on all trails.

*Season:* Memorial Day weekend through October, depending on the coopera-
tion of the weather.

---

# 27. OOHWAH LAKE

*Reference:* **In Manti–La Sal National Forest; map B3, grid d7.**

*Campsites, facilities:* There are six sites. Picnic tables, fire grills, and pit toilets
are available, but there is *no drinking water.*

*Reservations, fee:* Campsites are free and are first come, first served.

*Contact:* Contact the Moab Ranger District of Manti–La Sal National Forest at
(801) 259-7155.

*Location:* From Moab, drive eight miles south on U.S. 191, looking for the
sign to the La Sal Loop. Take the paved and then graveled road east to the
junction with Forest Road 76. Follow the dirt Forest Road 76 approximately
two miles to the camp.

*Trip notes:* This camp should have you saying "Ooh" and "Aah," especially if
you're looking to beat the desert heat in summer. Set at 8,800 feet in the La
Sal Mountains, it's a pretty, cool spot amid forest near a small lake. Here
you can fish for stocked rainbow trout, or follow a short, scenic hike to
nearby Warner Lake. For details on Warner Lake, see Warner Lake on page
238. The trail is open to horses and mountain bikers alike.

*Season:* May 29 through October 1.

---

# 28. JURASSIC PARK

*Reference:* **In Hanksville; map B3, grid e0.**

*Campsites, facilities:* There are 17 RV sites and 20 tent sites. Picnic tables, fire
pits, an RV disposal station, rest rooms, showers, and a public phone are
available.

*Reservations, fee:* Reservations are accepted. Full-hookup sites are $12, par-
tial hookups are $7, and tent sites are $5.

*Contact:* Call the campground at (801) 542-3433.

*Location:* In Hanksville, the campground is one block south of Center Street,
at 100 South Center.

*Trip notes:* Aside from views of the surrounding Henry Mountains, there's not
much to recommend this fairly open RV park. You might stop here on the
way from Capitol Reef National Park on the west to Lake Powell and Natural Bridges National Monuments to the south and east. While you're in town,
visit the Bureau of Land Management's Hanksville office, where you can
follow a short, self-guided tour of a restored grist mill.

*Season:* Open year-round.

---

# 29. RED ROCK RESTAURANT
##   AND CAMPGROUND

*Reference:* **In Hanksville; map B3, grid e0.**

*Campsites, facilities:* There are 45 sites with full hookups. A lawn area can
accommodate 15 tents and vans. Laundry facilities, showers, rest rooms, a
public phone, ice, picnic tables, and a restaurant are available.

---

*Reservations, fee:* Reservations are accepted. Fees are $14 for full hookups, $11 for vans, and $8 for tent sites.

*Contact:* Red Rock Restaurant and Campground, P.O. Box 55, Hanksville, UT 84734; (800) 452-7971.

*Location:* In Hanksville, the campground is on State Route 24, one block west of the junction of State Routes 24 and 95.

*Trip notes:* The camp offers a little lawn and some young but fast-growing shade trees in downtown Hanksville, a remote desert town that you probably won't visit unless you're headed on the way to one of the fine outdoor attractions in the area—Goblin Valley State Park, Natural Bridges National Monument, Capitol Reef National Park, Lake Powell, Canyonlands National Park, or the Henry Mountains. The restaurant next door to the campground does serve up the best food in town. You can also stop at the Bureau of Land Management's Hanksville office to take a short, self-guided tour of a restored grist mill.

*Season:* Spring through fall, depending on demand.

---

## 30. HATCH POINT

*Reference:* **Near Moab; map B3, grid e5.**

*Campsites, facilities:* There are 10 sites. Vault toilets, drinking water, picnic tables, and fire grills are available. The maximum length for self-contained RVs is 24 feet.

*Reservations, fee:* Campsites are $6 and are first come, first served.

*Contact:* Call the Bureau of Land Management in Moab at (801) 259-8193.

*Location:* From Moab, drive 32 miles south on U.S. 191. Follow the BLM Canyon Rims Recreation Area Road 25 miles northwest to the camp.

*Trip notes:* Although the better-developed campgrounds in this area tend to fill up fast, here you won't have to battle the crowds for a prime spot in redrock canyon country. Nearby you'll find two beautiful overlooks onto the Needles District of Canyonlands National Park: the Needles Overlook, approximately 12 miles away, and the Anticline Overlook, approximately five miles north of the camp. You can hike to the scenic vistas, or take a long drive to Moab or the entrance to Canyonlands to access four-wheel-drive roads in Lockhart Basin.

*Season:* April through September.

---

## 31. NEEDLES OUTPOST

*Reference:* **Near the Needles District of Canyonlands National Park; map B3, grid f4.**

*Campsites, facilities:* There are 20 RV sites without hookups and 26 tent sites. Showers, rest rooms, an RV disposal site, a grocery and gift shop, gasoline, four-by-four rentals, and scenic airplane charters are available.

*Reservations, fee:* Reservations are recommended most of the year. Campsites are $10.

*Contact:* Needles Outpost, P.O. Box 1349, Moab, UT 84532; (801) 979-4007 or (801) 259-8545.

---

*Location:* From Moab, follow U.S. 191 south 40 miles to State Route 211. Head 35 miles west on State Route 211. The campground is just outside Canyonlands National Park, near the entrance to the Needles District of the park.

*Trip notes:* A good alternative to the popular Squaw Flat campground in Canyonlands National Park's Needles District, this camp is set just outside of the park entrance. Many sites here are nestled in a juniper forest and bordered by red-rock cliffs. Although you won't get views over the national park itself, the scenic spires for which the Needles District is named are visible from most campsites. For details on hiking, four-wheeling, and mountain-biking options in Canyonlands National Park, see Squaw Flat on page 242.

*Season:* March 19 through October 31.

## 32. INDIAN CREEK

*Reference:* **Near the Needles District of Canyonlands National Park; map B3, grid f4.**

*Campsites, facilities:* There are two campsites with picnic tables and pit toilets. *No drinking water* is available.

*Reservations, fee:* Campsites are free and are first come, first served.

*Contact:* Call the Bureau of Land Management office in Monticello at (801) 587-2141.

*Location:* From Moab, follow U.S. 191 south 40 miles to State Route 211. Head approximately 33 miles west on State Route 211. Look for Lockhart Basin Road on the north (right) side of the road. Follow this dirt road approximately 2.5 miles north to the campground.

*Trip notes:* When Indian Creek is running, this can be a fine spot to take a splash on a hot day. Some of the sites are shaded, and the camp is within walking distance of the creek and a small waterfall. It is also located at the start of a popular but rugged four-wheel-drive and mountain-biking road. Canyonlands National Park is four miles away. For details on hiking, four-wheeling, and mountain-biking options in the national park, see Squaw Flat on page 242.

*Season:* Open year-round.

## 33. HAMBURGER ROCK

*Reference:* **Near the Needles District of Canyonlands National Park; map B3, grid f4.**

*Campsites, facilities:* There are eight campsites. Picnic tables and vault toilets are available, but there is *no drinking water.*

*Reservations, fee:* Campsites are free and are first come, first served.

*Contact:* Call the Bureau of Land Management office in Monticello at (801) 587-2141.

*Location:* From Moab, follow U.S. 191 south 40 miles to State Route 211. Head approximately 33 miles west on State Route 211. Look for Lockhart Basin Road on the north (right) side of the road. Follow this dirt road approximately 1.5 miles north to the campground.

*Trip notes:* The sandstone Hamburger Rock is approximately four to five acres in size. Sites at this unusual little campground are cut into the rock itself, providing protection from desert winds. The setting is rugged red-rock country, and much of it is dry and desolate, but the views of nearby Abajo or Blue Mountain offer glimpses of green. The dirt road beyond the campground is a popular four-wheel-drive and mountain-biking route. For details on hiking, four-wheeling, and mountain-biking options in nearby Canyonlands National Park, see Squaw Flat below.

*Season:* Open year-round.

## 34. SQUAW FLAT

*Reference:* **In the Needles District of Canyonlands National Park; map B3, grid f4.**

*Campsites, facilities:* There are 26 sites with picnic tables and fire grills. Drinking water can be obtained from a tank next to the rest rooms. Group sites are available. The maximum RV length is 20 feet.

*Reservations, fee:* Most campsites are $6 and are first come, first served. Group sites, backcountry four-wheel-drive sites, and backpacking sites can be reserved by calling park headquarters.

*Contact:* Call park headquarters at (801) 259-7164.

*Location:* From Moab, follow U.S. 191 south 40 miles to State Route 211. Head 37 miles west on State Route 211. Follow signs from the park entrance station to the campground.

*Trip notes:* Canyonlands' Needles District is one of the more visitor-friendly sections of this remote, rugged national park. From here, short hikes lead to wonderful sights such as Pothole Point, a pocked, petrified sand dune full of small—and some large—potholes, some of which hold water. Another trail winds toward Cave Spring, where an old cowboy line camp can be viewed. Longer day hikes, such as the Chessler Park Trail, lead through narrow slot canyons. The camp is also close to the Elephant Hill and Salt Creek four-wheel-drive routes, among the most famous, and difficult, four-wheel roads in the country. Popular with mountain bikers and four-wheelers, Squaw Flat campground tends to fill early in the day, especially during peak season. Surrounding the camp you'll see slickrock formations—sandstone that looks as though a sand dune has been petrified in place, leaving hard, slick rolling hills. It's textured enough for great rock scrambling, yet smooth enough for kids to safely play hide-and-go-seek around. Campsites are spaced a good distance from one another, many near sandstone overhangs. In the summer, park rangers lead evening programs at a small campfire circle near the campground.

*Season:* Open year-round.

## 35. WINDWHISTLE

*Reference:* **Near Moab; map B3, grid f5.**

*Campsites, facilities:* There are 19 sites. Drinking water, vault toilets, picnic tables, and fire grills are available.

*Reservations, fee:* Campsites are $6 and are first come, first served.

*Contact:* Call the Bureau of Land Management in Moab at (801) 259-8193.

*Location:* From Moab, drive 32 miles south on U.S. 191. Look for the BLM Canyon Rims Recreation Area Road, and follow it five miles west to the campground.

*Trip notes:* You won't encounter crowds at this mostly open Bureau of Land Management camp, a rarity for this part of popular southeastern Utah. Set on a high plateau at approximately 6,000 feet, the campground offers sweeping vistas of the surrounding country and the La Sal and Abajo Mountains on either side. In winter, it snows here occasionally, and you must bring your own water. Not far from here you'll find two scenic viewpoints onto Canyonlands National Park's Needles District: Anticline and Needles Overlooks. If you want to venture to the national park to enjoy its hiking, mountain biking, and four-wheel-drive recreation opportunities, you must drive 45 minutes each way.

*Season:* Open year-round, with no water from mid-October to mid-April.

## 36. NEWSPAPER ROCK

*Reference:* **Near Monticello; map B3, grid f5.**

*Campsites, facilities:* There are eight campsites with picnic tables and vault toilets. *No drinking water* is available.

*Reservations, fee:* Campsites are free and are first come, first served.

*Contact:* Call the Bureau of Land Management office in Monticello at (801) 587-2141.

*Location:* From Monticello, drive about 12 miles north on U.S. 191 to State Route 211. Follow State Route 211 west for 12 miles to the camp.

*Trip notes:* You'll find a grove of cottonwood trees along a small stream at this campground, although in periods of extreme drought the creek runs dry. The Native American rock writing panel near this campground is one of the most impressive in the Southwest, with rock writings dating back as many as 1,500 years. Technical climbers will find challenging routes nearby. Camping is not recommended during times of heavy rains because the area sits in a flood plain.

*Season:* Open year-round.

## 37. STARR SPRINGS

*Reference:* **On the east side of the Henry Mountains; map B3, grid g0.**

*Campsites, facilities:* There are 12 campsites. Vault toilets, picnic tables, fire grills, and drinking water are available.

*Reservations, fee:* Campsites are $4 and are first come, first served.

*Contact:* Call the Bureau of Land Management office in Hanksville at (801) 542-3461.

*Location:* From Hanksville, drive approximately 21 miles east on State Route 95. Take the turnoff to the Bullfrog Marina at the Glen Canyon National Recreation Area and State Route 278. The well-marked turnoff to the campground is in approximately 18 miles.

*Trip notes:* Set in a patch of oak trees, this campground is a cooler and quieter alternative to Hite Campground, the often crowded Lake Powell destination. Starr Springs has been used as a watering hole for livestock and wildlife since pioneers first settled the area in the late 1800s. A short hiking trail offers visitors views of Mount Hillers and the surrounding area. Equestrians can explore the open land leading to the Henry Mountains or journey down into the red-rock painted desert.

*Season:* January through October.

---

## 38. HITE

*Reference:* **On Lake Powell, in Glen Canyon National Recreation Area; map B3, grid g2.**

*Campsites, facilities:* Hundreds of dispersed campsites surround the large cement boat ramp near the edge of the water with a few scattered picnic tables. There are a few level spots for RVs. A rest room with cold water and flush toilets is available near the top of the boat ramp.

*Reservations, fee:* Camping is free and sites are first come, first served.

*Contact:* Call Glen Canyon National Recreation Area in Page, Arizona, at (602) 645-8200.

*Location:* Hite campground is 45 miles southeast of Hanksville, on the northern edge of Lake Powell along State Route 95.

*Trip notes:* The second largest manmade lake in the United States, Lake Powell encompasses nearly 2,000 miles of shoreline surrounded by towering sandstone cliffs. It's a primitive, spectacular setting, and folks flock here on weekends to boat, fish, swim, water-ski, and lounge beside the deep blue water. The lake is a power boater's paradise. Anglers cast for smallmouth, largemouth, and striped bass. The wildest whitewater trip in Utah, a three- to five-day excursion through Cataract Canyon, begins upriver in Moab and ends here. The campground offers beautiful views of the surrounding area and good access to the lake, with some leveled gravel spots and other spaces cut into the sandstone. Tenters may want to escape the crowds and set up camp at one of the side canyons within 10 minutes of the main area near the lake shore. A marina, gas station, and small store are approximately one mile away.

*Season:* Open year-round.

---

## 39. BUCKBOARD

*Reference:* **In Manti–La Sal National Forest; map B3, grid g6.**

*Campsites, facilities:* There are 13 sites for tents and RVs. Vault toilets, picnic tables, seasonal drinking water, and fire grills are available. At times, *no drinking water* is available; call the Monticello Ranger District to inquire if the water is on. The camp may not be suitable for larger trailers.

*Reservations, fee:* All sites are first come, first served. The fee is $5 per night when water is on; sites are free when the water is turned off.

*Contact:* Call the Monticello Ranger District of Manti–La Sal National Forest at (801) 587-2041.

---

*Location:* From Monticello, drive approximately 6.5 miles west on Forest Road 105 to the campground.

*Trip notes:* Set on a scenic loop a half hour away from the Needles District of Canyonlands National Park, this high-alpine campground is a good place to escape the summer desert heat. The Abajo Mountains tower above the camp, and below it you can see beautiful red-rock country. Anglers head to little Foy and Monticello Lakes, both a 10-minute drive away, to try for rainbow trout. In surrounding Manti–La Sal National Forest, horses are welcome on trails through meadows and pine forest. For details on hiking, four-wheeling, and mountain-biking options in Canyonlands, see Squaw Flat on page 242.

*Season:* June through September.

## 40. DALTON SPRINGS

*Reference:* **In Manti–La Sal National Forest; map B3, grid g6.**

*Campsites, facilities:* There are 16 campsites for tents, trailers, and RVs. Picnic tables, fire grills, vault toilets, and drinking water are available. At times, *no drinking water* is available; call the Monticello Ranger District to inquire if the water is on.

*Reservations, fee:* All sites are first come, first served. The fee is $5 per night when water is on; sites are free when the water is turned off.

*Contact:* Call the Monticello Ranger District of Manti–La Sal National Forest at (801) 587-2041.

*Location:* From Monticello, drive approximately five miles west on Forest Road 105 to the campground.

*Trip notes:* Dalton Springs is another good summertime spot to cool off from the prickly desert heat. Set at 8,400 feet, this mountain campground is shaded by pines and aspens. You can fish for rainbow trout at tiny Foy and Monticello Lakes, both of which are a 10-minute drive away. Canyonlands National Park is roughly a half-hour drive away from the campground. For details on hiking, four-wheeling, and mountain-biking options in the park, see Squaw Flat on page 242.

*Season:* June through September.

## 41. WESTERNER RV PARK

*Reference:* **In Monticello; map B3, grid g6.**

*Campsites, facilities:* This park has 28 sites with full hookups, laundry facilities, showers, picnic tables, and an RV disposal station.

*Reservations, fee:* Reservations are accepted. The fee is $14.

*Contact:* Westerner RV Park, Box 371, Monticello, UT 84535; (801) 587-2762.

*Location:* The campground is on the south end of Monticello on U.S. 191, adjacent to the public golf course.

*Trip notes:* You'll find shaded, grassy campsites here, and right next door is the pretty, nine-hole San Juan County Golf Course. A public swimming pool is in the neighborhood; inquire at the camp office. Monticello is a decent central location for exploring the region—Arches, Canyonlands, and Mesa Verde National Parks, as well as Hovenweep National Monument, are all within a

day's drive. Also close are Natural Bridges National Monument, Monument Valley, the Goosenecks of the San Juan River, and Lake Powell.
*Season:* April through December.

## 42. MONTICELLO KOA

*Reference:* **Near Monticello; map B3, grid g7.**
*Campsites, facilities:* There are six RV sites with full hookups, 16 sites with water and electricity hookups, 20 tent sites, and two camping cabins. Rest rooms, showers, laundry facilities, a game room, a grocery and gift store, barbecue grills, a play area, a nonheated pool, a public phone, and an RV disposal station are available. Pets are allowed on a leash.
*Reservations, fee:* Reservations are accepted. RV sites are $18.50, sites with water and electricity are $17, tent sites are $15, and camping cabins are $25.
*Contact:* Call the campground at (801) 587-2884.
*Location:* From Monticello, drive six miles east on U.S. 666, heading toward Cortez, Colorado. Look for the sign indicating the campground turnoff to the north.
*Trip notes:* This quiet RV park is set in open farmland, well off the highway. Views of the surrounding La Sal and Abajo Mountains are quite pretty. It's a decent overnight stop for travelers headed from Canyonlands and Arches National Parks towards Mesa Verde National Park in Colorado. Monticello offers a nine-hole public golf course. The park itself has plenty of amenities to keep children busy, including its own pool.
*Season:* May through October.

## 43. MOUNTAIN VIEW RV PARK

*Reference:* **In Monticello; map B3, grid g7.**
*Campsites, facilities:* There are 12 back-in sites with full hookups; eight pull-throughs with water, electricity, and cable; eight pull-throughs with no hookups; and eight tent sites. Rest rooms, showers, an RV disposal station, laundry facilities, barbecue grills for rent, cable TV, a play area with horseshoes, and a fenced pet area are available.
*Reservations, fee:* Reservations are recommended in summer; those with reservations must arrive by 7 P.M. to keep their places. RV sites are $14 and tent sites are $8.
*Contact:* Mountain View RV Park, P.O. Box 910, Monticello, UT 84535; (801) 587-2974.
*Location:* In Monticello, drive on U.S. 191 one mile north of its intersection with U.S. 666.
*Trip notes:* With Canyonlands National Park's Squaw Flat campground filling almost every night, this is a good place to beat the crowds. It's approximately a 45-minute drive from the national park. Consider driving into the nearby Blue Mountains, where you can fish for rainbow trout at little Foy and Monticello Lakes. If you want to golf nine holes, Monticello's San Juan County Golf Course is open to the public.
*Season:* Open year-round.

# 44. NIZHONI

*Reference:* In Manti–La Sal National Forest; map B3, grid g5.

*Campsites, facilities:* There are 21 campsites. Vault toilets, drinking water, picnic tables, and fire grills are available.

*Reservations, fee:* Campsites are $6 and are first come, first served.

*Contact:* Call the Monticello Ranger District of Manti–La Sal National Forest at (801) 587-2041.

*Location:* From Blanding, drive approximately six miles north on Forest Road 95 to the border of Manti–La Sal National Forest. Continue to drive straight on Forest Road 95, heading four miles to a fork in the road. Bear left to the campground.

*Trip notes:* This scenic, forested camp serves as a trailhead for a short, fascinating trail to the ruins of an Anasazi cliff dwelling. Hikers will find other short trails in the area. The town of Blanding is home to Edge of the Cedars State Park, which has a self-guided, quarter-mile walk through a restored cliff dwelling. Kids especially enjoy crawling down a ladder and into a restored kiva, an ancient, circular ceremonial room used by the Anasazi. The park's excellent museum features ancient pottery, figurines, and a slide show about the culture of the Fremont, Navajo, and Ute Indians, as well as the Mormon settlers.

*Season:* May 15 through October 30.

---

# 45. DEVIL'S CANYON

*Reference:* In Manti–La Sal National Forest; map B3, grid g6.

*Campsites, facilities:* There are 32 campsites for tents and RVs. Picnic tables, fire grills, vault toilets, and group camping areas are available.

*Reservations, fee:* Call the U.S. Forest Service National Reservation System at (800) 280-2267 for reservations. The fee is $6.

*Contact:* Call the Monticello Ranger District at (801) 587-2041.

*Location:* From Blanding, drive 9.5 miles northeast on U.S. 191. Look for a signed turnoff to the campground on the west (left) side of the road.

*Trip notes:* Perched in the cool Blue Mountains, this is one of the better public campgrounds in southeastern Utah. Pines, fir, and some juniper trees shade most of the campsites, which are spaced far apart from one another, offering privacy. The short Devil's Canyon Nature Trail features interpretive signs detailing the natural history of the area. A few miles to the south, boaters, anglers, and rafters will enjoy the deep blue water of lovely, large Recapture Reservoir, which is set among red hills and pinyon-juniper forest. Rainbow trout are stocked here annually.

*Season:* May through October.

---

# 46. NATURAL BRIDGES

*Reference:* In Natural Bridges National Monument; map B3, grid h3.

*Campsites, facilities:* There are 13 campsites for tents and RVs. Picnic tables, fire grills, and vault toilets are available. Drinking water and rest rooms with

---

flush toilets can be found at the visitors center, one-quarter mile away from the campground. The maximum RV length is 21 feet. Longer vehicles are allowed to use an overflow area occasionally; check with the visitors center for details.

*Reservations, fee:* Campsites are $5 and are first come, first served.

*Contact:* Call Natural Bridges National Monument at (801) 259-5174.

*Location:* From Blanding, drive 38 miles west on State Route 95. The campground is just north of State Route 95, one-quarter mile from the monument's visitors center.

*Trip notes:* You can explore this monument in a quick one-hour drive, or spend a day or two relaxing in its spectacular red-rock setting. The nine-mile Bridge View Road loop brings you to overlooks of the park's three natural rock bridges. The largest, Sipapu Bridge, stands 220 feet high, with a span of 268 feet. A 1.2-mile round-trip hike involves climbing down stairs and ladders, a fun experience. Kachina Bridge, 210 feet high and 204 feet across, is a 1.5-mile round-trip trek. A short and easy stroll brings you to the smallest of the trio, 106-foot-high and 180-foot-long Owachoma Bridge. The small campground here has a quiet feel to it. Shaded by pinyon trees and at 6,500 feet elevation, it's a good place to beat summer heat. The camp tends to fill up in the late afternoon, although rangers sometimes allow self-contained RVs and trailers to park in the visitors center lot. A small museum features displays on Native American history, solar power, and the formation of the natural bridges.

*Season:* Open year-round.

---

# 47. BLANDING KAMPARK

*Reference:* **In Blanding; map B3, grid h6.**

*Campsites, facilities:* There are 53 RV sites with full hookups and 16 tent sites. Rest rooms, showers, picnic tables, laundry facilities, an RV disposal site, a grocery and gift store, barbecue pits, and two public phones are available. Pets are allowed on a leash.

*Reservations, fee:* Reservations are accepted. Full hookups are $14 and tent sites are $10 for two people. Each additional person is $3.

*Contact:* Call the campground at (801) 678-2770.

*Location:* The campground is at the southern end of Blanding, at 861 South Main Street.

*Trip notes:* This city RV park is close to a pretty lake, Anasazi ruins, and a fascinating museum. The nearby Dinosaur Museum is more than just a roadside attraction. Its curators served as technical advisors on Steven Spielberg's *Jurassic Park*, and its exhibit on dinosaur skin is among the best you'll see anywhere. A five-minute drive north of town, beautiful Recapture Reservoir offers plenty of room to boaters, canoeists, and water-skiers. Anglers can fish here for stocked rainbow trout. For details on the restored Anasazi cliff dwelling and museum at nearby Edge of the Cedars State Park, see Nizhoni on page 247.

*Season:* Open year-round.

---

# 48. SAND ISLAND

**Reference:** Near Bluff, on the San Juan River; map B3, grid i6.

**Campsites, facilities:** This five-site campground features vault toilets, picnic tables, and a boat launch. *No drinking water* is available.

**Reservations, fee:** Campsites are $5 and are first come, first served.

**Contact:** Call the Bureau of Land Management at (801) 587-2141.

**Location:** From Bluff, drive approximately three miles west on U.S. 191 to the campground. It is along the San Juan River.

**Trip notes:** Set along a gentle stretch of the San Juan River, this camp is a popular spot to start canoeing and kayaking trips. You'll encounter a few small rapids, but it can be navigated by beginners. A short hike from camp leads to an Anasazi rock art panel that dates back 1,500 years.

**Season:** Open year-round.

# 49. CADILLAC RANCH

**Reference:** In Bluff; map B3, grid i6.

**Campsites, facilities:** There are 15 RV sites with full hookups and four tent sites. Rest rooms, showers, picnic tables, an RV disposal site, and fire grills are available.

**Reservations, fee:** Reservations are accepted. Campsites are $15.

**Contact:** Cadillac Ranch, P.O. Box 157, Bluff, UT 84512; (801) 672-2262.

**Location:** The campground is on U.S. 191 at the east end of Bluff.

**Trip notes:** Bluff is a tiny, pretty town on the edge of Monument Valley. You'll find some Navajo stands where you can purchase Native American jewelry. There's not much else around here aside from a few stores and restaurants. Anglers can cast for trout, bass, catfish, and bluegill at a fishing pond on Cadillac Ranch. No state fishing license is required, and there's no extra charge to fish.

**Season:** Open year-round.

# 50. K AND C RV PARK

**Reference:** In Bluff; map B3, grid i6.

**Campsites, facilities:** There are four RV sites with full hookups and picnic tables.

**Reservations, fee:** Reservations are accepted. The fee is $12.

**Contact:** K and C RV Park, P.O. Box 27, Bluff, UT 84512; (801) 672-2221.

**Location:** The park is in the center of Bluff on State Route 163.

**Trip notes:** This city RV park is a stopover on the way to Monument Valley and the Navajo Indian Reservation. The Four Corners Monument is a 45-minute drive away. It's the only place in the U.S. where a person can step in one spot and be in four states—Utah, Colorado, New Mexico, and Arizona—at the same time. Kids will love the geography lesson and stepping on the marker, hopscotching from state to state. The Navajo Tribe charges a small fee to visit the monument.

**Season:** Open year-round.

# 51. TURQUOISE

**RV** 6

*Reference:* **In Bluff; map B3, grid i6.**

*Campsites, facilities:* There are seven RV sites with full hookups and picnic tables.

*Reservations, fee:* Reservations are accepted. Each site is $10.

*Contact:* Turquoise, P.O. Box 66, Bluff, UT 84512; (801) 672-2219.

*Location:* The campground is on the corner of U.S. 191 and Fifth Street West in the center of Bluff.

*Trip notes:* Bluff stands on the edge of Monument Valley. It's a rugged, scenic spot, and it offers a few small shops and restaurants. Look for Native American jewelry in the area.

*Season:* Open year-round.

# 52. SQUARE TOWER CAMPGROUND

**RV** 8

*Reference:* **In Hovenweep National Monument; map B3, grid i8.**

*Campsites, facilities:* There are 31 campsites for RVs and tents. A rest room (with running cold water but no showers), fire grills, and picnic tables are available.

*Note:* At press time, this camp was closed due to budget cuts. It is unclear when the camp will reopen. Call Mesa Verde National Park at (303) 529-4461 before heading out.

*Reservations, fee:* Campsites are $6 and are first come, first served.

*Contact:* Call Mesa Verde National Park in Colorado at (303) 529-4461.

*Location:* From the tiny town of Aneth, drive 20 miles north on a partially paved and dirt road, following signs to the monument.

*Trip notes:* When it's open, this high-desert camp is a gem that's well off the beaten path. Unfortunately, as this book went to press, the campground was closed due to budget cuts, and no one seemed to know when it would reopen. Before driving a long way, call ahead and make sure it is open. The monument centers around an unusual Anasazi ruin complex featuring square and circular towers, cliff dwellings, and ancient petroglyphs. Some of the ruins date back more than 1,000 years. After checking in at the ranger station for directions, you can drive to the dispersed sites, or enjoy a two-mile, self-guided hike on the Square Tower Trail. Due the high elevation, the camp can be cold in the winter.

*Season:* Open year-round, but at press time, this camp was closed due to budget cuts. It is unclear when the camp will reopen. Call Mesa Verde National Park at (303) 529-4461 to confirm it's open before heading out.

# 53. GOOSENECKS STATE PARK

**RV** 9

*Reference:* **Near Mexican Hat; map B3, grid j3.**

*Campsites, facilities:* There are four campsites with picnic tables and vault toilets. *No water* is available.

*Reservations, fee:* Camping is free and sites are first come, first served.

*Contact:* Call Edge of the Cedars State Park in Blanding at (801) 678-2238.

*Location:* From Mexican Hat, drive approximately three miles north on State Route 163. Turn north onto State Route 261 and drive approximately one mile. Follow signs on State Route 318 to the state park.

*Trip notes:* The big draw here is the view. Visitors look down a 1,000-foot chasm at a place where the meandering San Juan River has cut "goosenecks" in the red-rock terrain. As it zigs and zags through the towering canyon walls, five miles of the river cover a distance of only one linear mile. The effect is, simply put, amazing. For hiking and backpacking trips, visit the Bureau of Land Management's Grand Gulch Primitive Area, approximately 30 miles away. Try a day hike to Junction Ruin, an Anasazi cliff dwelling; the trail begins at the Kane Gulch Ranger Station, just off State Route 261.

*Season:* Open year-round.

## 54. BURCHES TRADING POST

*Reference:* **In Mexican Hat; map B3, grid j8.**

*Campsites, facilities:* There are six RV sites with full hookups. Rest rooms, showers, picnic tables, laundry facilities, a grocery and gift shop, a public phone, and an RV disposal site are available. The Trading Post also has a restaurant and motel. Drinking water can be purchased at the store.

*Reservations, fee:* Reservations are accepted. Campsites are $10 to $15.

*Contact:* Burches Trading Post, P.O. Box 310337, Mexican Hat, UT 84531; (801) 683-2221.

*Location:* The campground is in the southeastern Utah town of Mexican Hat on State Route 163.

*Trip notes:* Nestled in rugged, pretty red-rock country, this city campground adjoins a motel-restaurant complex. For $7 a person, you can take a horse-back ride to view the unusual balanced rock formation that gives Mexican Hat its name, or a trip along the San Juan River. The river is approximately a half mile from the camp, and it's a good place to set off on a short rafting trip.

*Season:* Open year-round.

## 55. VALLES TRAILER PARK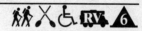

*Reference:* **In Mexican Hat; map B3, grid j3.**

*Campsites, facilities:* There are 20 RV sites with full hookups and eight tent sites. Rest rooms, showers, laundry facilities, picnic tables, a grocery and gift shop, barbecue grills, a public phone, and an RV disposal station are available.

*Reservations, fee:* Reservations are recommended in the summer months. The fee is $12 for two people. Each additional adult is $2.

*Contact:* Valles Trailer Park, P.O. Box 310216, Mexican Hat, UT 84531; (801) 683-2226.

*Location:* The campground is at the north end of Mexican Hat on U.S. 163.

*Trip notes:* Mexican Hat is a scenic little town surrounded by red-rock terrain. It's the gateway to spectacular Monument Valley, where John Wayne swaggered through many classic Westerns. River rafters can float the San Juan, which runs near town. Visitors should consider side trips to the Four Corners

Monument or Hovenweep National Monument, which features hiking trails among Anasazi ruins.

*Season:* Open year-round.

---

## 56. MITTEN VIEW CAMPGROUND

*Reference:* **In Monument Valley; map B3, grid j3.**

*Campsites, facilities:* There are 29 RV sites with no hookups, nine pull-through sites, 38 tent sites, and nine group areas for six or more people. No water is available, but there are coin-operated showers, rest rooms, picnic tables, and an RV disposal station. Drinking water must be purchased at Goulding's Trading Post or in Mexican Hat.

*Reservations, fee:* Reservations for groups of 10 or more are required. All other sites are first come, first served. RV sites are $10, group sites are $20, and tent sites are $10.

*Contact:* Mitten View Campground, P.O. Box 360289, Monument Valley, UT 84536; (801) 727-3353.

*Location:* The campground is on U.S. 163, 24 miles from Kayenta and eight miles from Goulding's Trading Post. Visitors need to enter the Navajo Tribal Park before they reach the campground. The fee to enter the Tribal Park is $2.50 a person between the ages of 8 and 59 and $1 for those over 60.

*Trip notes:* A surreal and beautiful region, Monument Valley features high sandstone monoliths rising from the desert floor like ships stranded on an ocean of sand. Pick up a brochure for the self-guiding drive through the area at the park entrance. The dirt road runs 17 miles round-trip, with 11 numbered stops at highlights such as Elephant and Camel Buttes, Totem Pole, and the Mittens rock formations. Survey the area from John Ford Point, where the director filmed classic Westerns such as *Stagecoach* and *The Searchers*. There is a snack shop and gift shop at the visitors center. Guided tours of Monument Valley, other restricted areas, and Mystery Valley are available from vendors in the visitors center parking lot. A three-hour Monument Valley tour costs $20 per person. It takes eight hours to see Monument Valley, Mystery Valley, and the restricted areas.

*Season:* Open year-round, except for Christmas Day, New Year's Day, and a half day on Thanksgiving.

---

## 57. GOULDING'S MONUMENT VALLEY CAMPGROUND

*Reference:* **In Monument Valley; map B3, grid j3.**

*Campsites, facilities:* There are 53 sites, 42 of which are full hookups, and 24 of which are pull-throughs. There are 40 tent sites. Camping cabins, rest rooms, showers, an RV disposal station, laundry facilities, a public phone, groceries, ice, picnic tables, and fire grills are available. There is a recreation room, coin games, a playground, and a hiking trail.

*Reservations, fee:* Reservations are recommended from June through September. Full hookups are $23.98 and tent sites are $15.26 for two people. Each additional person above the age of six is $3.

---

***Contact:*** Goulding's Monument Valley Campground, P.O. Box 360002, Monument Valley, UT 84536; (801) 727-3235.

***Location:*** Follow U.S. 163 to Monument Valley. The campground is 2.25 miles west on Monument Valley Road off of U.S. 163.

***Trip notes:*** Set on the edge of Monument Valley, this camp is adjacent to a trading post originally built in the 1920s. It's got all the amenities, and you can't beat the proximity to world-famous Monument Valley. Here you can follow the driving tour and try to identify places where John Ford filmed his famous movie Westerns. The nearby trip to the Four Corners Monument—the only place where you can stand in four states at the same time—is especially fun for children.

***Season:*** March 15 through October 31.

# Nevada Campgrounds

## Scenic Rating

Poor .................................... Fair ......................................... Great

## Key to the Symbols

|  Boating |  Canoeing/ Rafting |  Fishing |  Golf |  Hiking |  Historical Sites |
| Horseback Riding |  Hot Springs |  Swimming |  Waterskiing |  RV Sites |  Wheelchair Access |

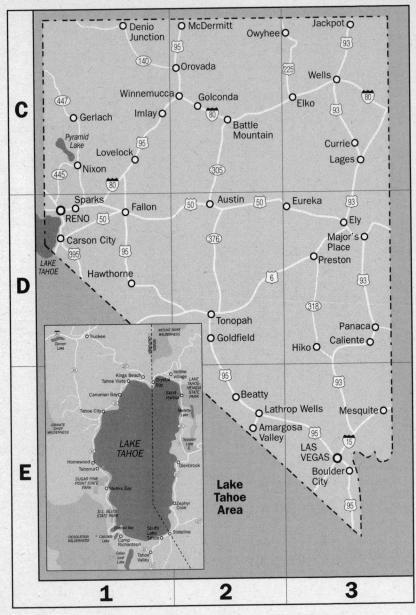

# Nevada Campgrounds—Pages 258-348

**Chapter C1** ............................. **258**
*Map on page 258.* Denio, Lovelock, Pyramid Lake, Pyramid Lake Paiute Reservation, Rye Patch Reservoir, Sheldon National Wildlife Refuge, Sutcliffe

**Chapter C2** ............................ 262
*Map on page 262.* Battle Mountain, Humboldt National Forest, Mountain City, Wilson Reservoir, Winnemucca

**Chapter C3** ............................ 268
*Map on page 268.* Angel Lake, Elko, Humboldt National Forest, Jackpot, Jarbridge Wilderness, Mountain City, Ruby Lake National Wildlife Refuge, Ruby Mountain Scenic Area, South Fork State Recreation Area, Wells, Wendover, Wildhorse Reservoir, Wildhorse State Recreation Area

**Chapter D1** ............................ 282
*Map on page 282.* Carson City, Carson River, Dayton, Dayton State Park, Fallon, Fort Churchill State Historic Park, Gardnerville, Genoa, Hawthorne, Lahontan State Recreation Area, Lake Lahontan, Lake Tahoe, Minden, Pyramid Lake Indian Reservation, Reno, Silver Springs, Sparks, Toiyabe National Forest, Topaz Lake, Truckee River, Virginia City, Wadsworth, Walker Lake, Walker River, Washoe Lake State Recreation Area, Yerington

**Chapter D2** ............................ 298
*Map on page 298.* Austin, Berlin–Ichthyosaur State Park, Gabbs, Mount Jefferson, Toiyabe National Forest, Tonopah

**Chapter D3** ............................ 304
*Map on page 304.* Baker, Beaver Dam State Park, Caliente, Cathedral Gorge State Park, Cave Lake State Recreation Area, Echo Canyon State Park, Ely, Great Basin National Park, Humboldt National Forest, Illipah Reservoir, Lehman Creek, Panaca, Pioche, Spring Valley State Park

**Chapter E2** ............................ 314
*Map on page 314.* Beatty, Death Valley National Park, Pahrump

**Chapter E3** ............................ 318
*Map on page 318.* Boulder City, Lake Mead National Recreation Area, Las Vegas, Laughlin, Mesquite, Overton, Overton Beach, Searchlight, Spring Mountains National Recreation Area, Toiyabe National Forest, Valley of Fire State Park

**Lake Tahoe Area Chapter** ....... 340
*Map on page 340.* D.L. Bliss State Park, Emerald Bay, Emerald Bay State Park, Fallen Leaf Lake, Homewood, Lake Tahoe, Meeks Bay, South Lake Tahoe, Stateline, Sugar Pine Point State Park, Tahoe City, Tahoe State Recreation Area, Tahoe Vista, Tahoma

# MAP C1

Map of Nevada .................. see page 256
Beyond This Region:
North ........................................ Oregon
East (Map C2) .................. see page 262
South (Map D1) ................ see page 282
West ...................................... California

4 Campgrounds
Pages 258–261

| C1 | C2 | C3 |
| D1 | D2 | D3 |
|    | E2 | E3 |

Nevada

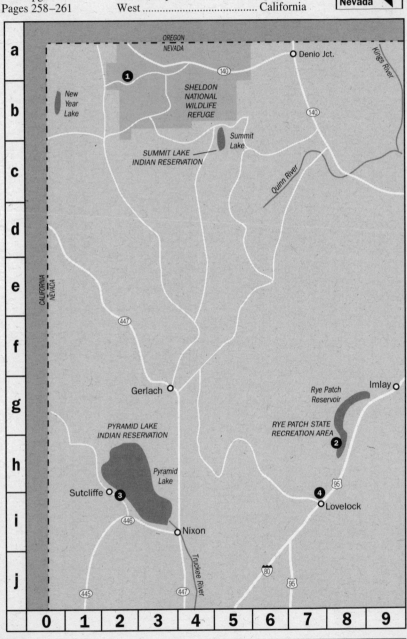

OREGON
NEVADA

❶

New Year Lake

SHELDON NATIONAL WILDLIFE REFUGE

Denio Jct.

Kings River

140

140

Summit Lake

SUMMIT LAKE INDIAN RESERVATION

Quinn River

CALIFORNIA
NEVADA

447

Gerlach

Rye Patch Reservoir

Imlay

PYRAMID LAKE INDIAN RESERVATION

RYE PATCH STATE RECREATION AREA

❷

Pyramid Lake

Sutcliffe ❸

95

❹ Lovelock

446

Nixon

Truckee River

80

95

445

447

| a | b | c | d | e | f | g | h | i | j |

| 0 | 1 | 2 | 3 | 4 | 5 | 6 | 7 | 8 | 9 |

**Chapter C1 features:**
1. Sheldon National Wildlife Refuge
2. Rye Patch State Recreation Area
3. Pyramid Lake Marina RV Park
4. Lazy K Campground and RV Park

---

# 1. SHELDON NATIONAL WILDLIFE REFUGE

*Reference:* **Near Denio; map C1, grid a2.**

*Campsites, facilities:* There are approximately a dozen primitive camps in the refuge, three of which (Fish Spring, Big Spring, and Virgin Valley) have vault toilets. There is *no drinking water.* Pets are permitted as long as they remain quiet, on leashes, or otherwise controlled. The maximum stay is 14 days. The nearest commercial services are in Cedarville (46 miles west of the western edge of the refuge) and Denio (14 miles east of the eastern edge).

*Reservations, fee:* No reservations are accepted. There is no camping fee.

*Contact:* Sheldon National Wildlife Refuge, P.O. Box 111, Lakeview, OR 97630; (503) 947-3315.

*Location:* From Cedarville, California, take Highway 229 east eight miles to the Nevada border, where the pavement ends and County Road 8A begins. Continue 12 miles to the first major intersection with another dirt road and follow the sign for Sheldon. In one mile is a second intersection; drive straight ahead on County Road 34. Go several miles and turn right at the sign for the refuge. Continue 19 miles and bear right into the refuge.

*Trip notes:* Sheldon National Wildlife Refuge, created in 1931 to protect native wildlife, covers more than 575,000 acres of high-desert habitat and is by far the best place to see wildlife en masse in Nevada. Especially around dawn and dusk, you might spot hundreds of pronghorn—fast, graceful, and very skittish, with big, white rump patches—grazing on the flats, drinking reservoir water, or bounding through the brush. Scan the sky and you might see golden eagles, falcons, or kestrels soaring overhead. The campsites are little more than dirt pads in the open desert. Lace up your hiking boots (or saddle up your horse) for a trek through the surrounding desert. Or fish in the reservoirs from the shore for trout. The primitive campsite at Virgin Valley has public hot springs.

*Season:* Open year-round, though access may be hampered in extreme weather (November through May).

---

# 2. RYE PATCH STATE RECREATION AREA

*Reference:* **Near Lovelock; map C1, grid h8.**

*Campsites, facilities:* The South Campground has 44 campsites for tents or self-contained RVs up to 30 feet long. Piped drinking water, flush toilets, showers, sewage disposal, public phones, picnic tables, grills, and fire rings are provided. The North Campground has 25 semi-developed sites, with hand-pumped water, vault toilets, picnic tables, and grills provided. Pets are

---

permitted as long as they remain quiet, on leashes, or otherwise controlled. The maximum stay is 14 days.

*Reservations, fee:* No reservations are accepted. The fee is $6 in summer, $3 in winter.

*Contact:* Rye Patch State Recreation Area, 2505 Rye Patch Reservoir Road, Lovelock, NV 89419; (702) 538-7321.

*Location:* From Lovelock, drive 23 miles east on Interstate 80 and take Exit 129. Drive one mile west to the park.

*Trip notes:* The South Campground is just downriver from the spillway of the Rye Patch dam, which impounds Humboldt River water to irrigate the alfalfa farms around Lovelock. It's well shaded, relatively quiet, and full of anglers fishing the reservoir for trout, walleye, and bass. The North Campground is on the reservoir in a treeless parking lot and is used mostly for overflow. There's a boat launch at water's edge and a little swimming beach on an inlet nearby.

*Season:* Open year-round.

---

## 3. PYRAMID LAKE MARINA RV PARK

*Reference:* **In Sutcliffe on the Pyramid Lake Paiute Reservation; map C1, grid h2.**

*Campsites, facilities:* There are 40 spaces for RVs, all with full hookups (30-amp receptacles) and all pull-throughs. Tent camping is allowed. Rest rooms have flush toilets and hot showers. Drinking water, a public phone, sewage disposal, laundry facilities, groceries, and a snack bar are available.

*Reservations, fee:* Reservations are accepted. The fee is $5 for day use, tent camping, and parking overnight on the beach, and $15 per vehicle for hookups at the RV park.

*Contact:* Pyramid Lake Marina, P.O. Box 309, Wadsworth, NV 89442; (702) 476-1156.

*Location:* From Reno, head east on Interstate 80. Take exit 43 in Sparks and drive 16 miles north on Highway 447. At the junction, bear left onto Highway 448 and drive 18 miles. Turn right at the sign to the marina.

*Trip notes:* The campground is just up from the bare, treeless shoreline of sparkling Pyramid Lake. All water activities are represented, especially fishing for large (10-pound) cutthroat trout during the season (October through June). You can also rent Jet Skis and boats, moor and launch a boat, and tour the excellent museum at the tribal visitors center, which has wildlife photography and historical black-and-whites, informational displays on Paiute history and lifestyles, and Paiute artifacts.

*Season:* Open year-round.

---

## 4. LAZY K CAMPGROUND AND RV PARK

*Reference:* **In Lovelock; map 1, grid i7.**

*Campsites, facilities:* There are 49 spaces for RVs, 30 with full hookups (30-amp receptacles); 27 are pull-throughs. There are 12 tent sites in the trees.

Rest rooms have flush toilets and hot showers. Drinking water, a public phone, sewage disposal, laundry facilities, groceries, a snack bar, and a playground are also available.

**Reservations, fee:** Reservations are accepted. The fee is $11 for tent camping and $14.95 to $18.50 for RVs.

**Contact:** Lazy K Campground and RV Park, 1550 Cornell, Lovelock, NV 89419; (702) 273-1116.

**Location:** In Lovelock, take exit 105 off Interstate 80 and go north to Cornell Street, then go right (east) for a mile to the campground.

**Trip notes:** The Lazy K was a KOA for years before closing in 1994. Friendly proprietor Ron Kiel reopened it in 1995 and has been restoring it to its prior shady and well-tended glory. It's right off the freeway, but fortunately, the large trees and landscaping hold down the noise—a definite plus since this is the only RV park in Lovelock.

**Season:** Open year-round.

# MAP C2

Map of Nevada .................. see page 256
Beyond This Region:
North ............................................. Oregon
East (Map C3) .................... see page 268
South (Map D2) ................ see page 298
West (Map C1) ................... see page 258

7 Campgrounds
Pages 262–267

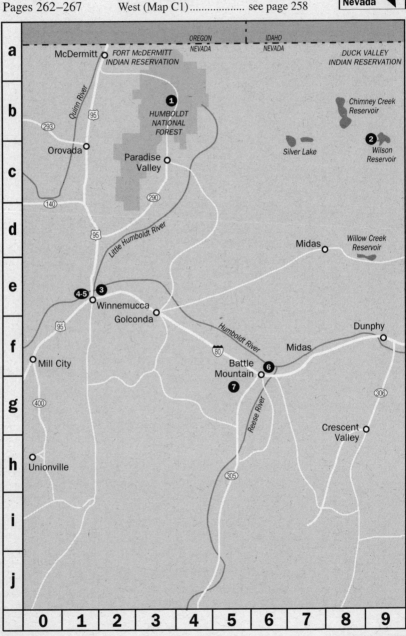

**Chapter C2 features:**

1. Lye Creek
2. Wilson Reservoir
3. Hi-Desert RV Park
4. Winnemucca RV Park

5. Model T RV Park
6. Colt Service Center RV Park
7. Mill Creek Recreation Area

# 1. LYE CREEK

*Reference:* **In Humboldt National Forest; map C2, grid b3.**

*Campsites, facilities:* There are 12 campsites for tents or self-contained RVs up to 20 feet long. Drinking water, accessible toilets, picnic tables, grills, and fire rings are provided. Pets are permitted as long as they remain quiet, on leashes, or otherwise controlled. There's a 14-day stay limit. The nearest phone and commercial services are in Paradise Valley (18 miles south). The U.S. Forest Service's Martin Creek Guard Station is nearby.

*Reservations, fee:* Reservations are accepted all year and are recommended for weekends in the summer. The fee is $4 per site.

*Contact:* For camping reservations, call Karen Dunham at the Santa Rosa Ranger District, 1200 Winnemucca Boulevard East, Winnemucca, NV 98445; (702) 623-5025 ext. 23. For information, contact Paradise Valley Ranger Station, (702) 578-3521.

*Location:* From Paradise Valley, take Highway 290 north for three miles. The pavement ends at the National Forest sign and the dirt begins. It's 10 miles up, up, and away to Hinckey Summit and five miles from there to the turnoff to the campground. Take a left (at road sign 087); it's another 1.5 miles down to the campground, for a total of 20 miles of dirt road.

*Trip notes:* Lye Creek, elevation 7,400 feet, was one of the nicest campgrounds in Nevada—and that was before the Forest Service completely refurbished it in the summer of 1995. It's in a protected draw right on the creek, which creates the perfect conditions for dense forest and lush vegetation. Play in the creek, stroll along the spur road, climb 10,000-foot Granite Peak, or just sit at your campsite and listen to the water rush over the rocks or the wind whiffle through the leaves. You might find some tiny brook trout in the creek. It's another 20 miles of gravel to complete the loop through the Santa Rosas; you meet up with U.S. 95 14 miles south of McDermitt.

*Season:* Early June through mid-October, depending on snowfall and snowmelt.

# 2. WILSON RESERVOIR

*Reference:* **Southwest of Mountain City; map C2, grid b9.**

*Campsites, facilities:* There are 15 sites for tents or self-contained RVs up to 16 feet long. Pumped drinking water, vault toilets, sewage disposal, picnic tables, grills, and fire pits are provided. Pets are permitted as long as they are quiet, leashed, or otherwise controlled. The maximum stay is 14 days.

*Reservations, fee:* No reservations are necessary. The fees are $3 for camping and $1 for boat launching.

*Contact:* Elko BLM District Office, 3900 East Idaho Street, Elko, NV 89803; (702) 753-0200.

*Location:* From Elko, drive 27 miles north on Highway 225 and bear left onto Highway 226. Continue roughly 40 miles on Highway 226. Where the pavement ends, turn left at the sign. Continue 16 miles, following the signs, to the campground.

*Trip notes:* This remote BLM campground is a favorite of trout (year-round) and largemouth bass (summer only) anglers. Ice-fishing is also popular, though the road in isn't maintained during the winter. If you bring your own boat or canoe, you can fish for trout anywhere they're biting. The elevation is 5,300 feet.

*Season:* Open year-round, but easily accessible from May through October.

## 3. HI-DESERT RV PARK

*Reference:* **In Winnemucca; map C2, grid e1.**

*Campsites, facilities:* There are 137 spaces for RVs, all with full hookups (20- and 30-amp receptacles); 80 are pull-throughs. Tent camping is allowed at 11 campsites. Handicapped-accessible rest rooms have flush toilets and hot showers. Drinking water, a public phone, sewage disposal, laundry facilities, groceries, video rentals, a game room, and a heated swimming pool are also available.

*Reservations, fee:* Reservations are accepted year-round and are recommended from June through September. The fees are $13 for tent camping and $19 for RVs. Noncampers can pay $2 to take a shower. A 10-percent Good Sam discount is available.

*Contact:* 5575 East Winnemucca Boulevard, Winnemucca, NV 89445; (702) 623-4513.

*Location:* In Winnemucca, take exit 180 off Interstate 80 and go right (west) a half mile on East Winnemucca Boulevard to the RV park.

*Trip notes:* Hi-Desert is one of the larger and better RV stopovers for Interstate 80 travelers, with grassy sites and good shade. The game room has a pool table, video games, and a TV; a weight room and hot tub are by the pool. A casino shuttle provides free 24-hour transportation to downtown Winnemucca, where there are four round-the-clock casinos.

*Season:* Open year-round.

## 4. WINNEMUCCA RV PARK

*Reference:* **In Winnemucca; map C2, grid e1.**

*Campsites, facilities:* There are 132 spaces for RVs, 84 with full hookups (20- and 30-amp receptacles); 74 are pull-throughs. Some sites are seasonal. Tent camping is allowed. Rest rooms have flush toilets and hot showers. Drinking water, a public phone, sewage disposal, laundry facilities, and groceries are also available.

*Reservations, fee:* Reservations are accepted. The fee is $14.50 to $18.50 for up to two people; additional children are $1 and adults are $2. KOA cardholders and seniors who pay cash receive a 10-percent discount.

*Contact:* Winnemucca RV Park, 5255 East Winnemucca Boulevard, Winnemucca, NV 89455; (702) 623-4458.

*Location:* In Winnemucca, take exit 178 off Interstate 80 and go right (west). At the Bullhead Motel, turn left (east) and drive 1.5 miles down East Winnemucca Boulevard to the RV park.

*Trip notes:* Winnemucca RV Park has been in the same location, about a mile east of downtown Winnemucca, for more than 20 years. The trees are mature, there's plenty of grass (nice for tent camping), and the campsites are spacious. The store has some slots and video poker machines.

*Season:* Open year-round.

## 5. MODEL T RV PARK

*Reference:* In Winnemucca; map C2, grid e1.

*Campsites, facilities:* There are 58 spaces for RVs, all with full hookups (20- and 30-amp receptacles) and pull-throughs. Tent camping is not allowed. Rest rooms have flush toilets and hot showers. Drinking water, a public phone, sewage disposal, laundry facilities, a convenience store, and a seasonal swimming pool are available.

*Reservations, fee:* Reservations are accepted. The camping fee is $10 to $16 per vehicle. A 10-percent AARP and Good Sam discount are offered.

*Contact:* Model T Casino and RV Park, 1130 West Winnemucca Boulevard, Winnemucca, NV 89455; (702) 623-2588.

*Location:* In Winnemucca, take exit 176 off Interstate 80 and go left (east) on Winnemucca Boulevard for half a mile to the RV park.

*Trip notes:* The parking lot of the Model T Casino right on the main drag near downtown Winnemucca provides a somewhat urban setting for this RV park. Inside the casino are blackjack tables, slot and video poker machines, a good cheap coffee shop, and a country-western lounge. The RV park is convenient to Raley's Supermarket and the cemetery (just in case you're in a "Monster Mash" kinda mood). Guests have use of the motel pool.

*Season:* Open year-round.

## 6. COLT SERVICE CENTER RV PARK

*Reference:* In Battle Mountain; map C2, grid f6.

*Campsites, facilities:* There are 96 spaces for RVs, all with full hookups (30-amp receptacles); 79 are pull-throughs. Tent camping is not allowed. Handicapped-accessible rest rooms (in the truck stop) have drinking water, flush toilets, and hot showers. A public phone, laundry facilities, and groceries are also available.

*Reservations, fee:* Reservations are accepted. The fee is $15 for two people, plus $3 for each additional person. Noncampers can use the showers for $5.

*Contact:* Colt Service Center, 650 West Front Street, Battle Mountain, NV 89820; (702) 635-5424.

*Location:* In Battle Mountain, take exit 229 off Interstate 80 and go right (east) a quarter-mile on Front Street (Business 80) to the RV park.

*Trip notes:* The Service Center consists of a motel, coffee shop, mini-mart, truck stop, Western Union window, and the RV park, all in a big lot right on the main drag a little west of downtown Battle Mountain. For picnic tables and some shade, head over to VFW Park (across the tracks on Reese Avenue at North First Street).

*Season:* Open year-round.

---

## 7. MILL CREEK RECREATION AREA

*Reference:* **Near Battle Mountain; map C2, grid g5.**

*Campsites, facilities:* There are 10 campsites for tent camping or self-contained RVs up to 24 feet long. Vault toilets, picnic tables, grills, and fire pits are provided. *No drinking water* is available. Pets are permitted as long as they remain quiet, on leashes, or otherwise controlled. The maximum stay at the campground is 14 days.

*Reservations, fee:* No reservations are necessary. Camping is free.

*Contact:* Battle Mountain BLM District Office, 50 Bastian Street (P.O. Box 1420), Battle Mountain, NV 89820; (702) 635-4000.

*Location:* From Battle Mountain, drive south 24 miles on Highway 305 and turn left at the sign for Mill Creek. The campground is another four miles away on a dirt road.

*Trip notes:* Mill Creek was the site of a 1930s Civilian Conservation Corps work camp, and the CCC built the eight-foot-high stone pillars at the campground entrance. Tall cottonwoods shade the sites and shelter myriad birds. Anglers can fish for brown trout in the creek.

*Season:* Open year-round, depending on weather conditions.

## LEAVE NO TRACE TIPS

**Plan ahead and prepare.**

- Learn about the regulations and special concerns of the area you are visiting.

- Visit the backcountry in small groups.

- Avoid popular areas during peak-use periods.

- Choose equipment and clothing in subdued colors.

- Pack food in reusable containers.

Map of Nevada ................. see page 256
Beyond This Region:
North ........................... Oregon
East ................................. Utah
South (Map D3) ................ see page 304
West (Map C2) .................. see page 262

24 Campgrounds
Pages 268–281

| C1 | C2 | C3 |
| D1 | D2 | D3 |
| | E2 | E3 |

**Nevada**

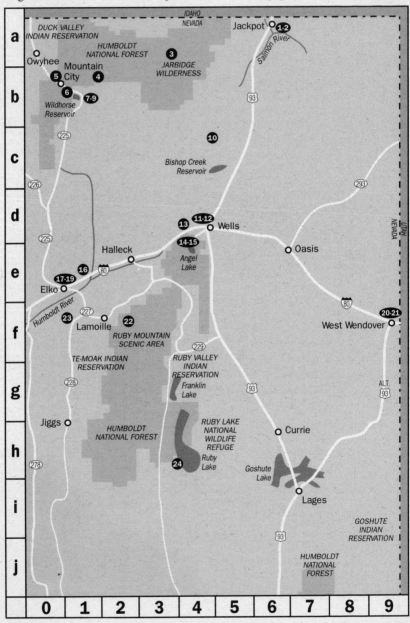

**Chapter C3 features:**

1. Cactus Pete's RV Park
2. Spanish Gardens RV Park
3. Jarbidge Campgrounds
4. Big Bend
5. Mountain City Motel and RV Park
6. Wildhorse Crossing
7. Wildhorse State Recreation Area
8. North Wildhorse Recreation Area
9. Wildhorse Campground
10. Tabor Creek Campground
11. Wells Chinatown RV Park
12. Mountain Shadows RV Park
13. Welcome Station RV Park
14. Angel Creek
15. Angel Lake
16. Ryndon Campground
17. Double Dice RV Park
18. Gold Country Motor Inn and RV Park
19. Cimarron West RV and Trailer Park
20. Wendover KOA
21. Stateline RV Park
22. Thomas Canyon
23. South Fork State Recreation Area
24. Ruby Marsh

## 1. CACTUS PETE'S RV PARK

*Reference:* **In Jackpot; map C3, grid a6.**

*Campsites, facilities:* The deluxe park has 52 spaces for RVs, all with full hookups (30-amp and 110-volt receptacles); all of the sites are pull-throughs. Tent camping is not permitted. Rest rooms have flush toilets and hot showers. A public phone, sewage disposal, laundry facilities, a heated swimming pool, a hot tub, and two tennis courts are available. The budget park has 15 spaces, all with full hookups; campers are not allowed use of the rest rooms, showers, or swimming facilities in the deluxe section. The water at both parks is shut off during the winter, but drinking water is available at the office. Groceries can be bought across the road at the general store.

*Reservations, fee:* Reservations are recommended for the deluxe park, which fills up fast in the summer. No reservations are accepted for the budget park. The fee is $8 to $12 per vehicle for the deluxe park, and $6 to $7 for the budget park.

*Contact:* Cactus Pete's Casino and RV Park, P.O. Box 508, Jackpot, NV 89825; (702) 755-2321.

*Location:* Jackpot is 45 miles south of Twin Falls, Idaho, and 68 miles north of Wells on U.S. 93; Cactus Pete's is 1.2 miles south of the Idaho border. The deluxe park is directly behind Cactus Pete's casino, next to the airport, while the budget park is south of the hotel tower.

*Trip notes:* This RV park and casino is as close as Las Vegas will ever get to Idaho. The larger deluxe park has showers, wide sites, and some greenery; the smaller budget park is little more than hookups in a gravel parking lot. Inside the casino, you'll find three pits with 28 table games, a slot club, $5 video poker, a buffet, a gourmet room, a showroom, a country lounge, and a convention center. If it happens to be a Wednesday evening, all food in the hotel is half price—the most astounding bargain in a state renowned for its

astounding bargains. Deluxe campers have use of the hotel facilities. Jackpot is on Mountain Time, so always turn your clocks ahead one hour.
*Season:* Open year-round.

---

## 2. SPANISH GARDENS RV PARK

*Reference:* **In Jackpot; map C3, grid a6.**

*Campsites, facilities:* There are 27 spaces for RVs, all with full hookups (30-amp receptacles); 11 are pull-throughs. Tent camping is allowed. Handicapped-accessible rest rooms have flush toilets and hot showers. Drinking water, a public phone, sewage disposal, laundry facilities, and cold storage game lockers (for hunters) are available.

*Reservations, fee:* Reservations are recommended during the summer and fall. The tent camping fee is $8 for the first person and $1 for each additional camper, while RVs are $13.50.

*Contact:* Spanish Gardens RV Park, P.O. Box 390, Jackpot, NV 89825; (702) 755-2333 or (800) 422-8233.

*Location:* Take U.S. 93 to the far south end of Jackpot. The RV park is at the corner of Gurley Street.

*Trip notes:* The park is right off the main highway, but a security wall, trees, and grassy areas buffer the impact. Jackpot is the closest gambling (by road) to Idaho and southwest Wyoming, and it's a destination in its own right. Many road warriors make reservations far in advance to stop here on their way south. If you can get a space at Spanish Gardens, grab it; though it's at the far south end of Jackpot, the park provides free taxi rides around town.

*Season:* Open year-round.

---

## 3. JARBIDGE CAMPGROUNDS

*Reference:* **In Humboldt National Forest; map C3, grid a3.**

*Campsites, facilities:* Two campgrounds (Jarbidge and Pine Creek) and three "dispersed areas" (Sawmill, Pavlak, and Bluster) combine for approximately 16 campsites over a one-mile stretch just beyond Jarbidge. Only Jarbidge and Pine Creek have piped drinking water (hand-pumped); all five campgrounds have picnic tables, fire rings, and vault toilets. Pine Creek is the largest and most luxurious, with six sites.

*Reservations, fee:* No reservations are accepted. There is no camping fee.

*Contact:* Jarbidge Ranger District, 1008 Burley Avenue, Buhl, ID 83316; (208) 543-4129.

*Location:* Two gravel roads run northeast from Highway 225, one about 55 miles north of Elko and 10 miles south of Wildhorse Reservoir, and the other approximately 65 miles north of Elko and directly across from the entrance to the Wildhorse State Recreation Area. The southern route is 60 miles of fair dirt road to Jarbidge, the northern route is 55 miles. Both take well over three hours, and both are well signed and straightforward.

*Trip notes:* Jarbidge, one of the remotest towns in the west, sits in the bottom of Jarbidge Canyon along Jarbidge River. Its permanent population hovers between 25 and 30, and the downtown consists of a grocery store, a gas

---

station, two restaurant/bars, a motel, and a bed-and-breakfast. The campgrounds are wooded, right on the river (with fishing for small bull trout), and surrounded by a vast tract of pristine mountain wilderness. Three great hiking trails—North Bear Street–Powerline Road, Copper Mountain, and Matterhorn Mountain—are close to camp. The sites get very crowded during the fall hunting season. Jarbidge, like Jackpot, is on Mountain Time; set your watch ahead one hour. The elevation ranges from 6,300 to 6,600 feet.
*Season:* June through October, depending on the weather.

## 4. BIG BEND    RV 6

*Reference:* **In Humboldt National Forest; map C3, grid b2.**
*Campsites, facilities:* There are 15 campsites for tents or self-contained RVs up to 30 feet long. Drinking water, vault toilets, picnic tables, grills, and fire rings are provided. The nearest commercial services are in Mountain City, 31 miles west, but there's a campground host during the season. Pets are permitted as long as they remain quiet, on leashes, or otherwise controlled. The stay limit is 14 days.
*Reservations, fee:* No reservations are accepted. The camping fee is $4.
*Contact:* Mountain City Ranger District, P.O. Box 276, Mountain City, NV 89831; (702) 763-6691.
*Location:* Take the north-access gravel road toward Jarbidge, which exits Highway 225 directly across from the entrance to Wildhorse State Recreation Area. Drive eight miles to the fork and bear left. Kick up dust another three miles and turn right into the campground.
*Trip notes:* If you don't have a full three hours of daylight to make it to Jarbidge, it's best to camp at Wildhorse State Recreation Area (see page 272), Wildhorse Crossing (see page 272), or right here at Big Bend for the night. The scenery (high-walled gorges and vast vistas) and your safety (on the long, narrow, and winding dirt road) are worth sleeping on. Pitch your tent under the quaking aspens, collect some of the plentiful dead wood for a nice little campfire, and count the stars. The elevation is 6,900 feet.
*Season:* Mid-June through mid-October, depending on snowfall.

## 5. MOUNTAIN CITY MOTEL AND RV PARK    RV 4

*Reference:* **In Mountain City; map C3, grid b0.**
*Campsites, facilities:* There are eight spaces for self-contained RVs, all with full hookups (20- and 30-amp receptacles). A public phone and sewage disposal are available. Rest rooms, complete with drinking water, can be found in the Steakhouse in the Mountain City Motel.
*Reservations, fee:* Reservations are accepted. The camping fee is $15.
*Contact:* Mountain City Motel, P.O. Box 102, Mountain City, NV 89831; (702) 763-6617.
*Location:* From Elko, drive north 84 miles on Highway 225 to the north side of Mountain City, where the RV park is located.
*Trip notes:* This is a small RV park behind Mountain City Motel and Steakhouse. There's a nice coffee shop and bar next door and a country store down the

road. Mountain City, like Jackpot and Jarbidge, is on Mountain Time, so turn your watches ahead an hour.

*Season:* Early April through November, depending on the weather.

## 6. WILDHORSE CROSSING

*Reference:* **In Humboldt National Forest; map C3, grid b1.**

*Campsites, facilities:* There are 37 campsites for tents or self-contained RVs up to 28 feet long. Piped drinking water, vault toilets, picnic tables, grills, and fire pits are provided. The nearest commercial services are in Mountain City, 20 miles north. Pets are permitted as long as they remain quiet, on leashes, or otherwise controlled. The stay limit is 14 days.

*Reservations, fee:* No reservations are accepted. The fee is $4 per campsite.

*Contact:* Mountain City Ranger District, P.O. Box 276, Mountain City, NV 89831; (702) 763-6691.

*Location:* From Mountain City, drive 15 miles south on Highway 225. The campground is just north of the Wildhorse Dam on the west side of the road.

*Trip notes:* This somewhat sparsely vegetated campground (mostly dirt with some scraggly shrubbery) on the flats of the Owyhee River is just downstream from the Wildhorse Dam. Wildhorse Crossing is generally uncrowded, since the first choice for most campers is the nearby Wildhorse State Recreation Area (see below). The campground occupies the flats between the highway and the river as it winds its way north through a scenic canyon. Anglers who camp here generally head up to the reservoir to fish.

*Season:* June through October.

## 7. WILDHORSE STATE RECREATION AREA

*Reference:* **On Wildhorse Reservoir; map C3, grid b1.**

*Campsites, facilities:* There are 32 campsites for tents or self-contained RVs up to 40 feet long; 10 are pull-throughs. Handicapped-accessible rest rooms have flush toilets and hot showers. Drinking water, a public phone, sewage disposal, a fish-cleaning area, and a boat-launching ramp are available. The stay limit is 14 days.

*Reservations, fee:* No reservations are accepted. The camping fee is $7 per vehicle; the day-use fee is $3.

*Contact:* Wildhorse State Recreation Area, District 4 Headquarters, Elko, NV 89801; (702) 758-6493.

*Location:* Drive 67 miles north of Elko or 19 miles south of Mountain City on Highway 225 to the campground.

*Trip notes:* Located on the northeast shore of Wildhorse Reservoir, this campground in the Wildhorse State Recreation Area sits among desert scrub with little shade. Yet the setting is idyllic, with a beautiful view of the Independence Range across the water, especially at sunset. The main recreation here is swimming, followed by boating and fishing (for trout, channel catfish, and small-mouth bass).

*Season:* Open year-round.

# 8. NORTH WILDHORSE RECREATION AREA

*Reference:* **On Wildhorse Reservoir; map C3, grid b1.**

*Campsites, facilities:* There are 18 campsites for tents or self-contained RVs up to 40 feet long. Pumped drinking water, vault toilets, sheltered picnic tables, grills, and fire pits are provided. Pets are permitted as long as they remain quiet, on leashes, or otherwise controlled. The maximum stay is 14 days.

*Reservations, fee:* No reservations are accepted. The camping fee is $4 per vehicle.

*Contact:* Elko Bureau of Land Management District Office, 3900 East Idaho Street, Elko, NV 89803; (702) 753-0200.

*Location:* Drive 67 miles north of Elko or 19 miles south of Mountain City on Highway 225 to the campground.

*Trip notes:* This Bureau of Land Management campground has a few advantages over the state-run Wildhorse State Recreation Area (see page 272): it's more sheltered (less exposed and with more trees) and there's no fee for day use. Hikers and mountain bikers love the two trails that lead to Sunflower Flat, where you can see wildflowers in season, and deer, maybe even elk, if you're lucky. Bring a bathing suit, boat, fishing pole (and rigging for trout, channel catfish, and small-mouth bass), outboard motor, and water skis to take full advantage of the reservoir.

*Season:* Open year-round, but generally more easily accessible from May 15 to November 15.

# 9. WILDHORSE CAMPGROUND

*Reference:* **On Wildhorse Reservoir; map C3, grid b1.**

*Campsites, facilities:* There are 23 campsites for tents or self-contained RVs up to 40 feet long, plus vault toilets and garbage cans. There is *no drinking water.*

*Reservations, fee:* No reservations are accepted. The camping fee is $3 to $3.50 per vehicle.

*Contact:* Shoshone-Paiute Business Council, P.O. Box 219, Owyhee, NV 89832; (702) 757-3161.

*Location:* Drive 67 miles north of Elko or 19 miles south of Mountain City on Highway 225 to the campground.

*Trip notes:* This Shoshone-Paiute campground falls between the nearby state and federal Wildhorse campgrounds (see page 272) for degree of development. Camping is on packed dirt, and facilities include pit toilets in concrete outhouses and garbage cans.

*Season:* Open year-round.

# 10. TABOR CREEK CAMPGROUND

*Reference:* **Near Wells; map C3, grid c4.**

*Campsites, facilities:* There are 10 campsites for tents or self-contained RVs up to 16 feet long. Piped drinking water, vault toilets, picnic tables, grills, and fire pits are provided. Pets are permitted as long as they remain quiet, on leashes, or otherwise controlled. The maximum stay is 14 days.

*Reservations, fee:* No reservations are accepted. Camping is free.

*Contact:* Elko Bureau of Land Management District Office, 3900 East Idaho Street, Elko, NV 89803; (702) 753-0200.

*Location:* From Wells, head west on Eighth Street toward the site of Metropolis, Nevada's only agricultural ghost town. Continue along the county road after the pavement ends for another 20 miles. At the sign, turn right and cross the cattle guard. The campground is about a mile in.

*Trip notes:* Tabor Creek is located on the west slope of the wildlife-rich Snake Mountains. Fences were constructed in the early 1980s to protect the creek from grazing and to improve the rainbow and brown trout fishery. The lush vegetation provides an ideal habitat for a wide variety of birds. Mule deer and pronghorn are abundant. Tabor Creek is most crowded in October during deer-hunting season.

*Season:* Open year-round, but most accessible from mid-April to late November, depending on snowfall.

## 11. WELLS CHINATOWN RV PARK

*Reference:* **In Wells; map C3, grid d4.**

*Campsites, facilities:* There are 18 spaces for RVs, all with full hookups (20- and 30-amp receptacles) and all pull-throughs. Tent camping is not allowed. Handicapped-accessible rest rooms have flush toilets and hot showers. Drinking water, a public phone, and sewage disposal are available. Stuart's Food Town supermarket is right next door.

*Reservations, fee:* Reservations are accepted. The camping fee is $13 for two people, and $2 for each additional adult.

*Contact:* Chinatown RV Park, 455 South Humboldt Avenue, Wells, NV 89835; (702) 752-2101.

*Location:* In Wells, take exit 351 off Interstate 80 and drive two blocks north to the RV park.

*Trip notes:* This RV park with some permanent residents is in the parking lot of a defunct casino and an unreliable restaurant called Chinatown, just off the interstate. Consider it as an overflow option in the event that Mountain Shadows up the street is full (see below).

*Season:* June through October.

## 12. MOUNTAIN SHADOWS RV PARK

*Reference:* **In Wells; map C3, grid d4.**

*Campsites, facilities:* There are 38 spaces for RVs, 33 with full hookups (30-amp receptacles); 13 are pull-throughs. Tent camping is allowed. Handicapped-accessible rest rooms have flush toilets and hot showers. Drinking water, a public phone, sewage disposal, and laundry facilities are available.

*Reservations, fee:* Reservations are recommended from Memorial Day to Labor Day, especially for pull-throughs. The fee is $16.50 for up to two people. Additional people are $2 apiece. Tent camping sites are $13. Noncampers can take showers for a $5 fee. AARP, AAA, Good Sam, and senior citizens discounts of 10 percent are offered.

*Contact:* Mountain Shadows RV Park, 405 S. Humboldt Avenue, Wells, NV 89835; (702) 752-3525.

*Location:* In Wells, take exit 351 off Interstate 80 and drive three blocks north to the RV park.

*Trip notes:* Mountain Shadows is one of the coziest, cleanest, and friendliest RV parks on the interstate through northern Nevada. Dick and Chickie Smith took it over in 1993 and have improved the bathhouse and laundry facilities, planted trees, and spruced up the landscaping. Rent videos and have a meal or fountain treat at Burger Bar, on the corner of South Humboldt Avenue and Sixth Street. Mountain Shadows is a good jumping-off spot for the East Humboldt Range, which towers over the park, and Ruby Valley and Mountains.

*Season:* March 1 through November 15.

---

## 13. WELCOME STATION RV PARK

*Reference:* **In Humboldt National Forest; map C3, grid d4.**

*Campsites, facilities:* There are 33 spaces for RVs, 15 with full hookups (30-amp receptacles); 13 are pull-throughs. Tent camping is allowed. Rest rooms have flush toilets and hot showers. Drinking water, a public phone, sewage disposal, laundry facilities, and limited groceries are available.

*Reservations, fee:* Reservations are accepted. The fees are $12 for tent camping and $12 to $15 for RVs.

*Contact:* Welcome Station RV Park, P.O. Box 340, Wells, NV 89835; (702) 752-3808.

*Location:* From Wells, head west on Interstate 80 and take exit 343 (Welcome/ Starr Valley). The RV park is right off the exit ramp.

*Trip notes:* This RV park has been around for more than 35 years, and the towering black elms and five acres of grass are there to prove it. A creek runs right through the property, with a few wary native trout living in its waters. Activities include volleyball, horseshoes, and counting the cars passing by on the Interstate.

*Season:* May 1 through November 1.

---

## 14. ANGEL CREEK

*Reference:* **In Humboldt National Forest; map C3, grid e4.**

*Campsites, facilities:* There are 18 campsites for tents or self-contained RVs up to 40 feet long. Piped drinking water, vault toilets, picnic tables, grills, and fire rings are provided. Pets are permitted as long as they remain quiet, on leashes, or otherwise controlled. The maximum stay is 14 days.

*Reservations, fee:* Reservations are accepted. The camping fee is $6.

*Contact:* Ruby Mountain Ranger District, 301 South Humboldt Avenue (P.O. Box 246), Wells, NV 89835; (702) 752-3357.

*Location:* In Wells, take exit 351 off Interstate 80 and head south (under the exit ramp). You'll immediately see a sign for Angel Lake; take a right here. Angel Creek campground is eight miles away.

---

*Trip notes:* Tucked in a small gully and shaded by leafy aspen trees, Angel Creek is peaceful and private compared to its sister campground four miles up the road (see Angel Lake below). A creek (no fish) runs behind the campground. The elevation is 6,800 feet.

*Season:* Early June through September, depending on snowfall and snowmelt.

---

# 15. ANGEL LAKE

*Reference:* **Near Wells; map C3, grid e4.**

*Campsites, facilities:* There are 26 campsites for tents or self-contained RVs up to 25 feet long. Piped drinking water and vault toilets, picnic tables, grills, and fire pits are provided. Pets are permitted as long as they remain quiet, on leashes, or otherwise controlled. The maximum stay is 14 days.

*Reservations, fee:* Reservations are accepted. The camping fee is $6.

*Contact:* Ruby Mountain Ranger District, 301 S. Humboldt Avenue (P.O. Box 246), Wells, NV 89835; (702) 752-3357.

*Location:* In Wells, take Exit 351 and head south (under the exit ramp). Go right at the sign for Angel Lake. Angel Lake campground is 12 miles away.

*Trip notes:* This relatively large campground set at the bottom of a sparsely vegetated cirque in the East Humboldt Range is popular with anglers in search of rainbow trout, as well as rowboaters, canoeists, hikers, and horseback riders. The lake is over a small rise and is not visible from the campsites. No motorboats are allowed on the water. The view east is of range upon range into the distance; Grey's Peak (10,674 feet) looms overhead. Hiking trails are unmaintained, but the Pole Canyon Trail, through alpine meadows, pasturelands, and aspen and pine forests, is nearby. The campground is at an elevation of 8,400 feet.

*Season:* Late June through September, depending on snowfall and snowmelt.

---

# 16. RYNDON CAMPGROUND

*Reference:* **Near Elko; map C3, grid e1.**

*Campsites, facilities:* There are 78 spaces for RVs, all with full hookups (30- and 50-amp receptacles) and all pull-throughs. Tent camping is available at 20 separate sites. Rest rooms have flush toilets and hot showers. Drinking water, a public phone, sewage disposal, laundry facilities, groceries, a recreation room, a heated swimming pool, and a full-service bar are available to campground visitors.

*Reservations, fee:* Reservations are accepted. The fee is $14.50 for tent camping and $16.50 to $18.50 for RVs, both with up to two people; additional people are $2. Noncampers can take showers for a $5 fee. Good Sam, AAA, and senior citizen discounts are offered.

*Contact:* Ryndon Campground, Box 1656, Elko, NV 89801; (702) 738-3448.

*Location:* From Elko, drive east on Interstate 80 and take exit 314 (Ryndon–Devils Gate), then drive one block on the frontage road to the RV park.

*Trip notes:* This RV resort is 13 miles east of the hustle and bustle of Elko, out in the desert a block from the interstate. The trout-and-bass-rich Humboldt River runs right through the property. The campground has a full-apparatus

---

playground for kids, along with volleyball, horseshoes, a putting green, a driving range, a swimming pool, video poker at the bar, and a fitness center.
*Season:* Open year-round.

## 17. DOUBLE DICE RV PARK

*Reference:* **In Elko; map C3, grid e1.**
*Campsites, facilities:* There are 140 spaces for RVs, all with full hookups (20-, 30-, and 50-amp receptacles); 55 are pull-throughs. Tent camping is allowed. Handicapped-accessible rest rooms have flush toilets and hot showers. Drinking water, a public phone, sewage disposal, and laundry facilities are available.
*Reservations, fee:* Reservations are recommended in the summer. The fees are $13 for tent camping and $20 per RV. Noncampers can take 20-minute showers for $3. Senior citizen and Good Sam discounts are offered.
*Contact:* Double Dice RV Park, 3730 East Idaho Street, Elko, NV 89801; (702) 738-5642.
*Location:* In Elko, take exit 303 off Interstate 80 and drive one block to Idaho Street. Go left (east) on Idaho Street and drive a little under a mile. Turn right into the park.
*Trip notes:* Set atop a hill in east Elko next door to the *Daily Free Press* newspaper offices, this full-scale urban RV park has its own bar and lounge, complete with video poker, slot machines, and sandwiches and burgers for sale. You can also catch the shuttle down the hill to town. Children can burn some energy at the playground here.
*Season:* Open year-round.

## 18. GOLD COUNTRY MOTOR INN AND RV PARK

*Reference:* **In Elko; map C3, grid e1.**
*Campsites, facilities:* There are 26 spaces for RVs, all 26 with full hookups (20-, 30-, and 50-amp receptacles). Rest rooms have flush toilets and hot showers. Drinking water, a public phone, sewage disposal, laundry facilities, and a heated swimming pool are available.
*Reservations, fee:* Reservations are recommended. The fee is $20 for up to two people and $2 for each additional person.
*Contact:* Best Western Gold Country Motor Inn, 2050 Idaho Street, Elko, NV 89801; (702) 738-8421 or (800) 621-1332.
*Location:* In Elko, take exit 303 off Interstate 80. Drive one block west on Idaho Street to the RV park.
*Trip notes:* Gold Country RV Park is right in the thick of the urban action at the east end of Elko, behind the motor inn. Inside the inn is a 24-hour coffee shop, fronted by slot and video poker machines. Across Idaho Street is the Red Lion, a full-scale casino with all table games, a buffet, a gourmet room, and a Las Vegas–style lounge. Take advantage of the swimming pool when weather permits (generally from Memorial Day through Labor Day).
*Season:* Open year-round.

# 19. CIMARRON WEST RV AND TRAILER PARK

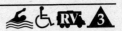

*Reference:* **In Elko; map C3, grid e1.**

*Campsites, facilities:* There are 12 spaces for RVs, all with full hookups (30-amp receptacles). (The RV park has a total of 73 spaces, but 61 are occupied by permanent residents.) No tent camping is allowed. There are handicapped-accessible rest rooms with flush toilets and hot showers. Drinking water, a public phone, sewage disposal, laundry facilities, a full-service mini-mart with an ice-cream parlor and slots, a 24-hour restaurant, video rentals, a gift store, a Texaco service station, and a drive-thru car wash are available.

*Reservations, fee:* Reservations are recommended. The fee is $16 for up to two people and $1 for each additional person.

*Contact:* Cimarron West RV Park, 1400 Mountain City Highway, Elko, NV 89801; (702) 738-8733.

*Location:* In Elko, take exit 301 off Interstate 80 and drive south for half a mile on Highway 225 to the RV park.

*Trip notes:* Elko is a busy little town and this is a busy little complex. It's just up the street from the airport and down the street from the Raley's shopping center. Accommodations are extremely tight in booming Elko (headquarters town for one of the largest gold mines in the world), and without reservations, especially in the summer, you might as well forget about staying here.

*Season:* Open year-round.

# 20. WENDOVER KOA

*Reference:* **In Wendover; map C3, grid f9.**

*Campsites, facilities:* There are 140 spaces for RVs, 72 with full hookups (30- and 50-amp receptacles); 85 are pull-throughs. Tent camping is allowed. Handicapped-accessible rest rooms have flush toilets and hot showers. Drinking water, a public phone, sewage disposal, laundry facilities, and a mini-mart and gift shop are available.

*Reservations, fee:* Reservations are recommended. The camping fee is $15 to $21 per vehicle. Noncampers can use the showers for $5. Good Sam and KOA discounts are offered.

*Contact:* Wendover KOA, 1250 Camper Drive (P.O. Box 2379), Wendover, NV 89883; (702) 664-3221.

*Location:* In West Wendover, take exit 410 off Interstate 80 to Wendover Boulevard, turn right, go approximately half a mile to Camper Drive, and turn left to the RV park.

*Trip notes:* This big, bustling RV park is on the southern edge of town, between the back door of the Red Garter Casino and the front door of the desert. A handy shuttle will pick you up and drop you off at the casino. Wendover KOA is the only place in town where you can pitch a tent. Proprietor Mike Cappa also rents a cabin that sleeps four for $22 from Sunday through Thursday and $27 a night on Friday and Saturday, but be sure to call ahead and make reservations far in advance for this great deal. Amenities at the camp-

ground include a heated swimming pool, a playground, tetherball, volleyball, horseshoes, and bike rentals.
*Season:* Open year-round.

---

## 21. STATELINE RV PARK

*Reference:* **In Wendover; map C3, grid f9.**
*Campsites, facilities:* There are 56 spaces for RVs, all with full hookups (20- and 30-amp receptacles). There are no pull-throughs. Tent camping is not allowed. Rest rooms have flush toilets and hot showers. Drinking water, a public phone, sewage disposal, and laundry facilities are available.
*Reservations, fee:* Reservations are recommended. The fee is $16 to $19 per vehicle. A 10-percent Good Sam discount is offered.
*Contact:* Stateline Hotel-Casino, P.O. Box 789, West Wendover, NV 89883; (702) 664-2221.
*Location:* In West Wendover, take exit 410 off Interstate 80, turn left on Wendover Boulevard, and drive one mile. Just across the Utah state line, turn right on First Street and continue for one block to the RV park.
*Trip notes:* Though in Utah, Stateline RV Park is connected to the Stateline casinos, just on the other side of the parking terrace. The park is graveled and has a few small trees. Overnighters get the use of the hotel's heated swimming pool and two tennis courts. Campers are also given the casino funbook and a discount coupon for the Wendover Golf Course. The Stateline has a dinner buffet, a gourmet restaurant, and a snack bar in the sports book, where sports bettors make their wagers and watch the games on TV monitors and large screens.
*Season:* Open year-round.

---

## 22. THOMAS CANYON

*Reference:* **In Humboldt National Forest, map C3, grid f2.**
*Campsites, facilities:* There are 17 campsites for tents or self-contained RVs up to 40 feet long. Piped drinking water, vault toilets, picnic tables, grills, and fire rings are provided. The closest commercial services are in Elko, nearly 30 miles northwest. Pets are permitted as long as they remain quiet, on leashes, or otherwise controlled. The maximum stay is 14 days.
*Reservations, fee:* Reservations are accepted. The fee is $6 per campsite.
*Contact:* Forest Supervisor, 976 Mountain City Highway, Elko, NV 89801; (702) 738-5171.
*Location:* From Elko, drive 20 miles southeast on Highway 227 to Lamoille. Turn right on Lamoille Canyon Byway and go eight miles to the campground.
*Trip notes:* Thomas Canyon, elevation 7,800 feet, is one of the most spectacularly set national forest campgrounds in Nevada. The glacial valley is surrounded by two rows of skyscraping outcrops and rugged ridges. At the terminus of the access road is a parking lot for the trailhead to the 40-mile Ruby Crest Trail. Thomas Creek flooded the campground in the spring of 1995, and the Forest Service hopes to have Loop A (seven sites) and Loop B (10 sites) reopened by sometime in 1997. Loop C (25 sites) is now and will

---

probably remain under water for the foreseeable future. Sites are well maintained and level, and there's plenty of vegetation for privacy.

*Season:* Late May through early September, depending on the weather.

## 23. SOUTH FORK STATE RECREATION AREA

*Reference:* **South of Elko; map C3, grid f1.**

*Campsites, facilities:* There are 25 campsites for tents or self-contained RVs up to 36 feet long. Piped drinking water, flush toilets, picnic tables, grills, and fire pits are provided. Pets are permitted as long as they remain quiet, on leashes, or otherwise controlled. The maximum stay is 14 days.

*Reservations, fee:* Reservations are accepted. The camping fee is $6.

*Contact:* South Fork State Recreation Area, Lower South Fork, HC 30 353-8, Elko, NV 89801; (702) 744-4346 or (702) 744-2010.

*Location:* From Elko, take Highway 227 southwest toward Lamoille. Seven miles from Elko, turn onto Highway 228 toward Jiggs. Drive 10 miles to the turnoff for the park and campground.

*Trip notes:* South Fork is the newest state recreation area, with power, water, and pavement completed in 1994. A 90-foot-high earthen dam on the South Fork River created the 40,000-acre-foot reservoir, which is stocked with rainbow and brown trout and black bass. Other popular activities include boating, waterskiing, and hiking.

*Season:* Open year-round, although access may be hampered by extreme weather in the off-season (November through May).

## 24. RUBY MARSH

*Reference:* **In Humboldt National Forest; map C3, grid h3.**

*Campsites, facilities:* There are 35 campsites for tents or self-contained RVs up to 22 feet long. Piped drinking water, vault toilets, picnic tables, grills, fire rings, and a fish-cleaning area are provided. A dump station is located across from the campground. Pets are permitted as long as they remain quiet, on leashes, or otherwise controlled. The maximum stay is 14 days.

*Reservations, fee:* Reservations are accepted. The fee is $6 per campsite.

*Contact:* Forest Supervisor, Humboldt National Forest, 976 Mountain City Highway, Elko, NV 89801; (702) 738-5171 or (702) 752-3357.

*Location:* From Elko, drive southeast seven miles on Highway 227 and turn right (south) on Highway 228. Go 30 miles until Highway 229's pavement runs out, then bear left. Drive 20 miles up and over the Ruby Mountains, then bear right at the junction for Ruby Lake National Wildlife Refuge and the campground.

*Trip notes:* This sparse campground is on a slight rise overlooking Ruby Lake, a freshwater bulrush marsh that hosts a large variety of birds, fish, and other critters. Boating and fishing for trout and bass keep campers busy.

*Season:* May through mid-October.

# LEAVE NO TRACE TIPS

**Travel and camp with care.**

*On the trail:*

• Stay on designated trails.

• Do not take shortcuts on switchbacks.

• When traveling cross-country where there are no trails,
follow animal trails or spread out your group so no new routes are created.
Walk along the most durable surfaces available,
such as rock, gravel, dry grasses, or snow.

• Use a map and compass to eliminate the need for
rock cairns, tree scars, or ribbons.

• If you encounter pack animals, step to the downhill side
of the trail and speak softly to avoid startling them.

*At camp:*

• Choose an established, legal site that will not be damaged by your stay.

• Restrict activities to areas where vegetation is compacted or absent.

• Keep pollutants out of the water by camping at least 200 feet
(about 70 adult steps) from lakes and streams.

• Control pets at all times, or leave them at home
with a sitter. Remove dog feces.

**MAP D1**

Map of Nevada ................ see page 256
Beyond This Region:
North (Map C1) ............... see page 258
East (Map D2) ................. see page 298
South ...................... California
West ...................... California

30 Campgrounds
Pages 282–297

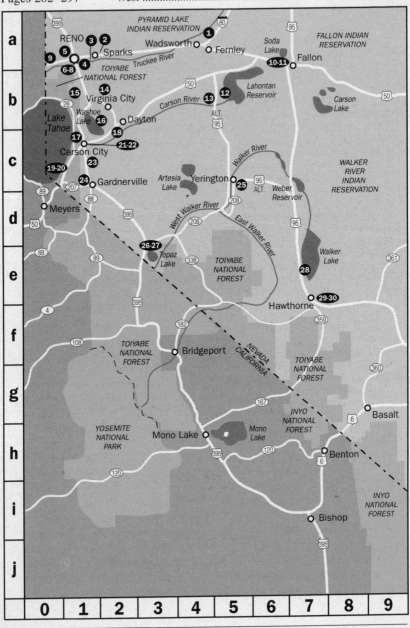

**Chapter D1 features:**

1. I-80 Campground
2. Victorian RV Park
3. River's Edge RV Park
4. Reno Hilton RV Camperland
5. Shamrock RV Park
6. Keystone RV Park
7. Chism's Trailer Park
8. Reno RV Park
9. Boomtown RV Park
10. Hub Totel RV Park
11. Fallon RV Park
12. Lahontan State Recreation Area
13. Fort Churchill Campground
14. Virginia City RV Park
15. Mt. Rose Campground
16. Washoe Lake State Recreation Area
17. Davis Creek County Park
18. Dayton State Park
19. Zephyr Cove RV Park
20. Nevada Beach Campground
21. Camp-N-Town RV Park
22. Comstock Country RV Resort
23. Silver City RV Park
24. Carson Valley RV Resort
25. Greenfield RV Park
26. Topaz Lodge RV Park
27. Topaz Lake Campground
28. Sportsman's Beach
29. Scotty's RV Park
30. Frontier Overnight RV Park

## 1. I-80 CAMPGROUND

*Reference:* **Near Wadsworth; map D1, grid a4.**

*Campsites, facilities:* There are 21 spaces for RVs, all with full hookups (20-, 30-, and 50-amp receptacles); all of these spaces are pull-throughs. Tents are allowed at the campground. Rest rooms have drinking water, flush toilets, and hot showers. A public phone, sewage disposal, and groceries are also available.

*Reservations, fee:* Reservations are accepted. The fees are $10 for tent camping and $15 for RVs.

*Contact:* I-80 Campground, Box 309, Wadsworth, NV 89442; (702) 575-2181.

*Location:* From Interstate 80, take exit 43 and drive under the bridge to reach the campground.

*Trip notes:* This is the sister RV park to the Pyramid Lake Marina (see page 260), both run by the Pyramid Lake Paiute and both on the Pyramid Lake Paiute Reservation. Opened in 1983, it's right off the interstate and has a gas station. The smoke shop sells Indian crafts.

*Season:* Open year-round.

## 2. VICTORIAN RV PARK

*Reference:* **In Sparks; map D1, grid a2.**

*Campsites, facilities:* There are 92 spaces for RVs, all with full hookups (30- and 50-amp receptacles); 46 of these pull-throughs. Tents are not allowed. Handicapped accessible rest rooms have drinking water, flush toilets, and hot showers; a public phone, sewage disposal, laundry facilities, groceries, and a heated swimming pool and spa are also available.

*Reservations, fee:* Reservations are accepted. The fee is $18 per vehicle. Good Sam, AAA, and AARP discounts are offered.

*Contact:* Victorian RV Park, 205 Nichols Boulevard, Sparks, NV 89431; (702) 355-4040 or (800) 955-6405.

*Location:* From Interstate 80 at Virginia Street in downtown Reno, drive east to exit 19 (McCarran Boulevard). Cross McCarran Boulevard and get on Victorian Avenue. Go west one block and turn right onto Nichols Boulevard. Drive half a block and turn right into the park.

*Trip notes:* This RV park is at the eastern edge of downtown Sparks's business district, right off Victorian Avenue (the main drag in Sparks). It's young, clean, and paved. RVers have access to the swimming pool and arcade across the street at the Thunderbird Resort.

*Season:* Open year-round.

## 3. RIVER'S EDGE RV PARK

*Reference:* **In Sparks; map D1, grid a1.**

*Campsites, facilities:* There are 164 spaces for RVs, all with full hookups (20-, 30-, and 50-amp receptacles); 98 of these are pull-throughs. Tents are not allowed. Rest rooms have drinking water, flush toilets, and hot showers; a public phone, sewage disposal, and laundry facilities are also available.

*Reservations, fee:* Reservations are accepted. The fee is $18 for two people, and $2 for each additional person. Good Sam and AAA discounts are offered.

*Contact:* River's Edge RV Park, 1405 South Rock Boulevard, Sparks, NV 89432; (702) 358-8533 or (800) 621-4792.

*Location:* From Interstate 80 at Virginia Street in downtown Reno, drive east to exit 17 (Rock Boulevard), then south 1.5 miles to the RV park, which is on the right.

*Trip notes:* This lush and well-shaded spot is an idyllic setting for an RV park, right on the Truckee River; you can fish for trout practically from your campsite. You also have direct access to many miles of paved riverside biking and hiking trails. A new owner took over in 1994 and is renovating everything. The RV park also happens to be right on the eastern landing route for Reno–Tahoe Airport, so big commercial airliners fly 300 feet overhead. But if you can stand an occasional jet engine or two, River's Edge is one of the nicer RV parks around.

*Season:* Open year-round.

## 4. RENO HILTON RV CAMPERLAND

*Reference:* **In Reno; map D1, grid a1.**

*Campsites, facilities:* There are 264 spaces for RVs, all with full hookups (20-, 30-, and 50-amp receptacles); 42 of these are pull-throughs. Tents are not allowed. Handicapped-accessible rest rooms have drinking water, flush toilets, and hot showers; a public phone, sewage disposal, laundry facilities, groceries, video rentals, and a heated swimming pool are also available. The stay limit is 28 days.

*Reservations, fee:* Reservations are accepted. The fee is $17 per vehicle.

*Contact:* Reno Hilton RV Camperland, 2500 East Second Street, Reno, NV 89595; (702) 789-2147 or (800) 648-5080.

*Location:* From Interstate 80 at Virginia Street in downtown Reno, drive east to U.S. 395. Go south on U.S. 395 for one mile. Take the Glendale Avenue exit and turn left (east). It's a half mile to the entrance of the hotel (right). The RV park is around on the north side of the hotel tower.

*Trip notes:* The largest hotel in northern Nevada also boasts the largest RV park. Expect parking-lot camping. Some sites overlook Hilton Bay, a square pond in the original gravel pit. Golfers line up on the edge of the pit and practice driving golf balls onto island-greens floating in the middle of the "bay." Like River's Edge RV Park (see page 284), this place is mighty close to the airport. But inside the Hilton is a veritable weekend's worth of attractions: a 100,000-square-foot casino, a race and sports book, an excellent buffet and four other restaurants, a Las Vegas–style floor show, a bowling alley, a shopping mall, a movie theater, and a huge arcade complete with bumper boats and an automated batting cage. Even if you don't camp here, the Reno Hilton is a must-see.

*Season:* Open year-round.

---

## 5. SHAMROCK RV PARK

*Reference:* In Reno; map D1, grid a1.

*Campsites, facilities:* There are 121 spaces for RVs, all with full hookups (30- and 50-amp receptacles); 75 of these are pull-throughs. Tents are not allowed. Handicapped-accessible rest rooms have drinking water, flush toilets, and hot showers; a public phone, sewage disposal, laundry facilities, groceries, a recreation room, a small playground, and a heated swimming pool are also available.

*Reservations, fee:* Reservations are accepted. The fee is $20 per vehicle. Good Sam discounts are offered.

*Contact:* Shamrock RV Park, 260 Parr Boulevard, Reno, NV 98512; call (702) 329-5222.

*Location:* From Interstate 80 heading east into Reno, take the Virginia Street exit and go left (north) about two miles to Parr Boulevard. Turn right on Parr Boulevard and drive down the hill; the park is on the right.

*Trip notes:* The Shamrock was new in 1985, but it's so clean you'd think it opened last week. It sits in a little depression, where the earthen walls separate it from its industrial neighborhood above. The camping area is big, all paved, and has trees and shrubs between wide sites. The rec hall has exercise equipment and a full kitchen. Two blocks away is the small but popular Bonanza Casino. A mile south is Rancho San Rafael Park, the largest park in the urban area, and two miles south of this is downtown Reno.

*Season:* Open year-round.

---

## 6. KEYSTONE RV PARK

*Reference:* In Reno; map D1, grid a1.

*Campsites, facilities:* There are 104 spaces for RVs, all with full hookups (30- and 50-amp receptacles); none of these are pull-throughs. Tents are not allowed. Handicapped-accessible rest rooms have drinking water, flush toilets,

---

and hot showers; a public phone, sewage disposal, and laundry facilities are also available.

*Reservations, fee:* Reservations are recommended during summer weekends and holidays. Campsites are $18. Good Sam discounts are offered.

*Contact:* Keystone RV Park, 1455 West Fourth Street, Reno, NV 89503; (702) 324-5000.

*Location:* From Interstate 80 heading west from Virginia Street in downtown Reno, go one exit to Keystone Street. Turn left (south) on Keystone and drive two blocks to Fourth Street. Turn right and drive two blocks to Keystone RV Park.

*Trip notes:* The Keystone is to Reno what the Victorian is to Sparks (see page 283). It's on the western edge of the downtown business district, within walking distance of plentiful fast food restaurants, a supermarket, an ice company, even a good bookstore. The front section opened in 1993; the back (which shares space with an 18-room motel) opened in 1992. It is parking lot camping, with a few trees and a little grass. The casinos are about eight blocks away, so the Keystone fills up fast for the nonstop events in Reno between Memorial Day and Labor Day, such as the State Fair, the Reno Rodeo, Hot August Nights, and the Balloon Races.

*Season:* Open year-round.

---

## 7. CHISM'S TRAILER PARK    ♿ 🚐 ▲ 5

*Reference:* **In Reno; map D1, grid a1.**

*Campsites, facilities:* There are a total of 152 spaces, but only 28 are for RVs; all 28 of these have full hookups (20-, 30-, and 50-amp receptacles) and six of these are pull-throughs. Tents are allowed. Handicapped-accessible rest rooms have drinking water, flush toilets, and hot showers; a public phone, sewage disposal, and laundry facilities are also available.

*Reservations, fee:* Reservations are recommended. The fee is $15 per vehicle.

*Contact:* Chism's Trailer Park, 1300 West Second Street, Reno, NV 89504; (702) 322-2281 or (800) 638-2281.

*Location:* From Interstate 80 heading west from Virginia Street in downtown Reno, go one exit to Keystone Street. Turn south on Keystone and drive four blocks to Second Street. Turn right and drive five blocks to the RV park, which is on the left.

*Trip notes:* Chism's is the oldest private campground in Nevada, having opened along the Truckee River just west of downtown in 1926. It's certainly the shadiest, with towering trees and lush landscaping. A lot of the park is occupied by permanent mobiles, but there are enough overnight sites to make it worth checking out. Also, it's the closest place to downtown to pitch a tent.

*Season:* Open year-round.

---

## 8. RENO RV PARK    ♿ 🚐 ▲ 2

*Reference:* **In Reno; map D1, grid a1.**

*Campsites, facilities:* There are 46 spaces for RVs, all with full hookups (20- and 30-amp receptacles); none of these are pull-throughs. Tents are not

---

allowed. Handicapped-accessible rest rooms have drinking water, flush toilets, and hot showers; a public phone, sewage disposal, and laundry facilities are available.

*Reservations, fee:* Reservations are recommended for weekends during the summer. The fee is $19 for two people, and $2 for each additional person. Good Sam and AAA discounts are offered.

*Contact:* Reno RV Park, 735 Mill Street, Reno, NV 89502; (702) 323-3381 or (800) 445-3381.

*Location:* From Interstate 80 heading east from Virginia Street in downtown Reno, take the Wells exit (exit 14) and drive south for a little less than a mile to Mill Street. Turn left on Mill Street and drive three blocks to the park, which is on the left.

*Trip notes:* This RV park consists of four rows of parking (all narrow back-in sites) off of two narrow alleys. The park's been here since 1984 and it's still the closest to downtown Reno. It's located in an older part of town: hospitals, medical offices, and the police station are all nearby. Security is beefy, with a high wall and gates in and out. Harrah's sends its shuttle around Fridays through Mondays.

*Season:* Open year-round.

## 9. BOOMTOWN RV PARK

*Reference:* In Reno; map D1, grid a1.

*Campsites, facilities:* There are 203 spaces for RVs, all with full hookups (20-, 30-, and 50-amp receptacles); 132 of these are pull-throughs. Tents are not allowed. Handicapped-accessible rest rooms have drinking water, flush toilets, and hot showers. Other amenities include a public phone, sewage disposal, laundry facilities, groceries, video rentals, a heated swimming pool, and two spas.

*Reservations, fee:* Reservations are recommended. The fee is $14 to $15 for two people, and $1 for each additional person. Good Sam and AARP discounts are offered.

*Contact:* Boomtown Hotel-Casino and RV Park, P.O. Box 399, Verdi, NV 89439; (702) 345-8650 or (800) 648-3790.

*Location:* From Reno, drive seven miles west on Interstate 80 and take the Garson Road exit (exit 4). The RV park is down the hill a half block behind the casino.

*Trip notes:* Like Reno Hilton RV Camperland (see page 284), Boomtown RV Park is its own destination. The park itself is a large self-contained area located below the casino, with wide RV parking spaces, some greenery, and its own swimming pool. You'll never lack for knowing the time, with the Boomtown clock tower looming high overhead. Inside the hotel is the Family Fun Center, featuring an 18-hole indoor miniature golf course, an antique carousel, a motion-simulation theater (the only one of its kind in northern Nevada), and video games galore. There is also a steakhouse, buffet, and 24-hour coffee shop.

*Season:* Open year-round.

## 10. HUB TOTEL RV PARK

*Reference:* In Fallon; map D1, grid a6.

*Campsites, facilities:* There are 44 spaces for RVs, all with full hookups (30- and 50-amp receptacles); all of these are pull-throughs. Tents are allowed. Rest rooms have drinking water, flush toilets, and hot showers; a public phone, sewage disposal, laundry facilities, and a recreation room with a pool table are also available.

*Reservations, fee:* Reservations are accepted. The fees are $10 for tents and $14 for RVs.

*Contact:* Hub Totel RV Park, 4800 U.S. 50, Fallon, NV 89406; (702) 867-3636.

*Location:* From the intersection of U.S. 95 and U.S. 50 in downtown Fallon, drive four miles west on U.S. 50 and turn left into the RV park.

*Trip notes:* Hub Totel (which isn't a play on Tub Hotel, by the way; the "Hub" refers to wheels and "Totel" is a contraction of Towing Motel) is right on the main drag just west of downtown Fallon. Mostly it's open parking-lot camping with the highway running by. Fallon is a good-sized town (for Nevada) where the main business is the Naval Air Station with its Top Gun fighter pilot school.

*Season:* Open year-round.

## 11. FALLON RV PARK

*Reference:* In Fallon; map D1, grid a7.

*Campsites, facilities:* There are 44 spaces for RVs, all with full hookups (30- and 50-amp receptacles); 20 of these are pull-throughs. Tents are allowed (there's one site). Rest rooms have drinking water, flush toilets, and hot showers; a public phone, sewage disposal, laundry facilities, groceries, a deli, a gas station, a recreation room, and a playground are also available.

*Reservations, fee:* Reservations are accepted. RV sites are $16 to $18, and tent sites are $10.

*Contact:* Fallon RV Park, 5787 U.S. 50, Fallon, NV 89406; (702) 867-2332.

*Location:* From the intersection of U.S. 95 and U.S. 50 in downtown Fallon, drive six miles west on U.S. 50 and turn left into the RV park.

*Trip notes:* This is the "Coke" RV park west of Fallon on U.S. 50 to the Hub Totel's "Pepsi" (see above); we're talking competition. Of the two, this is the nicer. The trees are larger, the grass is greener, and the spaces are wider. But it costs a couple of dollars more.

*Season:* Open year-round.

## 12. LAHONTAN STATE RECREATION AREA

*Reference:* Near Fallon; map D1, grid b5.

*Campsites, facilities:* There are 40 campsites for tents or self-contained RVs up to 30 feet long. Piped drinking water, flush toilets, showers, picnic tables, grills, and fire pits are provided. Pets are permitted as long as they remain quiet, on leashes, or otherwise controlled. The maximum stay is 14 days.

*Reservations, fee:* No reservations are accepted. The fee is $7 to camp (plus a $1 annual water-quality fee).

*Contact:* Park Headquarters, 16799 Lahontan Dam, Fallon, NV 89406, (702) 867-3500; or Silver Springs Ranger Station, (702) 577-2226.

*Location:* From the intersection of Alt. U.S. 95 and U.S. 50 at Silver Springs, drive south on Alt. U.S. 95 for three miles, turn left (east) on Fir Street, and continue 1.5 miles to the entrance to the park.

*Trip notes:* Lake Lahontan, elevation 4,200 feet, is a reservoir for the Truckee-Carson Irrigation District, the nation's original federal reclamations project. When full it has 70 miles of shoreline. Recreation here involves boating, fishing, and swimming at one of a dozen beaches. Open camping is allowed all the way around the lake. The improved campsites with the above amenities are found only here on the west side of the reservoir.

*Season:* Open year-round.

## 13. FORT CHURCHILL CAMPGROUND

*Reference:* **In Fort Churchill State Historic Park; map D1, grid b4.**

*Campsites, facilities:* There are 20 campsites for tents or self-contained RVs up to 24 feet long. Piped drinking water, vault toilets, sewage disposal, picnic tables, grills, and fire pits are provided. The nearest commercial services are in Silver Springs, eight miles north. Pets are permitted as long as they remain quiet, on leashes, or otherwise controlled. The maximum stay is 14 days.

*Reservations, fee:* No reservations are accepted. The fee is $7 per site.

*Contact:* Fort Churchill State Historic Park Headquarters, Silver Springs, NV 89429; (702) 577-2345.

*Location:* From the junction of U.S. 50 and Alt. U.S. 95 at Silver Springs, drive eight miles south on Alt. U.S. 95 and turn left into Fort Churchill State Historical Monument. Take the loop road around the ruins, and turn left into the campground.

*Trip notes:* This is one idyllic little campground, on bottomland that used to be the Bucklands Ranch just north of the Carson River. The trees here are as tall and full as in any campground in the state. The Army base ruins are a short stroll away, and a visitors center displays military, Pony Express, transcontinental telegraph, and Paiute history.

*Season:* Open year-round.

## 14. VIRGINIA CITY RV PARK

*Reference:* **In Virginia City; map D1, grid b2.**

*Campsites, facilities:* There are 50 spaces for RVs, all with full hookups (20-, 30-, and 50-amp receptacles); two of these are pull-throughs. Tents are allowed. Handicapped-accessible rest rooms have drinking water, flush toilets, and hot showers; a public phone, sewage disposal, laundry facilities, and groceries are also available.

*Reservations, fee:* Reservations are recommended all summer long. The fees are $8 for tents and $19 for RVs with two people, and $2 for each additional person. AAA and Good Sam discounts are offered.

*Contact:* Virginia City RV Park, Carson and F Streets, Virginia City, NV 89440; (702) 847-0999 or (800) 889-1240.

*Location:* From Reno, drive eight miles south on U.S. 395 and head east on Highway 341. Drive 14 miles to Virginia City. At Carson Street on the north side of town, turn left and drive three blocks to F Street and Virginia City RV Park.

*Trip notes:* This is one of the premier RV parks in Nevada—large, clean, and well run—in one of Nevada's premier tourist destinations. The bathrooms were recently remodeled, and the showers have individual dressing rooms. The spaces are wide and some are on the bluff overlooking the pioneer cemetery. The town park, with a pool and tennis courts, is right across the street. The RV park's market is large and sells gifts. Downtown Virginia City is a mere four-block walk.

*Season:* Open year-round.

---

## 15. MT. ROSE CAMPGROUND

*Reference:* **Toiyabe National Forest; map D1, grid b1.**

*Campsites, facilities:* There are 24 campsites for tents or self-contained RVs up to 16 feet long. Piped drinking water, flush toilets, picnic tables, grills, and fire rings are provided. The nearest commercial services are eight miles west in Incline Village. Pets are permitted as long as they remain quiet, on leashes, or otherwise controlled. The maximum stay is 14 days.

*Reservations, fee:* Reservations are accepted for some sites; call MISTIX at (800) 280-2267. Campsites are $7.

*Contact:* Carson Ranger District, 1536 South Carson Street, Carson City, NV 89701; (702) 882-2766.

*Location:* From Incline Village, drive eight miles uphill on Highway 431. The campground is on the right just before Mt. Rose summit.

*Trip notes:* Highway 431 is the route between Reno and the north shore of Lake Tahoe; it climbs to just under 9,000 feet. (It's the highest road over the Sierra that's kept open year-round.) The campground is at the summit, in a beautiful wooded mountain bowl. It's always 15 to 20 degrees cooler up here than it is in Reno or Carson. The trailhead to the peak of Mount Rose is by the maintenance shed on the other side of the highway.

*Season:* Open Memorial Day to Labor Day, depending on snow conditions.

---

## 16. WASHOE LAKE STATE RECREATION AREA

*Reference:* **In Washoe Valley; map D1, grid b2.**

*Campsites, facilities:* There are 49 campsites for tents or self-contained RVs up to 40 feet; 10 of these are pull-throughs. Piped drinking water, flush toilets, hot showers, picnic tables, grills, and fire rings are provided. The nearest commercial services are 12 miles south in Carson City. Pets are permitted as long as they remain quiet, on leashes, or otherwise controlled. The maximum stay is 14 days.

*Reservations, fee:* No reservations are accepted. The fee is $7 per campsite.

---

*Contact:* Washoe Lake State Recreation Area, 4855 Eastlake Boulevard, Carson City, NV 89701; (702) 687-4319.

*Location:* From Carson City, drive north on U.S. 395 for four miles. Bear right onto Highway 428 and drive eight miles to the park.

*Trip notes:* Washoe Lake reverted to playa during the eight-year drought between 1986 and 1994. The wet winters of 1995 and 1996 turned it back into a lake. The campground is just up from the lakeshore, where there's a small beach and a pier for boating and fishing. It's mostly open camping, but the view across the lake at the valley, foothills, and sheer eastern scarp of the Sierra is stunning. The elevation is 5,000 feet.

*Season:* Open year-round.

---

## 17. DAVIS CREEK COUNTY PARK

*Reference:* **Near Carson City; map D1, grid c1.**

*Campsites, facilities:* There are 63 campsites for tents or self-contained RVs up to 40 feet long; 19 of these are pull-throughs. Piped drinking water, flush toilets, showers, sewage disposal, picnic tables, grills, and fire pits are provided. The nearest commercial services are 11 miles south in Carson City. Pets are permitted as long as they remain quiet, on leashes, or otherwise controlled. The maximum stay is seven days.

*Reservations, fee:* No reservations are accepted. The fee is $10 per site.

*Contact:* Davis Creek County Park Headquarters, 25 Davis Creek Road, Carson City, NV 89704; (702) 849-0684.

*Location:* From Carson City, drive three miles north on U.S. 395 to Eastlake Boulevard and exit left onto old U.S. 395. Drive 6.5 miles to the park, which is on the left.

*Trip notes:* One of two county parks in Nevada with a campground (also see Topaz Lake Campground on page 296), this is a prime spot to spend some quality outdoor time. Both campground loops are in the trees of the Sierra foothills; the first loop is open year-round. Trails crisscross the park; a Forest Service trail climbs six miles up to Tahoe Meadows. A pond is stocked with rainbow trout and is used for ice skating in the winter. Just down the road a piece is Bowers Mansion County Park, with a historical house, a huge picnic area and playground, and a big swimming pool. The campground is at an elevation of 5,100 feet.

*Season:* Open year-round.

---

## 18. DAYTON STATE PARK

*Reference:* **Near Dayton, map D1, grid c2.**

*Campsites, facilities:* There are 10 campsites for tents or self-contained RVs up to 20 feet. Piped drinking water, flush toilets, picnic tables, grills, and fire rings are provided by the park. Pets are permitted as long as they remain quiet, on leashes, or otherwise controlled. The maximum stay within Dayton State Park is seven days.

*Reservations, fee:* No reservations are accepted. The fee is $5 per site.

*Contact:* Dayton State Park, Box 1478, Dayton, NV 89403; (702) 885-5678.

---

*Location:* From Dayton, drive four miles east on U.S. 50. The park is on the right (south) side of the road.

*Trip notes:* This is a small, quiet, partially shaded campground on the north bank of the Carson River. There's a campground host in the summer. One trail runs across an irrigation ditch to the river. Another goes under the highway to the ruins of an old stamp mill that dates back to the 1860s, when large stamp mills lined the river hereabouts, processing Comstock Lode ore.

*Season:* Open year-round.

## 19. ZEPHYR COVE RV PARK

*Reference:* In Toiyabe National Forest; map D1, grid c1.

*Campsites, facilities:* There are 100 spaces for RVs, all with full hookups (30-amp receptacles); seven of these are pull-throughs. There are 75 tent sites. Rest rooms have drinking water, flush toilets, and hot showers; a public phone, sewage disposal, and laundry facilities are also available at the park.

*Reservations, fee:* Reservations are recommended during the summer, especially on weekends. Camping fees for tents are $15 for up to four people and $23 for RVs with up to four people, plus $2 for each additional person.

*Contact:* Zephyr Cove RV Park, P.O. Box 830, Zephyr Cove, NV 89448; (702) 588-6644.

*Location:* From the intersection of U.S. 50 and Highway 207 at Kingsbury Grade north of Stateline, drive three miles north on U.S. 50 and turn right into the campground.

*Trip notes:* The RV park is rustic, under the trees at 6,200 feet, and sprawling—the largest at Tahoe on the Nevada side. The resort across the road has at least a week's worth of activities: swimming and sunbathing on a long sandy beach; canoe, Jet Ski, motorboat, and pedalboat rentals; waterskiing, fishing, parasailing, and horseback riding; cruising on the sternwheeler MS *Dixie II* and sailing on the *Whirlwind*. A snack shop and bar and grill overlook the pier. A free shuttle runs between the resort and the casinos at Stateline four miles away.

*Season:* Open year-round, depending on snow conditions.

## 20. NEVADA BEACH CAMPGROUND

*Reference:* In Toiyabe National Forest; map D1, grid c1.

*Campsites, facilities:* There are 54 campsites for tents or self-contained RVs up to 24 feet long. Piped drinking water, flush toilets, picnic tables, grills, and fire pits are provided. There is a campground host. Pets are permitted as long as they remain quiet, on leashes, or otherwise controlled. The maximum stay is 14 days.

*Reservations, fee:* Reservations are recommended. The fee is $16 per campsite.

*Contact:* For reservations, contact Biospherics at (800) 280-2267; for information about the campground, contact Tahoe Basin Management Unit, (916) 573-2600.

*Location:* From the intersection of U.S. 50 and Highway 207 at Kingsbury Grade north of Stateline, drive three miles north on U.S. 50. Turn left at Elk Point Road and drive a mile to Nevada Beach.

*Trip notes:* One of the most popular beaches and campgrounds on Lake Tahoe, this place fills up fast. Make reservations as far in advance as possible (up to 120 days) or try your luck between 9 A.M. and noon for a vacant site (see the host to pay for first come, first served sites). The campground, located at 6,200 feet and under the trees, is shared equally by tenters and RVers. The beach is a two-minute walk from most sites. Lake Tahoe warms up to a bracing 68 degrees on the surface the last week in July—eye-opening! But be careful of numbness and hypothermia, strong currents, deceptive depths and distances, and Tahoe Tessie, the local lake monster.

*Season:* Open from May through October.

---

## 21. CAMP-N-TOWN RV PARK

*Reference:* In Carson City; map D1, grid c1.

*Campsites, facilities:* There are 74 spaces for RVs, all with full hookups (20- and 30-amp receptacles); 38 of these are pull-throughs. Tents are allowed. Rest rooms have drinking water, flush toilets, and hot showers; a public phone, sewage disposal, laundry facilities, groceries, a game room, a bar, and a heated swimming pool are also available.

*Reservations, fee:* Reservations are recommended for summer weekends. The fee is $18 a campsite for two people, plus $2 for each additional person.

*Contact:* Camp-N-Town RV Park, 2438 North Carson Street (U.S. 395), Carson City, NV 89706; (702) 883-1123 or (800) 872-1123.

*Location:* From the downtown Carson City intersection of U.S. 50 and U.S. 395, go north on U.S. 395 for half a mile and turn left into the park.

*Trip notes:* Camp-N-Town is aptly named: it's right in downtown Carson City, a 15-minute stroll to the capitol, state museum, and casinos, and across the street from a large shopping center. It's atypically quiet for such a central location, behind the 49er Motel, but typically crowded. And it's shaded by the tall trees that help give downtown Carson its charm.

*Season:* Open year-round.

---

## 22. COMSTOCK COUNTRY RV RESORT

*Reference:* In Carson City; map D1, grid c1.

*Campsites, facilities:* Comstock Country Resort offers 163 spaces for RVs, all with full hookups (20-, 30-, and 50-amp receptacles); 133 of these are pull-throughs. Tents are allowed. Rest rooms have drinking water, flush toilets, and hot showers. Other amenities include a public phone, a sewage disposal site, laundry facilities, groceries, a game room, and a heated swimming pool and spa.

*Reservations, fee:* Reservations are accepted. The fee is $20 a campsite for two people, and $2 for each additional person.

*Contact:* Comstock Country RV Resort, 5400 South Carson Street (U.S. 395), Carson City, NV 89701; (702) 882-2445.

---

*Location:* Drive south on U.S. 395 through Carson City and pass the turnoff onto U.S. 50 west to Lake Tahoe. The RV park is just past the U.S. 50 intersection on the right.

*Trip notes:* This bustling RV park enclosed by a wood fence is in a terrific location. You can drive 30 minutes up the hill to Lake Tahoe, five minutes to the capitol, 15 minutes to Genoa and Carson Valley, or just laze around in the shade of Comstock Country.

*Season:* Open year-round.

## 23. SILVER CITY RV PARK

*Reference:* **Near Minden; map D1, grid c1.**

*Campsites, facilities:* There are 100 spaces for RVs, all with full hookups (20-, 30-, and 50-amp receptacles); 80 of these are pull-throughs. Tents are not allowed. Rest rooms have drinking water, flush toilets, and hot showers; a public phone, sewage disposal, laundry facilities, groceries, a game room, and a playground are also available.

*Reservations, fee:* Reservations are accepted. Campsites are $16 to $17. Good Sam discounts are available.

*Contact:* Silver City RV Park, 3165 U.S. 395, Minden, NV 89423; call (702) 267-3359.

*Location:* From the intersection of U.S. 395 and U.S. 50 (to Lake Tahoe), drive four miles south to the park, which is on the left.

*Trip notes:* Carson Valley is a beautiful pastoral place south of the urban hubbub of Reno and Carson City—the sheer Sierra to the west, the Washoe tribe's sacred Pine Nuts to the east, and green alfalfa fields dotted with cottonwoods and cattle all around. Silver City RV park is right in the middle of it.

*Season:* Open year-round.

## 24. CARSON VALLEY RV RESORT

*Reference:* **In Gardnerville; map D1, grid c1.**

*Campsites, facilities:* There are 59 spaces for RVs, all with full hookups (20-, 30-, and 50-amp receptacles); 26 of these are pull-throughs. Tents are not allowed. Handicapped-accessible rest rooms have drinking water, flush toilets, and hot showers; a public phone, sewage disposal, laundry facilities, groceries, and gas are available. The stay limit is 14 days during the summer months.

*Reservations, fee:* Reservations are accepted. Campsites are $16. Good Sam, AAA, and seniors-over-50 discounts are available.

*Contact:* Carson Valley RV Resort, 1627 U.S. 395, Minden, NV 89423; (702) 782-9711 or (800) 321-6983.

*Location:* From the intersection of U.S. 395 and Highway 88 just north of downtown Minden, drive south one mile on U.S. 395 and turn left into the RV park.

*Trip notes:* Carson Valley Inn is the major action in Minden: casino, hotel, motel, restaurants, wedding chapel, convenience store, arcade, and two spas. The RV park occupies one of the parking lots. Though it's town camping,

---

it's surprisingly quiet for being so close to the highway, and most sites have a grassy area.

*Season:* Open year-round.

---

# 25. GREENFIELD RV PARK

*Reference:* **In Yerington; map D1, grid c5.**

*Campsites, facilities:* There are 40 spaces for RVs, 24 with full hookups (20-, 30-, and 50-amp receptacles); all 40 are pull-throughs. Tents are allowed in the separate grassy area next to the laundry facilities. The rest rooms have drinking water, flush toilets, and hot showers; a public phone, sewage disposal, and laundry facilities are also available.

*Reservations, fee:* Reservations are accepted. Tent sites are $8 and RV sites are $15. Good Sam discounts are available.

*Contact:* Greenfield RV Park, 500 West Goldfield Avenue, Yerington, NV 89447; (702) 463-4912.

*Location:* Traveling south on Alt. U.S. 95 into Yerington, take a left at the intersection of Highway 208 onto Goldfield Avenue, and drive five blocks. The park is on the left.

*Trip notes:* Greenfield RV Park only opened in 1993, so there are young trees and new grass at every site. A new mobile home park abuts. Dairy Queen is next door, the new Warehouse Supermarket is across the street, and downtown Yerington is a short walk away.

*Season:* Open year-round.

---

# 26. TOPAZ LODGE RV PARK

*Reference:* **On Topaz Lake; map D1, grid e3.**

*Campsites, facilities:* There are 36 spaces for RVs, all with full hookups (30-amp receptacles); six of the spaces are pull-throughs. Tents are not allowed. Handicapped-accessible rest rooms have drinking water, flush toilets, and hot showers; a public phone, sewage disposal, groceries, and a heated swimming pool are available.

*Reservations, fee:* Reservations are recommended for summer. Campsites are $15 a night.

*Contact:* Topaz Lodge, 1979 U.S. 395 South, Gardnerville, NV 89410; (702) 266-3337 or (800) 862-0732.

*Location:* From Gardnerville, drive 19 miles south on U.S. 395. Pass the junction with Highway 208, drive one mile south on U.S. 395, and turn left into the RV park.

*Trip notes:* Next to Topaz Lodge (full-service casino, 24-hour coffee shop, and buffet), this RV park sits on a bluff right off the highway a half mile from Topaz Lake. Campsites are wide and a bit exposed. The reservoir was created in the early 1920s when the west fork of the Walker River was dammed. It's a beautiful treeless desert lake, right at the base of the eastern Sierra and at the head of Antelope Valley, one of the most pastoral scenes in the vicinity. Recreation on the lake includes swimming, boating, waterskiing, and

---

fishing for trout (check out the five-pound browns and seven-pound rainbows in the Shell station).

*Season:* Open year-round.

---

## 27. TOPAZ LAKE CAMPGROUND

*Reference:* **On Topaz Lake; map D1, grid e3.**

*Campsites, facilities:* There are 140 campsites for tents or RVs up to 35 feet long, 29 with water and electric hookups; 13 of the sites are pull-throughs. Piped drinking water, flush toilets and showers, a sewage disposal site, picnic tables, barbecue grills, and fire rings are provided. Pets are permitted as long as they remain quiet, on leashes, or otherwise controlled. The maximum stay is 14 days.

*Reservations, fee:* No reservations are accepted. Campsites are $8 to $10 a night.

*Contact:* Topaz Lake Park, 3700 Topaz Park Road, Gardnerville, NV 89410; (702) 266-3343.

*Location:* From Gardnerville, drive 19 miles south on U.S. 395. Pass the junction with Highway 208 and drive one more mile south on U.S. 395. At the sign for the campground, turn left and drive one mile (the last little bit is dirt) to the campground.

*Trip notes:* Topaz Lake Campground is the second of Nevada's two county parks with a campground (see Davis Creek County Park on page 291). This is a big spot, and it provides a mile of beachfront. After the ferocious winters of 1995 and 1996, the tent camping sites are right at the water on a sandy beach. The RV sites are found up the slope a little, and there's a grassy playground for the kids.

*Season:* Open year-round.

---

## 28. SPORTSMAN'S BEACH

*Reference:* **Near Hawthorne; map D1, grid e7.**

*Campsites, facilities:* There are 17 campsites for tents or self-contained RVs up to 30 feet in length. Vault toilets, picnic tables under shelters, grills, and fire pits are all provided for the use of visitors. Pets are permitted as long as they remain quiet, on leashes, or otherwise controlled. The maximum stay is 14 days.

*Reservations, fee:* No reservations are accepted. This campground is free.

*Contact:* Carson City Bureau of Land Management District Office, 1535 Hot Springs Road, Carson City, NV 89706; (702) 885-6000.

*Location:* From Hawthorne, drive 15 miles north on U.S. 95, and turn right into the campground.

*Trip notes:* The most accessible Bureau of Land Management campground in Nevada, Sportsman's Beach is a sparse, primitive camping area on the western shore of Walker Lake. The main amenity and the only shade are the shelters above the picnic tables. There's open camping right on the beach near the boat ramp.

*Season:* Open year-round.

---

Map of Nevada—Page 256

## 29. SCOTTY'S RV PARK

*Reference:* **In Hawthorne; map D1, grid e7.**

*Campsites, facilities:* There are 14 spaces for RVs, all with full hookups (20-, 30-, and 50-amp receptacles); 12 are pull-throughs. Tents are allowed. Rest rooms have drinking water, flush toilets, and hot showers; a public phone, sewage disposal, laundry facilities, and groceries are also available.

*Reservations, fee:* Reservations are accepted. Campsites are $12.50 a night per vehicle.

*Contact:* Scotty's RV Park, Fifth and J Streets, Hawthorne, NV 89415; (702) 945-2079.

*Location:* Driving south on U.S. 95 into Hawthorne, turn left at the traffic light at the main intersection in downtown Hawthorne (Fifth and E Streets). Continue four blocks and turn left into the park.

*Trip notes:* Two RV parks are within a block of each other here at the south end of downtown Hawthorne. Scotty's is younger and smaller than the Frontier (see below), but has the convenience store. If you're wondering about the thousands of concrete bunkers and pillboxes surrounding Hawthorne, the Army stores a bunch of bombs, bullets, grenades, mortars, and the like in them.

*Season:* Open year-round.

## 30. FRONTIER OVERNIGHT RV PARK

*Reference:* **In Hawthorne; map D1, grid e7.**

*Campsites, facilities:* There are 27 spaces for RVs, all with full hookups (20-, 30-, and 50-amp receptacles); all are pull-throughs. Tents are allowed. Rest rooms have drinking water, flush toilets, and hot showers; a public phone, sewage disposal, and laundry facilities are also available.

*Reservations, fee:* Reservations are accepted. Campsites are $11 a night.

*Contact:* Frontier Overnight RV Park, Fifth and L Streets, Hawthorne, NV 89415; (702) 945-2733.

*Location:* Driving south on U.S. 95, turn left at the traffic light in downtown Hawthorne (Fifth and E Streets). Continue five blocks and turn into the park on the left.

*Trip notes:* The Frontier has been here right on the highway in town since 1977. It's got some trees and fairly wide spaces, and is within walking distance of the El Capitan, Hawthorne's venerable casino.

*Season:* Open year-round.

# MAP D2

Map of Nevada .................. see page 256
Beyond This Region:
North (Map C2) ................. see page 262
East (Map D3) ................... see page 304
South (Map E2) ................. see page 314
West (Map D1) .................. see page 282

9 Campgrounds
Pages 298–303

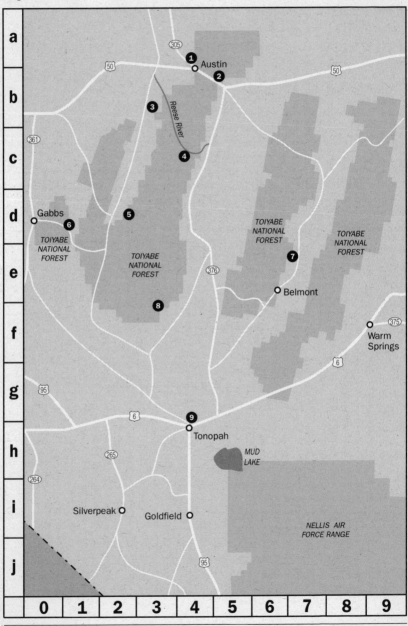

**Chapter D2 features:**

1. Austin RV Park
2. Bob Scott Campground
3. Big Creek Campground
4. Kingston Campground
5. Columbine Campground
6. Berlin-Ichthyosaur State Park Campground
7. Peavine Campground
8. Pine Creek Campground
9. Station House RV Park

# 1. AUSTIN RV PARK

*Reference:* **In Austin; map D2, grid a4.**

*Campsites, facilities:* There are 26 spaces for RVs, 24 with full hookups (30-amp receptacles). Tent campers can use the large grassy area. Rest rooms have drinking water, flush toilets, and hot showers. A public phone, sewage disposal, and laundry facilities are available.

*Reservations, fee:* Reservations are accepted. Sites are $10 for tent camping and $15 for RVs.

*Contact:* Austin RV Park, P.O. Box 173, Austin, NV 89310; (702) 964-1011.

*Location:* From the eastern side of Austin on U.S. 50, look for the campground sign. Turn north and the campground is up a small hill just above Main Street.

*Trip notes:* This RV park, set at an elevation of 6,900 feet, is the only one in Nevada that's connected to a Baptist church. The minister's wife, Donna White, leases the parking lot RV park from the church (there are too many potential conflicts for the church to be in the campground business). The RV office doubles as the Sunday school. Fee collecting is somewhat on the honor system (read the signs on the information boards and drop the night's payment in the drop box inside the Sunday school building). Mrs. White will come around at some point to see that everything is right and proper. Just down the hill on Main Street is the Gridley Store, still standing 135 years after it was built.

*Season:* Open year-round.

# 2. BOB SCOTT CAMPGROUND

*Reference:* **Near Austin in Toiyabe National Forest; map D2, grid b5.**

*Campsites, facilities:* There are 10 campsites for tents or self-contained RVs up to 20 feet long. Flush toilets, picnic tables, grills, and fire rings are provided. *No drinking water* is available. Pets are permitted as long as they remain quiet, on leashes, or otherwise controlled. The maximum stay is 14 days.

*Reservations, fee:* No reservations are accepted. Campsites are free.

*Contact:* Austin Ranger District, Box 130, Austin, NV 89310; (702) 964-2671.

*Location:* From Austin, drive east on U.S. 50 roughly 10 miles to the campground, which is right off the highway.

*Trip notes:* Bob Scott is a high-mountain campground (elevation 7,200 feet) set in the pinyon- and juniper-covered northern tip of the mighty Toiyabe Mountains. The campsites are shady and private. The Forest Service hopes to be able to provide drinking water in the near future; it's free to camp while there's no water. Sidetrips abound: Big Smoky Valley (the turnoff to

this scenic valley is three miles east), Hickison Petroglyph Recreation Area (seven miles east), and Spencer Hot Springs (six miles southeast).
*Season:* Mid-May through October.

## 3. BIG CREEK CAMPGROUND

*Reference:* In Toiyabe National Forest; map D2, grid b3.

*Campsites, facilities:* There are eight campsites for tents or self-contained RVs up to 20 feet long. Vault toilets, picnic tables, grills, and fire rings are provided. There is *no drinking water.* Pets are permitted as long as they remain quiet, on leashes, or otherwise controlled. The maximum stay is 14 days.

*Reservations, fee:* No reservations are accepted. Campsites are free.

*Contact:* Austin Ranger District Office, P.O. Box 130, Austin, NV 89310; (702) 964-2671.

*Location:* Drive 15 miles west of Austin on U.S. 50 and turn left (south) at the sign to Big Creek. The campground is 12 miles down a good dirt road.

*Trip notes:* Big Creek, elevation 6,500 feet, is located in an open canyon with some trees, plus dense vegetation mostly along the creekbed at the edge of the campground. Anglers can try for small rainbow and brook trout in Big Creek. Bring chemicals to treat the creek water if you're planning to drink it.

*Season:* May through October.

## 4. KINGSTON CAMPGROUND

*Reference:* In Toiyabe National Forest; map D2, grid c3.

*Campsites, facilities:* There are 12 campsites for tents or self-contained RVs up to 16 feet long. Vault toilets, picnic tables, grills, and fire rings are provided. There is *no drinking water.* Pets are permitted as long as they remain quiet, on leashes, or otherwise controlled. The maximum stay is 14 days.

*Reservations, fee:* No reservations are accepted. Campsites are free.

*Contact:* Austin Ranger District Office, P.O. Box 130, Austin, NV 89310; (702) 964-2671.

*Location:* From Austin, drive east 12 miles on U.S. 50, then south for 16 miles on Highway 376. Turn right at the sign for Kingston. The pavement runs out in two miles, and the campground is another two miles away on the dirt road.

*Trip notes:* These semiprivate campsites are on a creek at the lush bottom of Kingston Canyon, shaded by big trees and dense willows. A trout-filled Nevada Department of Wildlife reservoir can be found two miles up the dirt road beyond the campground, and another half mile from there is the trailhead to the 40-mile-long Toiyabe Crest Trail, which puts you on top of the range (above creeks and trees) and on top of the world. The campground's elevation is 6,900 feet.

*Season:* May through October.

## 5. COLUMBINE CAMPGROUND

*Reference:* In Toiyabe National Forest; map D2, grid d3.

*Campsites, facilities:* There are six campsites for tents; Columbine is not recommended for RVs or trailers of any size. Vault toilets, picnic tables, grills, and fire rings are provided. There is *no drinking water.* Pets are permitted as long as they remain quiet, on leashes, or otherwise controlled. The maximum stay is 14 days.

*Reservations, fee:* No reservations are accepted. There is no camping fee.

*Contact:* Austin Ranger District Office, P.O. Box 130, Austin, NV 89310; (702) 964-2671.

*Location:* Drive west on U.S. 50 from Austin for two miles, then bear left (southwest) on Highway 722 (old U.S. 50). In eight miles, turn left (south) onto County Road 21 (Reese River Valley Road). From there, it's approximately 23 miles of well-graded dirt road to the headquarters of the Yomba-Shoshone Tribe. Take a left (east) at the headquarters and follow the signs up Stewart Creek. It's another eight miles up the west face of the mighty Toiyabes to the campground.

*Trip notes:* Set at 9,000 feet, Columbine is a semiprimitive mountain campground high up under the aspen trees.

*Season:* Mid-June through early September.

# 6. BERLIN-ICHTHYOSAUR STATE PARK CAMPGROUND

*Reference:* **Near Gabbs; map D2, grid d1.**

*Campsites, facilities:* There are 14 campsites for tents or self-contained RVs up to 28 feet long. Piped drinking water, vault toilets, sewage disposal, picnic tables, barbecue grills, and fire pits are provided. Pets are permitted as long as they remain quiet, on leashes, or otherwise controlled. The maximum stay is 14 days.

*Reservations, fee:* No reservations are accepted. Sites are $6 per night.

*Contact:* State Park District Headquarters in Fallon, 16799 Lahontan Dam, Fallon, NV 89406; (702) 867-3001.

*Location:* From U.S. 95 between Hawthorne and Luning, take Highway 361 two miles north of Gabbs. Go right (east) on State Road 844 for 18 miles to the turnoff to Berlin-Ichthyosaur State Park. The campground is 2.5 miles away on a good dirt road.

*Trip notes:* This state park campground perched up on a ridge in the Shoshone Range has large sites, some overlooking Ione Valley. A half-mile nature trail leads from campsite #8 to the A-frame fossil shelter, which preserves a quarry site where the bones of prehistoric *ichthyosaurs* (giant sea lizards) were unearthed. You pass through Berlin—the best-preserved ghost town in Nevada—on the way to the campground. Be sure to stop and wander among the abandoned shops, offices, homes, cemetery, and the big mill building.

*Season:* Open year-round.

# 7. PEAVINE CAMPGROUND

*Reference:* **In Toiyabe National Forest; map D2, grid e6.**

*Campsites, facilities:* There are 11 campsites for tents or self-contained RVs up to 25 feet long. Vault toilets, picnic tables, grills, and fire rings are provided. There is *no drinking water.* The nearest commercial services are in Tonopah

(25 miles south). Pets are permitted as long as they remain quiet, on leashes, or otherwise controlled. The maximum stay is 14 days.

*Reservations, fee:* No reservations are accepted. Campsites are free.

*Contact:* Tonopah Ranger District, P.O. Box 3940, Tonopah, NV 89049; (702) 482-6286.

*Location:* From Tonopah, drive east for five miles on U.S. 6, then turn north on Highway 376. Drive 10 miles to the Peavine turnoff and go left (west) at the sign. It's another 10 miles on a decent dirt road to the campground.

*Trip notes:* The primitive drive to this campground involves a small creek crossing. During the height of spring runoff season, and at other rainy times of the year, it may be impassable; call for road conditions. Bring chemicals to treat the creek water if you're planning to drink it. The sites are shady, and there's fishing for small trout in the creek. The elevation is 5,500 feet.

*Season:* May through October.

## 8. PINE CREEK CAMPGROUND

*Reference:* **In Toiyabe National Forest; map D2, grid f3.**

*Campsites, facilities:* There are 24 campsites for tents or self-contained RVs up to 24 feet long. Vault toilets, picnic tables, grills, and fire rings are provided. There is *no drinking water.* The nearest commercial services are in Tonopah. Pets are permitted as long as they remain quiet, on leashes, or otherwise controlled. The maximum stay is 14 days.

*Reservations, fee:* No reservations are accepted. There is no camping fee.

*Contact:* Tonopah Ranger District, P.O. Box 3940, Tonopah, NV 89049; (702) 482-6286.

*Location:* From Tonopah, drive east five miles on U.S. 6 and turn north onto Highway 376. Drive 13 miles to County Road 82 (Monitor Valley Road), bear right, and drive 27 miles to the semi–ghost town of Belmont (no facilities). Continue on the Monitor Valley Road for another 17 miles to the sign for Pine Creek. Go right (west) 2.5 miles to the campground.

*Trip notes:* This is one of the larger Forest Service campgrounds in central Nevada, with a set-up similar to Peavine's (see page 301): shaded sites and small trout in the stream. Mount Jefferson towers overhead.

*Season:* May through October.

## 9. STATION HOUSE RV PARK

*Reference:* **In Tonopah; map D2, grid g4.**

*Campsites, facilities:* There are 20 spaces for RVs, all with full hookups (20-amp receptacles). Tent camping is not allowed. Handicapped-accessible rest rooms are located in the casino complex and have flush toilets and hot showers. Drinking water, a public phone, laundry facilities, sundries, a coffee shop, a snack bar, a bakery, video rentals, and a game room are also available inside.

*Reservations, fee:* Reservations are recommended, especially during the summer. Sites are $12 each.

*Contact:* Station House Hotel-Casino, P.O. Box 1351, Tonopah, NV 89049; (702) 482-9777.

***Location:*** From the south end of Tonopah, go two blocks south of the U.S. 6 intersection on U.S. 95 to the campground.

***Trip notes:*** The Station House is the largest casino in Tonopah and the RV park is in the parking lot in back. It's not exactly shady, private, or quiet, but the snack shop inside is the best on U.S. 95 between Las Vegas and Reno, where you can avail yourself of filling tacos, burritos, hot dogs, chili, root beer floats, and milkshakes, all for under $3 each. The Warehouse Supermarket is right next door.

***Season:*** Open year-round.

Map of Nevada ................. see page 256
Beyond This Region:
North (Map C3) ................ see page 268
East .................................................. Utah

**18 Campgrounds**
**Pages 304–313**

South (Map E3) ................ see page 318
West (Map D2) ................ see page 298

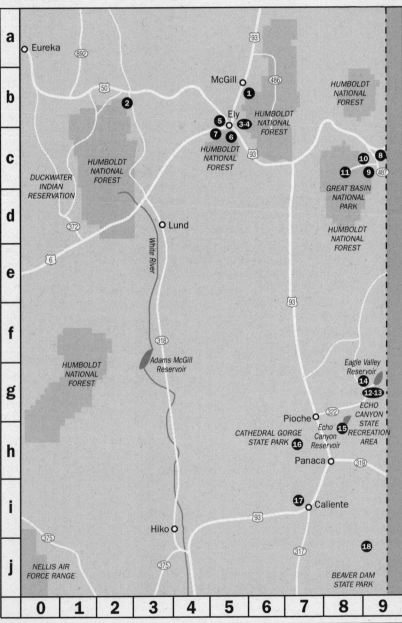

**Chapter D3 features:**

1. Cleve Creek Campground
2. Illipah Reservoir Campground
3. Cave Lake State Recreation Area
4. Valley View RV Park
5. West End RV Park
6. KOA of Ely
7. Ward Mountain
8. Whispering Elms RV Park
9. Baker Creek Campground
10. Lower and Upper Lehman Creek Campgrounds
11. Wheeler Peak Campground
12. Meadow Valley Campground
13. Spring Valley State Park
14. Eagle Valley Resort
15. Echo Canyon State Park
16. Cathedral Gorge State Park
17. Young's RV Park
18. Beaver Dam State Park

# 1. CLEVE CREEK CAMPGROUND

*Reference:* **Near Ely; map D3, grid b6.**

*Campsites, facilities:* There are 12 campsites for tents or self-contained RVs up to 24 feet long. Handicapped-accessible vault toilets, picnic tables, grills, and fire pits are provided. Pets are permitted as long as they remain quiet, on leashes, or otherwise controlled. The maximum stay is 14 days.

*Reservations, fee:* No reservations are accepted. Campsites are free.

*Contact:* Ely BLM District Office, 702 North Industrial Way (HC33 Box 33500), Ely, NV 89301; (702) 289-4865.

*Location:* From Ely, drive east on U.S. 50/6/93 and continue east on U.S. 50/6 toward Great Basin National Park at Major's Place. Turn north (left) on Highway 893 and drive 12 miles. Turn left at the sign and drive a little more than two miles on a graded dirt road to the campground.

*Trip notes:* Deep in the Schell Creek Range, dense cottonwoods tower over Cleve Creek, where you can catch wily brown and rainbow trout. Swap fishing yarns with your fellow campers on the Liar's Bench, a natural-stone and concrete structure at the group barbecue site built by volunteers from Las Vegas, of all places. Indian pictographs abound in this area.

*Season:* Open year-round, but accessibility is determined entirely by weather conditions.

# 2. ILLIPAH RESERVOIR CAMPGROUND

*Reference:* **Near Ely; map D3, grid b2.**

*Campsites, facilities:* There are 17 campsites for tents or self-contained RVs up to 35 feet long. Vault toilets, picnic tables, grills, and fire pits are provided. Pets are permitted as long as they remain quiet, on leashes, or otherwise controlled. The maximum stay is 14 days.

*Reservations, fee:* No reservations are accepted. Campsites are free.

*Contact:* Ely BLM District Office, 702 North Industrial Way (HC33 Box 33500), Ely, NV 89301; (702) 289-4865.

*Location:* Head west on U.S. 50 from Ely for 37 miles. At the sign for the campground, take a left, drive 150 yards, and turn left again. Continue another mile and a third to the reservoir.

*Trip notes:* This 100-acre reservoir is in a little valley between the big White Pine Range and the minor Mormon Ridge. Trout fishing and staring into space are the activities of choice.

*Season:* Open year-round.

## 3. CAVE LAKE STATE RECREATION AREA

*Reference:* **Near Ely; map D3, grid b5.**

*Campsites, facilities:* There are 35 campsites for tents or self-contained RVs up to 35 feet long. Piped drinking water, flush toilets, hot showers, sewage disposal, picnic tables, grills, and fire rings are provided. Pets are permitted as long as they remain quiet, on leashes, or otherwise controlled. The maximum stay is 14 days.

*Reservations, fee:* No reservations are accepted. Campsites are $7 a night.

*Contact:* State Parks District Office, P.O. Box 176, Panaca, NV 89042; (702) 728-4467.

*Location:* From Ely, drive southeast seven miles on U.S. 50/93. At Highway 486, turn right (east) and drive another seven miles up to the campground.

*Trip notes:* High up in the Schell Creek Range at an elevation of 7,300 feet, Cave Lake is a reservoir created by an earthen dam. The older campground (Lakeview) is a little uphill from the lake, with 20 sites and all facilities; the newer campground is across the road on Elk Flat, with 15 sites and all facilities. The lake hosts boating (ramp and dock available), fishing (brown and rainbow trout), and swimming (cold year-round). A five-mile trail departs from the main entrance and heads into the pinyon and juniper hills. In winter, the lower part of Lakeview is kept open for ice fishing, ice skating, and cross-country skiing.

*Season:* Open year-round.

## 4. VALLEY VIEW RV PARK

*Reference:* **In Ely; map D3, grid b5.**

*Campsites, facilities:* There are 83 spaces for RVs, all with full hookups (20-, 30-, and 50-amp receptacles); 12 of these are pull-throughs. Tents are allowed. Handicapped-accessible rest rooms have drinking water, flush toilets, and hot showers; a public phone, sewage disposal, laundry facilities, and limited groceries are also available.

*Reservations, fee:* Reservations are recommended from spring through fall, especially for the pull-throughs. The camping fee is $14 per vehicle.

*Contact:* Valley View RV Park, 65 McGill Highway, Ely, NV 89301; (702) 289-3303.

*Location:* Drive two miles north of Ely on U.S. 93 to the RV park, which is on the right.

*Trip notes:* Opened in 1976, this is one of the most mature RV parks in Nevada, and the tall trees, lush grass, and double-wide RV sites are there to prove it. It's quiet, friendly, and convenient to U.S. 93 heading northbound from Ely.

*Season:* Open year-round.

## 5. WEST END RV PARK

*Reference:* **In Ely; map D3, grid b5.**

*Campsites, facilities:* There are 11 spaces for RVs, all with full hookups (30- and 50-amp receptacles); none of the sites are pull-throughs. Tents are allowed. Rest rooms have drinking water, flush toilets, and hot showers. A public phone, sewage disposal, and laundry facilities are also available.

*Reservations, fee:* Reservations are accepted. The fee is $11 for two people, and $2 for each additional person.

*Contact:* West End RV Park, 50 Aultman Street, Ely, NV 89301; call (702) 289-2231.

*Location:* From the corner of Aultman and Fourth Street in downtown Ely, drive three blocks west on Aultman Street. The RV park is on the right.

*Trip notes:* This mini RV park is on Ely's main drag, a three-minute walk from the Nevada Hotel and the Jailhouse Casino. The trees are large enough to shade the whole park. Sometimes West End fills up with long-termers, but you should try your luck if you want to be right in the thick of the Ely action.

*Season:* Open year-round.

## 6. KOA OF ELY

*Reference:* **In Ely; map D3, grid c5.**

*Campsites, facilities:* There are 60 spaces for RVs, 37 with full hookups (20-, 30-, and 50-amp receptacles); all are pull-throughs. Tents are allowed in a separate grassy area. Handicapped-accessible rest rooms have drinking water, flush toilets, and hot showers. A public phone, sewage disposal, laundry facilities, groceries, corrals, a playground, and volleyball are also available.

*Reservations, fee:* Reservations are accepted. Campsites are $15 to $18.50 for two people, and $2 for each additional person. KOA and Good Sam discounts are offered.

*Contact:* KOA of Ely, HC 10, Box 10800, Ely, NV 89301; (702) 289-3413.

*Location:* From the intersection of U.S. 50/93 and U.S. 6 (south of the Motel 6 and Copper Queen) in central East Ely, drive three miles south on the Pioche Highway (U.S. 50/6 and U.S. 93). The RV park is on the right.

*Trip notes:* This is the largest RV park in all of eastern Nevada. Mature cottonwoods rim the perimeter and Chinese elms line the sites. Ward Mountain of the Egan Range towers over the park, which sits up above the valley a little, so at night you can look down at the lights of town. The KOA is most convenient to the southern and eastern side trips: Great Basin National Park (60 miles east), Cave Lake State Park (12 miles southeast), Ward Charcoal Ovens (3 miles east), and Pioche (120 miles south).

*Season:* Open year-round.

## 7. WARD MOUNTAIN

*Reference:* **In Humboldt National Forest; map D3, grid c5.**

*Campsites, facilities:* There are 29 campsites for tents or self-contained RVs up to 28 feet long; five of these are pull-throughs. Piped drinking water, vault toilets, picnic tables, grills, and fire pits are provided. Pets are permitted as long as they remain quiet, on leashes, or otherwise controlled. The maximum stay is 14 days.

*Reservations, fee:* No reservations are accepted. Campsites are $4 a night.

*Contact:* Ely Ranger District, 350 Eighth Street, Ely, NV 89301; call (702) 289-3031.

*Location:* From Ely, drive seven miles west on U.S. 6. Turn left at the sign and drive in a half mile to the campground.

*Trip notes:* This is a relatively large Forest Service campground in the pinyon and juniper forest of Ward Mountain in the Egan Range, elevation 7,400 feet. It offers a number of activities in the group picnic area: badminton, volleyball, horseshoes, a big barbecue pit for roasting whole pigs, even a field for baseball and softball (really just a rough open area), and hiking (and cross-country) trails into the hills.

*Season:* Open year-round, but the water runs only mid-May through September.

## 8. WHISPERING ELMS RV PARK

*Reference:* **In Baker; map D3, grid c9.**

*Campsites, facilities:* There are 16 spaces for RVs, all with full hookups (20-, 30-, and 50-amp receptacles) and all pull-throughs. Tents are allowed. Rest rooms have flush toilets and hot showers. A public phone and sewage disposal are also available.

*Reservations, fee:* Reservations are accepted. All campsites are $15 a night.

*Contact:* Whispering Elms, P.O. Box 8, Baker, NV 89311; (702) 234-7343.

*Location:* From the intersection of U.S. 50 and Highway 487, bear right on Highway 487 and continue into Baker. The RV park is on the left behind some Park Service buildings.

*Trip notes:* This is the nearest RV park to Great Basin National Park (where there are no hookups); Whispering Elms is a block from the park entrance. There's a separate grassy area for tents, and each site has a barbecue grill. The park is named after five or six dozen big elm trees that shade the fenced RV enclosure and whisper in the wind.

*Season:* May through September.

## 9. BAKER CREEK CAMPGROUND

*Reference:* **In Great Basin National Park; map D3, grid c8.**

*Campsites, facilities:* There are 34 campsites for tents or self-contained RVs up to 40 feet long; four of these are pull-throughs. Drinking water from the creek is treated and piped, but sometimes signs warn to boil it before drinking. Vault toilets, picnic tables, grills, and fire pits are provided. Pets are permitted as long as they remain quiet, on leashes, or otherwise controlled. The maximum stay is 14 days.

*Reservations, fee:* No reservations are accepted. Campsites are $5 a night.

*Contact:* Great Basin National Park, Baker, NV 89311; (702) 234-7331.

*Location:* From Ely, take U.S. 50/6 east 56 miles to the Y intersection. Bear right onto Highway 487 and drive five miles into Baker. Turn right (west) onto Highway 488 and drive five miles into the park. Just before the National Park visitors center, turn left and drive three miles on a dirt road.

*Trip notes:* Located at an elevation of approximately 7,000 feet, this campground has three loops. The choice spots are under big evergreens right on Baker Creek. A mile past the campground is the somewhat strenuous Baker Lake and Johnson Lake Loop Trail, which passes both lakes and crosses Johnson Pass at 10,800 feet.

*Season:* May through October.

## 10. LOWER AND UPPER LEHMAN CREEK CAMPGROUNDS

*Reference:* **In Great Basin National Park; map D3, grid c8.**

*Campsites, facilities:* Lower Campground has 11 campsites for tents or self-contained RVs up to 40 feet long; these are all pull-throughs and large sites. Upper Campground has 24 sites for RVs up to 20 feet long. Both have running water from the creek; although it's piped and treated, it's sometimes necessary to boil it before drinking. Both provide vault toilets, picnic tables, grills, and fire pits. Pets are permitted as long as they remain quiet, on leashes, or otherwise controlled. The maximum stay is 14 days.

*Reservations, fee:* No reservations are accepted. Campsites are $5 a night.

*Contact:* Great Basin National Park, Baker, NV 89311; (702) 234-7331.

*Location:* From Ely, take U.S. 50/6 east 56 miles to the Y intersection. Bear right onto Highway 487 and drive five miles into Baker. Turn right (west) onto Highway 488 and drive five miles up to the park and bear right on Wheeler Peak Scenic Drive. Continue for 1.5 miles to Lower Campground and 2.5 miles to Upper Campground.

*Trip notes:* Lower Campground, at an elevation of 7,400 feet, is used mostly by RVs and trailers, while Upper Campground, at 7,600 feet, is stretched out along three levels of the slope; upper Upper is on Lehman Creek, with a few little fish in it. The four-mile hiking trail to Wheeler Peak Campground leaves from upper Upper.

*Season:* Lower Campground is open year-round; Upper Campground is open mid-May to mid-September.

## 11. WHEELER PEAK CAMPGROUND

*Reference:* **In Great Basin National Park; map D3, grid c8.**

*Campsites, facilities:* There are 37 campsites for tents; RVs longer than 24 feet are not recommended due to the steepness and curviness of the Scenic Road. Drinking water from the creek is treated and piped, but sometimes signs warn to boil it before drinking. Vault toilets, picnic tables, grills, and fire pits are provided. Pets are permitted as long as they remain quiet, on leashes, or otherwise controlled. The maximum stay is 14 days.

*Reservations, fee:* No reservations are accepted. The fee is $5 per campsite.

*Contact:* Great Basin National Park, Baker, NV 89311; (702) 234-7331.

*Location:* From Ely, take U.S. 50/6 east 56 miles to the Y intersection. Bear right onto Highway 487 and drive five miles into Baker. Turn right (west) onto Highway 488 and drive five miles up to the park. Bear right on Wheeler Peak Scenic Drive. Continue for six miles up to the end of the road and the campground parking lot.

*Trip notes:* This is mountain camping at its peak. The Scenic Road is the highest paved road in Nevada, so the campground is the highest accessible by paved road. (The elevation—hang onto your lungs!—is 10,000 feet.) It's big, woodsy, and full of downy pine needles for a soft night's sleep. Hikers will appreciate the access to two short lake trails, a longer trail to a divine forest of bristlecone pines and the southernmost ice field in the contiguous United States, and a major huff and puff to Wheeler Peak at 13,063 feet, the second highest point in Nevada.

*Season:* June through September.

## 12. MEADOW VALLEY CAMPGROUND

*Reference:* **Near Pioche; map D3, grid g9.**

*Campsites, facilities:* There are six campsites for tents or self-contained RVs up to 16 feet long. Vault toilets, picnic tables, grills, and fire pits are provided. Pets are permitted as long as they remain quiet, on leashes, or otherwise controlled. The maximum stay is 14 days.

*Reservations, fee:* No reservations are accepted. Campsites are free.

*Contact:* Ely BLM District Office, 702 North Industrial Way (HC33 Box 33500), Ely, NV 89301; (702) 289-4865.

*Location:* From Pioche, take Highway 322 east for 17 miles. At the sign for the campground, take a left and drive 100 yards into a small canyon that towers over the road and shelters the campground.

*Trip notes:* This secluded campground is tucked away in Nicanor Canyon only a mile before Spring Valley State Park, where boating, fishing, and swimming are favorite pastimes. It serves as an overflow camping area for Spring Valley (see below), and it's free.

*Season:* Open year-round.

## 13. SPRING VALLEY STATE PARK

*Reference:* **Near Pioche; map D3, grid g9.**

*Campsites, facilities:* Horsethief Gulch Campground in Spring Valley State Park has 37 campsites for tents or self-contained RVs up to 28 feet long. Piped drinking water, flush toilets, showers, sewage disposal, a fish-cleaning shed, public telephones, picnic tables, grills, and fire pits are provided. The nearest commercial facilities are at Eagle Valley Resort (see page 311). Pets are permitted as long as they remain quiet, on leashes, or otherwise controlled. The maximum stay is seven days.

*Reservations, fee:* No reservations are accepted. The fees are $3 for day use and $7 a night for campsites.

*Contact:* Park Headquarters, (702) 962-5102; or the State Parks District Office, P.O. Box 176, Panaca, NV 89042, (702) 728-4467.

*Location:* From Pioche, take Highway 322 east and drive for 18 miles to the campground.

*Trip notes:* This is a shady campground next to a 65-acre reservoir stocked with rainbow and cutthroat trout. There's a pier for fishing and docking and a small stony and mossy beach for swimming (the water's very brisk). The elevation is 5,800 feet.

*Season:* Open year-round.

---

## 14. EAGLE VALLEY RESORT

*Reference:* **Near Pioche; map D3, grid g9.**

*Campsites, facilities:* There are 40 spaces for RVs, 36 with full hookups (20- and 30-amp receptacles); none of these are pull-throughs. Tents are allowed in a separate grassy area. Rest rooms have drinking water, flush toilets, and hot showers. A public phone, sewage disposal, laundry facilities, and groceries are available.

*Reservations, fee:* Reservations are accepted. The fee is $7.50 for tents and $11.50 to $15 for RVs.

*Contact:* Eagle Valley Resort, Box 262-2, Pioche, NV 89043; (702) 962-5293.

*Location:* From Pioche, take Highway 322 east for 16 miles to the resort.

*Trip notes:* Eagle Valley Resort offers basic RV camping, a place to park the rig and make excursions to Spring Valley (2.5 miles) and Echo Canyon (seven miles). The grocery store and bar, which has slots and video poker, are right across the road.

*Season:* Open year-round.

---

## 15. ECHO CANYON STATE PARK

*Reference:* **Near Pioche; map D3, grid h8.**

*Campsites, facilities:* There are 34 campsites for tents or self-contained RVs up to 30 feet long. Piped drinking water, flush toilets (turned off at the end of October), sewage disposal, public telephones, picnic tables under shelters, grills, fire pits, and a fish-cleaning shed are provided by the park. The nearest commercial services are located in Pioche. Pets are permitted as long as they remain quiet, on leashes, or otherwise controlled. The maximum stay is 14 days.

*Reservations, fee:* No reservations are accepted. Campsites are $7 a night.

*Contact:* Park Headquarters, (702) 962-5103; or State Parks District Office, P.O. Box 176, Panaca, NV 89042, (702) 728-4467.

*Location:* From Pioche, drive four miles east on NV 322. Turn right (south) on County Route 86 and drive eight miles to the campground.

*Trip notes:* The sites at this campground (elevation 5,800 feet) are large, lush, and level, and full of anglers fishing for stocked rainbow trout and naturally spawning crappie and largemouth bass. Between spring and fall, the fields downriver from the dam are some of the most verdant in eastern Nevada. The group picnic area is prime.

*Season:* Open year-round.

---

# 16. CATHEDRAL GORGE STATE PARK

*Reference:* **Near Panaca; map D3, grid h7.**

*Campsites, facilities:* There are 22 campsites for tents or self-contained RVs up to 30 feet long; the two pull-throughs can handle longer RVs. Piped drinking water, flush toilets, heavenly showers, sewage disposal, public telephones, picnic tables, grills, and fire pits are provided. Pets are permitted as long as they remain quiet, on leashes, or otherwise controlled. The maximum stay is 14 days.

*Reservations, fee:* No reservations are accepted. The fee is $3 for day use and $7 to camp.

*Contact:* State Parks District Office, P.O. Box 176, Panaca, NV 89042; (702) 728-4467.

*Location:* From the junction of U.S. 93 and Highway 319 (to Panaca), drive one mile north on U.S. 93 and turn left (west) into the park entrance. Drive 1.5 miles past headquarters and the district offices to the campground.

*Trip notes:* Cathedral Gorge is a small canyon that's been eroded over the past million years or so into a strange and wondrous place. The campground is on the desert floor with a great view of the gorge. It's marginally shaded by introduced locust and Russian olive trees. A quarter-mile nature trail connects the campground with the formations, and a four-mile trail runs into the backcountry. The elevation is 5,000 feet.

*Season:* Open year-round; showers run April 15 to November 15.

---

# 17. YOUNG'S RV PARK

*Reference:* **In Caliente; map D3, grid i7.**

*Campsites, facilities:* There are 27 spaces for RVs, all with full hookups (20- and 30-amp receptacles); 16 of these are pull-throughs. Tents are allowed in a separate grassy area. Rest rooms have drinking water, flush toilets, and hot showers. Sewage disposal is also available.

*Reservations, fee:* Reservations are accepted. The fee is $7 for tents and $12 for RVs.

*Contact:* Young's RV Park, P.O. Box 84, Caliente, NV 89008; (702) 726-3418.

*Location:* Take U.S. 93 to the southwest end of Caliente. The RV park is behind the BLM office.

*Trip notes:* This is the only bona fide RV park between Las Vegas and Ely on U.S. 93. Campsites are wide, with trees and grass. The facilities are basic, but it's right in town, where there's a Laundromat, public phones, and all services.

*Season:* Open year-round.

---

# 18. BEAVER DAM STATE PARK

*Reference:* **Near Caliente; map D3, grid j9.**

*Campsites, facilities:* There are 35 campsites for tents or self-contained RVs up to 24 feet long. Piped drinking water (turned off from October through May),

---

vault toilets, picnic tables, grills, and fire rings are provided. Pets are permitted as long as they remain quiet, on leashes, or otherwise controlled. The maximum stay is 14 days.

*Reservations, fee:* No reservations are accepted. Campsites are $7 a night.

*Contact:* State Parks District Office, P.O. Box 176, Panaca, NV 89042; (702) 728-4467.

*Location:* From Caliente, drive six miles north on U.S. 93, then turn right (east) at the sign onto the sometimes steep and twisty access road (in winter it's muddy, snowy, nasty). It's 28 miles of graded gravel (adequately signposted) to get to Beaver Dam, Nevada's remotest state park.

*Trip notes:* Beaver Dam (elevation 5,000 feet) is in canyon country right on the Utah state line. There's a reservoir stocked with trout. Three campgrounds are strung along a few miles: A (the old CCC camp from the 1930s) is on a ridge above the reservoir, but you can walk down the hill and over to it; B is on top of a hill from where a nature trail leads to an overlook; and C is a few miles beyond the dam on the creek. Hiking is plentiful through the forest and canyons.

*Season:* May through October.

# MAP E2

Map of Nevada .................. see page 256
Beyond This Region:
North (Map D2) ................ see page 298
East (Map E3) .................. see page 318
South ........................ California
West ......................... California

6 Campgrounds
Pages 314–317

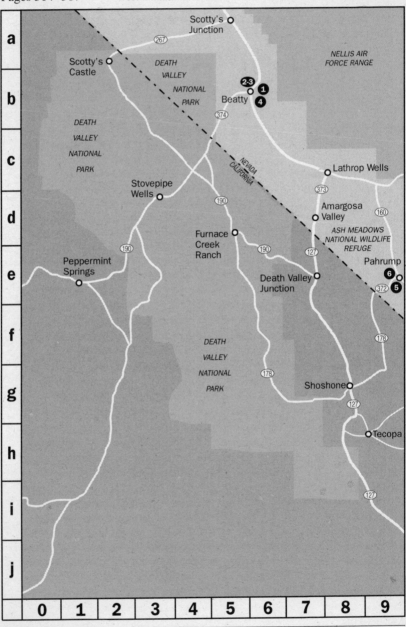

**Chapter E2 features:**
1. Bailey's Hot Springs
2. Rio Rancho RV Park
3. Space Station RV Park
4. Burro Inn RV Park
5. Pahrump Station RV Park
6. Seven Palms RV Park

# 1. BAILEY'S HOT SPRINGS

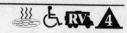

*Reference:* **Near Beatty; map E2, grid b6.**

*Campsites, facilities:* There are 17 spaces for RVs, all with full hookups (20-, 30-, and 50-amp receptacles); 14 of these are pull-throughs. Tents are allowed. Handicapped-accessible rest rooms have drinking water, flush toilets, and hot showers. A public phone, sewage disposal, and mineral hot spring pools are also available. The nearest commercial services are in Beatty, five miles down the road.

*Reservations, fee:* Reservations are accepted. Campsites are $10 a night.

*Contact:* Bailey's Hot Springs, Box 387, Beatty, NV 89002; (702) 553-2395.

*Location:* Drive five miles north of Beatty on U.S. 95, and turn right into the facility.

*Trip notes:* The Baileys have run this little hot springs resort since 1969. It's a small RV park wedged between a little hill and the highway at an elevation of 3,300 feet. At the base of the hill are three bathhouses built over natural pools of pure 100- to 105-degree mineral water. Noncampers can soak in the pools for $2 per person per half hour (but nobody watches the clock too closely).

*Season:* Open year-round.

# 2. RIO RANCHO RV PARK

*Reference:* **In Beatty; map E2, grid b6.**

*Campsites, facilities:* There are 70 spaces for RVs, all with full hookups (20- and 30-amp receptacles); 48 of these spaces are pull-throughs. Tents are allowed in the campground during the summer only. Rest rooms include drinking water, flush toilets, and hot showers. A public phone, sewage disposal, laundry facilities, video rentals, and a recreation room are also made available by Rio Rancho RV Park.

*Reservations, fee:* Reservations are accepted. Campsites are $14 a night for two people, and $2 for each additional person. Good Sam discounts are offered.

*Contact:* Rio Rancho RV Park, Box 905, Beatty, NV 89003; (702) 553-2238.

*Location:* From the intersection of U.S. 95 and Highway 374 in downtown Beatty, proceed north on U.S. 95 for one-half mile and turn left into Rio Rancho RV Park.

*Trip notes:* This is a well-established RV park with some trees, which are large for Beatty. Rio Rancho is located right next to the Beatty post office, and it's one short block from the Stagecoach Casino, which has a 24-hour coffee shop for weary or hungry travelers. The recreation room at the RV park has a pool table and TV.

*Season:* Open year-round.

## 3. SPACE STATION RV PARK

*Reference:* **In Beatty; map E2, grid b6.**

*Campsites, facilities:* There are 24 spaces for RVs, 19 with full hookups (20- and 30-amp receptacles); 18 of the sites are pull-throughs. Tents are allowed. Rest rooms have drinking water, flush toilets, and hot showers. A public phone, sewage disposal, and laundry facilities are also available.

*Reservations, fee:* Reservations are accepted. The fee is $12 for two people.

*Contact:* Space Station, P.O. Box 568, Beatty, NV 89003; (702) 553-9039.

*Location:* From the intersection of U.S. 95 and Highway 374 in downtown Beatty, drive north on U.S. 95 a quarter mile, and turn left into the park.

*Trip notes:* Just down the street from the Rio Rancho (see page 315), the Space Station is similar, though a little newer and less shaded. Beatty is the jumping-off point in Nevada for the north side of Death Valley National Park, Scotty's Castle in particular, which is 15 miles southwest on Highway 374.

*Season:* Open year-round.

## 4. BURRO INN RV PARK

*Reference:* **In Beatty; map E2, grid b6.**

*Campsites, facilities:* There are 43 spaces for RVs, all with full hookups (30- and 50-amp receptacles) and all pull-throughs. Tents are allowed. Rest rooms have drinking water, flush toilets, and hot showers. A public phone, sewage disposal, and laundry facilities are also available.

*Reservations, fee:* Reservations are accepted. The fee is $12 per vehicle.

*Contact:* Burro Inn, P.O. Box 7, Beatty, NV 89003; (702) 553-2225.

*Location:* From the intersection of U.S. 95 and Highway 374, drive south on U.S. 95 a half mile to the RV park.

*Trip notes:* In a dirt parking lot behind the Burro Inn Casino, this RV park is two blocks from the city pool and the town supermarket. Inside the Burro Inn are the casino, a 24-hour coffee shop, and a bar.

*Season:* Open year-round.

## 5. PAHRUMP STATION RV PARK

*Reference:* **In Pahrump; map E2, grid e9.**

*Campsites, facilities:* There are 43 spaces for RVs, all with full hookups (30- and 50-amp receptacles) and all pull-throughs. Tent camping is not allowed. Handicapped-accessible rest rooms have drinking water, flush toilets, and hot showers. A public phone, sewage disposal, laundry facilities, and a heated swimming pool are also available.

*Reservations, fee:* Reservations are accepted. The fee is $13 per RV.

*Contact:* Days Inn, P.O. Box 38, Pahrump, NV 89041; (702) 727-5100.

*Location:* This campground is located at the corner of Highway 160 and Loop Road in the middle of "town" ("downtown" Pahrump stretches along the highway for several miles).

*Trip notes:* Register at the Days Inn, which fronts Pahrump Station RV Park. Each site is surfaced with graded rock and graced by a few trees. It's in a good location near the center of the business district and across the street from Pahrump's biggest casino, Saddle West.

*Season:* Open year-round.

---

# 6. SEVEN PALMS RV PARK

*Reference:* **In Pahrump; map E2, grid e9.**

*Campsites, facilities:* There are 59 spaces for RVs, all with full hookups (30- and 50-amp receptacles); 49 of these are pull-throughs. Tents are allowed. Rest rooms have drinking water, flush toilets, and hot showers (for sale to noncampers for $3). A public phone, sewage disposal, and laundry facilities are also available.

*Reservations, fee:* Reservations are accepted. The fee is $13 per campsite.

*Contact:* Seven Palms, HCR 73 Box 28050, Pahrump, NV 89041; call (702) 727-6091.

*Location:* From the intersection of Highways 160 and 372 in downtown Pahrump, take 372 west for 2.5 miles to Linda Road. Turn right (north), drive for one mile, and turn right into the RV park.

*Trip notes:* Stanley Braithwaite built this RV park in 1984, and planted the hundreds of trees that shade the sites. Half the park is for permanents, but the RV section is separate.

*Season:* Open year-round.

# MAP E3

Map of Nevada .................. see page 256
Beyond This Region:
North (Map D3) ................. see page 304
East ........................... Arizona and Utah
South ....................................... California
West (Map E2) .................. see page 314

37 Campgrounds
Pages 318–339

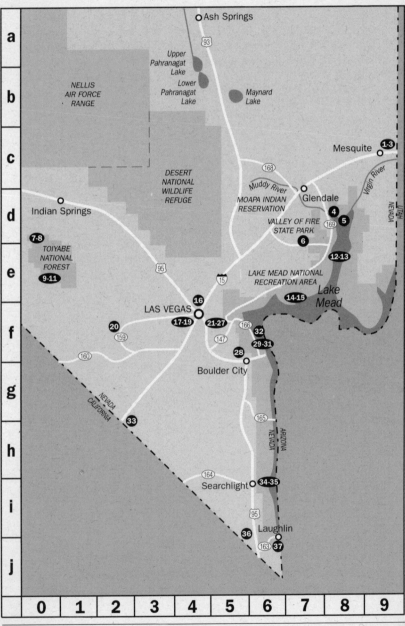

**Chapter E3 features:**

1. Si Redd's Oasis RV Park
2. Virgin River RV Park
3. Player's Island RV Park
4. Fun & Sun RV Park
5. Overton Beach RV Park
6. Valley of Fire State Park
7. Dolomite Campground
8. McWilliams Campground
9. Hilltop Campground
10. Kyle Canyon Campground
11. Fletcher View Campground
12. Echo Bay Campground
13. Echo Bay Trailer Village
14. Callville Bay Campground
15. Callville Bay Trailer Village
16. Hitchin' Post RV Park
17. Circusland RV Park
18. Boomtown RV Park
19. Oasis RV Park
20. Oak Creek Campground
21. King's Row Trailer Park
22. Las Vegas KOA
23. Road Runner RV Park
24. Holiday Travel Park
25. Sam's Town Nellis RV Park
26. Sam's Town Boulder RV Park
27. Boulder Lakes RV Resort
28. Canyon Trail RV Park
29. Hemenway Campground
30. Lakeshore Trailer Village
31. Boulder Beach Campground
32. Las Vegas Bay Campground
33. Primadonna RV Village
34. Cottonwood Cove Marina and Resort
35. Cottonwood Cove Campground
36. Cal-Nev-Ari RV Park
37. Riverside Resort RV Park

## 1. SI REDD'S OASIS RV PARK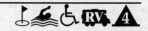

*Reference:* **In Mesquite; map E3, grid c9.**

*Campsites, facilities:* There are 91 spaces for RVs, all with full hookups (20-, 30-, and 50-amp receptacles); 30 of these are pull-throughs. Tents are not allowed. Handicapped-accessible rest rooms have drinking water, flush toilets, and hot showers. A public phone, sewage disposal, laundry facilities, groceries, a game room, and a heated swimming pool are available.

*Reservations, fee:* Reservations are recommended. The fee is $12.50 per RV. Good Sam discounts are offered.

*Contact:* Si Redd's Oasis RV Park, P.O. Box 360, Mesquite, NV 89024; (702) 346-5232 or (800) 621-0187.

*Location:* Take exit 120 off Interstate 15 right before the Arizona border, and drive a half mile east on Mesquite Boulevard to the RV park.

*Trip notes:* Mesquite is a typical Nevada stateline boomtown, and it's anchored by the Oasis. The RV park is in the casino's parking lot, and is little more than asphalt and hookups. But the Oasis has six swimming pools, its own championship (and miniature) golf course, a health club, restaurants, and a casino—all included in the price of a site.

*Season:* Open year-round.

## 2. VIRGIN RIVER RV PARK

*Reference:* **In Mesquite; map E3, grid c9.**

*Campsites, facilities:* There are 47 spaces for RVs, all with full hookups (20- and 30-amp receptacles); none of the sites are pull-throughs. Tents are not allowed. Handicapped-accessible rest rooms have drinking water, flush toilets,

---

and hot showers. A public phone, sewage disposal, laundry facilities, and a heated swimming pool are available.

*Reservations, fee:* Reservations are recommended. The fee is $10 per RV.

*Contact:* Virgin River RV Park, 100 East Pioneer Boulevard, Mesquite, NV 89024; (702) 346-7777 or (800) 346-7721.

*Location:* Take exit 122 off Interstate 15 near the Arizona border and drive north one block on Mesquite Boulevard to the RV park.

*Trip notes:* One of the newest RV parks in Nevada, Virgin River, in back of the casino, is small, sparse, and clean—only differentiated from the motel parking lot by a low retaining wall. Register at the front desk of the hotel. The casino has bingo and a two-screen movie theater. The pool has a spa.

*Season:* Open year-round.

## 3. PLAYER'S ISLAND RV PARK

*Reference:* In Mesquite; map E3, grid c9.

*Campsites, facilities:* There are 45 spaces for RVs, all with full hookups (20-, 30-, and 50-amp receptacles); 16 of these are pull-throughs. Tents are not allowed. Handicapped-accessible rest rooms have drinking water, flush toilets, and hot showers. A public phone, sewage disposal, and a swimming pool are also available.

*Reservations, fee:* Reservations are recommended. The fee is $16.20 a night for people under 50, and $12.96 a night for people over 50.

*Contact:* Player's Island RV Park, 930 Mesquite Boulevard (P.O. Box 2737), Mesquite, NV 89024; (702) 346-7529 or (800) 896-4567.

*Location:* Take exit 120 off Interstate 15 just before the Arizona state line and drive a half mile east on Mesquite Boulevard to the RV park.

*Trip notes:* Player's Island opened in July 1995, so its RV park, across a small service road on the same side of the boulevard, is still newish. It has what could be the widest parking spaces in the state, wide enough to fit a big motor home with a slide-out and a car. Or two cars and a motor home. Or a trailer, pickup truck, and car. The RV park is all asphalt with young trees, but offers a fine view of the Virgin Mountains across the Virgin Valley. The hotel-casino has a buffet, steakhouse, and coffee shop, a luxurious pool, and a European-style spa, complete with mud baths, watsu pool, and 14 therapists practicing all manner of bodywork. Very hedonistic and upscale.

*Season:* Open year-round.

## 4. FUN & SUN RV PARK

*Reference:* In Overton; map E3, grid d8.

*Campsites, facilities:* There are 112 spaces for RVs, all with full hookups (15-, 30-, and 50-amp receptacles); 66 of these are pull-throughs. Tents are not allowed. Rest rooms have drinking water, flush toilets, and hot showers. A public phone, sewage disposal, laundry facilities, a recreation room, and a heated swimming pool and spa are also available.

*Reservations, fee:* Reservations are accepted. The fee is $13.75 a night for two people, and $2 for each additional person.

*Contact:* Fun & Sun RV Park, 280 North Cooper Street, Overton, NV 89040; (702) 397-8894.

*Location:* From exit 93 off Interstate 15 at Moapa/Glendale, drive 12 miles south to Overton. Pass the post office, turn left on Cooper Street, and then right into the park.

*Trip notes:* Fun & Sun was originally designed to be a trailer park (some people still live here), so the spaces are big enough to contain double-wide mobile homes. And the facility as a whole is also big and wide, as well as open (with only a little greenery around the edges) and high-density, bordered by two walls, a wash, and the road. The recreation room has a full kitchen. Lake Mead is 11 miles south, with Valley of Fire in between.

*Season:* Open year-round.

## 5. OVERTON BEACH RV PARK

*Reference:* **In Lake Mead National Recreation Area; map E3, grid d8.**

*Campsites, facilities:* There are 54 spaces for RVs, all with full hookups (30- and 50-amp receptacles); 12 of these are pull-throughs. Tents are allowed. Rest rooms have drinking water, flush toilets, and hot showers ($1 for noncampers). A public phone, sewage disposal, laundry facilities, groceries, a gas dock, a marina, and a swimming beach are also available.

*Reservations, fee:* Reservations are accepted. Campsites are $16 a night.

*Contact:* Overton Beach Resort, Overton, NV 89040; (702) 394-4040.

*Location:* From Overton, drive 11 miles south on Highway 169. The RV park is at the end of the road near the lake.

*Trip notes:* Overton Beach is the farthest resort from the dam, up at Overton Arm. The best fishing on the lake is up here, thanks to its location three miles from both the Muddy and Virgin Rivers (which dump a lot of fish food into the shallow water). Every site here has a view of the lake and is a two-minute walk to the water. The marina has a convenience store and cafe, and the beach is a bearable combination of stone and sand.

*Season:* Open year-round.

## 6. VALLEY OF FIRE STATE PARK

*Reference:* **Near Overton; map E3, grid d7.**

*Campsites, facilities:* Campgrounds A and B have a total of 51 campsites for tents or self-contained RVs up to 30 feet long. Campground A has drinking water, flush toilets, and showers; Campground B has drinking water and vault toilets. Picnic tables under ramadas, grills, and fire rings are also provided. Pets are permitted as long as they remain quiet, on leashes, or otherwise controlled. The maximum stay is 14 days.

*Reservations, fee:* No reservations are accepted. The fee is $7 per campsite.

*Contact:* Valley of Fire State Park, Overton, NV 89040; (702) 397-2088.

*Location:* From Overton, drive six miles south on Highway 169. Turn right into the park and drive another five miles to the campgrounds.

*Trip notes:* Campground A is the larger of the two, so it's more crowded with RVs; three walk-in campsites are in the rear of the campground. Campground

B is more compact and scenic; the back campsites, under the fiery red cliffs, are the most spectacular in Nevada. The sites at both are gravelly, semi-private, and vegetated. It's an easy stroll to Atlatl Rock, a sheer face high up on a cliff littered with petroglyphs. The state's longest outdoor staircase provides access.

*Season:* Campground A is open year-round; Campground B is closed for two to three months every summer (to regenerate).

## 7. DOLOMITE CAMPGROUND

*Reference:* **In Spring Mountains National Recreation Area (Toiyabe National Forest); map E3, grid e0.**

*Campsites, facilities:* There are 31 campsites for tents or self-contained RVs up to 40 feet long. Piped drinking water, flush toilets, picnic tables, barbecue grills, and fire rings are provided. There is a campground host. Pets are permitted as long as they remain on leashes six feet long or less. The maximum stay is 16 days.

*Reservations, fee:* Reservations are accepted for the multi-family sites; the rest are first come, first served. For reservations, call (800) 280-CAMP. The fee is $10 for single-family sites, and $20 for multi-family sites.

*Contact:* Toiyabe National Forest, 2881 South Valley View Boulevard, Las Vegas, NV 89102; (702) 873-8800.

*Location:* From Las Vegas, drive 30 miles north on U.S. 95 and turn left onto Highway 156. Drive another 16 miles to the campground.

*Trip notes:* This big campground, elevation 8,500 feet, is just down the hill from the Lee Canyon ski resort (hike up the ski slope in summer). It's less crowded, less developed, and less densely vegetated than Kyle Canyon, Fletcher View, and Hilltop, the other campgrounds up here on Mount Charleston (see pages 323 and 324). The sites at the back (and highest point) of the campground are the most secluded and attractive. Trails crisscross the national recreation area. Contact National Forest headquarters in Las Vegas for the trailguide.

*Season:* May through September, depending on snowfall.

## 8. McWILLIAMS CAMPGROUND

*Reference:* **In Spring Mountains National Recreation Area (Toiyabe National Forest); map E3, grid e0.**

*Campsites, facilities:* There are 40 campsites for tents or self-contained RVs up to 35 feet long. Piped drinking water, one flush toilet and four vault toilets, picnic tables, grills, and fire rings are provided. There is a campground host. Pets are permitted as long as they remain on leashes six feet long or less. The maximum stay is 16 days.

*Reservations, fee:* Reservations are accepted for the multi-family sites; the rest are first come, first served. For reservations, call (800) 280-CAMP. The fee is $10 for single-family sites, and $20 for multi-family sites.

*Contact:* Toiyabe National Forest, 2881 South Valley View Boulevard, Las Vegas, NV 89102; (702) 873-8800.

*Location:* From Las Vegas, drive 30 miles north on U.S. 95 and turn left onto Highway 156. Drive another 15 miles to the campground.

*Trip notes:* This campground is down the hill slightly from Dolomite (see page 322); the two are so close that they might as well be the same. The sites are all off one large loop, and the ones in the middle are the most private. The elevation is 8,500 feet.

*Season:* May through September, depending on snowfall.

## 9. HILLTOP CAMPGROUND

*Reference:* **In Spring Mountains National Recreation Area (Toiyabe National Forest); map E3, grid e0.**

*Campsites, facilities:* There are 35 campsites for tents or self-contained RVs up to 40 feet long. Handicapped-accessible rest rooms with piped drinking water and flush toilets, as well as picnic tables, grills, and fire rings are provided. There is a campground host. Pets are permitted as long as they remain on leashes six feet long or less. The maximum stay is 16 days.

*Reservations, fee:* Reservations are accepted for the multi-family sites; the rest are first come, first served. For reservations, call (800) 280-CAMP. The fee is $10 for single-family sites, and $20 for multi-family sites.

*Contact:* Toiyabe National Forest, 2881 South Valley View Boulevard, Las Vegas, NV 89102; (702) 873-8800.

*Location:* From Las Vegas, drive 30 miles north on U.S. 95 to Highway 156. At the intersection of Highways 156 and 158, turn left on Highway 158 and drive six miles to the campground.

*Trip notes:* Hilltop was completely renovated in 1994 and has new asphalt pavement complete with curb, plus new picnic tables and grills, wide staircases from parking areas to uphill tent sites, and Mr. Clean rest rooms. At an elevation of 8,400 feet, this aptly named campground is situated high up on a bluff. A few sites have a fine view over the valley floor, but little shade. Other sites have more shade but less view. It's also cooler and breezier than the two campgrounds down in Kyle Canyon (see Kyle Canyon and Fletcher View Campgrounds below and on page 324).

*Season:* May through September, depending on snowfall.

## 10. KYLE CANYON CAMPGROUND

*Reference:* **In Spring Mountains National Recreation Area (Toiyabe National Forest); map E3, grid e0.**

*Campsites, facilities:* There are 25 sites for tents or self-contained RVs up to 40 feet long. Piped drinking water, vault toilets, picnic tables, grills, fire pits, and a campground host are available. Pets are permitted as long as they remain on leashes six feet long or less. The maximum stay is 16 days.

*Reservations, fee:* Reservations are accepted for the multi-family sites; the rest are first come, first served. For reservations, call (800) 280-CAMP. The fee is $10 for single-family sites, and $20 for multi-family sites.

*Contact:* Toiyabe National Forest, 2881 South Valley View Boulevard, Las Vegas, NV 89102; (702) 873-8800.

*Location:* From Las Vegas, drive 16 miles north on U.S. 95 and turn left (west) onto Highway 157. Drive another 15 miles to the campground.

*Trip notes:* This is the lowest of the five high-mountain campgrounds in the vicinity. At an elevation of 7,000 feet, it's roughly 5,000 feet higher than downtown Las Vegas (and usually at least 20 degrees cooler). It's also the closest to the city, a mere 45 minutes away. It has big sites, fairly far apart. Most are shaded by tall pines, with plenty of greenery in between. The front gate to the campground closes at 10 P.M.

*Season:* May through September, depending on snowfall.

## 11. FLETCHER VIEW CAMPGROUND

*Reference:* **In Spring Mountains National Recreation Area (Toiyabe National Forest); map E3, grid e0.**

*Campsites, facilities:* There are 12 campsites for tents or self-contained RVs up to 32 feet long. Piped drinking water, vault toilets, picnic tables, grills, fire pits, and a campground host are available. Pets are permitted as long as they remain on leashes six feet long or less. The maximum stay is 16 days.

*Reservations, fee:* No reservations are accepted. Campsites are $10 a night.

*Contact:* Toiyabe National Forest, 2881 South Valley View Boulevard, Las Vegas, NV 89102; (702) 873-8800.

*Location:* From Las Vegas, drive 16 miles north on U.S. 95 and turn left (west) onto Highway 157. Drive another 15 miles to the campground.

*Trip notes:* Fletcher View, elevation 7,000 feet, is a quarter mile up the road from Kyle Canyon Campground (see page 323), with the ranger station in between. Fletcher View is smaller and more compact than Kyle Canyon, just one road in and out. Sites are a little closer together and a bit shadier. If both campgrounds are full, the Kyle RV overflow area is across the road. It has no facilities, just a parking lot with room for about a dozen rigs.

*Season:* May through September, depending on snowfall.

## 12. ECHO BAY CAMPGROUND

*Reference:* **Lake Mead National Recreation Area; map E3, grid e8.**

*Campsites, facilities:* There are 155 campsites for tents or self-contained RVs up to 35 feet long. Piped drinking water, flush toilets, sewage disposal, picnic tables, and grills are provided. Pets are permitted as long as they remain quiet, on leashes, or otherwise controlled. The maximum stay is 90 days.

*Reservations, fee:* No reservations are accepted. Campsites are $8 a night.

*Contact:* National Park Service, 601 Nevada Highway, Boulder City, NV 89005; (702) 293-8990.

*Location:* From Las Vegas, take U.S. 93/95/Interstate 515 southeast for six miles. Exit on Lake Mead Boulevard (aka Highway 147) and go left (east). At the intersection of Highway 147 and Northshore Road, take a left and drive northeast on Northshore Road for 33 miles. Turn right on the access road and drive four miles down to the campgrounds.

*Trip notes:* Near the bottom of the access road (which traverses Bitter Spring Valley), there's an upper and a lower campground. The lower campground overlooks the houseboating area, is closer to the marina action, and has 20-foot-tall oleander bushes that give much-needed shade to the sites on blistering summer afternoons. The upper campground is similar, but closer to the RV and trailer parks (see below) and farther from the action. The marina has a lodge (check out the crow's nest four flights high), restaurant, bar, gas station and convenience store, and boat rentals. Here also is the best easily accessible beach on the Nevada side of the lake: small, sandy, uncrowded.

*Season:* Open year-round.

## 13. ECHO BAY TRAILER VILLAGE

*Reference:* **Lake Mead National Recreation Area; map E3, grid e8.**

*Campsites, facilities:* There are 35 spaces for RVs, all with full hookups (20-, 30-, and 50-amp receptacles); none of these are pull-throughs. Tents are not allowed. Rest rooms have drinking water, flush toilets, and hot showers. A public phone, sewage disposal, laundry facilities, and groceries are available.

*Reservations, fee:* Reservations are accepted. The fee is $9 per vehicle in winter, and $18 per vehicle in summer.

*Contact:* Echo Bay Trailer Village, Overton, NV 89040; (702) 394-4066 or (800) 752-9669.

*Location:* From Las Vegas, take U.S. 93/95/Interstate 515 southeast for six miles. Exit on Lake Mead Boulevard (aka Highway 147) and go left (east). At the intersection of Highway 147 and Northshore Road, take a left and drive northeast on Northshore Road for 33 miles. Turn right on the access road and drive four miles down to the RV park.

*Trip notes:* Echo Bay also boasts the best RV park on Lake Mead's Nevada side. Spaces are nice and wide, with telephone-pole stumps separating them. Every site has a tree or two. And there are no permanents: all the mobiles and trailers are in the trailer village across the way, and this lot is only for RVs. Register at the front desk of Echo Bay Seven Crowns Resort, just down the access road in the marina.

*Season:* Open year-round.

## 14. CALLVILLE BAY CAMPGROUND

*Reference:* **Lake Mead National Recreation Area; map E3, grid e7.**

*Campsites, facilities:* There are 80 campsites for tents or self-contained RVs up to 35 feet long. Piped drinking water, flush toilets, picnic tables, and grills are provided. There is a campground host. Pets are permitted as long as they remain quiet, on leashes, or otherwise controlled. The maximum stay is 90 days.

*Reservations, fee:* No reservations are accepted. Campsites are $8 a night.

*Contact:* National Park Service, 601 Nevada Highway, Boulder City, NV 89005; (702) 293-8990.

*Location:* From Las Vegas, take U.S. 93/95/Interstate 515 southeast for six miles. Exit on Lake Mead Boulevard (aka Highway 147) and go left (east).

At the intersection of Highway 147 and Northshore Road, take a left and drive northeast on Northshore Road for nine miles. Turn right on the access road and drive four miles down to the campground.

*Trip notes:* A beautiful grassy area greets you at the entrance to the campground, with stone picnic benches under shelters and a rest room. The sites closer to the front entrance have the taller shade-giving oleanders; those toward the rear of the campground are more exposed. Like Echo Bay (see page 324), Callville Bay has a marina with a restaurant and bar, a grocery store (with a snack bar), and boat rentals (including houseboats). Unlike Echo Bay, Callville (a half-hour closer to Las Vegas) attracts the lion share of the crowds and has no beach to speak of.

*Season:* Open year-round.

---

## 15. CALLVILLE BAY TRAILER VILLAGE

*Reference:* **Lake Mead National Recreation Area; map E3, grid e7.**

*Campsites, facilities:* There are only six spaces for overnight RVs, all with full hookups (20-, 30-, and 50-amp receptacles); three of these are pull-throughs. Tents are not allowed. Handicapped-accessible rest rooms have drinking water, flush toilets, and hot showers. A public phone, sewage disposal, laundry facilities, and groceries are available.

*Reservations, fee:* Reservations are recommended, especially on weekends. Campsites are $17.

*Contact:* Callville Bay Trailer Village, P.O. Box 100 HCR-30, Las Vegas, NV 89124; (702) 565-8958.

*Location:* From Las Vegas, take U.S. 93/95/Interstate 515 southeast for six miles. Exit on Lake Mead Boulevard (a.k.a. Highway 147) and go left (east). At the intersection of Highway 147 and Northshore Road, take a left and drive northeast on Northshore Road for nine miles. Turn right on the access road and drive four miles down to the RV park.

*Trip notes:* Callville Bay has only a handful of spaces for overnighters (at the end of the loop road); most of the "park" is occupied by permanent mobiles and trailers. Register at the administration office by the marina. RVs can always park without hookups at the campground across the way (see Callville Bay Campground on page 325). Better yet, drive another 30 minutes to Echo Bay (see page 325), the best RV parking on the lake.

*Season:* Open year-round.

---

## 16. HITCHIN' POST RV PARK

*Reference:* **In North Las Vegas; map E3, grid f4.**

*Campsites, facilities:* There are 100 spaces for RVs, all with full hookups (30- and 50-amp receptacles); all of these are pull-throughs. Tents and pets are not allowed. Handicapped-accessible rest rooms have drinking water, flush toilets, and hot showers. A public phone, sewage disposal, laundry facilities, groceries, video rentals, a game room, and a heated swimming pool are available.

---

**Reservations, fee:** Reservations are accepted. The fee is $18 for two people, and $3 for each additional person. Good Sam discounts are accepted.

**Contact:** Hitchin' Post RV Park, 3640 Las Vegas Boulevard North, North Las Vegas, NV 89115; (702) 644-1043.

**Location:** From downtown Las Vegas, drive 5.5 miles north on Las Vegas Boulevard North. The park is on the right.

**Trip notes:** The Hitchin' Post actually has a total of 200 spaces, with 100 for overnighters only. The rest are residential mobile homes. This RV park has the tightest security in Las Vegas, with a big security wall and gate. Inside the RV park it's clean, spacious, and paved.

**Season:** Open year-round.

# 17. CIRCUSLAND RV PARK

**Reference:** On the north Strip in Las Vegas; map E3, grid f4.

**Campsites, facilities:** There are 370 spaces for RVs, all with full hookups (20-, 30-, and 50-amp receptacles); 280 of these are pull-throughs. Tents are not allowed. Handicapped-accessible rest rooms have drinking water, flush toilets, and hot showers. A public phone, sewage disposal, laundry facilities, groceries, a game room, a fenced playground, a heated swimming pool, a children's pool, a spa, and a sauna are available.

**Reservations, fee:** Reservations are recommended year-round. Campsites are $12 to $22 a night.

**Contact:** Circusland RV Park, 500 Circus Circus Drive, Las Vegas, NV 89109; (702) 734-0410 or (800) 634-3450.

**Location:** From Interstate 15, take the Sahara Avenue exit and drive one mile east on Sahara Avenue to Las Vegas Boulevard South. Turn right (south) on Las Vegas Boulevard, drive half a mile to Circus Circus Drive, and turn right. Drive down the block about halfway, turn right, and follow the signs into the park.

**Trip notes:** This is a prime spot for RVers, especially those with kids. Those who stay here are right in the thick of things, and have the run of very good facilities. The park itself is big and all paved, with a grassy island here and a shade tree there. The pool and spa, fenced playground, and video arcade are convenient, and the convenience store is open 24 hours. Circus Circus, with its very cheap buffets, carnival midway, and Grand Slam Canyon indoor amusement park, are next door. The Stratosphere Tower hovers over it, and Wet 'N Wild water park is directly across the street. Ten minutes spent learning the Industrial Road back entrance will save you the frustration of sitting in traffic on the Strip.

**Season:** Open year-round.

# 18. BOOMTOWN RV PARK

**Reference:** South of Las Vegas; map E3, grid f4.

**Campsites, facilities:** There are 460 spaces for RVs, all with full hookups (20-, 30-, and 50-amp receptacles); 260 of these are pull-throughs. Tents are not allowed. Handicapped-accessible rest rooms have drinking water, flush

---

toilets, and hot showers. A public phone, sewage disposal, laundry facilities, groceries, a recreation room, a heated swimming pool, a wading pool with play apparatus, and a spa are available. The maximum stay is 14 days.

*Reservations, fee:* Reservations are recommended September through April. The fee is $12 to $16 per vehicle. Good Sam discounts are available.

*Contact:* 3333 Blue Diamond Road, Las Vegas, NV 89139; (702) 263-7777 or (800) 588-7711.

*Location:* From Las Vegas, take Interstate 15 south out of town and exit at Blue Diamond Road (exit 33, three miles south of Russell Road). Go west one block to Boomtown.

*Trip notes:* This RV park opened in May 1994. The spaces are ample, almost as wide as two spaces at more crowded parks. Each has a two-year-old pine tree and a verdant square of grass. There's also a two-acre grassy picnic area and two pools, one for adults and the other for children, complete with a play apparatus and fountains. It's convenient to the highway, but far enough off the road that traffic noise is at a minimum. Inside Boomtown is a full-service casino, buffet and 24-hour coffee shop (don't miss the strawberry "tall" cake for $1), and live country and western bands.

*Season:* Open year-round.

---

## 19. OASIS RV PARK

*Reference:* **South of Las Vegas; map E3, grid f4.**

*Campsites, facilities:* There are 707 spaces for RVs, all with full hookups (20-, 30-, and 50-amp receptacles); approximately 500 of these are pull-throughs. Tents are allowed. Handicapped-accessible rest rooms have drinking water, flush toilets, and hot showers. A public phone, sewage disposal, laundry facilities, groceries, a bar and lounge, an arcade, an exercise room, a putting course, and a heated swimming pool are available. The maximum stay is 30 days.

*Reservations, fee:* Reservations are accepted. The camping fee is $12 to $27 per site.

*Contact:* Oasis RV Park, 2711 West Windmill Road, Las Vegas, NV 89139; (702) 258-9978 or (800) 566-4707.

*Location:* From Las Vegas, take Interstate 15 south out of town and exit at Blue Diamond Road (exit 33, three miles south of Russell Road). Go east to Las Vegas Boulevard South. Turn right and drive one block to West Windmill Road, then turn right into the park.

*Trip notes:* Oasis opened just after Christmas 1995 and is now a major boon to RVers looking for quality parking in Las Vegas. In fact, Oasis's 707 spaces (second largest in Nevada, after Riverside Resort RV Park; see page 337), combined with Boomtown's nearly 500 spaces directly across Interstate 15, render exit 33 the most concentrated RV locale in the state. (By the way, don't try to run across the freeway to get to Boomtown; several people die in the attempt every year.) Five rows of towering date palms usher you from the park entrance to the cavernous clubhouse, 24,000 square feet of it. Each space is wide enough for a car and motor home, and comes with a picnic

---

table and patio. The horticulture is plentiful, though it needs a few years to mature. Be sure to grab a map from the front desk; this is Nevada's easiest RV park to get lost in!

*Season:* Open year-round.

## 20. OAK CREEK CAMPGROUND

*Reference:* **Near Las Vegas; map E3, grid f2.**

*Campsites, facilities:* There are 15 campsites for tents or self-contained RVs up to 12 feet long. Drinking water (from a tank), vault toilets, picnic tables, and fire pits are provided. Pets are permitted as long as they remain quiet, on leashes, or otherwise controlled. The maximum stay is 14 days.

*Reservations, fee:* No reservations are accepted. Campsites are $10 a night.

*Contact:* Las Vegas BLM District Office, 4765 West Vegas Drive (P.O. Box 26569), Las Vegas, NV 89126; (702) 647-5000.

*Location:* From Las Vegas, drive west on Charleston Boulevard. Oak Creek is three miles past the turnoff for Red Rock Canyon. Take a right at the sign to reach the campground.

*Trip notes:* This is the closest public campground to the bright lights of Las Vegas, 20 minutes from downtown and a stone's throw from Red Rock Canyon (BLM's southern Nevada showpiece), Spring Mountain Ranch State Park, and Bonnie Springs/Old Nevada. The campground is in the middle of the desert: dry, usually windy, either hot or cold (with little in between). The sites are good-sized and some have shade, and the mountain backdrop is stunning. Wild burros are plentiful in this area. They're docile and friendly, but please don't feed them.

*Season:* Open year-round.

## 21. KING'S ROW TRAILER PARK

*Reference:* **In southeast Las Vegas; map E3, grid f5.**

*Campsites, facilities:* There are 407 spaces for RVs, all with full hookups (15-, 30-, and 50-amp receptacles); 60 of these are pull-throughs. Tents are not allowed. Handicapped-accessible rest rooms have drinking water, flush toilets, and hot showers. A public phone, sewage disposal, laundry facilities, a recreation room, and a heated swimming pool are available.

*Reservations, fee:* Reservations are not accepted. Campsites are $11.

*Contact:* King's Row Trailer Park, 3660 Boulder Highway, Las Vegas, NV 89121; (702) 457-3606.

*Location:* From Las Vegas, take U.S. 93/95/Interstate 515 southeast to the Boulder Highway exit (exit 70), go left (west), head a half mile on Boulder Highway (back toward downtown), and turn left into the park.

*Trip notes:* King's Row is primarily a residential trailer and mobile home park, so big that it seems like a subdivision. It's usually full of permanents. During the winter months, when all the overnighter RV parks in town are filled up with snowbirds, you might park here in a pinch if you can get a space. Boulder Station Hotel-Casino is across and east (away from downtown) a bit.

*Season:* Open year-round.

# 22. LAS VEGAS KOA

*Reference:* **In southeast Las Vegas; map E3, grid f5.**

*Campsites, facilities:* There are 180 spaces for RVs, most with full hookups (20-, 30-, and 50-amp receptacles), and all pull-throughs. Tents are allowed. Handicapped-accessible rest rooms have drinking water, flush toilets, and hot showers. A public phone, sewage disposal, laundry facilities, groceries, a game room, a playground, two heated swimming pools, a wading pool, a spa, an RV wash, and a shuttle are available.

*Reservations, fee:* Reservations are accepted. The fees are $22 for tents and $24 to $26 for RV sites with two people, plus $5 for each additional person.

*Contact:* Las Vegas KOA, 4315 Boulder Highway, Las Vegas, NV 89121; (702) 451-5527.

*Location:* From Las Vegas, take U.S.93/95/Interstate 515 southeast to the Boulder Highway exit (exit 70). Turn right (southeast), go one mile on Boulder Highway, and turn left into the park.

*Trip notes:* This is a well-established RV park/campground, pleasantly rustic around the edges. The trees, oleander, and pool area are large and the sites aren't at all cramped. A little less than half the spaces are taken up by residential units, but the rest are reserved for overnighters. Tents are welcome here, the closest place to downtown and the Strip to pitch a little A-frame or dome (60 tent spaces). Boulder Station Casino right up the street has the best salad bar in town (in the Broiler restaurant) and one of the best buffets. It also has an 11-plex movie theater and a giant kids' play area.

*Season:* Open year-round.

# 23. ROAD RUNNER RV PARK

*Reference:* **In southeast Las Vegas; map E3, grid f5.**

*Campsites, facilities:* There are 200 spaces for RVs, all with full hookups (20-, 30-, and 50-amp receptacles); 72 of these are pull-throughs. Tents are not allowed. Handicapped-accessible rest rooms have drinking water, flush toilets, and hot showers. A public phone, sewage disposal, laundry facilities, a TV room (with slots), a heated swimming pool, and a spa are available.

*Reservations, fee:* Reservations are not accepted. Campsites are $16.

*Contact:* Road Runner RV Park, 4711 Boulder Highway, Las Vegas, NV 89121; (702) 456-4711.

*Location:* From Las Vegas, take U.S. 93/95/Interstate 515 southeast to the Boulder Highway exit (exit 70), go right (southeast), drive 1.5 miles on Boulder Highway, and turn left into the park.

*Trip notes:* This park is much newer than the KOA (see above), all paved and little shade (a few small cypress trees separate the sites). A large part of it is residential, but there's more likely to be an overnight space here than at King's Row (see page 329). It's across the street from an RV repair facility and an Albertsons supermarket. Sam's Town, one of the premier casinos in Las Vegas, is just down the street.

*Season:* Open year-round.

## 24. HOLIDAY TRAVEL PARK

*Reference:* **In southeast Las Vegas; map E3, grid f5.**

*Campsites, facilities:* There are 403 spaces for RVs, all with full hookups (20-, 30-, and 50-amp receptacles); 25 of these are pull-throughs. Tents and pets are not allowed. Handicapped-accessible rest rooms have drinking water, flush toilets, and hot showers. A public phone, sewage disposal, laundry facilities, a game room, and a heated swimming pool are available.

*Reservations, fee:* Reservations are accepted. The fee is $14 for two people.

*Contact:* Holiday Travel Park, 3890 South Nellis Avenue, Las Vegas, NV 89121; (702) 451-8005.

*Location:* From Las Vegas, take U.S. 93/95/Interstate 515 southeast to the Flamingo Avenue exit, go right, drive a mile east on Flamingo, then cross Boulder Highway. Take your first left onto Nellis Boulevard. Drive two blocks and turn right into the park.

*Trip notes:* Catering mostly to seniors and residential units, the Holiday is a big park with paved streets, gravel spaces, and little shade (cactus and small palms for greenery). It's generally full between December and April with snowbirds and permanents. It's one of three RV parks in a row around Sam's Town Casino, which combine for a total of nearly 1,000 spaces, though 300 are residential and 200 are for snowbirds. Still, with Sam's Town within walking distance and all the spaces, this neck of Las Vegas is a pretty safe bet for landing a parking space for your RV.

*Season:* Open year-round.

---

## 25. SAM'S TOWN NELLIS RV PARK

*Reference:* **In southeast Las Vegas; map E3, grid f5.**

*Campsites, facilities:* There are 207 spaces for RVs, all with full hookups (20-, 30-, and 50-amp receptacles); 14 of these are pull-throughs. Tents are not allowed. Handicapped-accessible rest rooms have drinking water, flush toilets, and hot showers. A public phone, sewage disposal, laundry facilities, a recreation hall, a heated swimming pool, and a spa are available.

*Reservations, fee:* Reservations are recommended. Campsites are $16.

*Contact:* Sam's Town Nellis RV Park, 4040 South Nellis Boulevard, Las Vegas, NV 89121; (702) 456-7777 or (800) 634-6371.

*Location:* From Las Vegas, take U.S. 93/95/Interstate 515 southeast to the Flamingo Avenue exit, go right, drive a mile on Flamingo, then cross Boulder Highway. Take your first left onto Nellis Boulevard. Drive one block and turn right into the park.

*Trip notes:* Sam's Town Nellis is on the north side, across Flamingo Avenue, from Sam's Town Casino. It's mostly a gravel parking lot with precious little shade but spacious sites and a pool. The recreation hall has a pool table and kitchen. This is the snowbird park, which closes down in the summer. The minimum stay to qualify for the discounted snowbird monthly rate is three months, and the maximum stay is six months.

*Season:* September through May.

---

## 26. SAM'S TOWN BOULDER RV PARK

*Reference:* **In southeast Las Vegas; map E3, grid f5.**

*Campsites, facilities:* There are 291 spaces for RVs, all with full hookups (20-, 30-, and 50-amp receptacles); 93 of these are pull-throughs. Tents are not allowed. Handicapped-accessible rest rooms have drinking water, flush toilets, and hot showers. A public phone, sewage disposal, laundry facilities, limited groceries, a heated swimming pool, and a spa are available. The maximum stay is 14 days.

*Reservations, fee:* Reservations are recommended during the winter. Campsites are $16.

*Contact:* Sam's Town Boulder RV Park, 5225 Boulder Highway, Las Vegas, NV 89121; (702) 456-7777 or (800) 634-6371.

*Location:* From Las Vegas, take U.S. 93/95/Interstate 515 southeast to the Flamingo Avenue exit, drive east one mile on Flamingo Avenue, then turn right (southeast) on Boulder Highway. Drive one block south and turn left into the park.

*Trip notes:* One step above a parking lot, this RV park on the other (east) side of the casino from the Holiday and Sam's Town Nellis RV parks (see page 331) is fairly roomy with little shade. But it's a two-minute walk across the auto parking lot to the casino. Sam's Town features a nine-story indoor atrium with trees, stone paths, and a big rock waterfall; an engaging laser-and-dancing-waters show (free) is presented twice a night in front of the waterfall. There are also half a dozen restaurants, a great sports bar, a bowling alley, a Western-wear emporium, and one of the best slot clubs in Las Vegas—a lot to recommend the three RV parks hereabouts.

*Season:* Open year-round.

## 27. BOULDER LAKES RV RESORT

*Reference:* **In southeast Las Vegas; map E3, grid f5.**

*Campsites, facilities:* There are 417 total spaces here, 75 of these held for overnight RVs, all with full hookups (20- and 30-amp receptacles). There are no pull-throughs. Tents are not allowed. Handicapped-accessible rest rooms have drinking water, flush toilets, and hot showers. A public phone, sewage disposal, laundry facilities, limited groceries, a recreation hall, and four heated swimming pools are also available.

*Reservations, fee:* Reservations are accepted. The fee is $18 for two people, and $2 for each additional person.

*Contact:* Boulder Lakes RV Resort, 6201 Boulder Highway, Las Vegas, NV 89122; (702) 435-1157.

*Location:* From Las Vegas, take U.S. 93/95/Interstate 515 southeast to the Tropicana Avenue exit, drive two miles east on Tropicana Avenue, and turn right (southeast) on Boulder Highway. Go a mile and turn left into the park.

*Trip notes:* A long and winding road leads from the highway to this large residential park, of which a portion is reserved for overnighters. If you're staying long-term, this one is as good as any of the residential parks on Boulder Highway, maybe better. If you're only visiting, you'll probably have a better shot here than at King's Row, Road Runner, or Holiday (see pages 329, 330, and 331).

*Season:* Open year-round.

## 28. CANYON TRAIL RV PARK

*Reference:* **In Boulder City; map E3, grid f6.**

*Campsites, facilities:* There are 156 spaces for RVs, all with full hookups (30- and 50-amp receptacles); 86 of these are pull-throughs. Tents are not allowed. Handicapped-accessible rest rooms have drinking water, flush toilets, and hot showers. A public phone, sewage disposal, and laundry facilities are also available.

*Reservations, fee:* Reservations are recommended during the winter. The fee is $17 for two people, and $3 for each additional person. Good Sam discounts are offered.

*Contact:* Canyon Trail RV Park, 1200 Industrial Road, Boulder City, NV 89005; (702) 293-1200.

*Location:* Coming into Boulder City from Las Vegas, there's a traffic light where U.S. 93 (the truck route through town) veers off to the left. Take a left at the light and go one block to Canyon Road. Turn left on Canyon Road, drive to the end, and turn left on Industrial Road. Drive half a block and turn right into the RV park.

*Trip notes:* This is the only RV park in Boulder City, the first master-planned community to be built by the U.S. government (in 1931) to house Hoover Dam workers. Like most of the hooking-up spots hereabouts, it's mostly residential, with no shade, precious little greenery, and craggy sandstone mountains rising behind the park. Lake Mead and Hoover Dam are a four-mile drive away, and the nearest casinos are three miles away: Boulder City is the only town in the state of Nevada where gambling is illegal (a holdover from its federal days).

*Season:* Open year-round.

## 29. HEMENWAY CAMPGROUND

*Reference:* **In Lake Mead National Recreation Area; map E3, grid f6.**

*Campsites, facilities:* There are 158 campsites for tents or self-contained RVs up to 35 feet long. Piped drinking water, flush toilets, sewage disposal, picnic tables, grills, and fire rings are provided. Pets are permitted as long as they remain quiet, on leashes, or otherwise controlled. The maximum stay is 30 days.

*Reservations, fee:* No reservations are accepted. The fee is $8 per site.

*Contact:* National Park Service, 601 Nevada Highway, Boulder City, NV 89005; (702) 293-8990.

*Location:* From Las Vegas, drive to and through Boulder City and take a left at the light where the U.S. 93 truck route bypasses town. At the intersection of

U.S. 93 and Highway 166 (Lakeshore Road, just past the Alan Bible Visitors Center), turn left on Highway 166 and drive one mile to the RV park on the right.

*Trip notes:* This is the closest camping on Lake Mead to Las Vegas, Boulder City, and Hoover Dam. Like Boulder Beach just up the road (see below), Hemenway is a sprawling campground on a wide sandy flat near the water, with shade trees and big sites—and it's rarely full.

*Season:* Open year-round.

## 30. LAKESHORE TRAILER VILLAGE

*Reference:* In Lake Mead National Recreation Area; map E3, grid f6.

*Campsites, facilities:* There are 75 spaces for overnight RVs, all with full hookups (20-, 30-, and 50-amp receptacles); 23 of these are pull-throughs. Tents are not allowed, and only one pet is allowed per site. Rest rooms have drinking water, flush toilets, and hot showers. A public phone, sewage disposal, laundry facilities, and groceries are available.

*Reservations, fee:* Reservations are not accepted (except for Memorial Day, the Fourth of July, and Labor Day weekends). The fee is $15 for two people, and $1.50 for each additional person.

*Contact:* Lakeshore RV Park, 268 Lakeshore Road, Boulder City, NV 89005; (702) 293-2540.

*Location:* From Las Vegas, drive to and through Boulder City and take a left at the light where the U.S. 93 truck route bypasses town. At the intersection of U.S. 93 and Highway 166 (Lakeshore Road, just past the Alan Bible Visitors Center), turn left on Highway 166 and drive two miles. Turn right into the entrance and right to the trailer village.

*Trip notes:* Like Echo Bay and Callville Bay (see pages 325 and 326), Lakeshore is a trailer village of permanent mobiles and trailers, with a compact area near the entrance dedicated to overnight RVers (register at the office near the entrance). It's at Boulder Beach, the most popular sunning and swimming stretch of Lake Mead. All the recreation of the lake is just down the hill: boating, waterskiing, swimming, and fishing.

*Season:* Open year-round.

## 31. BOULDER BEACH CAMPGROUND

*Reference:* In Lake Mead National Recreation Area; map E3, grid f6.

*Campsites, facilities:* There are 140 campsites for tents or self-contained RVs up to 35 feet long. Piped drinking water, flush toilets, sewage disposal, picnic tables, and grills are provided. There is a campground host. Pets are permitted as long as they remain quiet, on leashes, or otherwise controlled. The maximum stay is 30 days.

*Reservations, fee:* No reservations are accepted. The fee is $8 per site.

*Contact:* National Park Service, 601 Nevada Highway, Boulder City, NV 89005; (702) 293-8906.

*Location:* From Las Vegas, drive to and through Boulder City and take a left at the light where the U.S. 93 truck route bypasses town. At the intersection of U.S. 93 and Highway 166 (Lakeshore Road, just past the Alan Bible Visitors Center), turn left on Highway 166 and drive two miles. Turn right into the entrance, then left into the campground.

*Trip notes:* This sprawling and somewhat rustic campground with plenty of shade under cottonwoods and pines is a three-minute walk to the water (or a half-mile drive north on Lakeshore Drive to the beach parking lot). They don't call it Boulder Beach for nothing: the bottom is rocky and hard on the feet (wear your zoris). But the water is bathtub warm, 80 degrees or so all summer long. Sheltered picnic tables and rest rooms are available waterside.

*Season:* Open year-round.

## 32. LAS VEGAS BAY CAMPGROUND

*Reference:* **In Lake Mead National Recreation Area; map E3, grid f6.**

*Campsites, facilities:* There are 86 campsites for tents or self-contained RVs up to 35 feet long. Piped drinking water, flush toilets, picnic tables, grills, and fire pits are provided. There is a campground host. Pets are permitted as long as they remain quiet, on leashes, or otherwise controlled. The maximum stay is 30 days.

*Reservations, fee:* No reservations are accepted. The fee is $8 per site.

*Contact:* National Park Service, 601 Nevada Highway, Boulder City, NV 89005; (702) 293-8906.

*Location:* From Las Vegas, drive to and through Boulder City and take a left at the light where the U.S. 93 truck route bypasses town. At the intersection of U.S. 93 and Highway 166 (Lakeshore Road, just past the Alan Bible Visitors Center), turn left on Highway 166 and drive nine miles. Turn right into the marina, and then take the first left; the campground is about a mile down this spur road.

*Trip notes:* This facility sits on a bluff over the lake. It's not quite as shady or large as Boulder Beach (see page 334). Also, you've got to climb down a pretty steep slope to get to the water, and there's no real beach here. The marina is also a bit of a trek (1.4 miles by vehicle). It has a convenience store, restaurant, and bar. It's also home to the sternwheeler *Desert Princess,* which offers a variety of sightseeing and food cruises around the lake.

*Season:* Open year-round.

## 33. PRIMADONNA RV VILLAGE

*Reference:* **At the California state line on Interstate 15; map E3, grid g2.**

*Campsites, facilities:* There are 198 spaces for RVs, all with full hookups (30- and 50-amp receptacles); 157 of these are pull-throughs. Tents are not allowed. Handicapped-accessible rest rooms have drinking water, flush toilets, and hot showers. A public phone, sewage disposal, laundry facilities, groceries, a recreation room, a playground, a heated swimming pool (open year-round), and a spa are available. The maximum stay is 60 days.

*Reservations, fee:* Reservations are recommended from October through May. The fee is $12 per vehicle.

*Contact:* Primadonna RV Village, P.O. Box 93718, Las Vegas, NV 89193; (702) 382-1212 or (800) 248-8453.

*Location:* From Las Vegas, take Interstate 15 south 40 miles to the Stateline exit (exit 1) and drive east two blocks on the exit road. The park is on the east side of the Primadonna Casino.

*Trip notes:* Since this RV park only opened in 1993, the trees are still small, but the park itself is large. You won't want to spend too much time in your RV around here. There are three casinos (one on the other side of the highway, to which a monorail runs above the highway), 11 restaurants, a ferris wheel (free), a merry-go-round (free), a kiddie choo-choo (free), and a bowling center, as well as movie and motion-simulation theaters. Need more? How about a flume ride through one of the casinos, and—hang onto your hats, not to mention your breakfast—the tallest and fastest roller coaster in the world.

*Season:* Open year-round.

---

## 34. COTTONWOOD COVE MARINA AND RESORT

*Reference:* **In Lake Mead National Recreation Area; map E3, grid i6.**

*Campsites, facilities:* There are 75 spaces for RVs, all with full hookups (30- and 50-amp receptacles); 15 of these are pull-throughs. Tents are not allowed. Rest rooms have drinking water, flush toilets, and hot showers. A public phone, sewage disposal, laundry facilities, groceries, and a volleyball court are available.

*Reservations, fee:* Reservations are accepted for pull-through sites. Campsites are $17 to $20.

*Contact:* Cottonwood Cove Marina and Resort, 100 Cottonwood Cove Road, Cottonwood Cove, NV 89046; (702) 297-1464.

*Location:* From U.S. 95 at Searchlight, drive 14 miles east (all downhill) on Highway 164 (Cottonwood Cove Road) to the campground.

*Trip notes:* Cottonwood Cove is a protected "bay" on Lake Mohave. The RV park is the epitome of "desert landscaping" (bring sunscreen), but the sites are wide enough to park a boat next to an RV. The trailer village that surrounds it is the largest on the Nevada side of the lake. There are some activities at the marina, but the main action is on the water: houseboat, deck cruiser, and motorboat rentals, fishing, waterskiing, canoeing, and of course swimming, at the small beach in front of the tent campground. Also here are a motel, cafe, and general store.

*Season:* Open year-round.

---

## 35. COTTONWOOD COVE CAMPGROUND

*Reference:* **In Lake Mead National Recreation Area; map E3, grid i6.**

*Campsites, facilities:* There are 144 campsites for tents or self-contained RVs up to 35 feet long. Piped drinking water, flush toilets, sewage disposal, laundry facilities, picnic tables, grills, and fire rings are provided. Pets are permitted as long as they remain quiet, on leashes, or otherwise controlled. The maximum stay is 90 days.

*Reservations, fee:* No reservations are accepted. The fee is $8 per site.

*Contact:* National Park Service, 601 Nevada Highway, Boulder City, NV 89005; (702) 293-8990.

*Location:* From U.S. 95 at Searchlight, drive 14 miles east on Highway 164 (Cottonwood Cove Road) to the campground.

*Trip notes:* A typical campground in Lake Mead National Recreation Area, Cottonwood Cove is actually on Lake Mohave, a long, thin reservoir of water impounded by Davis Dam in Laughlin. The campground is very close to the water, just across a parking lot from the beach and a sheltered picnic area. Campsites are large and shady.

*Season:* Open year-round.

---

## 36. CAL-NEV-ARI RV PARK

*Reference:* **Near Searchlight; map E3, grid i6.**

*Campsites, facilities:* There are 25 spaces for RVs, all with full hookups (20-, 30- and 50-amp receptacles), and all pull-throughs. Tents and pets are not allowed. Rest rooms have drinking water, flush toilets, and hot showers. A public phone, sewage disposal, laundry facilities, groceries, and a heated swimming pool (at the Blue Sky Motel next door) are available.

*Reservations, fee:* Reservations are accepted. Campsites are $13.

*Contact:* Cal-Nev-Ari RV Park, P.O. Box 430, Cal-Nev-Ari, NV 89039; (702) 297-1115.

*Location:* From Searchlight, drive 10 miles south on U.S. 95 to Cal-Nev-Ari. The RV park is on the left.

*Trip notes:* Cal-Nev-Ari is a small village strung along U.S. 95 for half a mile. The RV park is "downtown," next to the convenience store where you register. It's gravel parking, though the sites are large and well-shaded. Across the highway is the cafe/casino, with slots, poker, and blackjack. Cal-Nev-Ari was founded by Slim and Nancy Kidwell in 1965; Nancy runs the whole show to this day.

*Season:* Open year-round.

---

## 37. RIVERSIDE RESORT RV PARK

*Reference:* **In Laughlin; map E3, grid j6.**

*Campsites, facilities:* There are a whopping 830 spaces for RVs, all with full hookups (20-, 30-, and 50-amp receptacles); 72 of these are pull-throughs. Tents are not allowed. Handicapped-accessible rest rooms have drinking water, flush toilets, and hot showers. A public phone, sewage disposal, laundry facilities, and a heated swimming pool (at the casino across the street) are also available. Maximum stay is 14 days.

*Reservations, fee:* Reservations are recommended at least three weeks in advance. The fee is $14 to $16 per vehicle.

---

***Contact:*** Riverside Resort RV Park, 1650 Casino Drive, Laughlin, NV 89029; (702) 298-2535 or (800) 227-3849.

***Location:*** From the intersection of U.S. 95 and Highway 163 a few miles south of Cal-Nev-Ari, drive 18 miles east on Highway 163 to Casino Drive and turn right. Drive one mile on Casino Drive and turn right into the RV park (across from the Riverside Hotel).

***Trip notes:*** This is far and away the largest RV park in Nevada, nearly twice as big as the second largest (Oasis RV Park in Las Vegas; see page 328). It's so sprawling, occupying eight levels up the hillside, that a casino shuttle comes around regularly to take RVers to the Riverside Casino. There's also an overhead bridge between the RV park and the hotel. Some of the sites at the top of the RV park have a great view of the Colorado River and casino strip next to it. Don Laughlin, owner of the Riverside, is the founder of the town and the big landowner hereabouts. His Riverside is the oldest hotel in this resort town, and has a classic-car collection, a six-screen movie complex, a showroom, and several restaurants. It also offers boat tours on the river (up to Davis Dam) and Jet Ski rentals.

***Season:*** Open year-round.

## LEAVE NO TRACE TIPS

**Pack it in and pack it out.**

• Take everything you bring into the wild back out with you.

• Protect wildlife and your food by storing
rations securely. Pick up all spilled foods.

• Use toilet paper or wipes sparingly; pack them out.

• Inspect your campsite for trash and any evidence of your stay.
Pack out all trash—even if it's not yours!

# TAHOE MAP

Map of Nevada .............. see page 256
Beyond This Region:
North (Map C1) ............. see page 258
East (Map D1) ............... see page 282
South .................................. California
West .................................. California

17 Campgrounds
Pages 340–349

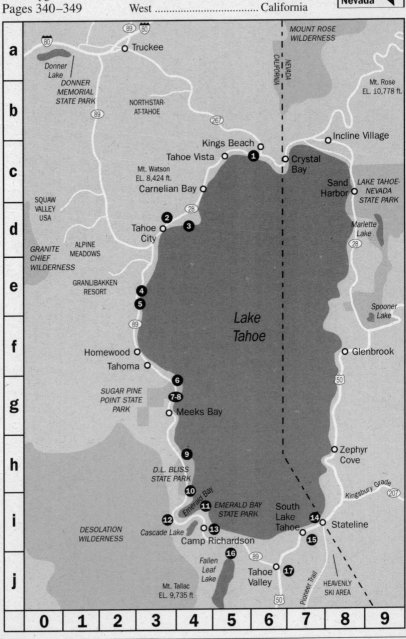

**Lake Tahoe Area chapter features:**

1. Sandy Beach Campground
2. Tahoe State Recreation Area
3. Lake Forest Campground
4. William Kent Campground
5. Kaspian Campground
6. Sugar Pine Point State Park
7. Meeks Bay Campground
8. Meeks Bay Resort
9. D. L. Bliss State Park
10. Emerald Bay Boat-In Camp
11. Emerald Bay State Park
12. Bayview Campground
13. Camp Richardson
14. Lakeside RV Park
15. Campground By The Lake
16. Fallen Leaf Campground
17. Tahoe Valley Campground

## 1. SANDY BEACH CAMPGROUND

*Reference:* **In Tahoe Vista; Tahoe map, grid c6.**

*Campsites, facilities:* There are 44 spaces, 22 with full hookups (20- and 30-amp receptacles); 7 are pull-throughs. Tents are allowed. Rest rooms have drinking water, flush toilets, and hot showers. A public phone, sewage disposal, laundry facilities, and firewood are available.

*Reservations, fee:* Reservations are accepted. The fee is $15 to $20 for up to four people.

*Contact:* Sandy Beach Campground, 6873 North Lake Tahoe Boulevard (Highway 28), Tahoe Vista, CA 96145; (916) 546-7682.

*Location:* From King's Beach, drive one mile west on North Lake Tahoe Boulevard. The campground is on the right in tiny downtown Tahoe Vista.

*Trip notes:* Tall pines shade the gravel sites at this private campground near the lake, with access to fishing, swimming beaches, marinas, restaurants, and the well-lit nightlife of Crystal Bay on the Nevada side.

*Season:* May 1 through October 1.

## 2. TAHOE STATE RECREATION AREA

*Reference:* **Near Tahoe City; Tahoe map, grid d3.**

*Campsites, facilities:* There are 39 campsites for tents or self-contained RVs up to 20 feet long. Piped drinking water, flush toilets, hot showers, picnic tables, grills, and fire pits are provided. Pets are permitted as long as they remain quiet, on leashes, or otherwise controlled. The maximum stay is 10 days.

*Reservations, fee:* Reservations are accepted; call MISTIX at (800) 444-7275. Campsites are $14.

*Contact:* California State Department of Parks and Recreation, P.O. Box D, Tahoma, CA 96142; (916) 583-3074.

*Location:* Drive a quarter mile north on North Lake Tahoe Boulevard (Highway 28) from downtown Tahoe City.

*Trip notes:* With the lake on one side, the main road around the lake on the other, and the paved West Shore Bike Trail between the campground and the road, Tahoe State Recreation Area is convenient for campers who want to be right on the beach, RVers who want to be right on the road, or cyclists who want quick and easy access to the trail. For tent campers, however, it might prove a bit too noisy and exposed.

*Season:* May 22 through September 15.

## 3. LAKE FOREST CAMPGROUND

*Reference:* **Near Tahoe City; Tahoe map, grid d4.**

*Campsites, facilities:* There are 20 campsites for tents or self-contained RVs up to 20 feet long. Piped drinking water, flush toilets, picnic tables, grills, and fire pits are provided. Pets are permitted as long as they remain quiet, on leashes, or otherwise controlled. The maximum stay is 10 days.

*Reservations, fee:* No reservations are accepted. Campsites are $10.

*Contact:* Tahoe City Public Utilities District, P.O. Box 33, Tahoe City, CA 96145; (916) 583-5544.

*Location:* Drive two miles north of Tahoe City on North Lake Tahoe Boulevard (Highway 28), then turn onto Lake Forest Road near the Coast Guard station.

*Trip notes:* This site is next to the only public boat-launching ramp on the north shore. It's a good place for boaters and water-skiers to camp. It's also within walking distance of a public beach. Tahoe's surface water warms up to 68 degrees during the hottest part of the summer. It's brisk swimming!

*Season:* Mid-May through mid-September.

## 4. WILLIAM KENT CAMPGROUND

*Reference:* **Near Tahoe City; Tahoe map, grid e3.**

*Campsites, facilities:* There are 95 campsites for tents or self-contained RVs up to 35 feet long, plus piped drinking water, flush toilets, sewage disposal, picnic tables, grills, and fire pits. Pets are permitted as long as they remain quiet, on leashes, or otherwise controlled. The maximum stay is 14 days.

*Reservations, fee:* Reservations are accepted; call (800) 280-CAMP. Campsites are $12.

*Contact:* U.S. Forest Service Lake Tahoe Visitors Center, 870 Emerald Bay Road, South Lake Tahoe, CA 96150; (916) 573-2600.

*Location:* From Tahoe City, drive three miles south on Highway 89, then turn right into the campground.

*Trip notes:* Though sites here are heavily wooded, they're fairly close together (the best ones are farthest from the road). Nearby are the U.S. Forest Service's William Kent Beach, the excellent West Shore Bike Trail, a TART (Tahoe Area Rapid Transit) bus stop, and the hectic Sunnyside Lodge.

*Season:* Mid-May through September.

## 5. KASPIAN CAMPGROUND

*Reference:* **Halfway between Tahoe City and Homewood; Tahoe map, grid e3.**

*Campsites, facilities:* There are 10 campsites for tents or self-contained RVs up to 20 feet long. Piped drinking water, flush toilets, picnic tables, grills, and fire pits are provided. Pets are permitted as long as they remain quiet, on leashes, or otherwise controlled. The maximum stay is 14 days.

*Reservations, fee:* Reservations are accepted; call (800) 280-CAMP. Campsites are $10.

*Contact:* U.S. Forest Service Lake Tahoe Visitors Center, 870 Emerald Bay Road, South Lake Tahoe, CA 96150; (916) 573-2600.

*Location:* From Tahoe City, drive five miles south on Highway 89 to Kaspian Campground.

*Trip notes:* This is a tiny Forest Service campground hemmed in by the lake and the highway. It's noisy but nice.

*Season:* Mid-May through mid-September.

---

# 6. SUGAR PINE POINT STATE PARK

*Reference:* **Near Tahoma; Tahoe map, grid g4.**

*Campsites, facilities:* There are 175 campsites for tents or self-contained RVs up to 30 feet long. Piped drinking water, flush toilets, hot showers and sewage disposal (summer only), picnic tables, grills, and fire pits are provided. Pets are permitted as long as they remain quiet, on leashes, or otherwise controlled. The maximum stay is 15 days.

*Reservations, fee:* Reservations are strongly recommended during the summer months; call MISTIX at (800) 444-7275. Campsites are $14.

*Contact:* Sugar Pine Point State Park, P.O. Box 266, Tahoma, CA 96142; (916) 525-7982.

*Location:* From the intersection of Highways 28 and 89 in Tahoe City, drive seven miles south on Highway 89 to Tahoma. Sugar Pine Point is a mile south of there on the inland side of the highway.

*Trip notes:* Sugar Pine Point State Park is an extremely busy campground in summer and one of the few Tahoe campgrounds open throughout the winter. This state park is also home to the 12,000-square-foot Ehrman Mansion, built by a west coast moneyman in 1902 and acquired by the state park system in 1965. It also offers a trails system from General Creek up to alpine lakes in Desolation Wilderness of El Dorado National Forest. And this is where the West Shore Bike Trail originates. This is a great location for a recreation installation, which is why a congregation of civilization comes here for vacation.

*Season:* Open year-round.

---

# 7. MEEKS BAY CAMPGROUND

*Reference:* **In Meeks Bay; Tahoe map, grid g4.**

*Campsites, facilities:* There are 40 campsites for tents or self-contained RVs up to 18 feet long. Piped drinking water, flush toilets, picnic tables, grills, and fire pits are provided. The maximum stay is 14 days.

*Reservations, fee:* Reservations are accepted; call (800) 280-CAMP. Campsites are $14.

---

*Contact:* U.S. Forest Service Lake Tahoe Visitors Center, 870 Emerald Bay Road, South Lake Tahoe, CA 96150; (916) 573-2600.

*Location:* From Tahoe City, drive 10 miles south on Highway 89 to Meeks Bay and the campground.

*Trip notes:* Of all the campgrounds on the north and west shores of Lake Tahoe fronted by the lake and backed by the highway, Meeks Bay is the most exposed and exhausticized. Still, the shallow white-sand beach in a sheltered cove is great for wading, splashing, and shore-hugging in a kayak or canoe; a private boat launch is nearby; and Meeks Bay Resort has the amenities.

*Season:* Mid-May through early October.

## 8. MEEKS BAY RESORT

*Reference:* **In Meeks Bay; Tahoe map, grid g4.**

*Campsites, facilities:* There are 28 campsites for tents or self-contained RVs up to 30 feet long. Piped drinking water, flush toilets, hot showers, picnic tables, grills, and fire pits are provided. Pets are not allowed here. The maximum stay is 14 days.

*Reservations, fee:* Reservations are not accepted. Campsites are $15 to $25.

*Contact:* Meeks Bay Resort, 7901 Highway 89 (Box 411), Meeks Bay, CA 96142; (916) 525-7242.

*Location:* From Tahoe City, go 10 miles south on Highway 89 to the resort.

*Trip notes:* This resort has a seven-bedroom mansion, 20 cabins and condos, a general store and snack bar, and the campground right on the highway. The beach is one of the most popular on the lake for families, thanks to a roped-off swimming area and lots of water toys for rent.

*Season:* May through September.

## 9. D. L. BLISS STATE PARK

*Reference:* **South of Meeks Bay; Tahoe map, grid h4.**

*Campsites, facilities:* There are 170 campsites for tents or self-contained RVs up to 16 feet long. Piped drinking water, flush toilets, hot showers, sewage disposal, picnic tables, grills, and fire pits are provided. Pets are permitted as long as they remain quiet, on leashes, or otherwise controlled. The maximum stay is 15 days.

*Reservations, fee:* Reservations are recommended; call MISTIX at (800) 444-7275. Campsites are $14 to $19.

*Contact:* D. L. Bliss State Park, Box 266, Tahoma, CA 96142; (916) 525-7277.

*Location:* From Meeks Bay, drive south on Highway 89 for five miles, and turn left into the state park.

*Trip notes:* Bliss State Park is, well, blissful. With its wooded, secluded, and hilly campsites, its well-protected white-sand beach and convenient coves, it could be the best campground on the lake. It's also one of the favorites, so reserve early. Emerald Bay Trail is a minimally strenuous five-mile day hike from the south end of the park to Emerald Bay.

*Season:* Mid-June through September.

## 10. EMERALD BAY BOAT-IN CAMP

*Reference:* **On Emerald Bay; Tahoe map, grid h4.**

*Campsites, facilities:* There are 20 campsites for tents only. Piped drinking water, chemical toilets, picnic tables, grills, and fire pits are provided. Pets are permitted as long as they remain quiet, on leashes, or otherwise controlled. The maximum stay is 14 days.

*Reservations, fee:* No reservations are accepted. Campsites are $9.

*Contact:* Emerald Bay State Park, P.O. Box 266, Tahoma, CA 96142; (916) 525-7277.

*Location:* This campground on the north shore of Emerald Bay is inaccessible except by boat.

*Trip notes:* This is the only boat-in campground on Lake Tahoe, making it the least accessible and thus the most secluded. However, the big pier can handle many boats from small to large, and the bay starts getting crowded with pleasure craft in the late afternoon. The beach is also big. It's an easy hike to Vikingsholm Castle and D. L. Bliss State Park.

*Season:* Memorial Day through Labor Day.

## 11. EMERALD BAY STATE PARK

*Reference:* **On Emerald Bay; Tahoe map, grid i4.**

*Campsites, facilities:* There are 100 campsites for tents or self-contained RVs up to 20 feet long. Piped drinking water, flush toilets, hot showers, picnic tables, barbecue grills, and fire pits are provided. Pets are permitted as long as they remain quiet, on leashes, or otherwise controlled. The maximum stay is 15 days.

*Reservations, fee:* Reservations are recommended; call (800) 444-7275. Campsites are $14.

*Contact:* Emerald Bay State Park, P.O. Box 266, Tahoma, CA 96142; (916) 525-7277.

*Location:* From the intersection of U.S. 50 and Highway 89 near South Lake Tahoe, drive northwest on Highway 89 for eight miles to the campground.

*Trip notes:* This campground, elevation 6,800 feet, has the best views over the lake of any Tahoe campground and, along with sister park D. L. Bliss (see page 344), is the most popular on the lake. The sites are small and crowded, and the beach is a steep quarter-mile slog down the slope.

*Season:* June through September.

## 12. BAYVIEW CAMPGROUND

*Reference:* **At Emerald Bay; Tahoe map, grid i3.**

*Campsites, facilities:* There are 100 campsites for tents or self-contained RVs up to 30 feet long. Vault toilets and fire pits are provided. Pets are permitted as long as they remain quiet, on leashes, or otherwise controlled. The maximum stay is 14 days.

*Reservations, fee:* No reservations are accepted. Camping is free.

*Contact:* U.S. Forest Service Lake Tahoe Visitors Center, 870 Emerald Bay Road, South Lake Tahoe, CA 96150; (916) 573-2600.

*Location:* This campground is on Highway 89 across from the Emerald Bay overlook, roughly six miles northwest of the intersection of U.S. 50 and Highway 89.

*Trip notes:* This is the only free campground on the lake and the least developed. Trailheads lead into Desolation Wilderness, Cascade Lake and Falls, Granite Lake, and Velma Lakes.

*Season:* June to September.

## 13. CAMP RICHARDSON

*Reference:* **Near South Lake Tahoe; Tahoe map, grid i5.**

*Campsites, facilities:* There are 123 spaces for RVs, 33 with full hookups (30-amp receptacles); two of the sites are pull-throughs. Tents are allowed. Rest rooms have flush toilets and hot showers. A public phone, sewage disposal, laundry facilities, groceries, and firewood are available. No pets are allowed.

*Reservations, fee:* Reservations are recommended. Campsites are $17 to $22.

*Contact:* Richardson's Resort and Marina, P.O. Box 9028, South Lake Tahoe, CA 96158; (916) 541-1801 or (800) 544-1801.

*Location:* From the intersection of U.S. 50 and Highway 89 near South Lake Tahoe, drive northwest on Highway 89 for eight miles to the campground.

*Trip notes:* This is the premier family resort on Lake Tahoe, and one of the few privately operated Forest Service campgrounds. It boasts a great restaurant, a marina, boat rentals of all kinds, a shallow roped-off swimming area for children (with toys for rent), white-sand beaches, horseback riding, volleyball, a bike trail and rentals, hiking trails, and the historic Tallac estates.

*Season:* April 15 to October 15.

## 14. LAKESIDE RV PARK

*Reference:* **At Stateline; Tahoe map, grid i7.**

*Campsites, facilities:* There are 43 spaces for RVs, 12 with full hookups (30- and 50-amp receptacles). Tents are allowed. Rest rooms have drinking water, flush toilets, and hot showers. A public phone, sewage disposal, and laundry facilities are available.

*Reservations, fee:* Reservations are recommended during the summer. Campsites are $22.

*Contact:* Lakeside RV Park, P.O. Box 4493, South Lake Tahoe, CA 96157; (916) 544-4704.

*Location:* From the Nevada state line, drive west on U.S. 50 half a mile to Park Avenue. Take a left on Park Avenue, then go right on Cedar Avenue, and drive one block to the RV park.

*Trip notes:* The only private RV park in South Lake Tahoe, Lakeside is quiet, shaded by mature pine trees, and two blocks from the highway and the lake.

*Season:* Open year-round.

## 15. CAMPGROUND BY THE LAKE

*Reference:* **In South Lake Tahoe; Tahoe map, grid i7.**

*Campsites, facilities:* There are 170 campsites for tents or self-contained RVs up to 35 feet long; 10 are pull-throughs. Piped drinking water, flush toilets, hot showers, picnic tables, grills, and fire pits are provided. Pets are permitted as long as they remain quiet, on leashes, or otherwise controlled. The maximum stay is 15 days.

*Reservations, fee:* Reservations are accepted. Campsites are $16.50.

*Contact:* South Lake Tahoe Recreation Area, 1180 Rufus Allen Boulevard, South Lake Tahoe, CA 96150; (916) 542-6096.

*Location:* From South Lake Tahoe, drive north on U.S. 50 and take a right on Lyons Avenue, which turns into North Rufus Allen Boulevard. The campground is on the right.

*Trip notes:* This well-maintained campground is in a convenient location for lake and commercial-district access, and big enough to handle the crowds, but it's somewhat noisy. Next door is a recreation center with a pool and fitness facilities.

*Season:* April through October.

---

## 16. FALLEN LEAF CAMPGROUND

*Reference:* **Near South Lake Tahoe; Tahoe map; grid j5.**

*Campsites, facilities:* There are 205 campsites for tents or self-contained RVs up to 40 feet. Piped drinking water, flush toilets, picnic tables, grills, and fire pits are provided. Pets are permitted as long as they remain quiet, on leashes, or otherwise controlled. The maximum stay is 15 days.

*Reservations, fee:* Reservations are accepted; call (800) 280-CAMP. Campsites are $14.

*Contact:* U.S. Forest Service Lake Tahoe Visitors Center, 870 Emerald Bay Road, South Lake Tahoe, CA 96150; (916) 573-2600.

*Location:* From the intersection of U.S. 50 and Highway 89 near South Lake Tahoe, drive northwest on Highway 89 for two miles. Turn left at the Fallen Leaf Lake turnoff and drive another mile to the campground.

*Trip notes:* Lotta tenters here. Lake Tahoe is several miles away, but the highway is also a good enough distance for some respite from traffic noise. Fallen Leaf Lake, with fishing and boating, is nearby. Trailheads into Desolation Wilderness are accessible from here.

*Season:* May through October.

---

## 17. TAHOE VALLEY CAMPGROUND

*Reference:* **Near South Lake Tahoe; Tahoe map, grid j7.**

*Campsites, facilities:* There are 410 spaces for RVs, 300 with full hookups (20-, 30-, and 50-amp receptacles); 40 are pull-throughs. Tents are allowed. Handicapped-accessible rest rooms have drinking water, flush toilets, and hot showers. A public phone, sewage disposal, laundry facilities, groceries,

---

a heated swimming pool, tennis courts, a recreation hall, and a playground are available.

***Reservations, fee:*** Reservations are recommended. Campsites are $20 to $27.

***Contact:*** Tahoe Valley Campground, P.O. Box 9026, South Lake Tahoe, CA 96158; (916) 541-2222.

***Location:*** From the intersection of U.S. 50 and Highway 89, proceed south a quarter mile on U.S. 50 to C Street and turn left. Continue one block to the campground.

***Trip notes:*** This is the kind of RV park where any traveler can settle down, dust off, and revitalize. There's so much to do nearby that you could spend all summer here. The Upper Truckee River and a factory outlet mall are walkable. Two 18-hole golf courses are within a stone's throw. The Nevada casinos regularly send around a free shuttle, and public buses also stop. There are bike and horse trails, concierge services, even a visitors center.

***Season:*** April 15 to October 15.

## Leave No Trace Tips

**Travel and camp with care.**

*On the trail:*

• Stay on designated trails.

• Do not take shortcuts on switchbacks.

• When traveling cross-country where there are no trails,
follow animal trails or spread out your group so no new routes are created.
Walk along the most durable surfaces available,
such as rock, gravel, dry grasses, or snow.

• Use a map and compass to eliminate the need for
rock cairns, tree scars, or ribbons.

• If you encounter pack animals, step to the downhill side
of the trail and speak softly to avoid startling them.

*At camp:*

• Choose an established, legal site that will not be damaged by your stay.

• Restrict activities to areas where vegetation is compacted or absent.

• Keep pollutants out of the water by camping at least 200 feet
(about 70 adult steps) from lakes and streams.

• Control pets at all times, or leave them at home
with a sitter. Remove dog feces.

# Index

## A

AAA (see Automobile Association of America)

AARP (see American Association of Retired Persons)

Abajo Mountains (see Blue. Mountains)

Adelaide **153**

Alan Bible Visitors Center  334, 335

Albion **102**

Alpine Loop  104

Alta ski resort  30, 102

American Association of Retired Persons (AARP)  265, 275, 283, 287

American Campground **108**

American Fork Canyon  30, 102, 103, 104

(North Fork)  103

American Fork Creek  102

American Fork, UT  35, 108

Anaho Island National Wildlife Refuge  42

Anasazi cliff dwelling  247, 248, 251

Anasazi State Park  209, 213

Anderson Cove **75**

Anderson Meadow **158**

Anderson Meadow Reservoir  158

Aneth, UT  250

Angel Creek **275,** 276

Angel Lake  275, 276

Angel Lake (campground)  40, **276**

Antelope Flat  127, **128,** 129

(boat ramp)  127, 132

Antelope Island  78

Antelope Island State Park **78**

Antelope Valley  295

Antelope Valley RV Park **152**

Anticline Overlook  240, 243

Antimony, UT  208

Aquarius Mobile and RV **204**

Aquarius Motel  204

Arch View Campground **228**

Arches National Park  31, 34, 35, 195, 227, 228, 229, 233, 236, 245, 246

Ash Meadows National Wildlife Refuge  42

Ashdown Gorge Wilderness Area  31

Ashley National Forest  30, 31, 32, 134, 135, 136, 137, 138, 139, 140, 141, 142, 143, 148

(Duchesne Ranger District)  32, 137, 138, 139, 148

(Flaming Gorge Dutch John Office)  32

(Flaming Gorge Headquarters)  32

(Headquarters)  32

(Roosevelt Ranger District)  32, 139, 140, 141, 142

(Vernal Ranger District)  32, 135, 136, 137, 143

Aspen Grove (Ashley National Forest, UT) **138**

Aspen Grove (Strawberry Reservoir, NV) **114**

Atlatl Rock  322

ATV Trail  153, 154, 190, 195

Austin, NV  41, 299, 300, 301

Austin Ranger District  41, 299

(Office)  300, 301

Austin RV Park **299**

Automobile Association of America (AAA)  275, 276, 283, 284, 287, 289, 294

Avintaquin **148**

# B

Bailey's Hot Springs **315**
Baker Creek 309
Baker Creek Campground **308**
Baker Dam **174**
Baker Lake 309
Baker, NV 41, 308, 309
Baker Reservoir 174
Bald Mountain 92, 93, 94
Balloon Races (Reno, NV) 286
Balsam **115**
Bandits Cove **63**
Barker Reservoir **212**
Barn Pole Hollow 171
Battle Mountain, NV 42, 265, 266
Bauer's Canyon Ranch **179**
Bayview Campground **345**
Bear Lake 59, 60, 61, 62, 63, 67
  (Cisco Beach) 63
Bear Lake Marina 60, 61
Bear Lake Rendezvous Beach State
  Park **62**
  (Big Creek campground) 62
  (Cottonwood campground) 62
  (Willow campground) 62
Bear Lake South Eden **62**
Bear Lake State Recreation Area
  **59,** 62
Bear Lake, UT 60, 61
Bear River 96
  (Blacks Fork) 97
  (Hayden Fork) 94, 95
  (Stillwater Fork) 96
Bear River (campground) **96**
Bear River Migratory Bird
  Refuge 37
Beatty, NV 315, 316
Beaver Canyon 155, 157, 158
Beaver Canyon Campground **156**
Beaver Creek 89, 90
Beaver Creek (campground) **89**
Beaver Dam State Park **312,** 313

Beaver Mountain (ski area) 30
Beaver Pond 95
Beaver Ranger District 33, 157, 158
Beaver River 157, 158
Beaver, UT 33, 152, 153, 154, 155,
  156, 157, 158, 159, 169
  (public golf course) 156
Beaver View **95**
Bed and Breakfast Inns of Utah
  (organization) 39
Belmont Hot Springs **58**
Belmont, NV 302
Berlin, NV 301
Berlin-Ichthyosaur State Park 41, **301**
Best Western
  (Gold Country Motor Inn—
  Elko, NV) 277
  (Green River, UT) 228
  (Parowan, UT) 159
Bicknell, UT 204
Bicycle Vacation Guide
  (organization) 39
Big Bend (Moab, UT) **236,** 237
Big Bend (Humboldt National
  Forest, NV) **271**
Big Cottonwood Canyon 32, 100, 101
Big Cottonwood Creek 100
Big Creek 300
Big Creek campground (Bear Lake
  Rendezvous Beach State
  Park, UT) 62
Big Creek Campground (Toiyabe
  National Forest, NV) **300**
Big Lyman Lake 97
Big Smoky Valley 299
Big Spring camp 259
Birch Creek **73**
Bitter Spring Valley 324
Blackhawk **117,** 118
Blacksmith Fork Canyon 70
Blacksmith Fork River 69
  (Left Fork) 68

Blanding Kampark **248**
Blanding, UT 221, 222, 247, 248, 251
Blind Lake 207
Bliss State Park (see D. L. Bliss
    State Park)
blisters 24
BLM (see Bureau of Land
    Management)
Blue Bell Knoll (peak) 31
Blue Mountains 31, 242, 243, 245,
    246, 247
Blue Sky Motel 337
Blue Spring **171**
Blue Springs Reservoir 177
Blue Spruce **211**
Bluewater Beach Campground **61**
Bluff, UT 249, 250
Bluster campground 270
Bob Scott Campground **299**
Bonneville Salt Flats 50
Bonnie Springs/Old Nevada **329**
Boomtown Casino (Las Vegas,
    NV) 328
Boomtown RV Park (Las Vegas, NV)
    **327,** 328
Boomtown RV Park (Reno, NV) **287**
    (Family Fun Center) 287
Bootleg Amphitheater 130
Botts **73,** 74
Boulder Beach 334, 335
Boulder Beach Campground **334,** 335
Boulder City, NV 41, 324, 325, 333,
    334, 335, 337
Boulder Creek 213
Boulder Lakes RV Resort **332**
Boulder Mountain 31, 204, 205,
    206, 207, 209, 210, 217
Boulder Mountain Homestead **207**
Boulder Station Hotel-Casino (Las
    Vegas, NV) 329, 330
Boulder, UT 213
Boulger Reservoir 119

Bountiful Peak 80
Bountiful Peak (campground) **80**
Bountiful, UT 80
Bowers Mansion County Park 291
Bowery **200**
Bowery Creek 160
Bowery Haven **199**
Bown Reservoir 206, 209, 210
    (Lower) 210
Box Death Hollow Wilderness Area 31
Box Elder **71**
Boy Scout **51**
Braithwaite, Stanley 317
Brentwood Utah RV Park **175,** 176
Brian Head Ski Resort 31, 159, 169
Bridal Veil Falls 109, 111
Bridge **141**
Bridge Hollow **133**
Bridge View Road loop 248
Bridger **66**
Bridger Lake 99
Bridger Lake (campground) **99**
Brigham City, UT 35, 37, 58, 60, 61,
    69, 70, 71
Brighton (ski area) 30
Bristlecone Ridge Hiking and Nature
    Trail 121
Browne Lake 134, 135
Browne Lake (campground) **134**
Browne's Park State Waterfowl
    Management Area 133
Bryce Amphitheater 218
Bryce Canyon 35, 161, 162, 165,
    201, 216, 218, 219
Bryce Canyon Lodge 218, 220
Bryce Canyon National Park 31, 34,
    35, 160, 161, 162, 168, 169,
    179, 180, 187, 195, 208, 214,
    215, 216, 217, 218, 219, 220
Bryce Canyon Pines Country
    Store & Campground,
    RV Park & Motel **216**

Bryce, UT  216, 217
Buckboard  **244**
Buckhorn Wash (geographic
    feature)  226
Buhl, ID  270
Bull Flat (geographic feature)  49
Bull Flat Trail  49
Bull Lake  49
Bullfrog  **221**
Bullfrog Lodge  220
Bullfrog Marina  220, 243
Bullfrog RV Park  **220**
Bullhead Motel  265
Burches Trading Post  **251**
Bureau of Land Management
    (BLM)  36, 38, 42, 52, 53, 54,
    55, 73, 120, 133, 147, 156,
    174, 185, 213, 214, 222, 225,
    226, 229, 233, 236, 237, 238,
    240, 243, 249, 251, 264, 273,
    296, 312, 329
    (Battle Mountain District Office)
    42, 266
    (Carson City District Office)
    42, 296
    (Cedar City District Office)  156,
    174, 186
    (Cedar City Field Office)  37
    (Dixie Field Office)  37
    (Elko District Office)  263, 273, 274
    (Ely District Office)  42, 305, 310
    (Escalante Field Office)  37, 212
    (Fillmore Field Office)  37
    (Hanksville Field Office)  211, 239,
    240, 243
    (Kanab Field Office)  37
    (Las Vegas District Office)  42, 329
    (Moab Field Office)  37
    (Monticello Field Office)  241, 243
    (Nevada State Office)  42
    (Price Field Office)  37
    (Richfield Field Office)  37
    (Salt Lake Field Office)  37, 73
    (San Juan Field Office)  37
    (Utah State Office)  37
    (Vernal District Office)  133, 147
    (Vernal Field Office)  37
    (Winnemuca District Office)  42
Burley Ranger District  49
Burr Trail  213
Burro Inn RV Park  **316**
    (Casino—Beatty, NV)  316
Burro Pass  238
Butch Cassidy Campground  **195**
Butch Cassidy Water Park  233
Butterfly  **94**

**C**

Cactus Pete's RV Park  **269**
Cadillac Ranch  **249**
Caineville, UT  202
Cal-Nev-Ari, NV  337, 338
Cal-Nev-Ari RV Park  **337**
Calf Creek Falls Recreation Area  36,
    **212,** 214
Caliente, NV  312, 313
California State Department of Parks
    and Recreation  341
Callville Bay  326
Callville Bay Campground  **325,**
    326, 334
Callville Bay Trailer Village  **326**
Camel Butte  252
Camp Richardson  **346**
Camp-N-Town RV Park  **293**
Campground By The Lake  **347**
campground ethics  16, 17
camping with children  27
Cannonville, UT  219
Canyon Rim  129
Canyon Rim (campground)  **128**
Canyon Rim hiking trail  129, 130
Canyon Rims Recreation Area
    240, 243

Canyon Trail RV Park **333**

Canyonlands Campark **234**

Canyonlands National Forest 230
(Island in the Sky District) 230

Canyonlands National Park 31, 34,
35, 211, 226, 227, 228, 230,
231, 240, 241, 242, 245, 246
(Island in the Sky District) 230
(Needles District) 240, 241,
242, 243

Capitol Gorge 205

Capitol Reef 209

Capitol Reef National Monument 206

Capitol Reef National Park 34, 35,
201, 202, 203, 204, 205, 206, 207,
209, 210, 214, 218, 239, 240

Cappa, Mike 278

Carmel **126**

Carmel Canyon Trail 230

Carson City, NV 41, 42, 43, 44, 290,
291, 290, 293, 294, 296

Carson Ranger District 41, 290

Carson River 289, 292

Carson Valley Inn 294

Carson Valley, NV 294

Carson Valley RV Resort **294**

Cascade Falls 346

Cascade Lake 346

Cascade Springs 103, 107

Cassidy, Butch 134

Castle Dale, UT 31, 193

Castle Rock **198**

Cataract Canyon 244

Cathedral Gorge 312

Cathedral Gorge State Park
41, **312**

Cathedral Valley 202, 203

Cathedral Valley (campground) **202**

Cathedral Valley Loop (four-wheel
driving tour) 202

Cave Lake 306

Cave Lake State Park 41, 307

Cave Lake State Recreation Area **306**

Cave Spring 242

CCC (see Civilian Conservation
Corps)

Cecret Lake 102

Cedar Breaks National Monument
35, 160, 161, 165, 168, 169,
180, 187
(Visitors Center) 165

Cedar Canyon 166

Cedar Canyon (campground) **165**

Cedar City Ranger District 33, 159,
162, 163, 165, 166, 167

Cedar City, UT 32, 33, 35, 36, 37,
159, 165, 166, 167, 168, 169,
170, 182

Cedar Mesa **210**

Cedar Point campground 85

Cedar Springs **131**

Cedar Springs Marina 131

Cedarville, CA 259

Central, UT 171, 172, 173

Central Utah Project 139

Century RV Park **77**

Charleston, Mount 40, 322

Cherry **115**

Cherry Hill Campground **79**

Chessler Park Trail 242

Chicken Creek 121

Chicken Creek (campground) **121**

Chimney Rock 205

China Meadows **97,** 99

China Meadows Lake 97

China Meadows Trailhead **98**

Chinatown RV Park 274

Chism's Trailer Park **286**

Christmas Meadows **96**

Chuckwagon Campground **205**

Cimarron West RV and Trailer
Park **278**

Circle L. Mobile Home Park **78**

Circleville, UT 207

Circus Circus Casino (Las Vegas, NV) 327
Circusland RV Park **327**
Cisco Beach 63
Civilian Conservation Corps (CCC) 153, 266
Clay Wash (geographic feature) 171
Clear Creek 165
Clear Creek (campground) **49**
Cleve Creek 305
Cleve Creek Campground **305**
Cleveland, UT 225
Clover Springs **52**
Coalville, UT 82, 84
Cobblerest **91**
Cohab Canyon 206
Colorado River 139, 227, 231, 232, 233, 236, 237, 238, 338 (camping complex) 36
Colt Service Center RV Park **265**
Columbine Campground **300,** 301
Comstock Country RV Resort **293,** 294
cooking utensils 12, 13
coolers 12, 14
Copper Mountain Trail 271
Coral Pink Sand Dunes State Park 180, **185,** 186, 187
Corn Creek 153
Corn Creek Canyon 153
Cortez, CO 246
Cottonwood (Rockport State Park, UT) **85**
Cottonwood (Wasatch–Cache National Forest, UT) **50,** 51, 52
Cottonwood (Wasatch Mountain State Park, UT) **106**
Cottonwood campground (Bear Lake Rendezvous Beach State Park, UT) 62
Cottonwood Cove 336, 337
Cottonwood Cove Campground **336**

Cottonwood Cove Marina and Resort **336**
Cottonwood Cove, NV 336
Country Aire **169,** 170
Country Cuzzins RV Park **64**
Crandall's **86**
Crazy Horse Campark **186**
Croyden, UT 78
Crystal Bay 341
Crystal Hot Springs 69
Crystal Springs Resort **69**
Currant Creek **112**
Currant Creek Lodge 112
Currant Creek Reservoir 30, 112
Curtis Bench Trail 230
cuts 24

**D**

D. L. Bliss State Park **344,** 345
*Daily Free Press* 277
Dalton Springs **245**
Daniels Canyon 112
Dark Canyon Wilderness 31
Davis County, UT 80
Davis Creek County Park **291,** 296 (Headquarters) 291
Davis Dam 337, 338
daypacks 19, 20
Days Inn (Pahrump, NV) 316
Dayton, NV 291, 292
Dayton State Park **291**
Dead Horse Point 231
Dead Horse Point Nature Trail 231
Dead Horse Point State Park 36, **231**
Death Valley National Park 316
Deep Creek **135**
Deer Creek 213
Deer Creek (campground) **106,** 107
Deer Creek Park 104, **111**
Deer Creek Recreation Area **213,** 214
Deer Creek Reservoir 104, 105, 106, 111, 112

Deer Run **131**
Deer Trail Lodge **165**
Defas Dude Ranch 137, 138
dehydration 22
Delano Motel and RV Park **155**
Delano Peak 153
Delicate Arch 229
DeLorme Mapping Company 38
Delta, UT 54, 152
Denio, NV 259
Denver, CO 21, 44
Deseret Peak 50, 51, 52
Deseret Peak Wilderness Area 51
Desert National Wildlife Refuge 42
*Desert Princess* (cruise ship) 335
Desolation Canyon 226
Desolation Wilderness 343, 346, 347
Devil's Canyon **247**
Devil's Canyon Nature Trail 247
Devil's Garden **229,** 233
Devil's Garden Natural Area 214
Devils Kitchen (see Little Bryce
    Canyon)
Dewey Bridge **237,** 238
Diamond **116**
Diamond Fork Canyon 115, 116
Dinosaur, CO 35
Dinosaur Museum 248
Dinosaur National Monument 35,
    126, 144, 145, 147
    (Dinosaur Quarry Visitors Center)
    35, 144, 145
    (Headquarters) 144, 145
Dixie National Forest 30, 31, 32,
    159, 160, 161, 162, 165, 166,
    167, 169, 170, 171, 172, 173,
    208, 209, 210, 211, 212, 215,
    216, 217, 219, 220
    (Cedar City Ranger District) 33,
    159, 162, 166, 167
    (Escalante Ranger District) 33,
    211, 212, 219

    (Headquarters) 32
    (Pine Valley Ranger District) 33,
    170, 171, 172, 173
    (Powell Ranger District) 33,
    215, 220
    (Teasdale Ranger District) 33,
    208, 209, 210
Dixie Red Cliffs (campground) **185**
Dixie Red Cliffs Recreation Area 36,
    181, 182, 184
Doctor Creek 202
Doctor Creek (campground) **201**
Dolomite Campground **322,** 323
Donkey Lake 207
Donut Falls 100
Double Dice RV Park **277**
Double W Campground **207**
Dowd Mountain Overlook 127
Draper, UT 83, 84
Dripping Springs **132**
Duchesne Ranger District 32, 137,
    138, 139, 148
Duchesne River
    (North Fork) 108, 137, 138
    (West Fork) 138
Duchesne, UT 32, 137, 138, 139,
    140, 141, 147, 148
Duck Creek 168
Duck Creek (campground) **167**
Duck Creek Village, UT 167
Duck Valley Indian Reservation 43
Dunham, Karen 263
Dutch John, UT 32, 133, 134

**E**
Eagle Valley Resort 310, **311**
East Canyon Reservoir 80
East Canyon State Park 36, 78,
    **80,** 81
East Ely, NV 307
East Fork **97**
East Humboldt Range 275, 276

East Park **136**
East Park Reservoir 136, 137
East Zion Trailer Park **180**
Echo Bay 326
Echo Bay Campground **324**
Echo Bay Seven Crowns Resort 325
Echo Bay Trailer Village **325,** 326, 334
Echo Canyon 311
Echo Canyon State Park **311** (Headquarters) 311
Echo Reservoir 81, 82
Echo Resort on Echo Reservoir **81**
Edge of the Cedars State Park 247, 248, 251
Egan Range 307, 308
El Capitan Casino (Hawthorne, NV) 297
El Dorado National Forest 343
Electric Lake 120
Elephant Butte 252
Elephant Hill 242
Elk Flat 306
Elk Meadows Ski Resort 155, 156, 157
Elkhorn, UT 203
Elko, NV 40, 42, 43, 263, 264, 270, 271, 272, 273, 274, 276, 277, 278, 279, 280
Ellen, Mount 211
Ely, NV 40, 42, 305, 306, 307, 308, 309, 310, 312
(East) 307
Ely Ranger District 40, 308
Emerald Bay 344, 345, 346
Emerald Bay Boat-In Camp **345**
Emerald Bay State Park **345**
Emerald Bay Trail 344
Emery County, UT 194, 196, 225
Enterprise Reservoir
(Lower) 170
(Upper) 170

Enterprise, UT 170, 171
Ephraim Canyon 192
Ephraim, UT 31, 33, 192, 194
Equestrian **171**
Escalante Petrified Forest State Park **213,** 214, 215
Escalante Ranger District 33, 211, 212, 219
Escalante River 213
Escalante, UT 31, 33, 36, 37, 211, 212, 213, 214, 215, 217
Escalante–Grand Staircase National Monument 35, 214
*Essential Wilderness Navigator: How to Find Your Way in the Great Outdoors* (book) 21
Eureka, UT 54, 55
Evanston Ranger District 34, 94, 95, 96, 97
Evanston, WY 30, 34, 97, 98, 99, 100
Evergreen, CO 38

**F**

Fairview, UT 119
Fallen Leaf Campground **347**
Fallen Leaf Lake 347
Fallon, NV 43, 288, 289, 301
Fallon RV Park **288**
Farmington, UT 80, 82
Ferron Canyon 196
Ferron Canyon (campground) **196**
Ferron Ranger District 33, 119, 120, 193, 194, 196
Ferron Reservoir 194
Ferron Reservoir (campground) **194**
Ferron, UT 31, 33, 194, 196
Fielding, UT 58
Fiery Furnace (geographic feature) 229
Fillmore Ranger District 33, 152, 153, 190
Fillmore, UT 33, 37, 54, 55, 152, 153, 154

Firefighters Memorial **130**
first-aid 12, 22, 26
Fish Lake 31, 199, 200, 201, 202
Fish Lake Lodge and Lakeside
    Resort **200**
Fish Lake, UT 199, 200
Fish Spring camp 259
Fish Springs National Wildlife Refuge
    37, 53
Fishlake National Forest 30, 31, 33,
    120, 152, 153, 157, 158, 189,
    198, 201, 203, 204
    (Beaver Ranger District) 33,
    157, 158
    (Fillmore Ranger District) 33,
    152, 153, 190
    (Headquarters) 33
    (Loa Ranger District) 33, 198,
    200, 201, 203, 204
    (Richfield Ranger District) 33, 197
Flaming Gorge Dutch John Office 32
Flaming Gorge Dam 31, 127, 129,
    130, 131, 132, 133
Flaming Gorge Lodge 130
Flaming Gorge National Recreation
    Area 30, 34, 35, 126, 127,
    128, 129, 130, 131, 132, 133,
    134, 135
    (Flaming Gorge Ranger District)
    126, 127, 128, 129, 130, 131,
    132, 134, 135
    (Headquarters) 32
    (Red Canyon Visitors Center)
    128, 129
Flaming Gorge Natural History
    Association 130
Flaming Gorge Ranger District 126,
    127, 128, 129, 130, 131, 132,
    134, 135
Flaming Gorge Reservoir 126, 127,
    129, 130, 131, 132, 135, 136,
    144, 146

Flat Canyon **119**
Fletcher View Campground 322,
    323, **324**
Flying U Campground **199**
Ford, John 252, 253
Forks of the Huntington **120**
Forsythe Reservoir 203
Fort Bridger 98, 99, 100
Fort Churchill Campground **289**
Fort Churchill State Historic Park 289
    (Headquarters) 289
    (Visitors Center) 289
Fort Churchill State Historical
    Monument 289
49er Motel 293
Fossil Valley **145,** 146
Fountain Green, UT 122
Four Corners Monument 38, 220,
    249, 252, 253
Foy Lake 245, 246
Francis, UT 88, 107
Frazier Trailer Park **110**
free campsites 49, 53, 59, 68, 72–
    73, 77, 80, 95, 126–127, 129,
    132, 134–135, 137, 140, 145,
    147, 152, 244–245
Freedom, UT 122
Freeport, ME 38
Fremont Indian State Park 198, 199
Fremont River 203
Fremont River Overlook 206
Fremont State Park 197
Friendship **68**
Front Boy (map company) 44
Frontier Overnight RV Park **297**
Fruita **206**
Frying Pan **198**
Fun & Sun RV Park **320,** 321

**G**
Gabbs, NV 301
Garden City, UT 60, 61

Gardnerville, NV 294, 295, 296

General Creek 343

General Store Gift Shop and RV Park **164**

Genoa, NV 294

Glen Canyon National Recreation Area 34, 35, 222, 243, 244

Glendale, UT 160, 179, 180

Globe Theatre (Cedar City, UT) 166, 169

Goblin Valley 230

Goblin Valley State Park 36, **229,** 230, 240

Gold Country Motor Inn and RV Park **277**

Golden Spike National Historic Site 34, 35, 49

Golden Spike RV Park **70**

Gooseberry (Gooseberry Creek, UT) **197**

Gooseberry (Manti–La Sal National Forest, UT) **119**

Gooseberry Creek 197

Gooseneck **129**

Goosenecks State Park **250**

Goulding's Monument Valley Campground **252,** 253

Goulding's Trading Post 252

Grand Canyon National Park 169, 187, 222

(North Rim) 187

Grand Gulch Primitive Area 251

Grand Parade Trail 220

Grand Slam Canyon indoor amusement park 327

Grandview Point 230

Grandview Trailhead 137

Granite Flat **103**

Granite Lake 346

Granite Peak 263

Grantsville Reservoir 51, 52

Grantsville, UT 50, 51, 52

Gravel Pit 126, 127

Gravel Pit/Stateline/Swim Beach **126**

Great Basin 50, 53, 152

Great Basin History Museum 152

Great Basin National Park 41, 305, 307, 308, 309

Great Salt Lake 37, 38, 50, 72, 78, 79, 80, 81

Great Salt Lake State Park 52, 79, **81**

Great Western Trail 31, 104, 195, 197, 198, 199

Green River 130, 131, 133, 144, 145, 226, 227, 228

Green River (campground) **145**

Green River State Park **226,** 227, 228, 230

(Golf Course) 226, 227

Green River, UT 226, 227, 228, 229, 230

Greendale West **130**

Greenfield RV Park **295**

Greens Lake 128, 129

Greens Lake (campground) **129**

Grey's Peak 276

Grosvenor Arch 220

Guinavah-Malibu **67**

Gunlock Reservoir 173

Gunlock State Park **173**

Gunlock, UT 173

Gunnison, UT 194

*Gunsmoke* (television series) 186

**H**

Hades **137**

Hailstone Campground **88**

Hal Canyon **236,** 237

Hall's Crossing 220, 221

Hall's Crossing (campground) **222**

Hall's Crossing RV Park **221,** 222

Hamblin, Jacob 183

Hamburger Rock 242

Hamburger Rock (campground) **241**

Hanksville, UT  211, 220, 221, 229, 239, 240, 243, 244

Hanna, UT  137, 138

Hantavirus Pulmonary Syndrome  26

Hardware Ranch (see Wildlife's Hardware Ranch)

Harrah's Casino (Reno, NV)  287

Harrisburg Lakeside RV Resort  **181,** 182

Harrisburg, UT  182

Hatch Point  **240**

Hatch, UT  168, 169

Hawthorne, NV  296, 297, 301

Hayden Fork  **95**

Hayden Peak  94

heatstroke  22, 23

Heber City, UT  34, 36, 85, 86, 87, 88, 104, 112, 113, 114

Heber Ranger District  34, 107, 108, 112, 113, 114

Heber, UT  113

Heber Valley  106, 111

Heber Valley RV Park  **107**

Hemenway Campground  **333,** 334

Henry Mountains  36, 206, 209, 210, 211, 220, 239, 240, 244

Hi-Desert RV Park  **264**

Hickison Petroglyph Recreation Area  300

Hidden Haven Campground  **84**

Hidden Peak  101

Hideout Canyon  **127**

Hideout Trail  127

High Creek  59

High Creek (campground)  **59**

High Uintas Wilderness Area  30, 31, 87, 90, 93, 94, 98, 100, 134, 135, 137, 138, 139, 140, 141, 142, 143

Highline Trail  94

hiking gear  19, 20, 24

Hillers, Mount  244

Hilltop Campground  322, **323**

Hilton (see Reno Hilton RV Camperland)

Hilton Bay  285

Hinckey Summit  263

Hitch 'N Post (campground)  **187**

Hitch 'N Post, UT  187

Hitch-N-Post RV Park and Campground (Panguitch Lake, UT)  **161,** 162

Hitchin' Post RV Park (Las Vegas, NV)  **326,** 327

Hite  **244**

Hittle Bottom  **237**

Hobble  **77**

Hobble Creek Canyon  115

Hobble Creek Golf Course  115

Holiday Hills Campground  **82**

Holiday Travel Park  **331,** 332, 333

Holly, Mount  153

Homestead Resort  105

Homewood, CA  342

Honeycomb Rocks  **170**

Honeyville, UT  69

Hoop Lake  **100**

Hoover Dam  333, 334

Hope, UT  109

Horsethief Gulch Campground  310

Hovenweep National Monument  34, 246, 250, 252

Hub Totel RV Park  **288**

Humboldt National Forest  40, 270, 271, 272, 275, 279, 280, 307

(Ely Ranger District)  40, 308

(Jarbidge Ranger District)  270

(Mountain City Ranger District) 40, 271, 272

(Ruby Mountain Ranger District) 41, 275, 276

(Santa Rosa Ranger District) 41, 263

Humboldt River  260, 276

Huntington Creek  120

Huntington Reservoir  193

Huntington State Park **193**
Huntington, UT 31, 119, 193
Huntsville, UT 73, 74, 75, 76, 77
Hurrah Pass 232
Hurricane, UT 174, 175, 176,
    177, 184
hypothermia 22, 23
Hyrum Reservoir 69, 70
Hyrum State Park **69**
Hyrum, UT 68, 69

**I**

I-80 Campground **283**
Ideal Beach Resort 61, 62
Illipah Reservoir Campground **305**
Incline Village, NV 290
Independence Range 272
Indian Creek 241
Indian Creek (campground—
    Canyonlands National Park,
    UT) **241**
Indian Creek (campground—Fishlake
    National Forest, UT) **120**
Indian Crossing **133**
insects 22
Intake **50**
Ione Valley 301
Iron County, UT 166
Iron Mine **137**
Island Boat Camp 104
Island in the Sky District 230

**J**

Jackpot, NV 269, 270, 271, 272
Jailhouse Casino (Ely, NV) 307
Jarbidge Campgrounds **270**
    (Bluster campground) 270
    (Pavlak campground) 270
    (Pine Creek campground) 270
    (Sawmill campground) 270
Jarbidge Canyon 270
Jarbidge, NV 270, 271, 272

Jarbidge Ranger District 270
Jarbidge River 270
Jardine Juniper Trailhead 65
Jarvie Historic Ranch 133
Jarvie, John 134
Jarvies Canyon **132**
Jefferson Hunt **76**
Jefferson, Mount 302
Jensen, UT 144, 145
*Jeremiah Johnson* (movie) 103
Jericho **54**
Jericho Junction, UT 54, 55
Jesse Ewing Canyon 133
Joe's Valley **192**
Joe's Valley Reservoir 192, 193
*John Atlantic Burr* (ferry) 220
John Ford Point 252
John Jarvie Historic Site 133, 134
John Wesley Powell River Running
    Museum (Green River, UT) 227,
    228, 229
Johnson Lake Loop Trail 309
Johnson Pass 309
Johnson Reservoir 198, 201
Jones Hole Creek 145
Jones Hole Fish Hatchery 145
Jordanelle Dam 107
Jordanelle Reservoir 88, 107
Jordanelle State Park 36, 88
Joseph, UT 199
Josie Morris Ranch 145
JR Munchies Campground **196,** 197
Junction Ruin 251
Juniper and Cedar Point **85**
Juniper campground 85
Jurassic Park **239**
*Jurassic Park* (movie) 248

**K**

K and C RV Park **249**
Kachina Bridge (geographic
    feature) 248

Kaler Hollow **137**
Kamas Ranger District 34, 87, 89, 90, 91, 92, 93, 94
Kamas, UT 30, 34, 89, 90, 91, 92, 93, 94, 95, 96, 97, 107
Kanab RV Corral **187**
Kanab, UT 35, 37, 161, 178, 179, 180, 185, 186, 187, 222
Kanarraville, UT 170
Kane Creek 232
Kane Gulch Ranger Station 251
Kane Springs Campground **231**
Kanosh, UT 153
Kaspian Campground **342,** 343
Kayenta, UT 252
Kaysville, UT 79
Ken's Lake 235
Kents Lake 153
Kents Lake (campground) **157**
Keystone RV Park **285,** 286
Kiel, Ron 261
Kingfisher Island, UT 127
Kings Creek **220**
King's Beach 341
King's Peak 140
King's Row Trailer Park **329,** 330, 333
Kingsbury Grade, NV 292, 293
Kingston Campground **300**
Kingston Canyon 300
Klondike Bluff 228
KOA 261, 264, 278, 307
  (Bear Lake) **60**
  (Beaver) **154,** 155
  (Brigham City) **70**
  (Cedar City) **169**
  (Ely) **307**
  (Fillmore) **153**
  (Green River) **226**
  (Las Vegas) **330**
  (Manila/Flaming Gorge) **146**
  (Moab) **235**
  (Monticello) **246**
  (Nephi) **121**
  (Panguitch) **161**
  (Provo) **110**
  (Richfield) **197**
  (Vernal) **125**
  (Wendover) **278**
  (Zion/Bryce) **179**
Kodachrome Basin State Park 36, 216, **219**
Kolob Canyon 170
Kolob Reservoir 177
Kyle Canyon 323
Kyle Canyon Campground 322, **323,** 324

**L**

La Sal Loop 238, 239
La Sal Mountains 31, 228, 230, 238, 239, 243, 246
La Verkin, UT 174
Lagoon Pioneer Village Campground **82**
Lahontan, Lake 289
Lahontan State Park 41
Lahontan State Recreation Area **288**
  (Headquarters) 289
Lake Forest Campground **342**
Lake Fork Trail 49
Lake Hill **192**
Lake Lahontan 289
Lake Mead 41, 221, 321, 333, 334
Lake Mead National Recreation Area 41, 321, 324, 325, 326, 333, 334, 335, 336, 337
Lake Mohave 336, 337
Lake Powell 187, 211, 220, 221, 222, 239, 240, 244, 246
Lake Powell, UT 35
Lake Tahoe 40, 290, 292, 293, 294, 342, 343, 344, 345, 346, 347
  (Visitors Center) 342, 343, 344, 346, 347

Lake Tahoe–Nevada State
   Park 41
Lake View Resort **162**
Lakeshore Trailer Village **334**
Lakeside Campground **109**
Lakeside RV Park **346**
Laketown, UT 62, 63
Lakeview Campground 306
Lakeview, OR 259
Lamoille, NV 279, 280
Lapoint, UT 143
Las Vegas **327**
Las Vegas Bay Campground **335**
Las Vegas, NV 40, 41, 42, 43, 44,
   269, 277, 285, 303, 305, 312,
   322, 323, 324, 325, 326, 327,
   328, 329, 330, 331, 332, 333,
   334, 335, 336, 338
   (North) 326, 327
Las Vegas Ranger District 41
Laughlin, Don 338
Laughlin, NV 337, 338
Lava Point **177**
Layton, UT 78
Lazy K Campground and RV Park
   **260,** 261
Ledgefork **87**
Lee Canyon ski resort 322
Leeds RV Park **181**
Leeds, UT 173, 181, 182, 185
Lee's Ferry 222
Lehi, UT 53
Lehman Caves 41
Lehman Creek 309
Lehman Creek Campground 309
   (Lower) **309**
   (Upper) **309**
Levan, UT 121
Lewis M. Turner **65**
Liar's Bench (geographic feature) 305
Lilly Lake 92
Lilly Lake (campground) **92**

Limber Pine Trailhead 67
Little Bryce Canyon 179, 191
Little Cottonwood **157**
Little Cottonwood Canyon 32, 100,
   101, 102
Little Grand Canyon (see Wedge, The)
Little Hole 133
   (boat ramp) 133
Little Lyman Lake 97
Little Lyman Lake (campground) **97**
Little Mill **102**
Little Pine Lake 219
Little Reservoir 158
Little Reservoir (campground) **158**
Little Sahara Recreation Area 54, 55
Loa Ranger District 33, 198, 200,
   201, 203, 204
Loa, UT 33, 203
Lockhart Basin 240
Lodge **65**
Lodgepole (Ashley National Forest,
   UT) **135**
Lodgepole (Daniels Canyon, UT) **112**
Logan Canyon 60, 64, 65, 66, 67, 68
Logan Ranger District 34, 59, 64,
   65, 66, 67, 68, 69
Logan River 65, 66
Logan, UT 30, 34, 59, 60, 61, 63,
   64, 65, 66, 67, 68, 69
Lone Peak 30, 84
Lone Peak Wilderness
   Area 103
Lonesome Beaver **210,** 211
Loop **52**
Loop, The (see Alpine Loop)
Lopeman's Frontier Movie Town
   (Kanab, UT) 186
Lost Creek 93
Lost Creek (campground) **93**
Lost Creek Reservoir 78
Lost Creek State Park **78**
Lost Lake 93

Lottie Dell Campground **49**
Lovelock, NV 259, 260, 261
Lower Beach **148**
Lower Bown **210**
Lower Calf Creek Falls 213
Lower Gooseberry Reservoir 119
Lower Meadows **74,** 75
Lower Narrows **51**
Lower Provo **90**
Lower Provo River 90
Lucerne Marina 126
Lucerne Valley 127
Lucerne Valley (campground) **126,** 129
Lund's Campground **194**
Luning, NV 301
Lye Creek 40, **263**

# M

Mackinaw **201,** 202
Madsen Bay **118**
Magic Waters (water-slide park—Salt Lake City, UT) 84
Magpie **76**
Mahagony **105**
Mahogany Cove **157**
Major's Place 305
Malibu campground 67
Manila, UT 32, 35, 125, 126, 146
Manti Community **192**
Manti Mormon Temple 191
Manti Mountain 192, 194, 196
Manti, UT 31, 191, 192
Manti–La Sal National Forest 30, 31, 33, 119, 120, 121, 122, 192, 193, 194, 196, 238, 239, 244, 245, 247
(Ferron Ranger District) 33, 119, 120, 193, 194, 196
(Headquarters) 33
(Moab Ranger District) 33, 238, 239
(Monticello Ranger District) 33, 244, 245, 247
(Price Ranger District) 33, 119
(Sanpete Ranger District) 33, 121, 122, 192, 194
Mantua Reservoir 71
Mantua, UT 71, 72
Maple Bench **116**
Maple Canyon 122
Maple Canyon (campground) **122**
Maple Grove **189,** 190
Maple Hollow **152**
Maples, The **77**
Mapleton, UT 114
Marsh Lake 98
Marsh Lake (campground) **98**
Marysville, UT 202, 203, 207
Matheson Wetlands Preserve 232, 233
Matterhorn Mountain Trail 271
Mayfield, UT 194
McArthur's Temple View RV Resort **182,** 183
McDermitt, NV 263
McMillan Springs 36, **211**
McWilliams Campground **322**
Mead, Lake 41, 221, 321, 333, 334
Meadow Valley Campground **310**
Medford, OR 43
Meeks Bay, CA 343, 344
Meeks Bay Campground **343,** 344
Meeks Bay Resort **344**
Melon Days Festival (Green River, UT) 226
Mesa Arch 230
Mesa Verde National Park 245, 246, 250
Mesquite, NV 319, 320
Metropolis, NV 274
Mexican Hat, UT 250, 251, 252
Midvale, UT 39
Midway, UT 104, 105
Milford, UT 156
Mill Creek (Battle Mountain, NV) 266
Mill Creek (Moab, UT) 235

Mill Creek Canyon  229
Mill Creek Recreation Area  **266**
Mill Hollow  **108**
Mill Hollow Reservoir  108
Mill Meadow Reservoir  203
Miller Flat Reservoir  120
Millsite Reservoir  196
Millsite State Park  **196**
Minden, NV  294
Mineral Canyon  226
Mineral Mountains  156
Minersville Reservoir  159
Minersville State Park  **159**
Mirror Lake  94
Mirror Lake (campground)  **93**
Mitten View Campground  **252**
Moab  **241**
Moab Ranger District  33, 238, 239
Moab Slickrock Bike Trail  238
Moab, UT  33, 35, 36, 37, 38, 227,
    228, 229, 230, 231, 232, 233,
    234, 235, 236, 237, 238, 239,
    240, 241, 242, 243, 244
    (Information Center)  229, 233
Moab Valley  236
Moab Valley RV and Campark  **233,**
    234, 235
Model T RV Park  **265**
Mohave, Lake  336, 337
Monroe Mystic Hot Springs  **203**
Monroe, UT  203
Monte Cristo  **73**
Monticello Lake  245, 246
Monticello Ranger District  33, 244,
    245, 247
Monticello, UT  31, 33, 37, 241, 243,
    245, 246
Monument Valley  38, 246, 249,
    250, 251, 252, 253
Monument Valley, UT  38, 252, 253
Moon Lake  139
Moon Lake (campground)  31, **139**

Moosehorn  **93**
Moosehorn Lake  93
Moqui Motel and Campground  **214**
Morgan, UT  78, 81
Mormon Ridge  306
Morning Glory Bridge  236
mosquitoes  25
Motel 6 (Ely, NV)  307
Mount Charleston  40, 322
Mount Ellen  211
Mount Ellen Trail  211
Mount Hillers  244
Mount Holly  153
Mount Jefferson  302
Mount Naomi Wilderness Area
    30, 65
Mount Nebo  117, 191
Mount Nebo Wilderness Area
    30, 117
Mount Olympus Wilderness Area  30
Mount Rose  290
Mount Timpanogos  103, 104,
    110, 111
Mount Timpanogos
    (campground)  **103**
Mount Timpanogos Wilderness Area
    30, 103
Mountain City Motel and RV
    Park  **271**
Mountain City, NV  40, 263, 271,
    272, 273
Mountain City Ranger District  40,
    271, 272
Mountain Haven Campground  **71**
Mountain Home, UT  138, 139
Mountain Shadows RV Park (Salt
    Lake City, UT)  **83,** 84
Mountain Shadows RV Park (Wells,
    NV)  **274,** 275
Mountain Spa  **104,** 105
Mountain View (Scofield State Park,
    UT)  **118**

Mountain View (Starvation Reservoir, UT) **147**
Mountain View Ranger District 34, 97, 98, 99, 100
Mountain View RV Park **246**
Mountain View, WY 34, 97, 98, 99, 100
Mountainridge **168**
MS *Dixie II* (ship) 292
Mt. Carmel Junction, UT 178, 180
Mt. Rose Campground **290**
Muddy River 321
Mukuntuweep RV Park and Campground **178**
Muley Twist Canyon 210
Mustang Ridge 131
Mystery Valley 252

**N**

Narrows hike (see Zion Narrows hike)
National Forest Service 59, 117, 126
National Park Service 165, 216, 308, 324, 325, 333, 334, 335, 337
National Park System 229
National Register of Historic Places 237
National Reservation System 127, 128, 129, 130, 131, 132, 135, 137, 138, 139
Natural Bridges **247**
Natural Bridges National Monument 35, 239, 240, 246, 247, 248
Nature Conservancy 232
Navajo Indian Reservation 249
Navajo Lake 166, 167, 168
Navajo Lake (campground) **166**
Navajo Lake Lodge 167
Navajo Loop Trail 218
Navajo Reservation 38
Navajo Tribal Park 38, 252 (Visitors Center) 38
Naval Air Station (Fallon, NV) 288

Nebo, Mount 117, 191
Needles District 240, 241, 242, 245
Needles Outpost **240**
Needles Overlook 240, 243
Neff Reservoir 203
Negro Bill Canyon 236, 237
Nephi, UT 30, 36, 121, 122, 190
Nevada Beach 293
Nevada Beach Campground **292**
Nevada Bureau of Mines and Geology 44
Nevada Commission on Tourism 44
Nevada Department of Conservation and National Resources 42
Nevada Department of Transportation 43
Nevada Department of Wildlife 44, 300
Nevada State Fair 286
Nevada State Parks 301, 306, 310, 311, 312, 313 (District Headquarters) 301 (District Office) 306, 310, 311, 312, 313
Newspaper Rock **243**
Nicanor Canyon 310
Nixon, NV 43
Nizhoni **247,** 248
Noah's Ark hiking trail 160
North Bear Street-Powerline Road Trail 271
North Campground **217,** 218, 219, 220
North Juniper Park **172**
North Las Vegas, NV 326, 327
North Wildhorse Recreation Area **273**
Notom, UT 210

**O**
Oak City, UT 152
Oak Creek (Dixie National Forest, UT) **209**

Oak Creek Campground (Las Vegas, NV) **329**
Oak Creek Canyon **152**
Oak Grove (Dixie National Forest, UT) **173**
Oak Grove (Moab, UT) **236**
Oak Hollow **105**
Oak Park Reservoir 137
Oakley, UT 87
Oaks Park **136**
Oaks Park Reservoir 136
Oasis **54**
Oasis Casino (Mesquite, NV) 319
Oasis RV Park **328,** 338
Office of Museum Services (Salt Lake City, UT) 39
Ogden Canyon 76, 77
Ogden Ranger District 71, 72, 73, 74, 75, 76, 77
Ogden River (South Fork) 74, 75, 76, 77
Ogden, UT 30, 38, 70, 72, 73, 74, 75, 76, 77, 78, 79, 80
Old Folks Flat **119**
Onaqui Mountains 52
Oohwah Lake 238
Oohwah Lake (campground) **239**
Orangeville, UT 120, 193
Orderville, UT 168, 180
Orem, UT 103, 109, 111
orienteering 21
Otter Creek 208
Otter Creek Reservoir 203, 208
Otter Creek State Park 207, **208**
Ouray National Wildlife Refuge 37, 147
Overton Beach Resort 321
Overton Beach RV Park **321**
Overton, NV 320, 321, 325
Owachoma Bridge 248
Owyhee, NV 43, 273
Owyhee River 272

**P**
Pack Creek 235
Pack Creek Campground **235**
Page, AZ 35, 244
Pahranagat National Wildlife Refuge 42
Pahrump, NV 316, 317
Pahrump Station RV Park **316**
Pahvant Range 31
Painted Rocks Recreation Area 194
Paiute ATV Trail 31, 153, 154, 190, 195, 197, 199
Palisade Reservoir 191, 192
Palisade State Park **191,** 192
Palmyra **115**
Panaca, NV 306, 310, 311, 312, 313
Panguitch Lake 31, 160, 161, 162, 163, 164, 165, 166, 167, 168
(North) **163,** 164
(South) **163**
Panguitch Lake Resort **163**
Panguitch, UT 33, 160, 161, 162, 163, 164, 165, 168, 179, 215, 217, 218
Paradise Park **142**
Paradise Reservoir 143
Paradise Valley 263
(Ranger Station) 263
Paria Canyon 222
Paria River 222
Park City, UT 39, 82, 84, 85, 86, 87, 88, 107
Parowan, UT 159, 160
Paungausant Plateau 168, 169
Pavant Mountains 154
Pavlak campground 270
Payson Canyon 30, 116, 117
Payson Lakes **117**
Payson, UT 30, 116, 117, 118, 190
Peavine Campground **301,** 302
Pelican Lake 147
Pelican Lake (campground) **147**

Perception Park **74**
Phoenix, AZ 220
Pine Creek 302
Pine Creek (Humboldt National
    Forest, NV) 270
Pine Creek Campground (Toiyabe
    National Forest, NV) **302**
Pine Lake (campground) **219**
Pine Lake (Dixie National Forest, UT)
    216, 217
    (Little) 219
Pine Lake (Panguitch, UT) 161
Pine Park **171**
Pine Valley **172**
Pine Valley Lodge 171, 172
Pine Valley Mountains 172, 173, 184
Pine Valley Mountains Wilderness
    Area 31
Pine Valley Ranger District 33, 170,
    171, 172, 173
Pine Valley, UT 171, 172, 173
Pine Valley Wilderness Area 171,
    172, 174
Pinery **86**
Pines **173**
Pineview Reservoir 73, 74, 76, 77
Pink Cliffs Village **216**
Pinks Trail 166
Pioche, NV 307, 310, 311
Pioneer **68,** 69
Pioneer Village 79, 83
Pit Stop **159**
Piute County, UT 158
Piute Reservoir 202, 207, 208
Piute State Park **207**
plague 25, 26
Player's Island RV Park **320**
Pleasant Creek **209,** 210
Pleasant Grove Ranger District 34,
    102, 103, 104, 109
Pleasant Grove, UT 34, 108
Plymouth, UT 58

Point Supreme **165**
poisonous plants 22
Pole Canyon Trail 276
Pole Creek **142**
Pole Creek Lake 142
Ponderosa **190**
Ponderosa Grove **186**
Pony Express Trail 36, 37, 53
Portal RV Park and Fishery **232**
Posy Lake **212**
Pothole Point 242
Powell, Lake 187, 211, 220, 221,
    222, 239, 240, 244, 246
Powell Ranger District 33, 215, 220
Preston Valley **67**
Price Canyon 120
Price Canyon Recreation Area **120**
Price Ranger District 33, 119
Price, UT 33, 37, 120, 225
Primadonna RV Village **335,** 336
    (Casino—Las Vegas, NV) 336
Provo Canyon 30, 107, 109, 110, 111
Provo River 88, 91, 92, 107, 109, 111
    (Lower) 90
Provo River Parkway (riverside hiking
    path) 110
Provo, UT 34, 38, 53, 107, 108,
    109, 110, 111, 117, 121
Puffer Lake 153
Pyramid Lake 42, 260
Pyramid Lake Marina RV Park
    **260,** 283
Pyramid Lake Paiute Reservation 43,
    260, 283
Pyramid Lake Paiute Tribal
    Council 43

**Q**
Quail Creek 185
Quail Creek Reservoir 182, 184, 185
Quail Creek State Park 36, 181, 182,
    **184,** 185

Quail Lake RV Park **174,** 175
Queen's Garden Trail  218

# R

R and R  **154**
Rainbow Bridge  221
Rainbow Bridge National Monument
    35, 221
Rainbow Park  **145**
Rancho San Rafael Park  285
Raven Maps (map company)  43
Recapture Reservoir  247, 248
Red Banks  **65**
Red Canyon  31, 161, 168, 215,
    216, 219, 220
Red Canyon (campground—
    Panguitch, UT)  **215**
Red Canyon Lodge  128
Red Canyon Nature Trail  129
Red Canyon RV Park and Camp-
    ground (Red Canyon, UT)  **215**
Red Canyons RV Park (Panguitch,
    UT)  **160,** 161
Red Castle (geographic feature)  98
Red Fleet Reservoir  135, 136, 144
Red Fleet State Park  125, **144**
Red Garter Casino (Wendover,
    NV)  278
Red Ledge Campground  **170**
Red Lion Casino (Elko, NV)  277
Red Rock Canyon (Las Vegas, NV)  329
Red Rock Canyon (Moab, UT)  232
Red Rock Restaurant and Camp-
    ground  **239,** 240
Red Springs  **135**
Redlands RV Park  **183,** 184
Redman  **101**
Renegade Point  **113**
Reno Hilton RV Camperland  **284,**
    285, 287
Reno, NV  42, 43, 44, 260, 284,
    285, 286, 287, 290, 294, 303

Reno Rodeo  286
Reno RV Park  **286,** 287
Reno-Tahoe Airport  284
Reservoir  **140**
Richardson's Resort and Marina  346
Richfield Ranger District  33, 197
Richfield, UT  33, 37, 196, 197, 199,
    200, 201, 203
Richmond, UT  59
Rim Rock Ranch Motel and RV Park
    204, **206**
Rio Rancho RV Park  **315,** 316
River Bend Trailer Park  **111**
River Side RV Park and Campground
    (Logan, UT)  **63**
River's Edge RV Park  **284,** 285
Riverside Campground (Red Canyon,
    UT)  **168**
Riverside Casino (Laughlin, NV)  338
Riverside Resort RV Park (Laughlin,
    NV)  328, **337,** 338
Riverton, UT  84
Riverview  **140**
Road Runner RV Park  **330,** 333
Rock Cliff Campground  **88**
Rock Corral (campground)  **156**
Rock Corral, UT  156
Rock Creek  139
Rock Lake
    (Lower)  142
    (Middle)  142
    (Upper)  142
Rockport Reservoir  85, 86, 87
Rockport State Park  36, 85, 86, 87
Ronald Jensen Historical Farm
    (Hyrum, UT)  70
Roosevelt Ranger District  32, 139,
    140, 141, 142
Roosevelt, UT  32, 37, 142
Rose, Mount  290
Round Lake  203
Ruby Crest Trail  279

Ruby Lake  280
Ruby Lake National Wildlife Refuge
    42, 280
Ruby Marsh  **280**
Ruby Mountain Ranger District  41,
    275, 276
Ruby Mountains  275, 280
Ruby Valley  275
Ruby's Inn RV Campground  216,
    **217,** 220
Rustic Lodge  **164**
Rye Patch State Recreation Area
    **259,** 260
    (North Campground)  259, 260
    (South Campground)  259, 260
Ryndon Campground  **276**
Ryndon–Devils Gate  276

## S

Saddle West Casino (Pahrump,
    NV)  317
Salina Canyon  195
Salina Creek RV and Campground  **195**
Salina, UT  31, 194, 195, 197
Salt Creek  121
Salt Creek Canyon  121
Salt Lake City, UT  30, 32, 34, 35,
    36, 37, 38, 39, 50, 51, 52, 53,
    60, 61, 62, 70, 71, 73, 78, 79,
    80, 81, 82, 83, 84, 85, 86, 87,
    88, 100, 101, 102, 103, 104,
    105, 106, 107, 121
    (Office of Museum Services)  39
Salt Lake City VIP  **83**
Salt Lake County, UT  30, 32
Salt Lake International Airport  83
Salt Lake Ranger District  34, 50, 51,
    52, 100, 101, 102
Salt Lake Tabernacle and Mormon
    Temple  83
Salt Lake Valley  101, 102
Saltair Resort  81

Sam's Town Boulder RV Park  **332**
Sam's Town Casino (Las Vegas, NV)
    330, 331, 332
Sam's Town Nellis RV Park
    **331,** 332
San Francisco, CA  40
San Juan County Golf Course
    (Monticello, UT)  245, 246
San Juan River  246, 249, 251
    (Goosenecks)  246
San Pitch Mountains  121
San Rafael  **225**
San Rafael Swell (geographic feature)
    193, 225, 230
San Rafael, UT  193
Sand Flats  **238**
Sand Flats Recreation Area  238
Sand Island  **249**
Sand Mountain  **55**
Sandy Beach Campground  **341**
Sandy, UT  84
Sanpete County, UT  121, 194
Sanpete Ranger District  33, 121,
    122, 192, 194
Santa Clara River  171
Santa Rosa Ranger District  41, 263
Santaquin Canyon  117
Sawmill Basin  211
Sawmill campground  270
Sawtooth National Forest  49
    (Burley Ranger District)  49
Schell Creek Range  305, 306
Schurz, NV  43
Scipio, UT  190
Scofield Reservoir  118, 119
Scofield State Park  118
scorpions  25
Scotty's Castle  316
Scotty's RV Park  **297**
Searchers, The (movie)  252
Searchlight, NV  337
Sego Canyon  238

Seidman, David  21
Settlers RV Park  **182**
Seven Palms RV Park  **317**
Sevier County, UT  203
Sevier River  160, 168, 169
Shady Acres  **227**
Shady Dell  **91**
Shady Haven RV Park  **84**
Shakespeare Arch  219
Shamrock RV Park  **285**
Sheep Creek Bay  127
Sheep Creek Canyon  126
Sheldon National Wildlife Refuge
    43, **259**
    (Big Spring camp)  259
    (Fish Spring camp)  259
    (Virgin Valley camp)  259
Shingle Creek  90
Shingle Creek (campground)  **90**
Shingle Creek Lake  90
Shivwits Campground  **180**
Shoal Creek  171
Shoshone Range  301
Si Redd's Oasis RV Park  **319**
Sierra Mountains  290, 291, 294, 295
Sigurd, UT  199, 200, 201
Silver City RV Park  **294**
Silver Flat Lake  103
Silver Lake  101
Silver Reef ghost town  173, 184
Silver Reef Museum (Leeds, UT)  181
Silver Springs, NV  289
Silver Springs Ranger Station  289
Silver Springs RV Park  **174**
Simpson Springs  36, **53**
Singletree  **208**
Singletree Falls  209
Sipapu Bridge  248
Six-Mile Canyon  192
Ski Utah (organization)  39
Skull Creek  **129**
Skyline Arch  229

Skyline Drive (four-wheel-drive scenic
    route)  120, 192, 194, 195, 196
sleeping bags  12
Slickrock Bicycle Trail  36, 234, 235
Slickrock Campground  **232,** 233
Smith and Morehouse  **87**
Smith and Morehouse Reservoir  87
Smith, Chickie  275
Smith, Dick  275
Smithfield Canyon  59
Smithfield Canyon (campground)  **59**
Smithfield, UT  59
Snake Mountains  274
snakebites  24, 25
Snow Canyon  36, 183
Snow Canyon State Park  173, 180,
    181, 183
Snowbasin Ski Area  30, 77
Snowbird ski resort  30, 101
Snowville, UT  49
Soapstone  **91**
Soapstone Basin  91
Soldier Creek  **113**
Soldier Summit  118, 119
Solitude (ski area)  30
South  **177**
South Beach  82
South Fork  **74**
South Fork River  280
South Fork State Recreation Area  **280**
South Juniper Park  **172**
South Lake Tahoe, CA  342, 343,
    344, 345, 346, 347, 348
South Lake Tahoe Recreation Area  347
South Willow Canyon  50, 51, 52
Space Station RV Park  **316**
Spanish Fork, UT  118, 119
Spanish Fork Canyon  31, 116,
    194, 195
Spanish Fork Ranger District  34, 53,
    114, 115, 116, 117, 118, 190
Spanish Fork Ranger Station  117

Spanish Fork, UT  34, 116
Spanish Gardens RV Park  **270**
Spanish Trail RV Park and
    Campground  **233,** 234
Spanish Valley Golf Course (Moab,
    UT)  233, 235
Sparks, NV  41, 260, 284, 286
Spencer Hot Springs  300
Spielberg, Steven  248
Spirit Lake  31, 134
Spirit Lake (campground)  **134**
Split Mountain  **144,** 145
Sportsman's Beach  **296**
Sportsman's Paradise Park and
    Campground  **160**
Spring  **68**
Spring Hollow  **66**
Spring Mountain Ranch State
    Park  329
Spring Mountains National
    Recreation Area  322, 323, 324
Spring Valley  311
Spring Valley State Park  **310**
    (Headquarters)  310
Springdale, UT  35, 176, 177, 178
Springville Art Museum  115
Springville, UT  115
Spruces (Big Cottonwood Canyon,
    UT)  **100**
Spruces (Dixie National Forest,
    UT)  **167**
Square Tower Campground  **250**
Square Tower Trail  250
Squaw Flat  241, **242,** 245, 246
Squaw Peak  109
St. George Campground and RV
    Park  **183**
St. George, UT  31, 33, 36, 37, 38,
    170, 172, 173, 174, 176, 181,
    182, 183, 184, 185
    (city park)  183
*Stagecoach* (movie)  252

Stagecoach Casino (Beatty, NV)  315
Starr Springs  36, **243,** 244
Starr Valley  275
Starvation Reservoir  147, 148
Starvation State Park  147, 148
State Line  **99**
State Line Reservoir  99
Stateline Hotel-Casino  279
Stateline, NV  292, 293, 346
Stateline RV Park  **279**
Station House Hotel-Casino
    (Tonopah, NV)  302, 303
Station House RV Park  **302**
Steinaker Reservoir  135, 143
Steinaker State Park  125, **143**
Sterling, UT  192
Stewart Creek  301
Stillwater  **96**
Stillwater National Wildlife Refuge  43
stoves  12, 13
Stratosphere Tower  327
Strawberry Bay  **112**
Strawberry Dam  114
Strawberry Reservoir  30, 112,
    113, 114
Strawberry River  114
Sugar Pine Point State Park  **343**
Sulphur  **94**
sunburns  22
Sundance ski area  103
Sundance, UT  107, 111
Sunflower Flat (geographic
    feature)  273
Sunglow  **204**
Sunnyside Lodge  342
Sunrise (Garden City, UT)  **60**
Sunrise (Wasatch–Cache National
    Forest, UT)  **67**
Sunrise Point Overlook  218
sunscreen  19, 22
Sunset (Wasatch National Forest,
    UT)  **80**

Sunset Campground (Bryce Canyon
    National Park, UT) **218**
Sunset Peak 102
Sunset Point 217, 218
sunstroke 22
Sutcliffe, NV 260
Sweetwater RV Park and Marina **61**
Swift Creek **140**
Swift Creek Trailhead 140
Swim Beach 126, 127
Syracuse, UT 79

**T**
Tabiona, UT 137, 138
Tabor Creek Campground **273,** 274
Tahoe Area Rapid Transit (TART) 342
Tahoe Basin Management Unit 292
Tahoe City, CA 341, 342, 343, 344
Tahoe, Lake 40, 290, 292, 293, 294,
    342, 343, 344, 345, 346, 347
    (Visitors Center) 342, 343, 344,
    346, 347
Tahoe Meadows 291
Tahoe State Recreation Area **341**
Tahoe Valley Campground **347,** 348
    (Visitors Center) 348
Tahoe Vista, CA 341
Tahoma, CA 341, 343, 344, 345
Tanners Flat **101**
Tasha, UT 198
Taylor Fork **89**
Te-Ah **166**
Teapot Lake 92
Teasdale Ranger District 33, 208,
    209, 210
Teasdale Ranger Station 209
Teasdale, UT 33, 208, 209, 210
Temple Square (Salt Lake City, UT) 38
tents 12, 13, 15
Thomas Canyon 279
Thomas Canyon (campground)
    40, **279**

Thomas Creek 279
Thompson, UT 238
Thousand Lakes Mountain 205
Thousand Lakes RV Park **204,** 205
Thunderbird Resort 284
Tibble Fork Reservoir 102, 103
ticks 25
Timothy Lake 140
Timpanogos Cave 102, 103
Timpanogos Cave National
    Monument 35
Timpanogos, Mount 103, 104,
    110, 111
Timpanoke **103**
Tinney Flat **117**
Toiyabe Crest Trail 300
Toiyabe Mountains 299, 301
Toiyabe National Forest 41, 290,
    292, 299, **300,** 301, 302, 322,
    323, 324
    (Austin Ranger District) 41, 299,
    300, 301
    (Carson Ranger District) 41, 290
    (Las Vegas Ranger District) 41
    (Superintendent) 41
    (Tonopah Ranger District) 41, 302
Tonopah, NV 41, 301, 302, 303
Tonopah Ranger District 41, 302
Tony Grove 59, **66**
Tony Grove Lake 65, 66
Tooele County, UT 52
Tooele, UT 37, 50, 53
Topaz Lake 295, 296
Topaz Lake Campground 291, **296**
Topaz Lake Park 296
Topaz Lodge RV Park **295**
Torrey, UT 35, 202, 204, 205, 206,
    207, 210
Tortoise and Hare Trailer Court **180**
Totem Pole (geographic
    formation) 252
Trading Post (see Burches Trading Post)

Trails Illustrated (map company) 38
Transcontinental Railroad 49
Trappist Monastery (Huntsville, UT) 76
Trial Lake 92
Trial Lake (campground) **92**
Trial Lake Dam 92
Triple S RV Park and
    Campground **214**
Tropic Reservoir 161, 215, 216, 220
Truckee River 284, 286
    (Upper) 348
Truckee-Carson Irrigation District 289
Tule Lake 212
Turquoise **250**
Tushar Mountains 155, 156, 157,
    158, 208
Twelvemile Flat **193**
Twin Coves **86**
Twin Falls, ID 269
Twin Peaks Wilderness Area 30

**U**
U.S. Army 297
U.S. Fish and Wildlife Service 37, 43
U.S. Forest Service 30, 38, 40, 43,
    50, 67, 74, 75, 77, 97, 98, 112,
    134, 146, 153, 193, 214, 215,
    220, 233, 263, 279, 299, 302,
    308, 342, 343, 346
U.S. Forest Service National Reserva-
    tion System 32, 40, 66, 67, 71,
    74, 76, 87, 90, 91, 92, 93, 98,
    99, 100, 101, 102, 103, 104,
    112, 113, 114, 115, 117, 118,
    131, 132, 159, 162, 163, 166,
    167, 171, 190, 193, 198, 200,
    201, 208, 215, 219, 247
U.S. Geological Survey 39, 43, 44
Uinta and Ouray Indian
    Reservation 143
Uinta Canyon **142**
Uinta Little Valley **53**

Uinta Mountains 91, 94, 134
Uinta National Forest 30, 34, 54,
    102, 103, 107, 108, 109, 114,
    118, 121
    (Heber Ranger District) 34, 107,
    108, 112, 113, 114
    (Pleasant Grove Ranger District)
    34, 102, 103, 104, 109
    (Spanish Fork Ranger District) 34,
    53, 114, 115, 116, 117, 118, 190
    (Supervisor's Office) 34
Uinta River 142
Uinta Wilderness 98
Union Pacific Rail Trail 82
Union Pacific Rail Trail State Park 88
United Beaver Camperland **155**
United Campground **228**
Up the Creek Camp Park **234**
Upheaval Dome 230
Upper Birch Creek Reservoir 73
Upper Meadows **75**
Upper Narrows **52**
Upper Stillwater **139**
Upper Stillwater Reservoir 31, 139
Utah Campground Owners
    Association 39
Utah County, UT 30, 114, 117
Utah Department of Natural
    Resources 39
Utah Department of Transportation 39
Utah Division of Parks and Recreation
    State Office 36
    (Northeast Region Office) 36
    (Northwest Region Office) 36
    (Southeast Region Office) 36
    (Southwest Region Office) 36
Utah Division of Wildlife Resources
    39, 73, 108, 158, 159, 167, 172,
    174, 203, 204, 235
    (fish hatchery) 168
Utah Field House of Natural
    History 125

Utah Geological Survey (map company) 39
Utah Guides and Outfitters (organization) 39
Utah Hotel-Motel Association 39
Utah Lake 108, 109, 110
Utah Lake State Park **108,** 110
Utah River Runner's Hall of Fame 227
Utah Shakespearean Festival (Cedar City, UT) 166, 169
Utah State Fairpark 83
Utah Travel Council 35, 38, 39
Ute Indian Reservation 139
Ute Mountain 135

**V**

Valles Trailer Park **251**
Valley City, UT 39
Valley of Fire 321
Valley of Fire State Park 41, **321**
Valley View RV Park **306**
Velma Lakes 346
Verdi, NV 287
Vermillion Castle **159**
Vermillion Castle hiking trail 160
Vernal Campground Dina **146**
Vernal Ranger District 32, 135, 136, 137, 143
Vernal, UT 32, 37, 125, 126, 127, 128, 129, 130, 131, 132, 133, 134, 135, 136, 137, 143, 144, 145, 146, 147
(Visitors Center) 137
Vernon Reservoir 53
Vernon, UT 53
Veyo, UT 171, 172, 173
VFW Park 266
Victorian RV Park **283,** 284, 286
Virgin Mountains 320
Virgin River (Nevada) 321
Virgin River (Utah) 176, 177
Virgin River Basin 166

Virgin River Rim Trail 166, 167
Virgin River RV Park **319,** 320
Virgin River Valley 167
Virgin, UT 177
Virgin Valley 259, 320
Virgin Valley camp 259
Virginia City, NV 289, 290
Virginia City RV Park **289,** 290

**W**

Wadsworth, NV 260, 283
Wagons West **154**
Walker Lake 296
Walker River 295
Walker River Indian Reservation 43
Wandin **141**
Wanship Reservoir 86
Wanship, UT 85, 86, 87
Ward Charcoal Ovens (recreation area) 307
Ward Mountain 307, 308
Ward Mountain (campground) **307**
Warner Lake 238, 239
Warner Lake (campground) **238,** 239
Wasatch County, UT 30
Wasatch Front 30, 51, 72, 73, 76, 100, 101, 102, 104, 139, 148
Wasatch Mountain State Park 36, 105, 106, 107
Wasatch Mountains 50, 103
Wasatch National Forest 32, 50, 51, 52, 71, 73, 74, 75, 76, 77, 80, 89, 90, 91, 92, 93, 94, 95, 96, 97, 98, 99, 100
(Ogden Ranger District) 71, 72, 73, 74, 75, 76, 77
Wasatch National Forest Recreation Areas 50
(North Willow) 50
(South Willow) 50
Wasatch Plateau 31, 121, 193, 194, 195, 198

Wasatch–Cache National Forest  30, 34, 50, 51, 52, 53, 54, **64,** 65, 66, 67, 68, 80, 87
(Evanston Ranger District)  34, 94, 95, 96, 97
(Kamas Ranger District)  34, 87, 89, 90, 91, 92, 93, 94
(Logan Ranger District)  34, 59, 64, 65, 66, 67, 68, 69
(Mountain View Ranger District)  34, 97, 98, 99, 100
(Salt Lake Ranger District)  34, 50, 51, 52, 100, 101, 102
(Wasatch–Cache Supervisor's Office)  34
Washington, UT  184, 185
Washoe Lake  291
Washoe Lake State Recreation Area  **290,** 291
Washoe Valley  290
Watchman  **176**
Water Lily Lake  141
water treatment  23
Waterpocket Fold (geographic feature)  209, 210, 211
Wayne, John  251
weather conditions  12
Weber River  82, 85, 86, 87
Wedge, The (geographic area)  225
Welcome Station RV Park  **275**
Wells Chinatown RV Park  **274**
Wells, NV  41, 269, 273, 274, 275, 276
Wellsville Mountain Wilderness Area  30
Wendover Golf Course  279
Wendover, NV  278, 279
(West)  278, 279
West Desert  36, 37
West End RV Park  **307**
West Shore Bike Trail  341, 342, 343
West Wendover, NV  278, 279

Western Park Campground  **63**
Westerner RV Park  **245**
Westin Plaza (Manila, UT)  125
Westwater Canyon  238
Wet 'N Wild water park (Las Vegas, NV)  327
Whale Rock  230
wheelchair-accessible campsites  59, 61, 62–63, 69, 72, 74, 76, 79, 87, 92–93, 96, 98–99, 100, 105, 106, 108, 112–115, 117–119, 138, 139, 147–148, 152–154, 157–158, 160, 165, 167, 169, 174–177, 179–180, 182–185, 187, 189, 191–193, 196, 237, 264–265, 270, 272, 274, 277–278, 283, 284–287, 289, 294–295, 302, 305–307, 315–316, 319–320, 323, 326–333, 335, 337, 347
Wheeler Peak  41, 310
Wheeler Peak Campground  **309**
*Whirlwind* (ship)  292
Whispering Elms RV Park  **308**
White Bridge Campground  **162**
White, Donna  299
White House  **222**
White Pine Range  306
White Rim Trail  231
White Rocks Canyon  31
White Sands  **54**
Whiterocks  **143**
Whiterocks, UT  143
Whiting  **114**
Wide Hollow Reservoir  213, 214, 215
Wilderness Study Areas  226
Wildflower RV  **202**
Wildhorse Campground  **273**
Wildhorse Crossing  271, **272**
Wildhorse Dam  272
Wildhorse Reservoir  270, 272, 273

Wildhorse State Recreation Area 270, 271, **272**, 273
Wildlife's Hardware Ranch 68, 69, 70
Willard Basin **71**
Willard Bay 72
  (North) **72**, 73
  (South) **72**, 73
Willard Bay State Park 36, 72
Willard Peak 72
Willard, UT 72
William Kent Beach 342
William Kent Campground **342**
Willow campground 62
Willow Flat **230**, 231
Willow Park **175**
Willows **75**
Wilson Reservoir **263**
Window Rock, AZ 38
Windwhistle **242**
Winnemucca, NV 41, 42, 263, 264, 265
Winnemucca RV Park **264**, 265
Wolf Creek **107**
Wolverine ATV Trailhead **95**, 96
Wood Camp **64**
Woodland, UT 107, 108
Woodruff, UT 73

**Y**
Yankee Meadows Reservoir 160
Yearns Reservoir 192
Yellow Pine RV (Wasatch National Forest, UT) **89**
Yellowpine (Ashley National Forest, UT) **138**
Yellowstone **141**
Yellowstone Park 200
Yellowstone River 140, 141
Yerington, NV 295
Yogi Bear's Jellystone Park **191**
Yomba-Shoshone Tribe Headquarters 301

Young's RV Park **312**
Yuba Lake State Park **190**
Yuba Reservoir 190, 194

**Z**
Zephyr Cove, NV 292
Zephyr Cove RV Park **292**
Zion Canyon 176
Zion Canyon Campground **176**
Zion Narrows hike 178
Zion National Park 31, 34, 35, 160, 166, 167, 168, 169, 170, 174, 175, 176, 177, 178, 179, 180, 181, 184, 187, 195, 201, 213, 218
  (Zion Nature Center) 177
  (Zion Visitors Center) 177
Zion Ponderosa Resort **178**

# Leave No Trace

Leave No Trace, Inc., is a program dedicated to maintaining the integrity of outdoor recreation areas through education and public awareness. Foghorn Press is a proud supporter of this program and its ethics.

## Here's how you can Leave No Trace:

### Plan Ahead and Prepare

- Learn about the regulations and special concerns of the area you are visiting.
- Visit the backcountry in small groups.
- Avoid popular areas during peak-use periods.
- Choose equipment and clothing in subdued colors.
- Pack food in reusable containers.

### Travel and Camp with Care

*On the trail:*

- Stay on designated trails.
- Do not take shortcuts on switchbacks.
- When traveling cross-country where there are no trails, follow animal trails or spread out your group so no new routes are created. Walk along the most durable surfaces available, such as rock, gravel, dry grasses, or snow.
- Use a map and compass to eliminate the need for rock cairns, tree scars, or ribbons.
- If you encounter pack animals, step to the downhill side of the trail and speak softly to avoid startling them.

*At camp:*

- Choose an established, legal site that will not be damaged by your stay.
- Restrict activities to areas where vegetation is compacted or absent.
- Keep pollutants out of the water by camping at least 200 feet (about 70 adult steps) from lakes and streams.
- Control pets at all times, or leave them at home with a sitter. Remove dog feces.

### Pack It In and Pack It Out

- Take everything you bring into the wild back out with you.
- Protect yourself, the wildlife, and your food by storing rations securely. Pick up all spilled foods.
- Use toilet paper or wipes sparingly; pack them out.
- Inspect your campsite for trash and any evidence of your stay. Pack out all trash—even if it's not yours!

### Properly Dispose of What You Can't Pack Out

- If no refuse facility is available, deposit human waste in catholes dug six to eight inches deep at least 200 feet from water, camps, or trails. Cover and disguise the catholes when you're finished.
- To wash yourself or your dishes, carry the water 200 feet from streams or lakes and use small amounts of biodegradable soap. Scatter the strained dishwater.

### Keep the Wilderness Wild

- Treat our natural heritage with respect. Leave plants, rocks, and historical artifacts as you found them.
- Good campsites are found, not made. Do not alter a campsite.
- Let nature's sounds prevail; keep loud voices and noises to a minimum.
- Do not build structures or furniture or dig trenches.

### Minimize Use and Impact of Fires

- Campfires can have a lasting impact on the backcountry. Always carry a light-weight stove for cooking, and use a candle lantern instead of building a fire whenever possible.
- Where fires are permitted, use established fire rings only.
- Do not scar the natural setting by snapping the branches off live, dead, or downed trees.
- Completely extinguish your campfire and make sure it is cold before departing. Remove all unburned trash from the fire ring and scatter the cold ashes over a large area well away from any camp.

## For more information, call 1-800-332-4100.

# About the Authors

**Gayen** and **Tom Wharton** have spent the last 25 years exploring Utah, the U.S., and the rest of the world with their four children. Avid outdoor enthusiasts and campers, the couple has carved out writing careers while camping, hiking, skiing, fishing, and exploring Utah's varied backcountry.

Gayen Wharton is an award-winning elementary school teacher and past president of the Utah Society of Environmental Education, which named her Environmental Educator of the Year in 1994. Tom Wharton is the editor of the *Salt Lake Tribune's* outdoor section.

The Whartons are the authors of *Utah for the Discover America Series* and *An Outdoor Family Guide to the Southwest's Four Corners.* Tom is also the author of *Utah! A Family Travel Guide,* published in 1987, and a contributor to seven other books, including *Wild Places,* published by Foghorn Press in 1996.

Nevada has been **Deke Castleman's** beat since 1986. Author of the *Nevada Handbook* (now in its fourth edition), he knows Nevada inside and out, from the down-and-dirty casino pits to the high-and-mighty mountaintops. Over the years, he has camped in the high desert with sage, rattlers, and cattle; in the low desert with yucca, scorpions, and mustangs; along the side of dirt roads, on the edge of ghost towns, and outside abandoned gold mines; and, for this book, in actual campgrounds and RV parks.

Castleman is also a regular contributor to *Nevada* magazine and the author of several guidebooks to Las Vegas and one to Alaska. He lives in Las Vegas with his wife and two children.

# FOGHORN 🕭 OUTDOORS

Foghorn Press books are sold throughout the U.S. Call 1-800-FOGHORN (8:30–5:30 PST) for the location of a bookstore near you that carries Foghorn Press titles or visit our Web site at www.foghorn.com. If you prefer, you may place an order directly with Foghorn Press using your Visa or MasterCard. All of the titles listed below are now available, unless otherwise noted.

To receive a free copy of our complete booklist, call 1-800-FOGHORN, or write to: Foghorn Press, 555 DeHaro Street, Suite 220, San Francisco, CA 94107.

## The Complete Guide Series

The Complete Guides are the books that have given Foghorn Press its reputation for excellence. Each book is a comprehensive resource for its subject, from *every* camping spot in California to hundreds of the best hikes in New England. With extensive cross-references and detailed maps, the Complete Guides offer readers a quick and easy way to get the best recreational information available.

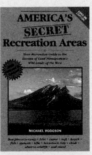

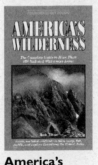

**Alaska Fishing**
The Complete Guide to Hundreds of Fishing Spots on Rivers, Lakes, Streams, and the Coast
*640 pp., $21.95*
*available April 1997*

**America's Secret Recreation Areas**
Your Recreation Guide to the Bureau of Land Management's Wild Lands of the West
*640 pp., $17.95*

**America's Wilderness**
The Complete Guide to More Than 600 National Wilderness Areas
*592 pp., $19.95*

**Baja Camping**
Featuring all the Campgrounds From Tijuana to Cabo San Lucas, Including 1,000 Miles of Shoreline Beaches
*296 pp., $12.95*

**California Beaches**
The Complete Guide to More Than 400 Beaches and 1,200 Miles of Coastline
*640 pp., $19.95*

## California Boating and Water Sports
The Complete Guide to More Than 400 Lakes, Rivers, and Marinas
*552 pp., $19.95*

## California Camping
The Complete Guide to More Than 50,000 Campsites for Tenters, RVers, and Car Campers
*848 pp., $19.95*

## California Fishing
The Complete Guide to Hundreds of Fishing Spots on Lakes, Streams, Rivers, and the Coast
*700 pp., $20.95*
*available March 1997*

## California Golf
The Only Guide to Every Course in the Golden State
*896 pp., $19.95*

### California Hiking
The Complete Guide to 1,000 of the Best Hikes in the Golden State
*856 pp., $20.95*
*available April 1997*

## California In-Line Skating
The Complete Guide to the Best Places to Skate
*480 pp., $19.95*

## California Waterfalls
Where to Hike, Drive, Walk, Bike, and Backpack to 200 of the Golden State's Most Spectacular Falls
*300 pp., $17.95*
*available March 1997*

## The Camper's Companion
The Pack-Along Guide for Better Outdoor Trips
*458 pp., $15.95*

### New England Camping
The Complete Guide to More Than 15,000 Campsites in New England
*300 pp., $20.95*
*available June 1997*

### New England Hiking
The Complete Guide to 350 of the Best Hikes in New England
*300 pp., $20.95*
*available May 1997*

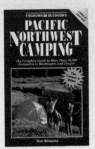

### Pacific Northwest Camping
The Complete Guide to More Than 45,000 Campsites in Washington and Oregon
*720 pp., $19.95*

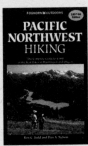

### Pacific Northwest Hiking
The Complete Guide to 1,000 of the Best Hikes in Washington and Oregon
*808 pp., $20.95*
*available May 1997*

### Southwest Camping
The Complete Guide to More Than 35,000 Campsites in Arizona and New Mexico
*544 pp., $17.95*

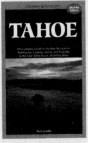

### Tahoe The Complete Guide to Outdoor Recreation, Sightseeing, Lodging, Dining, & Nightlife in Tahoe, Including Reno
*704 pp., $20.95*
*available June 1997*

### Utah & Nevada Camping
The Complete Guide to More Than 36,000 Campsites
*384 pp., $18.95*

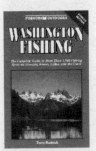

### Washington Fishing
The Complete Guide to More Than 1,000 Fishing Spots on Streams, Rivers, Lakes, and the Coast
*528 pp., $19.95*

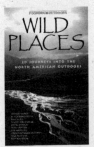

### Wild Places
20 Journeys Into the North American Outdoors
*320 pp., $15.95*

# Utah Chapter Reference Map

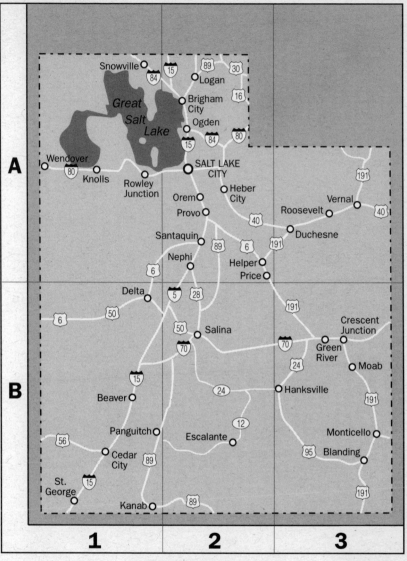

## Utah Campgrounds

Chapter A1 ..................... page 48

Chapter A2 ..................... page 56

Chapter A3 ..................... page 124

Chapter B1 ..................... page 150

Chapter B2 ..................... page 188

Chapter B3 ..................... page 224

# Nevada Chapter Reference Map

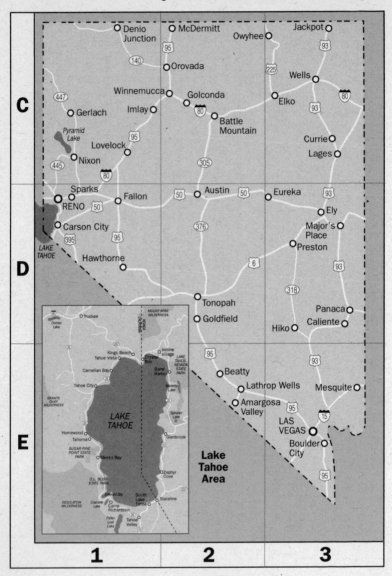

## Nevada Campgrounds

Chapter C1 ...................... page 258  
Chapter C2 ...................... page 262  
Chapter C3 ...................... page 268  
Chapter D1 ...................... page 282  
Chapter D2 ...................... page 298  
Chapter D3 ...................... page 304  
Chapter E2 ...................... page 314  
Chapter E3 ...................... page 318  
Lake Tahoe Area Campgrounds .............. page 340